Music East and West

Essays in Honor of Walter Kaufmann

Walter Kaufmann *Photo by* Philip Freed

Music East and West

Essays in Honor of Walter Kaufmann

Edited by Thomas Noblitt

FESTSCHRIFT SERIES NO. 3

Pendragon Press New York

From the Same Publisher

FESTSCHRIFT SERIES

No. 1. A Musical Offering: Essays in honor of Martin Bernstein, edited by E. Clinkscale and C. Brook (1977)

No. 2. Aspects of Medieval and Renaissance Music: A Birthday Offering to Gustave Reese, edited by Jan LaRue (Pendragon Edition 1978)

Library of Congress Cataloging in Publication Data
Main entry under title:

Music East and West.

(Pendragon Press Festschrift series; no. 3)
Bibliography: p.
Includes index.
1. Kaufmann, Walter, 1907- 2. Music—Addresses, essays, lectures. 3. Ethnomusicology—Addresses, essays, lectures. I. Noblitt, Thomas L. II. Series.
ML55.K37 1980 780 80-15060
ISBN 0-918728-15-0

162 W. 13 St., N.Y., N.Y. 10011

Table of Contents

Foreword

On April 1, 1977 Walter Kaufmann observed his seventieth birthday. At the celebration held at Indiana University marking that occasion, a number of his professional friends and colleagues, including former students who had written their doctoral dissertations under his supervision, announced their intention to honor him with a *Festschrift*. That intention has now been realized with the publication of the present volume, a tangible expression of the admiration which the contributors to this collection have for Walter Kaufmann.

Few individuals have had such a distinguished career in music as has Walter Kaufmann. The range of his professional activities is astonishing, but even more remarkable is the eminence that he has achieved in each sphere of endeavor. It was as a composer that he first acquired an international reputation. The list of his compositions is exceedingly long and varied, and his works have been performed with great success over the radio and in opera houses and concert halls throughout the world. Kaufmann's departure from Europe and immigration to India in 1934, where he became Director of European Music at All-India Radio in Bombay, marked the beginning of a long and successful career as a conductor, a career that was interrupted by the Second World War but continued afterwards in London at the British Broadcasting Corporation and, subsequently, in Canada as director of the Winnipeg Symphony Orchestra. In 1957 Walter Kaufmann joined the Faculty of the School of Music at Indiana University. In Bloomington the investigations into Hindu and other Eastern musics that he had initiated while in India began to yield fruit. Between 1959 and 1976 Kaufmann published, in addition to a number of articles, a remarkable series of books, studies which became widely recognized throughout the world as scholarly achievements of the highest order: *Musical Notations of the Orient, The Ragas of North India, Tibetan Buddhist Chant, The Rāgas of South India,* and *Musical References in the Chinese Classics*. Kaufmann's accomplishments in music were recognized by Indiana University in 1975, when he was named Distinguished Professor of Music. But it is not only to Kaufmann the composer, the conductor, and the scholar that this work is dedicated, it is also to a warm human being, whose friendship is treasured by all who have had the privilege of knowing him.

Publication of the present work would not have been possible without the generous financial support of Indiana University. The substantial contributions made to this project by the Office of Research and Graduate Development, the Indiana University Foundation, and the President's Council on the Humanities are gratefully acknowledged. I personally wish to express my appreciation to Dean Charles Webb, Dean Eugene Eoyang, and Dean Gene Faris for their crucial roles in identifying and obtaining the funds necessary to make this volume a reality.

Thomas Noblitt

Indiana University
Bloomington, Indiana

Note: The editor has respected the practices of those authors who have considered it inadvisable to form English plurals when referring to non-Western instruments.

Wayne Howard

A Yajurveda Festival in Kēraḷa

This study[1] would not have been possible without the generous assistance of my friend Śrī Māṭampu Nārāyaṇan Nampūtiri, who at my request initiated and promoted the celebration of the festival described in the following pages and who provided me with a large amount of information on the Yajurvedic practices of the Nampū-tiris. His valuable help was given both orally and in writing; the written communications were put in easily readable form by his son Satiścandran, and certain Sanskrit references were checked by his paternal uncle Subrahmaṇian. I am also deeply grateful to another well-known Nampūtiri Yajurvedī, Śrī Deśamaṅgalam Śaṅkaran Nampūtirippāṭ, who arranged to have the festival at his ancestral home in the village Kaṭalāśśēri. It could not have been held without the enthusiastic participation of the Yajurvedic reciters themselves, whom I am privileged to present, along with the names of their respective villages, in Figure 1; I trust that this study reflects in some way the high standards which they uphold in carrying out their sacred duty. I am therefore extremely fortunate to benefit from the knowledge of the above scholars in paying tribute to my esteemed friend and teacher Walter Kaufmann, who, in the year 1968, introduced me to the profound world of Veda recitation and chant.

[1]An earlier, much shorter version, presented orally on March 19, 1973 to the Dept. of South and Southeast Asian Studies, University of California at Berkeley, was given at the invitation of Prof. J. F. Staal, a pioneer in explaining the intricacies of Nampūtiri Veda recitation to the West.

Figure 1. *Assembly of Yajurvedic Paṇḍits. Seated (left to right): Śrī Māṭampu Padmanābhan Nampūtiri (Kirālūr). Śrī Alakkādu Nīlakaṇṭhan Nampūtiri (Puttañcira), Śrī Āyirit Śaktidharan Bhaṭṭatirippāṭ (Tṛppūṇittura), Śrī Kaplinnāṭṭa Vāsudevan Nampūtiri (Neṭumpura), Śrī Ampalappiḷḷi Citran Bhaṭṭatirippāṭ (Turavu), and Śrī Karōḷit Kuññuṇṇi Nampūtiri (Ūrakam). Standing (left to right): Śrī Kaplinnāṭṭa Vaidikan Divākaran Nampūtiri (Perumpiḷiśśēri), Śrī Ālakkāṭṭūr Nārāyaṇan Nampūtiri (Cēruśśēri), Śrī Kaplinnāṭṭa Vaidikan Anujan Nampūtiri (Ñāruviśśēri), Śrī Vaṭakkēṭattu Nārāyaṇan Nampūtiri (Perumpaṭappuñcēri), Śrī Kaṇṇamaṅgalam Vāsudevan Nampūtiri (Paḷḷiśśēri), Śrī Kaṇṇamaṅgalam Brahmadattan Nampūtiri (Perumpiḷiśśēri), Śrī Ayirit Nārāyaṇan Bhaṭṭatirippāṭ (Ūrakam), and Śrī Karōḷit Kuñcu Nampūtiri (Kaṭalāśśēri). All villages are in the Trichur District except Tṛppūṇittura, which is in Ernakalam District.*

Kēraḷa and Nampūtiri Yajurveda

Kēraḷa, state in southwestern India stretching some 750 miles from its northern- to southernmost extremities but never exceeding 180 miles in breadth, is situated as a natural entity between the dense slopes of the Western Ghāṭs to the east and the Arabian Sea to the west. Its physical boundaries have secured for the region's inhabitants a measure of isolation from the rest of the subcontinent, a separation which has promoted the development of several distinctive cultural phenomena. Hinduism is, of course, by far the predominant religion, and here as elsewhere the Brāhmaṇ caste exclusively is charged with the preservation and oral transmission of the ancient sacred texts, the Vedas. Although several classes of Brāhmaṇs presently reside within her boundaries, Kēraḷa knows only one such community whose roots cannot definitely be traced elsewhere—the Nampūtiri (pronounced Nam·bū'di·ri) sub-caste, which, until very recently, was a kind of landed aristocracy. Above everything else it is the duty of the Nampūtiris to perpetuate recitation of the Vedas, and this charge they have kept faithfully for centuries. The geographic and self-imposed segregation from other Brāhmaṇ communities, the generally orthodox and disciplined organization of Nampūtiri society, the passion for mental cultivation, and the scrupulousness and rigor of Vedic training have all contributed to the subsistence of styles and forms of Veda recitation approaching, perhaps more closely than those elsewhere in India, the Vedic recitation and chant of the remote past. Nampūtiri Veda recitation can best be heard in central Kēraḷa, in and around the Trichur District, where the principal Yajur- and Sāmaveda villages and important Ṛgveda academy (*maṭha*) may be found.

Of the three Vedas preserved by the Nampūtiris (Atharvaveda is not found among them), Yajurveda seems in the least danger of soon becoming extinct. This observation is confirmed by sporadic appearances of an *ōttūṭṭu,*[2] a Vedic festival in which large numbers of Yajurvedins, sometimes over a hundred, may take part. An *ōttūṭṭu* is an event of special significance due partly to the occurrence there of unusual modes of recitation not easily heard elsewhere.

All Nampūtiri Yajurvedīs belong to the Taittirīya[3] school of the Kṛṣṇa ("Black") Yajurveda. As is the case with the other three Vedas, the principal text or collection is the *saṃhitā*, to which was subsequently added a *brāhmaṇa*, an *āraṇyaka*, and an *upaniṣad*. The Taittirīya-Saṃhitā (TS), on which most *ōttuṭṭu* recitations are based, consists of *mantras* and prose formulas to be recited at the various Vedic sacrifices; however, an *ōttūṭṭu* is itself in no way connected with the sacrificial ritual. In the *saṃhitā*s of the Black Yajurveda, in addition to the verses and formulas, are also found explanatory or *brāhmana* portions; two of the seven books of the

[2]From *ōttu* ("Veda recitation") + *ūṭṭu* ("feasting"); see T. Burrow and M. B. Emeneau, *A Dravidian Etymological Dictionary* (Oxford: Clarendon Press, 1961), nos. 886 and 516 (cited hereafter as DED).

[3]*Taittirīya* comes from the Sanskrit *tittiri* ("partridge"). For the legend behind the use of this term, see M. Monier Williams, *A Sanskrit-English Dictionary* (Oxford, 1899; reprint ed., Delhi: Motilal Banarsidass, 1970), p. 455, col. 1 (henceforth referred to as SED).

TS consist entirely of such explanatory matter. *Saṃhitās* lacking the explanatory material are said to belong to the Śukla ("White") Yajurveda, but there are no Śukla Yajurvedīs among the Naṃpūtiris. To avoid confusion, it should be remembered that the TS has an extraneous *brāhmaṇa*, the Taittirīya-Brāhmaṇa (TB), apart from it. The *āraṇyaka* and *upaniṣad* associated with the TS are the Taittirīya-Āraṇyaka (TĀ) and Taittirīya-Upaniṣad (TU).

There is no hard and fast rule as to how long an *ōttūṭṭu* lasts, but it takes place usually within the first fifteen days (*tithi*s) of the lunar month, from *prathamā* to *paurṇamī*; during this period the moon is, of course, on the increase. The fifteen days are divided into *svādhyāya* and *anadhyāya*, more or less working days and holidays. *Prathamā*, the first day, is an *anadhyāya* day. The second through seventh days are working days, though at times the seventh (*saptamī*) may be a holiday. The eighth day is a holiday, and the next three are working days. The last four days are holidays, although the twelfth can be both. So in all there is about an equal number of *svādhyāya* and *anadhyāya* days. Veda recitation is conducted only on working days, and the *ōttūṭṭu* must be completed within as many of these as are available. One important factor to be considered is whether recitations of the TB, TĀ, and TU are to be included in the festival. If so, then the number of working days must be increased. The matter of expenses may also come into play. An extra day means so many rupees extra; therefore, Veda recitation may take place both day and night in order to shorten the *ōttūṭṭu* and thus minimize cost.

The *Ōttūṭṭu* Feast

Much of the expense arises from the preparation of certain foods for the often large number of participants and invited guests. Actually an *ōttūṭṭu* is a feast in a dual sense. Primarily it is a religious festival, a celebration of the intellectual abilities of participating scholars, skills used in sustaining the Vedic heritage through oral repetition. Secondarily it is a banquet, or series of banquets, in which certain foods deemed appropriate are served on the working days, at noon and in the evening. As is the custom throughout South India, food is placed by the servers on the large, glossy leaf (*ila*)[4] of the banana tree. Participants and guests who are *ādhyan*s (members of the highest Naṃpūtiri sub-caste) are served on a leaf placed over a second leaf which has been split lengthwise into two

[4]See DED, no. 423.

halves. The two halves protrude outwards from beneath the undivided leaf. A person with the title Bhaṭṭatirippāṭ or Nampūtirippāṭ would be served in this fashion. The menu is basically the same for all *ōttūṭṭus*; each item is offered to each person three times. The following are standard dishes: cooked rice (*cōru*);[5] a spiceless curry called *ōlan*,[6] prepared by boiling tender cucumber pumpkin (*kūśmāṇḍam*)[7] with salt, then sprinkling on it pure raw coconut oil; another curry called *kāḷan*,[8] prepared by boiling the plant *cēna*[9] and banana slices, mixing in salt, turmeric powder, pepper and buttermilk, then adding mashed coconut; fried banana slices (*kāya uppēri*);[10] fried *cēna* slices (*cēna uppēri*); mango or lime pickled in salt with some condiments (*uppiliṭṭatu*); sliced and boiled banana (*paḻannuṟukku*);[11] a white curry (*veḷuttakaṟi*)[12] consisting of green chillies and ginger mixed with salt and curd; and finally salt (*uppu*),[13] buttermilk (*mōru*),[14] and *pappaṭam*,[15] dough made to swell and become crisp by frying in coconut oil. *Pappaṭam* cannot be served at the evening feast, and *sambār*, the popular South Indian soup served over rice, is never used at an *ōttūṭṭu*. At the conclusion of the feast, one of two kinds of pudding is offered. *Pāyasam*[16] is made from rice and jaggery (*śarkkara*:[17] brown sugar made from palm sap).[18] The other pudding may be one of two

[5]See DED, no. 2360.

[6]See DED, no. 902.

[7]See DED, no. 1455; SED, p. 300, col. 3.

[8]See DED, no. 1256.

[9]See DED, no. 1682. *Cēna* is *Amorphophallus campanulatus* of the *araceae* family.

[10]See DED, no. 1220.

[11]See DED, nos. 3299 and 3089.

[12]See DED, nos. 4524 and 1171. It is known also as *iñcittairu*. *Iñci* = "ginger" (see DED, no. 363); *tairu* (from *tayir*) = "curd" (see DED, no. 2517).

[13]See DED, no. 2201.

[14]See DED, no. 4015.

[15]See DED, no. 3243.

[16]See SED, p. 619, col. 2: "prepared with or made of milk."

[17]See SED, p. 1058, col. 2.

[18]J. F. Staal, in his book *Nambudiri Veda Recitation* (The Hague: Mouton, 1961), p. 48, writes of temple feasts in which courses of the meal prior to the serving of *pāl-pāyasam* are to be completed by the time two Ṛgvedīs arrive at a certain spot in their *ratha* recitation. *Ratha* is a *vikṛti* (repetition formula) based upon the *padapāṭha* (word by word recitation). *Pāl-pāyasam* is compared by the Nampūtiris to the *svayamātṛṇṇā* ("naturally perforated") bricks or pebbles, which are placed in the first, third, and fifth layers of the bird-shaped fire altar of the *agnicayana* ritual. See Staal's *Agni: The Vedic Ritual of the Fire Altar*, pt. 1, pp. 175-96, 216 (prepublication version).

kinds of *prathaman*: either *pālaṭa*[19] or *paḻam*.[20] *Pālaṭa* is a mixture of milk and rice which is powdered in a mortar with a pestle, kneaded to a paste, baked, and spread on plantain leaves. *Paḻam* is banana ripe fruit which is first dehydrated (*varaṭṭi*),[21] then liquefied over a fire by adding water, jaggery, and coconut milk. A person signifies that he has finished his meal by folding over the lower right hand corner of the *ila*.

Ōttūṭṭu Modus Operandi

On September 26, 1971 tape recordings comprising approximately ten hours of Yajurveda recitations were made during a short *ōttūṭṭu* held, as previously stated, at Kaṭalāśśēri, one of several important Yajurveda villages south of Trichur City. Nowadays the event is by no means common; the most recent *ōttūṭṭu* had taken place one year earlier at a Śiva temple in the same village. These festivals normally are observed in temples; the 1971 performance, however, took place outside, in a private home, to appease several of the more conservative reciters who doubtlessly would have objected to the presence of a non-Hindu and his recording apparatus inside a temple, especially on so auspicious an occasion. The Kaṭalāśśēri *ōttūṭṭu* was held in three sessions, beginning respectively at 6:30 a.m., 1:30 p.m., and 6:30 p.m.

The morning session begins when one can see the pits of the hairs on his arms. By this time everyone must have completed his bath and morning worship, so it is necessary that all arise well before daybreak. While reciting, the Vaidikas (Vedic chanters) sit facing one another on two long, rectangular planks of wood which are slightly elevated and run parallel to each other. Each plank is called a *panti palaka*. *Panti* is a corrupt form of *paṅkti* ("row"), and *palaka*[22] indicates that it is used for sitting. At the Kaṭalāśśēri *ōttūṭṭu* there was room for about five men per plank, the others having sat both behind them and between the planks at either end. During the Veda recitation any participant is free to arise and depart at his leisure, but at no time should less than four reciters be present.

19 See DED, nos. 3370 and 77.

20 See DED, no. 3299.

21 See DED, no. 4355.

22 From Sanskrit *phalaka* ("board, plank, bench"); see SED, p. 717, col. 2.

Before recitation begins, a respectful gesture is made towards eminent scholars, teachers, and elders by each of the younger and less experienced Yajurvedīs. This is the *abhivādana* ("salutation"), a formality performed also during Vedic study (*vedādhyayana*). The disciple sits facing the more distinguished Vaidikas. If he has completed his Vedic training he is seated on a *phalaka* (not the same as the *panti palaka* mentioned above),[23] a solid, almost round object with a tail, in the shape of a tortoise (*kūrma*). A *phalaka* may be made from the wood of the jackfruit tree (*cakka*)[24] or from mango wood, but for religious rites only the jackwood *phalaka* is acceptable. The mango wood variety is employed at other functions—at mealtimes, for instance, where it serves simply as a seat. Kṣatriyas (members of the military or ruling caste) use round, oval, or rectangular *phalaka*s without the tails and other symbols of the tortoise.

There is a special symbolism associated with the *kūrma*-shaped *phalaka*. A characteristic of the tortoise is that it withdraws its limbs into a hard shell so that no enemy can do it harm. This explains why the term *kūrmāsana* is used to designate a particular sitting posture practiced by ascetics. Similarly, a *yogī* (or, for that matter, any Brāhmaṇ) withdraws all his senses from sense objects so that these cannot despoil him.[25] Hindus regard the tortoise as *kṣetravid*, having familiarity with localities. Therefore the *yajamāna* ("sacrificer") of the Vedic ritual is taken to heaven by the tortoise, who knows the place. During *vedādhyayana* only the *ācārya*, the preceptor, may sit on the *phalaka*. Its tail must always be to the left of the man sitting on it; he faces east during morning ceremonies, west during evening rituals.

Abhivādana is quite brief and consists of two actions. First, the disciple holds each of his ear lobes with thumb and ring finger as he speaks a particular sentence. A person whose personal name is, for example, Nārāyaṇa, will say, "*abhivādaye nārāyaṇa śarmā nāma, aham asmi bhoḥ*" ("my name is Nārāyaṇa Śarmā; I am here saluting thee, O teacher"). Next, the hands are crossed and placed on the feet of the *ācārya* (see Figures 2 and 3).

[23]To be distinguished also from the two *phalaka*s of the Vedic sacrifice, which are used to press the stalks of *soma*. See Louis Renou, *Vocabulaire du rituel védique* (Paris: Librairie C. Klincksieck, 1954), p. 118.

[24]See DED, no. 1876.

[25]Bhagavad-Gītā 2.58 describes as truly knowledgeable the person who retracts his senses from sense objects as the tortoise pulls in his limbs.

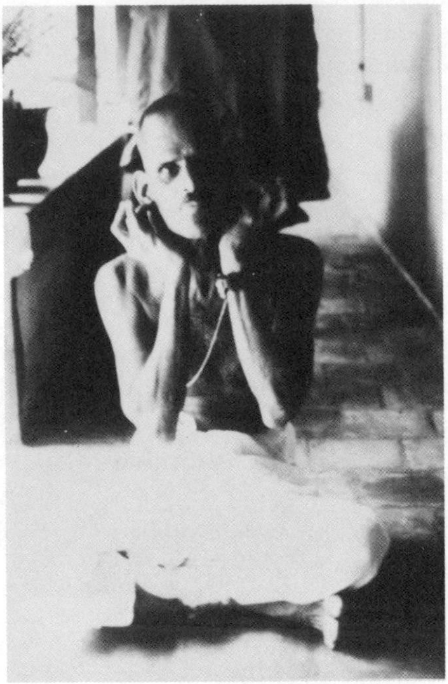

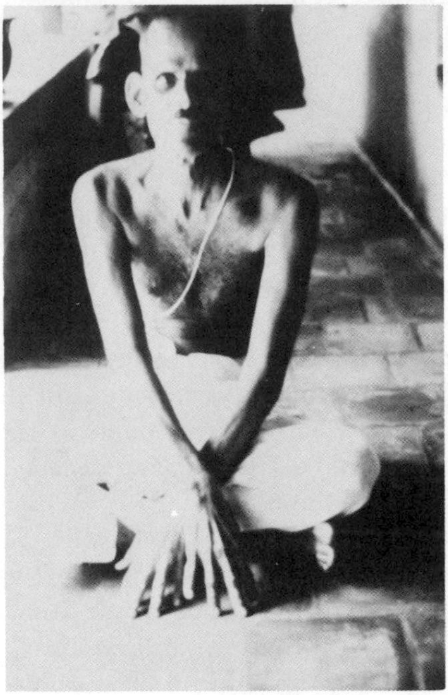

Figures 2 and 3. Abhivādana. *Demonstrated by Śrī Māṭampu Nārāyaṇan Nampūtiri (Vaṭakkañcēri).*

Yet another formality must be observed before recitation commences. This is the repetition of a short *anuvāka* ("section") of the TS, which reads as follows:

suśármāsi supratiṣṭhānó bṛhád ukṣé náma
eṣá te yónir víśvebhyas tvā devébyaḥ / om /[26]

Unlike the *abhivādana*, this passage is recited "with *svara*," with the accents (explained below) realized by means of musical pitches. Both *abhivādana* and the *mantras* beginning "*suśarmāsi* . . ." are used at the beginning of the recital of Veda in the morning and at night, after morning and evening worship (*sandhyāvandana*).

[26] Unless otherwise specified, TS references are to Dāmodar Sātvalekar, ed., *Taittirīya-Saṃhitā* (Pardi: Svādhyāya-Maṇḍala, 1957). The cited passage (TS 1.4.26) is rendered in English in A. B. Keith, trans., *The Veda of the Black Yajus School, Entitled Taittirīya-Saṃhitā*, Harvard Oriental Series, vol. 18 (Cambridge, 1914; reprint ed., Delhi: Motilal Banarsidass, 1967), pp. 59-60: "Thou givest good protection, and art well established. Homage to the great bull! This is thy birthplace; to the All-gods thee!"

The TS has four large divisions, namely, *kāṇḍa* (chapter), *prapāṭhaka* (lesson), *anuvāka* (section), and *paññāti* (group of fifty words). All are Sanskrit terms but the last, which belongs to the common dialect of Nampūtiri Yajurvedis but is doubtlessly derived from Sanskrit. The purpose of the division into groups of fifty is to facilitate study by the Vedic student. After he has finished an *anuvāka*, the Nampūtiri must state the number of words contained in it. If the number is less than fifty, the first word of the *anuvāka* is recited, followed by the total number of words. If this total exceeds fifty, each fiftieth word is stated, followed by the number left over, if any. For example, if an *anuvāka* contains eighty-eight words, the fiftieth word is specified, followed by "*aṣṭātriṃśac ca*" ("plus 38"; 88-50 = 38). If the total number is 115, the fiftieth and hundredth words are chanted, followed by "*pañcadaśa ca*" ("plus 15"; 115-100 = 15).[27] These enumerations are performed with tonal accents and in the same tempo as the respective *anuvāka*.

All *ōttūṭṭus* are composed of three parts: *saṃhitā*, in which the text is treated according to the euphonic laws of Sanskrit; *pada*, in which the words are given in their original form, without recourse to euphonic combination between words; and a special form of *pada* called *koṭṭu*, a word which means "beating a drum, clapping hands."[28] The festival begins with the chanting of *saṃhitā*, which lasts until the evening of the first working day. Then at night *koṭṭu* is also started, and it may continue until late hours. *Pada* recitation (*padapāṭha*) can begin only after *koṭṭu* has progressed a little. There may be no *pada* recitals at all during the first few days; but thereafter all three (*saṃhitā, koṭṭu*, and *pada*) go on simultaneously until the *ōttūṭṭu* is finished. *Saṃhitā* is concluded first, then *koṭṭu*, and finally *padapāṭha*; that is, they are finished in the order in which they are begun. *Padapāṭha*, then, is the last to be started because it takes less time to be performed than does *koṭṭu*.

In the course of a complete festival, *saṃhitā* and *pada* are each heard six times. Each *paññāti* is recited once by a single Vaidika; thereafter, as a rule (though there are exceptions) everyone recites the same *paññāti* five times *ekaśruti* (in a monotone). Therefore, the group of fifty words is chanted a total of six times in both *saṃhitā*- and *padapāṭha*. The very nature of *koṭṭu* (discussed below) requires a fourfold repetition. Hence, the entire TS is gone

27. This feature is indicated by Sātvalekar in his edition of the TS.
28. DED, no. 1717.

through a total of sixteen times (six in *saṃhitā*, six in *pada*, four in *koṭṭu*: 6+6+4 = 16). If a reciter makes a mistake while chanting alone, or should several Vaidikas distort the group recital at any point, then the mistake is instantly pointed out and the respective portion repeated correctly. In the end, therefore, all *ōttūṭṭus* are performed faultlessly, for every error is remedied.

One last procedural feature is worth noting. This concerns the recitation of TS 4.5, a small *prapāṭhaka* of eleven *anuvākas*—the *Rudrādhyāya*, also known among the Naṃpūtiris as *Śrī Rudra* ("The Magnificent Rudra," a Vedic god). Like the rest of the TS, it is chanted in *saṃhitā, pada*, and *koṭṭu*; but there is a rule which says that it is to be recited only in the early morning, before the Vaidikas have partaken of food or drink. A person who breaks the fast is not allowed to chant the *prapāṭhaka*. I am told by Śrī Māṭampu Nārāyaṇan Naṃpūtiri that a particular *mantra* of this section is recited in such a way that no inhaling or exhaling takes place (I am unable to identify the verse in question).

Saṃhitā Recitations

Sādhāraṇā Mātrā

Naṃpūtiri Yajurvedīs recite the TS in four ways, named *sādhāraṇā mātrā, śālā mātrā, valiya saṃhitā*, and *cantādikkat*. *Sādhāraṇa* ("ordinary") recitation is the quickest of the four and, like the others, is dependent on the Vedic accents for its proper realization. Each word (*pada*) generally has one principal accent, the *udātta* ("raised"), which normally is preceded by an *anudātta* ("unraised") and followed by a transition accent, *svarita* ("intoned"), to one or a series of accentless, unimportant syllables, *pracaya* ("multitude"). The position of the *udātta* is determined by grammatical considerations.[29] An *udātta* may be followed by an *anudātta* if the latter is itself followed by an *udātta*. Sometimes, for phonological reasons, an *udātta* is lost; in such cases a *svarita* is preceded by an *anudātta* rather than an *udātta* and is called, appropriately, an independent *svarita*—a *svarita* not dependent on a preceding *udātta* for its existence.

In its method of marking the accents, the TS follows the example of the Ṛgveda-Saṃhitā. Here the syllables bearing the *anudātta* are marked with a horizontal line below. *Udātta* and *pracaya* bear no

[29] See A. A. Macdonell, *Vedic Grammar, Grundriss der Indo-Arischen Philologie und Altertumskunde*, vol. 1, pt. 4 (Strasbourg: Karl J. Trübner, 1910), pp. 76-107.

markings at all, and the *svarita* is indicated by a vertical stroke above the syllable. For example, the following extract from the TS has the accents as marked (U = *udātta*, A = *anudātta*, S = *svarita*, P = *pracaya*):

i̱ṣé tvo̱rjé tvā̍ va̱yávā̍ḥ sthopā̱yávā̍ḥ stha (from TS 1.1.1.1).
AU AU S A U S P AU S P

The *udātta* syllables are denoted above by the acute sign (´), but it must be emphasized that the *udātta* of the printed texts is left completely undesignated. Occasionally, two or more consecutive syllables at the beginning of the line will bear the *anudātta*; for the purposes of this study, only the last of those syllables will be termed *anudātta*. The ones preceding will be called *pracaya* or *sarvānudātta* ("completely accentless") syllables. For example, the word *antaryāmatvam* occurring at the beginning of a line has the following accents:

a̱nta̱ryā̱ma̱tvám (from TS 6.4.6.1)
P P P A U
sarvānudātta

It is necessary to remember that the *udātta* is normally preceded by an *anudātta* and followed by a *svarita*. If, in normal word (*pada*, not *saṃhitā*) accentuation, the *udātta* occurs on the initial syllable of a word, the second syllable will have the *svarita* and any remaining syllables will be accentless (*pracaya*). If the *udātta* is found on the final syllable of a two-syllable word, the preceding syllable will be an *anudātta*. If the word has more than two syllables, those preceding *anudātta* will be *pracayas* (*sarvānudāttas*). In *saṃhitā* recitation, when the sentence, verse, or quarter-verse is taken as the accentual unit, certain changes from the normal *pada* or word accentuation may take place. But the principal accent, the *udātta*, always remains fixed. As a rule every word has only one *udātta*, but some words have a double accent and others have no accent at all. Among the latter are vocatives not initial in the line and finite verbs, in principal clauses, not initial in the line.[30]

The following transcription of *sādhāraṇā mātrā* (*mātrā* = "time unit") illustrates the tones associated with the accents in the most rapid of the *saṃhitā* styles. As is true regarding all the modes of non-sacrificial Naṃpūtiri Yajurvedic recitation, four pitch levels

[30]Ibid., pp. 81-82.

are discernible.[31] In *sādhāraṇa* recitation they are a middle pitch, a major second above, and a minor second and minor third below. I have endeavored to indicate the exact manner in which the text is uttered in recitation. The first pitch of the musical examples is set equal to the actual sung pitch; metronomic readings are given for all examples. A comma (,) marks spots where breath is taken, and a diagonal line (\) designates a glide. In order to facilitate discussion of accent, every fifth syllable has the appropriate number placed above. Tape numbers refer to a catalogue of recordings appearing in a previous publication.[32]

Example 1. *Sādhāraṇā Mātrā* (TS 1.1.1.1) [Tape Xb(3)C]

[31]Taittirīya recitation is described as consisting of four tones in Taittirīya-Prātiśākhya 23.15-19. See W. D. Whitney, *The Taittirīya-Prātiśākhya, with Its Commentary, the Tribhāṣyaratna: Text, Translation, and Notes* (New Haven, 1868; reprint ed., Delhi: Motilal Banarsidass, 1973), pp. 409-13.

[32]Wayne Howard, *Sāmavedic Chant* (New Haven: Yale University Press, 1977), pp. 455-500.

If, in the following analysis, the letters L (low), LM (lower middle), M (middle), and H (high) are used to indicate the four pitches, then the accents have the following tonal values: the superscribed "s" shows that the tone is short (less than an eighth note), "l" that it is long (an eighth note or more), "sl" that it is sometimes short, sometimes long.

(1) *Udātta* on Short Vowels
 A. One tone (M^{sl}) on 7, 11, 42, 47, 65, 70, 77, 78, 95, 106
 B. One tone (LM^{l}) on 74

C. Three tones ($L^{s}M^{s}LM^{s}$) on 29, 87. The first is an instance of short *udātta* followed by a semivowel (*r*) + consonant. The second is an example of short *udātta* followed by a nasal (*n*) + consonant. Both semivowel and nasal attach to the preceding vowel rather than to the following consonant (this is true in all the modes).

(2) *Udātta* on Long Vowels

A. One tone (LM^{l}) on 2

B. Two tones ($M^{s}L^{l}/LM^{l}L^{s}$) on 20, 62, 88

C. Two tones ($LM^{l}M^{sl}$) on 4, 105

D. Three tones ($L^{s}M^{s}LM^{s}$) on 52, 61, 69

E. Four tones ($M^{s}LM^{s}M^{s}LM^{s}$) on 15

F. Four tones ($L^{s}M^{s}LM^{s}M^{l}$) on 19, 24, 32, 43, 58, 85, 94, 101

(3) *Anudātta* on Short Vowels

A. One tone (L^{sl}) on 1, 18, 51, 84, 86, 104

B. One tone (M^{sl}) on 23, 28, 60, 73, 93

C. Two tones ($M^{s}L^{s}$) on 68, 100

(4) *Anudātta* on Long Vowels

A. One tone (L^{l}) on 64

B. Two tones ($M^{sl}L^{l}$) on 3, 6, 10, 14, 41, 46, 57, 76

(5) *Svarita* on Short Vowels

A. One tone (H^{sl}) on 8, 12, 16, 21, 25, 44, 48, 53, 63, 75, 79, 89, 96, 107

B. One tone (M^{s}) on 30. The high pitch was probably intended here, but the chanter was short of breath.

C. Five tones ($L^{s}M^{s}L^{s}H^{s}LM^{s}$) on 71. Followed by nasal + consonant, which makes this syllable long.

(6) *Svarita* on Long Vowels

A. Four tones ($M^{s}L^{s}H^{s}LM^{s}$) on 33

B. Five tones ($L^{s}M^{s}L^{s}H^{s}LM^{s}$) on 5, 66, 102. A and B are so similar that they should be considered the same.

(7) *Pracaya* on Short Vowels

A. One tone (LM^{s}) on 13, 17, 22, 26, 55, 56

B. One tone (M^{sl}) on 31, 34, 35, 36, 37, 40, 45, 49, 67, 81, 82, 83, 92, 98, 99, 109. A and B are similar to short *udātta*.

C. Five tones ($M^{s}LM^{s}M^{s}LM^{s}M^{l}$) on 103, 110. Both are finals in the line (that is, before pauses).

(8) *Pracaya* on Long Vowels

A. One tone (LM^{l}) on 9

B. One tone (M^{l}) on 39, 108
C. Two tones ($M^{sl}L^{l}$) on 72, 91
D. Two tones ($LM^{s}L^{l}$) on 80
E. Three tones ($LM^{s}M^{s}LM^{s}/L^{s}M^{s}LM^{sl}$) on 27, 38, 54, 90, 97
F. Four tones ($L^{s}M^{s}LM^{s}M^{l}$) on 50

Obviously the reciter has employed here much more than the simple tone scheme suggested by the phonetic treatises (*prātiśākhyas*).[33] The Taittirīya-Prātiśākhya, for instance, has the following to say regarding the accents:

> The *udātta* is high, the *anudātta* low, and the *svarita* a compound tone . . . it begins at the level of the *udātta* and the rest is at the level of the *anudātta*: so say the teachers: some say it is a continuous fall (*pravaṇa*).[34]

A different view is expressed by the Ṛk-Prātiśākhya:

> The first ½ or ¼ *mātrā* of the *svarita* is higher than the *udātta*: the rest is *anudātta*.[35]

Actually, this last statement comes closest to describing the accents of Nampūtiri *sādhāraṇa* recitation, for the *svarita* is invariably realized as a high pitch (H), a tone which does not occur in connection with the other accents. It also conforms to the manner in which the accents are indicated in the printed text: an *anudātta* by a horizontal stroke beneath the syllable, a *svarita* by a vertical stroke above, and *udātta* and *pracaya* with no marking at all. Walter Kaufmann has pointed out the usage of these signs in North Indian music notation to designate low and high (*komal* and *tīvra*) alterations of pitches.[36]

But the *sādhāraṇa* recitation does not fit so conveniently into the scheme just described. For instance, *udātta* and *pracaya* on long vowels are performed in six different ways. Similar non-conformity is detected in regard to *anudātta* and *pracaya* on short vowels. Inconsistencies of this type were noticed by J.E.B. Gray in his

[33]See W. S. Allen, *Phonetics in Ancient India* (London: Oxford University Press, 1953), pp. 87-93.

[34]Taittirīya-Prātiśākhya 1.38-40, 46-47, trans. Allen, *Phonetics*, p. 88.

[35]Ṛk-Prātiśākhya 3.4-5, trans. Allen, *Phonetics*, p. 88.

[36]"Some Reflections on the Notations of Vedic Chant," in *Essays in Musicology: A Birthday Offering for Willi Apel*, ed. Hans Tischler (Bloomington: Indiana University School of Music, 1968), p. 4.

analysis of Nampūtiri Ṛgvedic recitation.[37] He comes to the provocative conclusion that "it becomes irrelevant to talk about the Vedic accent in terms of pitch at all, which is a paradoxical conclusion, admittedly, to be drawn from an analysis which has used pitch as the sole instrument with which to measure."[38] Gray believes the chief operatives in realization of accent to be *alpaprāṇa* ("little breath") and *mahāprāṇa* ("big breath"), two terms used by Patañjali in his commentary (*Mahābhāṣya*) on the *Aṣṭādhyāyī* ("Eight Chapters") of the grammarian Pāṇini. Patañjali used the two terms to denote, respectively, non-aspirate and aspirate consonants. In a previous article dealing with Ṛgveda from Mahārāṣṭra, Gray has expanded the meanings of *alpa-* and *mahāprāṇa* so that each term implies three qualities.[39] In his view *alpaprāṇa* designates "(i) the quality of udātta, (ii) the quality of the initial component of svarita, and (iii) the quality of the absence of aspiration." *Mahāprāṇa*, on the other hand, implies "(iv) the quality of anudātta, (v) the quality of the final component of svarita, and (vi) the quality of aspiration."[40] He infers from all this that *anudātta* involves the process of relaxation and ordinary breath, *udātta* the process of tension and little breath, and *svarita* the process of tension and little breath returning to relaxation and normal breath.[41] Other features such as aspiration, hiatus (the gap between vowels),[42] and the occurrence of conjunct consonants affect the recitation.

The above considerations possibly are manifest to some extent in the *sādhāraṇa* Yajurvedic recitation, although the latter is not nearly as complicated as the Nampūtiri Ṛgvedic recitals described by Gray. It may be pointed out that Nampūtiri Yajurvedīs are always tonally consistent in their performances of the short and long *svarita*, a trait which may be compared to the practices of the Ṛgvedīs.[43] Gray, in a paragraph on Nampūtiri Yajurveda (presumably of the *sādhāraṇa* type), recognizes that "the svarita is always

[37]"An Analysis of Nambudiri Ṛgvedic Recitation and the Nature of the Vedic Accent," *Bulletin of the School of Oriental and African Studies* 22 (1959): 499-530.

[38]Ibid., p. 519.

[39]"An Analysis of Ṛgvedic Recitation," *Bulletin of the School of Oriental and African Studies* 22 (1959): 86-94.

[40]Ibid., p. 89.

[41]See Gray, "Nambudiri Ṛgvedic Recitation," p. 518.

[42]See Macdonell, *Vedic Grammar*, pp. 12-13.

[43]See Gray, "Nambudiri Ṛgvedic Recitation," pp. 501-2.

unerringly positioned."[44] He is also correct in observing "a tendency towards somewhat slurred recitation,"[45] which often results in tonal ambiguity. Forthcoming analyses will show that the slower recitation modes (*śālā mātrā, valiya saṃhitā, cantādikkat*) are much less ambiguous and generally are consistent in their interpretations of the accents. A further peculiarity of the *sādhāraṇa* mode is that, in the *mantra* portions of the TS, short vowels become long if followed by two or more consonants (including semivowels and *visarga* [-*ḥ*]), thus conforming to the requirements of meter (refer to syllables 8, 12, 16, 23, 34, 36, 44, 48, 60, 63, 65, 73, 74, 77, 82, 86, 93, 98, and 107 in the transcription above). The slower recitation modes ignore this rule of prosody.

Śālā Mātrā

Śālā mātrā, as the name implies, is a type of recitation used in the Vedic sacrifice,[46] *śālā* being equivalent to "sacrificial shed." Four pitches continue to be employed, but the intervallic relationships are different. The high pitch is now a minor third above the mid-tone, and the two lowest pitches (low, low middle) are a perfect fourth and major second below respectively.

Example 2. *Śālā Mātrā* (TS 1.1.1.1) [Tape Xb(3)C]

[44] Ibid., p. 509.

[45] Ibid.

[46] See Renou, *Vocabulaire*, pp. 148-49.

30 35
ya̱ kár - ma - ṇa̱ á pyā - ya - dhva -
40
m a - ghni - yā de - va - bhā̱ - gá - m ū́ - r - ja -
45 50
sva - tī̱ - ḥ pá - ya - sva - tī́ - ḥ pra̱ - já - va -
55 60
tī- r a - na - mī̱ - vá́ a - ya̱ - kṣmá́ má́
65 70
vaḥ ste̱ - ná i - śa - ta̱ má́ 'ghá - śam -
75 80
so ru̱ - drá - sya he̱ - tíḥ pá - ri vo vṛ - ṇa -
85 90
ktu dhru̱ - vá́ a̱ - smín gó - pa - tau syā -
95 100
ta ba̱ - hvī́ - r yá - ja - mā - na - sya pa̱ - śū́ - n pa -
105 110
hi i̱ - ṣé trí - ca - tvā - riṁ - śat

Śālā mātrā accents have the following tonal composition:

(1) *Udātta* on Short Vowels
- A. One tone (LM^{l}) on 42. Two tones ($LM^{s}M^{l}$) were probably intended, but the reciter was short of breath.
- B. One tone (M^{l}) on 106
- C. Two tones ($LM^{s}M^{sl}$) on 7, 11, 47, 65, 70, 74, 77, 78, 95
- D. Four tones ($LM^{s}M^{s}LM^{l}M^{l}$) on 29, 87. Same as *udātta* on long vowels because of the effect of (i) semivowel + consonant and (ii) nasal + consonant.

(2) *Udātta* on Long Vowels
- A. Four tones ($LM^{s}M^{sl}LM^{sl}M^{l}/L^{s}M^{sl}LM^{sl}M^{l}$) on 2, 4, 15, 19, 20, 24, 32, 43, 52, 58, 61, 62, 69, 85, 88, 94, 101, 105

(3) *Anudātta* on Short Vowels
- A. One tone (L^{sl}) on 1, 51, 104. Two of the three occur at the beginning of the line.
- B. Two tones ($M^{s}L^{sl}$) on 18, 28, 31, 60, 68, 73, 84, 86, 93, 100.

(4) *Anudātta* on Long Vowels
- A. Two tones ($M^{l}L^{l}$) on 3
- B. Three tones ($M^{s}L^{sl}M^{s}/LM^{s}L^{sl}M^{s}$) on 6, 10, 14, 41, 46, 57, 64, 76

(5) *Svarita* on Short Vowels
- A. One tone (H^{l}) on 21. Lack of breath here.
- B. Two tones ($LM^{s}H^{sl}/M^{s}H^{sl}$) on 8, 12, 16, 25, 30, 44, 48, 53, 59, 63, 79, 89, 96, 107
- C. Two tones ($LM^{s}M^{s}$) on 75. M^{s} appears instead of H^{s} due to lack of breath.
- D. Six tones ($LM^{s}M^{l}LM^{s}H^{s}LM^{l}M^{l}$) on 71. The effect of following nasal + consonant.

(6) *Svarita* on Long Vowels
- A. Six tones ($LM^{s}M^{l}LM^{s}H^{s}LM^{l}M^{l}$) on 5, 33, 66, 102

(7) *Pracaya* on Short Vowels
- A. One tone (M^{sl}) on 13, 17, 22, 23. Compare with (1)B.
- B. Two tones ($LM^{s}M^{sl}$) on 26, 34, 35, 36, 37, 40, 45, 49, 55, 56, 67, 81, 82, 83, 92, 98, 99. Same as (1)C.
- C. Four tones ($LM^{s}M^{s}LM^{s}M^{l}$) on 109. Effect of following nasal + consonant. Compare with (1)D.
- D. Five tones ($M^{s}LM^{l}M^{s}LM^{l}M^{l}$) on 103, 110. Both are finals in the line. A slight extension of (7)C.

(8) *Pracaya* on Long Vowels
- A. Four tones ($LM^{s}M^{sl}LM^{sl}M^{sl}/L^{s}M^{sl}LM^{sl}M^{sl}$) on 9, 27, 38, 39, 50, 54, 72, 80, 90, 91, 97, 108. Same as (2)A.

Valiya Saṃhitā

For some as yet unexplained reason, *valiya* ("strong, powerful, great")[47] *saṃhitā*, the only *saṃhitā* recitation style with a Dravidian name, falls outside the complex *sādhāraṇa-śālā-cantādikkat.* It was described for Staal as "something in between *śālā mātrā* and *cantādikkal.*"[48] In any case, the relationships of the four pitches are the same as in *śālā mātrā.*

Example 3. *Valiya Saṃhitā* (TS 6.5.6.1) [Tape XXIIb(2)]

[47]DED, no. 4317.

[48]Staal, *Nambudiri Veda Recitation*, p. 58.

The *valiya* accents can be described as follows:

(1) *Udātta* on Short Vowels

A. Two tones (L^sM^l) on 1, 5, 17, 21, 30, 38, 69, 70, 78, 86, 97, 102

B. Four tones ($LM^sM^sLM^lM^l$) on 112. It is final in the line.

(2) *Udātta* on Long Vowels

A. Four tones ($LM^sM^sLM^{sl}M^l$) on 9, 12, 24, 31, 33, 34, 41, 45, 50, 52, 57, 61, 74, 76, 88, 90, 92, 93, 107, 109

(3) *Anudātta* on Short Vowels

A. One tone (L^l) on 4, 16, 20, 23, 29, 37, 40, 44, 49, 51, 56, 65, 68, 73, 87, 96, 106, 108

B. Two tones (M^sL^l) on 85

(4) *Anudātta* on Long Vowels

A. Two tones ($M^{sl}L^l$) on 8, 11, 32, 60, 75, 77, 89, 91, 98, 111

B. Three tones ($M^lL^lLM^l$) on 101. Effect of following nasal + consonant.

(5) *Svarita* on Short Vowels

A. Two tones (LM^sH^l) on 2, 18, 25, 42, 46, 53, 62, 99, 103, 110

B. Six tones ($LM^lM^lLM^sH^sLM^lM^l$) on 58. Effect of following nasal + semivowel. Same as (6)A.

(6) *Svarita* on Long Vowels

A. Six tones ($LM^{sl}M^lLM^sH^sLM^lM^l$) on 6, 10, 13, 22, 35, 39, 66, 71, 79, 94

(7) *Pracaya* on Short Vowels

A. One tone (M^l) on 19

B. Two tones (L^sM^l) on 3, 26, 27, 28, 36, 54, 55, 59, 64, 67, 82, 83, 95, 100, 105. Same as (1)A.

C. Four tones ($LM^sM^sLM^lM^l$) on 14, 48, 84. Effect of following nasal + consonant (but see 14). Compare with (1)B and (8)A.

(8) *Pracaya* on Long Vowels

A. Four tones ($LM^sM^sLM^lM^l$) on 7, 15, 43, 47, 63, 72, 80, 81, 104. Same as (2)A.

Cantādikkat

The term *cantādikkat*, which designates the slowest of the four *saṃhitā* types, is perhaps a combination of the Sanskrit words *chanda* ("shape, form") and *ādi* ("beginning"),[49] an etymology which seems likely by the fact that the Dravidian word *cantam* is possibly derived from *chanda.*[50] Therefore *cantādikkat* may refer to the teaching of *saṃhitā* recitation and hence to the "first form" of the TS learned by the student. This theory tends to be confirmed by an observation of Staal, who writes:

> . . . *sādhāraṇā, śālā* and *cantādikkal* may be related to the three modes of speech *druta* [fast], *madhyama* [medium] and *vilambita* [slow] mentioned by the Ṛ[k-]Pr[ātiśākhya]. In the Prātiśākhya they are related to *abhyāsa*, "repetition (whilst reciting oneself)", to *prayoga* "(recitation for) sacrificial use" and *upadeśa*, "teaching (of recitation)", respecitvely.[51]

[49]SED, p. 404, col. 3, and p. 136, col. 3.

[50]See DED, no. 1921.

[51]Staal, *Nambudiri Veda Recitation*, p. 58.

Four tones continue to be employed, as in the other recitation modes. In relation to the middle pitch they are a minor (sometimes major) third above, a perfect fourth and minor second below.

Example 4. *Cantādikkat* (TS 6.4.6.1) [Tape XXa(1)]

50
tyā de - vā́ - n a - bhyā - yan -
55
ta té de - vā́ bí - bhyā -
60
ta ín - dra - m ú - pā -
65
dhā - van tā́ - n ín -
70
dro 'n - tar - yā - mé - ṇa
75
80
an - tá - rā - dha - tta tá - d an -
85
tar - yā - má - sya an - tar -
90
yā - ma - tvám yá - d an -

The accents are realized in the following manner:

(1) *Udātta* on Short Vowels

A. Two tones (LM^lM^l) on 4, 10, 11, 32, 36, 44, 47, 58, 63, 75, 79, 83, 90, 96, 102, 104, 108, 111. Note that 108 is not affected by the following semivowel + consonant. Does the aspiration prevent the change to a long *udātta*?

B. Six tones ($L^sM^lL^sM^lL^sM^l$) on 25, 61, 68, 89, 103. All are instances of (i) an *udātta* vowel followed by nasal + consonant, or (ii) final *udātta* in the line. Same as (2)A.

(2) *Udātta* on Long Vowels

A. Six tones ($L^sM^lL^sM^lL^sM^l$) on 2, 3, 6, 18, 20, 23, 27, 35, 41, 50, 55, 57, 67, 72, 94, 98

(3) *Anudātta* on Short Vowels

A. One tone (L^l) on 51. This is the treatment of a short *anudātta* before an independent *svarita*.

B. Two tones (L^lLM^l) on 5, 24, 46, 62, 95

C. Three tones ($LM^lL^sLM^l$) on 88. This is an *anudātta* following *sarvānudātta* syllables.

D. Four tones ($L^lLM^lL^sLM^l$) on 26, 74. Both followed by nasal + consonant; hence the same as (4)A.

(4) *Anudātta* on Long Vowels
   A. Four tones ($L^{sl}LM^{l}L^{s}LM^{l}$) on 1, 19, 22, 34, 43, 49, 56, 71, 82, 93, 101, 107, 110

(5) *Svarita* on Short Vowels
   A. Three tones ($LM^{s}H^{s}M^{l}/L^{s}H^{s}M^{l}$) on 12, 21, 28, 33, 37, 42, 45, 48, 59, 73, 76, 84, 105, 109
   B. Seven tones ($L^{s}M^{l}L^{s}M^{l}L^{s}H^{s}M^{l}$) on 7, 80, 91, 99. All are followed by (i) semivowel + consonant, or (ii) nasal + consonant. Therefore, the same as (6)B.

(6) *Svarita* on Long Vowels
   A. Six tones ($LM^{l}L^{s}LM^{l}L^{s}H^{s}M^{l}$) on 52. An independent *svarita*.
   B. Seven tones ($L^{s}M^{l}L^{s}M^{l}L^{s}H^{s}M^{l}$) on 64, 69, 97, 112

(7) *Pracaya* on Short Vowels
   A. One tone (L^{l}) on 85. This is the first in a series of *sarvānudātta* syllables.
   B. Two tones ($LM^{l}M^{l}$) on 8, 14, 16, 29, 30, 39, 77. Same as (1)A.
   C. Six tones ($L^{s}LM^{l}L^{s}LM^{l}L^{s}LM^{l}$) on 86. A short *sarvānudātta* syllable followed by two semivowels. Same as (8)B.
   D. Six tones ($L^{s}M^{l}L^{s}M^{l}L^{s}M^{l}$) on 9, 15, 17, 31, 40, 53, 54, 60, 66, 70, 78, 81, 92. All are *pracayas* which are (i) final in the line, (ii) followed by nasal + consonant, or (iii) followed by two semivowels. Compare with (1)B, (2)A, and (8)A.

(8) *Pracaya* on Long Vowels
   A. Six tones ($L^{s}M^{l}L^{s}M^{l}L^{s}M^{l}$) on 13, 38, 65, 100, 106
   B. Six tones ($L^{s}LM^{l}L^{s}LM^{l}L^{s}LM^{l}$) on 87. A long *sarvānudātta* syllable. Compare with (7)C.

In order to discern the tonal changes which the accents undergo from one recitation style to the next, a tabulation of pitch gradation is in order. So that an accurate picture of tonal evolution can emerge, the factors which cause modification of the normal accentual patterns (final position in the line, the presence of following nasal + consonant/semivowel [or semivowel + consonant/semivowel], independence of the *svarita, pracaya*s [*sarvānudātta*s] initial in the line, and so on) will not be taken into account; that is, only the customary accentuation scheme will be entered. *Sādhāraṇā mātrā* presents a problem in that there is little uniformity; here I use the pattern which occurs most frequently for each accent (Table 1).

Table 1

Accentual Pitch Patterns of the *Saṃhitā* Recitations

	Sādhāraṇā Mātrā	*Śālā Mātrā*	*Valiya Saṃhitā*	*Cantādikkat*
Short *Udātta*	M^{sl}	$LM^{s}M^{sl}$	$L^{s}M^{l}$	$LM^{l}M^{l}$
Long *Udātta*	$L^{s}M^{s}LM^{s}M^{l}$	$L^{s}(M^{l})M^{sl}LM^{sl}M^{l}$	$LM^{s}M^{s}LM^{sl}M^{l}$	$L^{s}M^{l}L^{s}M^{l}L^{s}M^{l}$
Short *Anudātta*	L^{sl}/M^{sl}	$M^{s}L^{sl}$	L^{l}	$L^{l}LM^{l}$
Long *Anudātta*	$M^{sl}L^{l}$	$(L^{l})M^{s}L^{sl}M^{s}$	$M^{sl}L^{l}$	$L^{sl}LM^{l}L^{s}LM^{l}$
Short *Svarita*	H^{sl}	$(L^{l})M^{s}H^{sl}$	$LM^{s}H^{l}$	$L^{s}(M^{l})H^{s}M^{l}$
Long *Svarita*	$L^{s}M^{s}L^{s}H^{s}LM^{s}$	$LM^{s}M^{l}LM^{s}H^{s}LM^{l}M^{l}$	$LM^{sl}M^{l}LM^{s}H^{s}LM^{l}M^{l}$	$L^{s}M^{l}L^{s}M^{l}L^{s}H^{s}M^{l}$
Short *Pracaya*	M^{sl}	$LM^{s}M^{sl}$	$L^{s}M^{l}$	$LM^{l}M^{l}$
Long *Pracaya*	$L^{s}(M^{l})M^{s}LM^{sl}$	$L^{s}(M^{l})M^{sl}LM^{sl}M^{sl}$	$LM^{s}M^{s}LM^{l}M^{l}$	$L^{s}M^{l}L^{s}M^{l}L^{s}M^{l}$

According to number of tones, the accents are realized in the four recitation modes as follows: short *udātta*, 1/2/2/2; long *udātta*, 4/4/4/6; short *anudātta*, 1/2/1/2; long *anudātta*, 2/3/2/4; short *svarita*, 1/2/2/3; long *svarita*, 5/6/6/7; short *pracaya*, 1/2/2/2; long *pracaya*, 3/4/4/6. Long *svarita* is therefore the most melismatic of the accents, and short *anudātta* has the fewest tones. *Udātta* and *pracaya* are practically identical.[52] The number of tones associated with an accent usually remains the same or increases as the reciter moves from one mode to another of increased duration. Exceptions are short and long *anudātta* in *valiya saṃhitā*; although (as previously noted) the latter is somewhat more lengthy than *śālā* recitation, the two *anudātta* types are tonally diminished by one tone each. This is not to say that *valiya* recitation is in fact more rapid than *śālā mātrā*. For example, as far as pitch is concerned the long *svarita* is exactly the same in the two modes; but a comparison of the transcriptions (Examples 2 and 3) shows that the *svarita* of the *valiya* genre is taken at a decidedly slower tempo.

Śālā, valiya, and *cantādikkat* performances are quite measured, but the same cannot be said for *sādhāraṇā mātrā*—at least not for the recitation transcribed above (Example 1), which draws its text from a *mantra* portion of the TS and is hence influenced by metrical considerations. However, the transcribed versions of the other three styles (Examples 2-4) have prose texts taken from *brāhmaṇa* (exegetical) parts of the TS, and it is possible to hear in them divisions into fixed time units (= *mātrā*s?). These units are shown in Table 2 (see facing page); again, those elements which change the value of an accent (nasality, and so on) are not taken into account. Therefore, the respective *śālā* and *valiya* accents are identical as far as time units are concerned. As a rule, *cantādikkat* increases the values of accents on long vowels by one unit; the sole exception is long *svarita*, which is comprised of three units in each of the modes.

Pada Recitations

Ordinary *Padapāṭha*

Vedic *saṃhitā*s, like the TS, are ordinarily recited according to the rule that the sentence, verse, quarter-verse, or section sung in a single breath (as in Examples 1-4 above) is considered the euphonic

[52]This is also the view of Taittirīya-Prātiśākhya 21.10. See Whitney's edition, p. 386.

Table 2
Accentual Time Units for Three *Saṃhitā* Modes

	Śālā Mātrā	*Valiya Saṃhitā*	*Cantādikkat*
Short *Udātta*	1	1	1
Long *Udātta*	2	2	3
Short *Anudātta*	1	1	1
Long *Anudātta*	1	1	2
Short *Svarita*	1	1	1
Long *Svarita*	3	3	3
Short *Pracaya*	1	1	1
Long *Pracaya*	2	2	3

and accentual unit. This type of recitation (*saṃhitāpāṭha*) has been the basis of the analyses presented thus far. But the *saṃhitās* can also be recited in such a way that the individual word (*pada*), not a group of words, is the basic entity of utterance; thus, the Sanskrit laws of coalescence (*sandhi*) of final and initial letters of words are ignored completely, and each word appears in its unchanged, radical form. The opening *mantra* of the TS, which has already been cited in order to explain the accents, may be repeated now in its two forms.

saṃhitāpāṭha: / i̱ṣé tvo̱rjé tvā̍ vā̱yáva̍ḥ sthopā̱yáva̍ḥ sthạ /
AU A U S A U S P A U S P

padapāṭha: / i̱ṣé / tvā̱ / ū̱rjé / tvā̱ / vā̱yáva̍ḥ / stha̱ /
AU P A U P A U S P

u̱pā̱yáva̱ íty u̍pa ā̱yáva̍ḥ / stha̱ /[53]
P A U A U S P A U S P

[53]See N. S. Sontakke and T. N. Dharmādhikārī, eds., *Taittirīya-Saṃhitā, with the Padapātha and the Commentaries of Bhaṭṭa Bhāskara Miśra and Sāyaṇācārya*, vol. I (Poona: Vaidika Saṃśodhana Maṇḍala, 1970), p. 12.

Clarification of two features of the *pada* text just presented is necessary. Firstly, it should be noted that two words, *tvā* and *stha* (both stated twice), are completely without accent. Although they are marked with the *anudātta* sign, I label them *pracayas*; this designation seems preferable, for the normal function of an *anudātta* is to introduce an *udātta*, which, of course, is absent in both cases. Secondly, it will be observed that the next to last unit is comprised not of one but of four words. The reason for this departure (which occurs often in *pada* texts) is that the word *upāyavaḥ* is a compound (*upa* + *āyavaḥ*). The method *(parigraha)* of presenting compounds in the TS *padapāṭha* is to follow the compound with the word *iti* ("in this manner") and then to assign each word of the compound its separate accent. Therefore, the units of accentuation of *upāyavaḥ* are the following (bracketed):

u̱pā̱yávā̱ íty upa-ā̱yávaḥ

In this example the final "i" of *iti* has been changed to "y" to satisfy one of the rules of vowel *sandhi* (these laws of junction are too numerous to be discussed in full in this study). The *pada* text utilizes *iti* also in other ways—specifically, to follow prepositions (*upasargas*), particles (*avyāyas*), and words whose final vowels are not subject to euphonic combination (*pragraha-padas*).[54]

The *padapāṭha* extract which I have transcribed (Example 5) makes use of four tones, as do the four kinds of *saṃhitāpāṭha*. In this particular performance the pitches are related in the same way as those of *cantādikkat* recitation.

Example 5. *Padapāṭha* (TS 5.6.8.3) [Tape XXIb(6)]

54The entire fourth chapter of the Taittirīya-Prātiśākhya is devoted to a full discussion of the *pragrahas* (see Whitney's edition, pp. 99-132). For an exhaustive study of the *padapāṭha*, see Albrecht Weber, "Über den Padapāṭha der Taittirīya-Saṃhitā," *Indische Studien* 13 (1873): 1-128.

lo - kám / a - bhí - ti / ja - ya - tí / jā - nu - daghnám í - ti
jā - nu da - ghnám / cin - vī - ta - ḥ / pra - tha - mám /
cin-vā - ná - ḥ / gā-ya - tri - yā́ / e - vá / i - mám /
lo-kám / a - bhyā́ ro - ha - tí - ty a - bhi ā́ - ro -
ha - ti / nā - bhi - daghnám í - ti nā - bhi da - ghnám /
cin- vī - ta - ḥ / dvi tí - yam / cin - vā - ná - ḥ / tri -
ṣṭú - bhā / e - vá / an - tá - ri - kṣam / a - bhyā́ - ro -
ha - tí - ty a - bhi ā́ - ro - ha - ti / grī - va - da - ghnám
í - ti grí - va da - ghnám / cin - vī - ta - ḥ / tr - tí -
yam / cin - vā - ná - ḥ / já - ga - tyā / e - vá /

a̱ - múm / lo̱ - kám / a̱ - bhyá̄ - ro haṯ - tī- ty a - bhi
á̄ - ro - ha - ti / ná / a̱ - gním / ci̱ - tvá̄ /
rā - má̄ - m / ú - pé - ti / i̱ - yā̱ - t / a̱ - yo̱ - náu /
ré - ta - ḥ / dhā̱ - syā̱ - mi̱ / í - ti / ná / dvi̱ -
tí̄ - yam / ci̱ - tvá̄ / a̱n - yá - sya /
strí - yam //

The various accents are constituted as follows:

(1) *Udātta* on Short Vowels

A. One tone (M^s) on 4, 35, 75, 96, 114, 129, 156, 169, 180. It occurs mostly on the first syllables of words and hence is often in initial position.

B. One tone (LM^{sl}) on 8, 34, 74, 91, 113, 178. It appears mainly on medial and final syllables of words.

C. Four tones ($LM^{sl}M^sLM^{sl}M^{sl}$) on 3, 10, 18, 20, 22, 24, 46, 49, 55, 57, 59, 80, 89, 94, 119, 128, 133, 135, 137, 149, 151, 171. All are finals before a pause.

D. Five tones ($M^sLM^sM^sLM^sM^s$) on 40. Extension of C.

(2) *Udātta* on Long Vowels

A. One tone (LM^{l}) on 64, 85, 103, 124, 142. All appear in medial position.

B. Two tones ($M^{sl}LM^{s}$) on 26, 61, 67, 100, 106, 139, 145, 164, 173. All are in initial or medial position. An extension of A.

C. Four tones ($LM^{l}M^{s}LM^{s}M^{l}$) on 14, 16, 153, 155, 163. All are finals before a pause.

D. Four tones ($M^{s}LM^{s}M^{s}LM^{l}$) on 157. The second of two successive *udātta*s.

E. Six tones ($LM^{l}M^{s}LM^{s}M^{s}LM^{s}M^{sl}$) on 53, 176. Finals before a pause. An extension of C.

(3) *Anudātta* on Short Vowels

A. One tone (M^{sl}) on 7, 9, 63, 102, 141. All in medial position.

B. One tone (LM^{sl}) on 33, 52, 73, 112. All in medial position.

C. One tone (L^{sl}) on 15, 19, 25, 39, 45, 56, 60, 79, 84, 90, 95, 99, 118, 123, 134, 138, 150, 152, 172, 175, 177. Nearly always in initial position.

(4) *Anudātta* on Long Vowels

A. One tone (L^{l}) on 17, 21, 23, 54, 58, 93, 132, 136, 154. All are in initial position.

B. One tone (LM^{l}) on 2, 48, 88, 127. All in medial position.

C. Two tones ($M^{s}LM^{s}$) on 162. Extension of B.

(5) *Svarita* on Short Vowels

A. One tone (H^{sl}) on 36, 65, 76, 97, 104, 115, 143. All are medial.

B. One tone (M^{l}) on 130. Probably an error.

C. Five tones ($M^{s}LM^{s}H^{s}LM^{s}M^{sl}$) on 27, 158, 165, 170, 179. All are finals before a pause.

D. Six tones ($LM^{l}M^{s}LM^{s}H^{s}LM^{s}M^{l}$) on 181. Final before a pause. An extension of C.

E. Seven tones ($M^{s}LM^{s}M^{s}LM^{s}H^{s}LM^{s}M^{sl}$) on 86, 125, 174. Finals before a pause (extensions of C and D).

(6) *Svarita* on Long Vowels

A. Four tones ($M^{sl}LM^{s}H^{s}LM^{s}$) on 62, 101, 140. All appear in medial position.

B. Five tones ($LM^{s}M^{s}LM^{s}H^{s}LM^{s}$) on 5, 68, 107, 146. All are in medial position (an extension of A).

C. Six tones ($LM^{l}M^{s}LM^{s}H^{s}LM^{s}M^{l}$) on 92. Final before a pause.

(7) *Pracaya* on Short Vowels

A. One tone (L^{sl}) on 1, 28, 29, 41, 44, 47, 81, 87, 120, 126, 159, 161. Most are in initial position and are hence *sarvānudāttas*.

B. One tone (LM^{l}) on 6. Medial position.

C. One tone (M^{sl}) on 12, 32, 51, 69, 72, 108, 111, 147. Medial.

D. Three tones ($LM^{l}L^{s}LM^{l}$) on 30. Final before a pause on an accentless word.

E. Four tones ($L^{s}LM^{l}L^{s}LM^{l}$) on 13, 43, 83, 122, 168. An extension of D.

F. Four tones ($LM^{sl}M^{s}LM^{s}M^{s}$) on 66, 70, 78, 98, 105, 109, 144, 148. Finals before a pause on an accented word.

G. Five tones ($M^{s}LM^{s}M^{s}LM^{s}M^{s}$) on 38, 117. Finals before a pause (an extension of F).

(8) *Pracaya* on Long Vowels

A. One tone (L^{l}) on 11, 31, 50, 166. All are initials (*sarvānudāttas*) in the line.

B. One tone (LM^{l}) on 37, 42, 71, 77, 82, 110, 116, 121. Medials.

C. Two tones ($M^{l}LM^{s}$) on 167. Medial.

D. Three tones ($LM^{l}L^{s}LM^{l}$) on 160. Final before a pause on an accentless word.

E. Six tones ($LM^{l}M^{s}LM^{s}M^{s}LM^{s}M^{l}$) on 131. Final before a pause on an accented word.

Here, therefore, the factors which most determine the tonal make-up of an accent appear to be the initiality, mediality, or finality of that accent in the word isolate or line (in case of a compound). Thus, this ordinary *padapāṭha* cannot be compared with any of the *saṃhitā* recitations, where the accents are almost entirely confined to medial position. Staal refers to a *valiya padapāṭha,*[55] which, with *valiya saṃhitā*, is considered an addition to the usual three components (*saṃhitā, pada, koṭṭu*) of an *ōttūṭṭu*, thus enlarging the feast to include five elements (hence: *pañcanta* or *pañcasandha*). The *pada* style discussed above, however, is clearly the normal type, for the speed of recitation is often faster than the *sādhāraṇā mātrā* of *saṃhitāpāṭha*.

[55] *Nambudiri Veda Recitation*, p. 61.

Koṭṭu

Koṭṭu is the tour de force of the Naṃpūtiri Yajurvedīs; nothing like it is heard among any of the other Brāhmaṇ communities of India. Actually it is a unique way of reciting the *padapāṭha*, except that here each *anuvāka* of the TS is divided into sets of four words. A reciter chants the first four words of the *anuvāka* by himself, in ordinary *padapāṭha*; these same four words are then repeated rapidly three times by the remaining Vaidikas, who are called collectively the *caṅgiṭikkār.*[56] Their recitation strikes the uninitiated listener as monotonous *ekaśruti* (recited on a single pitch), but I am told that the Vedic paṇḍits are able to hear in it all of the pitches peculiar to *udātta, svarita*, and so on. Approximately when the *caṅgiṭikkār* are beginning their third repetition, the soloist begins the next group of four words. As he approaches the fourth word of the set, the *caṅgiṭikkār* start their threefold repetition. So there is a continual overlapping of the parts of the soloist and the *caṅgiṭikkār*. This characteristic can be observed in Example 6; here the soloist is chanting the last word of the four-word group *rundhe candram asi mama* as the others are just beginning their three statements.

Example 6. *Koṭṭu* (TS 6.1.4.8) [Tape XXIVa(1)]

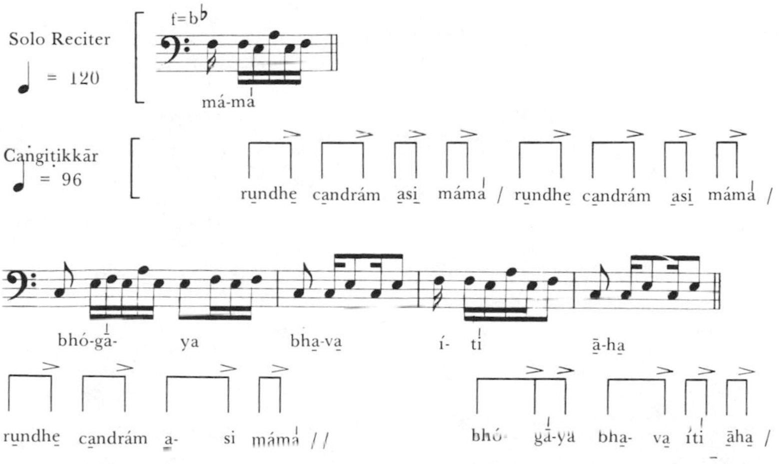

56This word is perhaps a combination of the Sanskrit *caṅga* ("being a judge of": see SED, p. 382, col. 2) and the Malayālam *iṭikka* ("to beat": see DED, no. 376). The *caṅgiṭikkār* are quite rhythmic in their recital (similar in fact to the "beating" of a drum), and they are also "judges" of the recitation of the solo reciter.

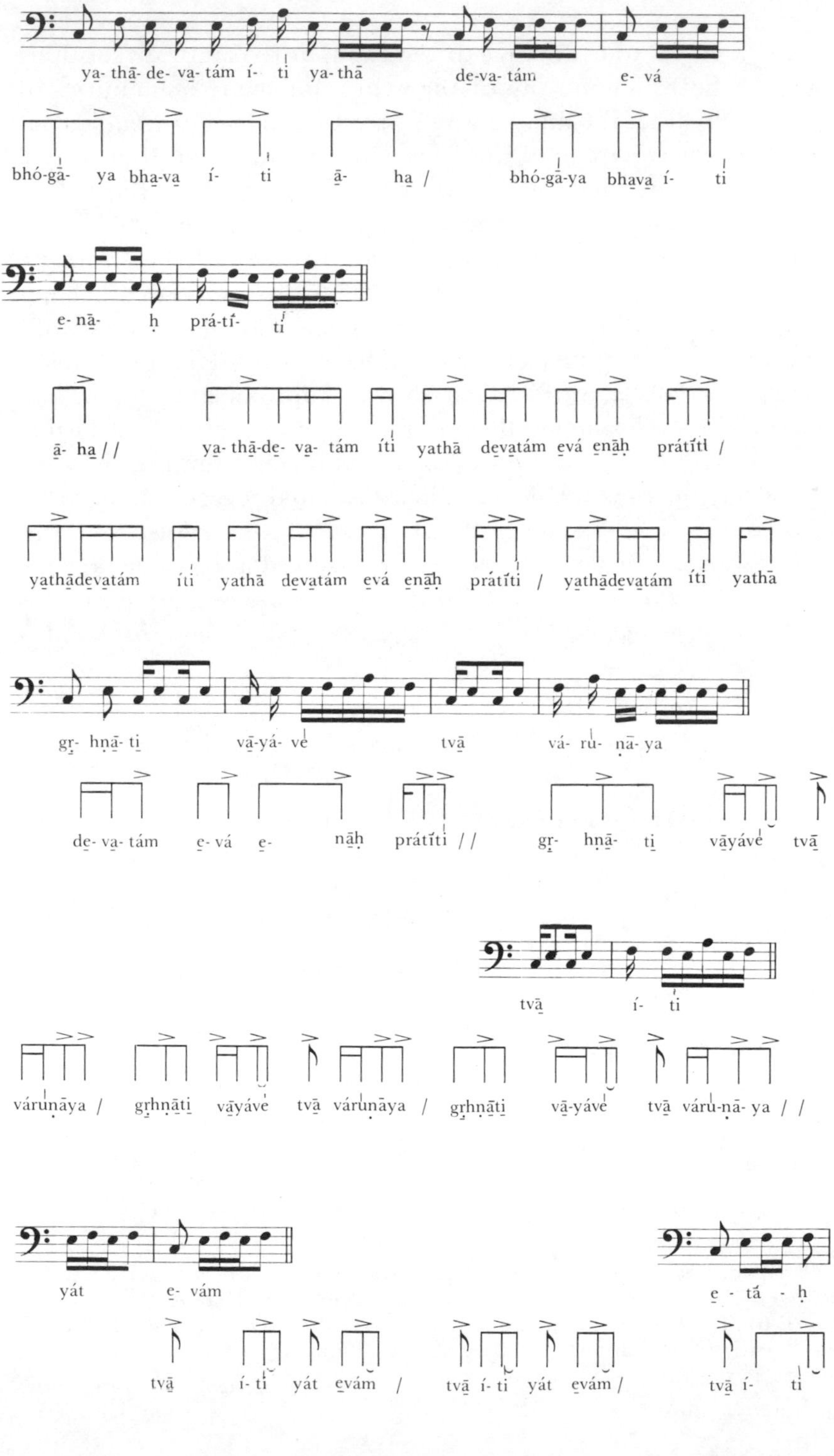
ya- thā- de- va- tám í- ti ya- thā de-va- tám e- vá
bhó-gā- ya bha-va í- ti ā- ha / bhó-gā-ya bhava í- ti
e- nā- ḥ prá-tī- ti
ā- ha / / ya- thā-de- va- tám íti yathā devatám evá enāḥ prátīti /
yathādevatám íti yathā devatám evá enāḥ prátīti / yathādevatám íti yathā
gr- hṇā- ti vā-yá- ve tvā vá- ru- ṇā- ya
de- va- tám e- vá e- nāḥ prátīti / / gr- hṇā- ti vāyáve tvā
tvā í- ti
várunāya / grhṇāti vāyáve tvā várunāya / grhṇāti vā-yáve tvā váru-ṇā- ya / /
yát e- vám
e - tā - ḥ
tvā í- ti yát evám / tvā í- ti yát evám / tvā í- ti

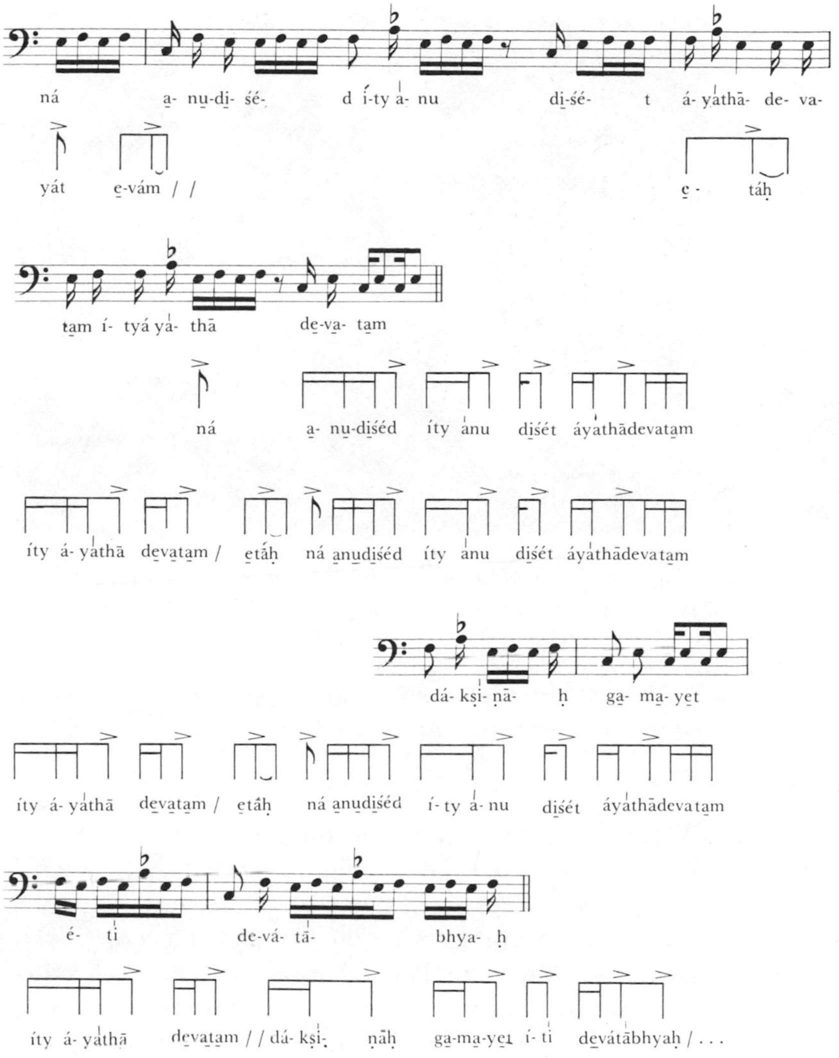

When a compound word (a *parigraha-pada*) appears in a four-word segment, the soloist must start his recitation earlier than usual due to the increased number of syllables (see, for example, his treatment of the compound *yathādevatam*, occurring early in Example 6). When a compound is found as the third word in the group of four, the *caṅgiṭikkār* ordinarily are silent as the soloist recites the compound (see, towards the end of Example 6, his recitation of the word *anudiśed*).

Figure 4. Ghoṣam. *The Ghoṣi, Śrī Kaplinnāṭṭa Vāsudevan Nampūtiri (back to camera), is seated in front of the nilaviḷakku, a bronze lamp with two flames. To his left are five members of the caṅgiṭikkār (left to right): Śrī Cittūr Nārāyanan Nampūṭirippāt, Śrī Deśamaṅgalam Śaṅkaran Nampūtirippāṭ (partially hidden), Śrī Ayirit Śaktidharan Bhaṭṭatirippāṭ, Śrī Vaṭakkēṭattu Nārāyaṇan Nampūtiri, and Śrī Karōḷit Kuññuṇṇi Nampūtiri.*

Ghoṣam

At times *koṭṭu* recitation may be interrupted by what the Yajurvedīs call *ghoṣam*, a Sanskrit word meaning "tumult."[57] The signal for beginning *ghoṣam* comes during *koṭṭu*, when certain textual syllables are shouted out by successive members of the *caṅgiṭikkār*. Usually only one syllable is emphasized in this way for each statement of the four-word group, although there is no set rule as to which syllable of the group will be shouted. However, in a word with several syllables the shout must take place only on the last syllable. The last shout to be made occurs on the final syllable of the four-word set and is the loudest yell of all. Actually the shouting continues only a minute or so, after which the *caṅgiṭikkār* begin reciting slower and with musical pitches—an anticipation of the start of *ghoṣam*. This lasts only a short time (just long enough to repeat the final set of words), and then *ghoṣam* proper begins. During *ghoṣam* only one particular Yajurvedī, called the *ghoṣi*, serves as the soloist (in *koṭṭu* the Vaidikas take turns in this role, each reciter being seated to the right of the previous soloist—that

[57] SED, p. 378, col. 1.

is, the change takes place in a counter-clockwise manner). Structurally *ghoṣam* is the same as *koṭṭu*: recitation proceeds in four-word segments, each segment stated once by the *ghoṣi*, three times by the *caṅgiṭikkār*, with the characteristic overlapping. There are two principal differences, however. Firstly, the words uttered by the *caṅgiṭikkār* are done so "with *svara*," in contrast to the *ekaśruti* (monotone) style of *koṭṭu*. Secondly, *koṭṭu* is carried on at a constant tempo and dynamic level (the shouting excepted), whereas *ghoṣam* starts very slowly and quietly, then gradually builds in intensity to a powerful, even vociferous climax, where the assembled Brāhmaṇs (at this point quite animated) raise their arms in rhythm with the chant (see Figure 4).[58]

A portion of the *caṅgiṭikkār*'s recital, without repeats, is presented in Example 7, although the transcription does not adequately convey the majesty of the performance. A certain vastness and feeling of timelessness, even immortality, is suggested by their rendition, especially in its early stages; this is partly because each of the *caṅgiṭikkār* recites at a completely arbitrary tonal level, even though he is careful to maintain the proper intervallic perspectives. Movement is therefore in huge blocks of sound, one gigantic tone cluster followed by another. Recitations of *saṃhitā* and ordinary *pada* are done this way when the full body participates; but these recitals take place at a constant tempo and dynamic plane, and they are minus the mournful interjections of a singer such as the *ghoṣi*.

Example 7. *Ghoṣam: Caṅgitikkār* Recitation (from TS 6.1.5.1) [Tape XXIVa(2)]

[58] See also the photograph in Staal, *Nambudiri Veda Recitation*, fig. 5.

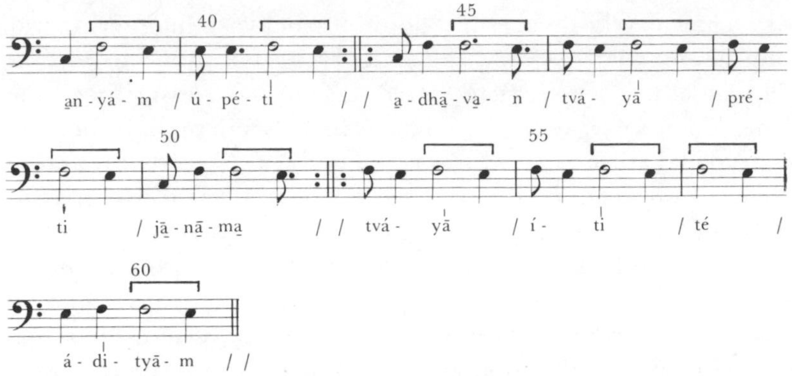

The *caṅgiṭikkār* part is chanted on three pitches; in relation to the highest, which is most prominent, the others are the perfect fourth and the minor second below (other *ōttūṭṭu* recitations with *svara* utilize four tones, as noted in previous analyses). A word with one syllable, or the final syllable of a word with two or more syllables, is sung with the elongated high pitch descending to middle level (this feature is bracketed in the transcription and holds regardless of accent). The same is true for the final syllables of the analyzed members of compounds (the two words following *iti*).

The accents are now examined, as far as analyzation is possible in this form. All notes except eighths and sixteenths will be counted long.

(1) *Udātta* on Short Vowels
- A. One tone (M^{sl}) on 6, 9, 13, 40, 58. All either occur in medial position or else are initials when the following syllable is not final.
- B. One tone (L^{l}) on 36. An initial followed by nasal + semivowel.
- C. Two tones ($H^{s}M^{l}$) on 27, 46, 53, 55. All are in initial position.
- D. Two tones ($H^{l}M^{l}$) on 29, 39. Both are finals.

(2) *Udātta* on Long Vowels
- A. One tone (L^{s}) on 20. A medial syllable which is not followed by a final.
- B. One tone (M^{l}) on 41. An *udātta* immediately following another *udātta*.
- C. Two tones ($H^{s}M^{l}$) on 25, 30, 48. An initial or medial syllable followed by a final.
- D. Two tones ($H^{l}M^{l}$) on 2, 3, 19, 57. All are finals except 19, which precedes a syllable absorbed through *sandhi*.

(3) *Anudātta* on Short Vowels
   A. One tone (L^{sl}) on 8, 38. One is in medial position; the other is an initial followed by nasal + semivowel.
   B. One tone (M^{l}) on 5, 18. An *anudātta* following a *sarvānudātta* syllable.
   C. One tone (H^{s}) on 24. Medial position.
   D. Two tones ($H^{l}M^{l}$) on 34, 45, 52. All are finals.

(4) *Anudātta* on Long Vowels: No examples.

(5) *Svarita* on Short Vowels
   A. One tone (H^{sl}) on 7, 10, 14, 21, 59. All are medials.
   B. Two tones ($H^{l}M^{l}$) on 26, 28, 31, 37, 42, 49, 56. Finals.

(6) *Svarita* on Long Vowels
   A. Two tones ($H^{l}M^{l}$) on 47, 54. Both are in final position.

(7) *Pracaya* on Short Vowels
   A. One tone (L^{s}) on 16, 23, 32, 43. All are *sarvānudātta*s.
   B. One tone (H^{s}) on 17. A *sarvānudātta* in medial position (those of A are initial in the line).
   C. Two tones ($H^{l}M^{l}$) on 12, 15, 22. All are finals.

(8) *Pracaya* on Long Vowels
   A. One tone (L^{s}) on 4, 50. Both are initial *sarvānudātta*s.
   B. One tone (H^{sl}) on 11, 33, 44, 51. Syllables in medial position, including *sarvānudātta*s not initial in the line.
   C. Two tones ($H^{l}M^{l}$) on 35, 60. Both are finals in the line.

The *ghoṣi*, whose recitation is similar to ordinary *padapāṭha*, may at any time shout out the third word of any four-word group; when this takes place the others are silent. If the word is a compound, only the second of the analyzed components can be shouted. Occasionally the *ghoṣi* intones a syllable with a great amount of wavering (*kampa*); for example, in the set "*te anyaḥ anyam upeti*" the final syllable *-yam* of the third word was recited with thirty-one tones. If ever the *ghoṣi* makes a mistake, *ghoṣam* must yield to *koṭṭu* recitation. If an error is not committed, then at the climax the *caṅgiṭikkār* begin again to shout out textual syllables as a sign that *koṭṭu* is soon to be resumed.

Koṭṭu and *ghoṣam* are always begun in the evening. In olden times there was, of course, no electricity, and a kind of bronze lamp with two flames, the *nilaviḷakku*,[59] was used for light. Its employment at ceremonies has been carried over to the present day; at

[59] *Nilam* = "ground" (DED, no. 3044); *viḷakku* = "lamp" (DED, no. 4524). This is therefore a type of lamp that is placed on the ground or floor.

the *ōttūṭṭu* it is situated between the two *panti palaka*s at one end, in front of the *ghoṣi*. Undoubtedly it has a symbolic function as well, for fire is Agni, a deity frequently invoked for favors in the Vedas. Fire dispels darkness everywhere, even darkness shrouding the heart. The *nilaviḷakku* is therefore present at all rites, whether they take place in a Naṃpūtiri home or temple.

As the *ōttūṭṭu* draws to a close, the last few words are chanted in a very slow *cantādikkat* manifesting the outburst of boundless joy (*ānanda*).

Bonnie C. Wade

Cadence Practice in Hindustānī Vocal Music: *Khyāl* in Three *Rāgs**

Cadences are created in Hindustānī classical music by the "coming together" of certain melodic and rhythmic elements in a particular fashion. Cadences are oriented to the first count (*sam*) in a metric cycle (*tāl*); for example, it is frequently said that "phrases end on count 1." Cadences also are said to be oriented to arriving at a particular pitch at the same time one arrives at count 1.

The association of a particular pitch or pitches in a *rāg* with points of rest is an ancient idea in Indian music. The naming of those particular pitches for particular rāgs has been important in rag theory. Those particular pitches have been spoken of in terms of categories: *aṁśa, vādī, saṁvādī*, and *viśrānti svar* (or *viśrāntisthān).* Aṁśa and vādī are terms that have been used to refer to the most important structural pitches in a rāg (however defined); saṁvādī is a second important pitch, usually at the interval of a fourth or fifth from vādī. Kaufmann usually refers to those pitches as "the vādīs" rather than vādī/saṁvādī. Viśrānti svar is a term with broader connotation, meaning any pitch within a rāg, including vādī or saṁvādī but probably also other pitches on which it is possible and desireable to pause.

Kaufmann, in his Introduction to *The Ragas of North India,* speaks to the expectancy of a relationship of a certain pitch coinciding with count 1 for cadences. He refers to the competition

*In this article I follow the orthographic practice of Hindi language and Hindustānī music in keeping with the subject matter, in preference to the Sanskrit and Karnatak usage, i.e., *rāg* rather than *rāga, tāl* rather than *tāla, sam* rather than *sama*, and the like.

This essay was written especially for the present volume. Please do not quote without written permission from the author.

between drummer and soloist whereby the former might cause the latter to "miss a *sam* and perform a wrong note on this important beat."[1] At another point Kaufmann speaks of a song ending "either on the vādī or SA, with the *sam* of the drummer."[2] Here things become somewhat complex. Vādī may very well be the particular pitch that coincides with count 1, but not all performers agree which pitch in a particular rāg is vādī. The situation with pitch Sa is obviously not ambiguous as far as naming the particular pitch concerned, but there is controversy in Hindustānī music theory now as to whether cadence on Sa is always as characteristic of a particular rāg as cadence on vādī would be or whether musical practice is assigning an increasingly important cadential role to pitch Sa regardless of which rāg the performance is in. Despite the controversy, the basic traditional idea of associating a particular pitch with cadence remains strong.

In the Hindustānī vocal genre *khyāl* (as in other genres) the melodic and rhythmic material in cadences includes more than just one pitch at one count. The "coming together" includes another basic structural idea, namely, that the movement toward sam is vital. A term advocated to refer to the movement toward sam as well as the arrival at sam is *āmad.*[3] Āmad literally means "arriving at," "entry," or "appearance." In Hindustānī music it ideally includes both melodic and rhythmic flow that keeps the form of the rāg and the tāl clearly visable, but is

> that *identifiable section* of the flowing form of a *sthāyi* (or *gat*) in and through which the flow seems to *activate or regulate itself perceptibly at a particular point of the rhythm-cycle,* and therefrom *to move towards,* and *attain the sama in a well-designed way*, which at once seems a *self*-completion of the entire bandish [form] as a dynamic design [italics mine]. . . . Aesthetically, the āmad determines, and is determined by the entire embedment in the bandish.[4]

In khyāl "that identifiable section of the flowing form of a sthāyi" is the *mukhṛā*. The mukhṛā is the initial phrase of each

[1](Bloomington: Indiana University Press, 1968), p. 29.

[2]Ibid., p. 26.

[3]This point was stressed by S.K. Saxena in "The Fabric of Āmad: A Study of Form and Flow in Hindustani Music," a paper read at the Seminar on Science and Music at Sangit Natak Akademi in New Delhi, 1970, published in *Sangeet Natak* 16 (1970):38-44. The term "āmad" usually is associated with Kathak dance, but Saxena applies it primarily to *tarānās, dhamārs*, and *dhrupads.* I think it can be applied to khyāl, as well.

[4]Saxena, "Fabric of Āmad," pp. 39-40.

section of the song (*chīz*). In Example 1 below, the song transnotated[5] by Kaufmann in *Rāg Jaunpurī,*[6] the first phrase of the first section (*sthāyi*) and that of the second section (*antarā*) are indicated by brackets.

Example 1. Rāg Jaunpurī (Tritāl)

A sample of initial phrases of khyāl compositions in Rāg Jaunpurī are shown in Example 2a below. The mukhṛās in Example 2a are transnotated from compositions in KPM, the source of most of Kaufmann's Hindustānī song notations. All happen to be in the same metric cycle, *tīntāl (tritāl)* of 16 counts. Count 1 of the cycle is shown by x above the note; count 5 by the Arabic numeral 2; count 9 by o; count 13 by the Arabic numeral 3. Barlines occur at the end of each cycle. Indian syllables for pitches are cited under each note of the first mukhṛā of the sample.

[5]Transnotation is the term I use to indicate the process of "renotating" from one notation to another; in this case, Kaufmann has transnotated from the Hindustānī to the Western system. Transcription is the term I use to refer to the process of notating from sound.

[6]*Ragas of North India*, pp. 470-71, from V.N. Bhatkhande, *Hindustānī Sangīt Paddhati: Krāmik Pustak Mālikā*, 6 vols. (Bombay: Malinibai B. Sukthankar, 1934-37), 3:640 (cited hereafter as KPM).

Example 2a. Rāg Jaunpurī: Initial Phrases in Notated Compositions

KPM 3: 646

KPM 3: 649

KPM 3: 650

KPM 3: 651

KPM 3: 652

KPM 3: 654

KPM 3: 656

Initial phrases, or mukhṛās, of songs in the same rāg are likely to have some similar characteristics. They share melodic phrases that are particularly associated with Rāg Jaunpurī, for example, Ni♭ Dha♭ and Pa, Pa Dha♭ Ma Pa Ga♭, pitches Ni♭ and Ma being oriented toward their lower neighbors Dha♭ and Ga♭. It is also distinctive to Jaunpurī that the range of even the beginning of the melody should be situated so high in the octave and include, especially, pitch *tār* Sa (Sȧ). The same characteristics can be seen in Example 2b, transcriptions of the most frequent forms of the mukhṛā in performances by three artists.[7] Each performance was in either medium speed (*madhya laya*) or fast speed (*drut laya*). In some cadences the accompanying stringed instrument, *sāraṅgī*, completed the melodic phrase.

Example 2b. Melodic Shape of Mukhṛā as Performed

[7]From this author's collection. The total number of cadences from which these mukhṛās were distilled is 129.

Another characteristic is shared among all the mukhṛās cited in Examples 2a and 2b. While these mukhṛās begin at various points in the cycle (counts 5, 12, 9, and 7), they all culminate either at count 1 (sam) or within the melodic and rhythmic context of count 1, i.e., extending just beyond count 1. It is most important to note that many mukhṛās do not just halt at that important pitch on sam. Count 1 may be the important count toward which to move, but the melodic phrase of the cadence is likely to extend beyond it.

Kaufmann tells us in *The Ragas of North India* which pitches we might expect to find on sam in Rāg Jaunpurī.[8] According to him and others there are two "most important" pitches in Jaunpurī: Dha♭ and Ga♭. Some scholars regard Dha♭ as vādī, with Ga♭ being the second-most-important pitch (saṁvādī).[9] We would expect by consensus to find Dha♭ on sam in mukhṛās, but Ga♭ is also likely to occur there. In Example 2a both Dha♭ and Ga♭ occur at sam, but so does Pa. Furthermore, the melodic movement involving Dha♭ encompasses Ni♭ Dha♭, with resolution beyond sam to Pa. Melodic movement involving Ga♭ either pauses at but proceeds beyond sam to Re Ma Pa or pauses at Ga♭ but proceeds to resolution Ga♭ Re Sa. Another mukhṛā focuses its approach and its arrival at sam on Pa:

Pa
Ma
Ga♭
Re Re
Sa

In Example 2b, Jaunpurī mukhṛās from performances, pitch Ṡa is most frequently the pitch on sam, but resolution is often made down to Dha♭ or Pa from it. Dha♭ on sam resolving to Pa is also prominent.

In these examples of notated mukhṛās and performed cadences in Rāg Jaunpurī, the association of a particular pitch at sam is carried through, in that one from a small selection of pitches usually will be placed there. The occurrence of the vādī(s)—in this case Dha♭ or Ga♭—or of pitch Sa also is fairly constant. However, pitch Pa is also prominent. Pa is a pitch in Jaunpurī on which pauses can be made. While Kaufmann is not verbally explicit about this in his discussion of the rāg, he does demonstrate the point in musical example. It is important to note that it is not only *the* pitch *at* sam that defines these cadences in Jaunpurī but also motion toward and just beyond sam that is important. All of these elements show the particular rāg very clearly.

[8] P. 470.
[9] KPM, 3:644.

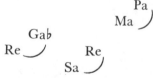

Another aspect of āmad as described in the quotation above is the integration of the cadential material into the total design: "Aesthetically, the āmad determines, and is determined by the entire embedment in the [form]."[10] This includes such considerations as the nature of the music which immediately precedes it and the manner in which the text fits in. In Example 3a the mukhṛā participates in the rise and fall of the melody in the phrase but provides a contrast to the setting of text immediately preceding it, i.e., from melismatic back to syllabic text treatment. Example 3b continues the rhythmic, textual, and melodic context of the phrase. In Example 3c the mukhṛā not only continues the syncopation created by the syllable placement just before it, it also accentuates it by the change from legato to "staccato" singing. Example 3d has a marked separation between the end of the phrase and the mukhṛā, but the singer prepares for the mukhṛā to smooth over that separation. In 3e the mukhṛā continues a descent to Sa.

Example 3. Descending Line and Mukhṛā Integrated for Cadence

[10]Saxena, "Fabric of Āmad," p. 40.

c. Tīntāl Madhya Rāg Desī

d. Tīntāl Drut Rāg Desī

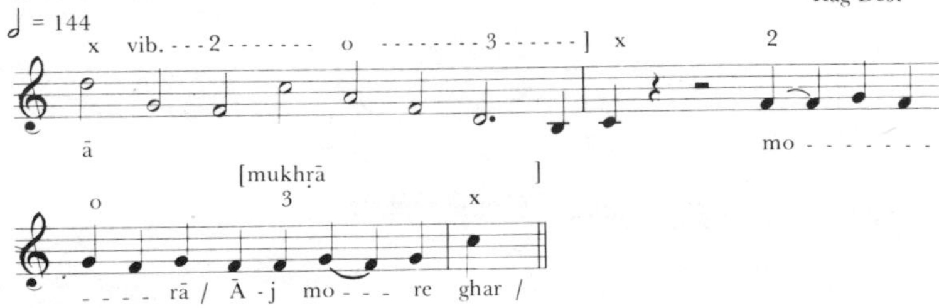

e. Tīntāl Drut Rāg Desī

Rather than integrating the melody of the mukhṛā into the melodic phrase just preceding it, as in Example 3e, however, many singers finish off the preceding melodic phrase, then sing the mukhṛā. Very often an approach is made to pitch Sa of the middle octave to close the melodic phrase before the mukhṛā is sung. This happens so frequently that a case could be made that there are more often than not *two* elements that combine to make the cadence: 1) a melodic approach to madhya Sa or some other pitch and 2) the mukhṛā that coincides with sam. Instances of such cases are shown in Examples 4a-d.

Example 4. Descending Line and Mukhṛā Separate Entities in Cadence

a. Tīntāl Madhya Rāg Desī

b. Ektāl Vilambit Rāg Todī

c. Tīntāl Drut Rāg Rāmkalī

d. Tīntāl Drut Rāg Desī

The melodic shape of the cadence in Indian music has occasioned comment from scholars. Gangoly mentions a suggestion made by Paṇḍit Kṛṣṇa Chandra Ghose Vedānta-Chintāmaṇi for determining the sex of a mode, i.e., whether it is a rāg or rāgiṇī:

> According to an ingenious suggestion by a modern scholar of music, it is the placing of the emphasis on the cadential notes (nyāsa, vinyāsa, apanyāsa, sannyāsa) on the stronger or the weaker pulses of the rhythm of a melody that determine its sex. And that when the musical phrases or structure of a melody have an upward or ascending tendency (arohana) with the cadential notes resting on the stronger pulses—then it is called a rāga (a masculine melody). And when the phrases and structure have a downward or descending tendency (avarohana) with the cadential notes resting on the weaker impulses,—it is characterized as a rāgiṇī (a feminine melody).[11]

Bhatkhande classified some rāgs in his ṭhāṭ system by their descending line,[12] an approach that Jairazbhoy thinks is "reasonable . . . since cadential phrases, which are of considerable importance in rāgs, are generally descending."[13] While it does appear that cadential phrases generally are descending, it might be more cautious to specify *which* portion of the cadence is descending. One reason for this suggestion is the nature of cadences in the antarā portion of performances and compositions; another reason is the ascending shape of the mukhṛā in particular rāgs. Both instances are discussed below.

Pitch Sȧ is the important pitch on count 1 when the second portion (antarā) of a khyāl composition is being sung. Most antarā mukhṛās have a similar shape, i.e., a rise from about mid-octave to tār Sȧ, no matter which rāg is being featured. Examples of antarā mukhṛās are given in Example 5. Occasionally a pitch other than Sȧ falls on the cadential sam, but Sȧ will appear very shortly and be emphasized as usual. Since relatively little time in khyāl performances is spent on antarā, however, this does not mean that pitch Sȧ predominates as the on-sam pitch throughout a performance. It would predominate only if it predominated in sthāyi cadences, as well.

[11]Ordhendra C. Gangoly, *Rāgas and Rāgiṇīs* (Bombay, n.p., 1935; reprint ed., Bombay: Nalanda Publications, 1948), pp. 70-71.

[12]See KPM.

[13]Nazir A. Jairazbhoy, *The Rāgs of North Indian Music* (Middletown, Conn: Wesleyan University Press, 1971), p. 52.

Example 5. Antarā Mukhṛā

The question of melodic shape in cadences is pertinent in Rāg Lālit (formerly classified as a rāgiṇī in Hindustānī music theory). The khyāl mukhṛās in this rāg (Lālit) usually approach sam with melodic ascent, as seen below in Example 6.

According to Kaufmann, the vādīs of Rāg Lālit are Ma and tār Sa.[14] In KPM Bhatkhande distinguishes Ma as vādī, Sa as saṁvādī, not specifying which Sa.[15] With Sa considered such an important pitch in the rāg, one might expect it to command the role of on-sam pitch in cadences. Of the thirty notated compositions in the KPM, however, only two settle on Sa in the initial phrase; rather, Ma predominates. In my transcribed performances of Rāg Lālit, Ma predominates, as well.

The khyāl mukhrās of Lālit provide good examples of the cadence ending "in the context of sam" rather than right on sam. In twelve of the twenty notated Lālit compositions in KPM, Ma♯ falls on count 1 of the initial tāl cycle, and in the performances transcribed it frequently fell on sam in cadences. As shown in Example 6, however, Ma♯ resolves to Ma♮ to complete the mukhṛā in those cases, as happened in the notated songs as well. According to Kaufmann, Ma♯ is a weak pitch.[16] Ma♯ is weak in that it will

[14]*Ragas of North India*, p. 325.
[15]4:489.
[16]*Ragas of North India*, p. 325.

always be resolved to Ma♮. This is one of the few Hindustānī rāgs in which such chromatic movement is permitted.

The mukhṛās in the first four chīz in Rāg Lālit in Example 6 below are remarkably similar; the interplay between the two Mas is accentuated by the rise from Ni a tritone or a perfect fifth below; sam falls on either of the Mas, as the pinnacle of an essentially descent-to-ascent melodic curve.

Example 6. Melodic Shape of Mukhṛā: Rāg Lālit

In five performances of Rāg Lālit the approaches to the mukhṛā came to rest on Sa 53 percent of the time, on the vādī Ma♮ 20.6 percent of the time, and on Ga 26.4 percent of a total of 68 cadences (see Table 1 below). While Ga is not designated vādī in Lālit, it is a viśrāntisthān, a pitch on which one can expect a pause to occur. The approach to the mukhṛā in khyāl singing is a resting place where such a pitch might regularly occur.

Table 1
Approaches to Sthāyi Mukhṛā in Lālit

Performer	↗Sa	↘Sa	↘Ga	To Ma♮
A (vil)	1	13	2	
B (vil)		9	10	5
C (vil)	1	4	5	4
B (drut)		8	1	5
Subtotal	2	34	18	14
Subtotal	——→	36	18	14
Total				68

The third rāg to be discussed here—Rāg Desī—is another rāg in which pitch Sa shares the on-sam spot in cadences with the designated strong pitches Pa and Re.[17] Among the sixteen notated compositions in Rāg Desī in KPM, the picture is diffuse: three mukhṛās land on Sa at sam, while one hits Ni and resolves up to Sa; five hit Re but four of those resolve to Sa; two hit Pa, one of which resolves to Sa; another lands on Dha♭ but resolves to Pa; four others are on other pitches. The sample of mukhṛās from transcribed performances (shown in Example 7a) reveals Ṡa and Re to be the predominant pitches on sam. And mukhṛās that land on Re at sam resolve to Sa, as may be seen in Example 7b.[18]

Example 7.

a. Pitches on Sam in the Mukhṛā

b. Resolution of Mukhṛā Terminating on Vādī/Saṁvādī

[17]Ibid., p. 479; KPM, 6:347.

[18]This is a clear instance of the necessity for drawing conclusions about such problems as cadence from performance practice as well as from notation of compositions.

As designated by Bhatkhande in KPM, Re is saṁvādī and Pa is vādī.[19] In those terms, saṁvādī is more prominent than vādī as an on-sam pitch in this sampling of cadences in Rāg Desī. One explanation for the predominance of saṁvādī on sam could be melodic shape. The general tendency to descend to the area of madhya Sa, for cadences, most likely causes saṁvādī Re to fall on sam. In any case, the vādī-saṁvādī interval Pa-Re is usually outlined in the melody of the mukhṛā. Furthermore, a resolution to Sa from either pitch frequently completes the cadence beyond sam.

To consider the approach made in khyāl improvisation to the mukhṛās in Rāg Desī, I examined performances of six compositions totaling 157 approaches to the sthāyi mukhṛā. The six performances are tabulated below according to the destination point of the melodic passage immediately preceding the mukhṛā. In 69.3 percent of the cadences, there was an approach to Sa, including both descent to madhya and ascent to tār Sa; the vādī (Pa) and saṁvādī (Re) accounted for 14.6 percent and 12.1 percent respectively, and only 4 percent fell on other pitches of Rāg Desī. It seemed to depend to some extent on the performance practice of individual artists rather than on the composition being rendered. Performer C was almost solely responsible for the high percentage of vādī and saṁvādī destinations of those pre-mukhṛā phrases.

Table 2
Approaches to Sthāyi Mukhṛā in Rāg Desī

Performer	Ga♭ ↘ Sa ↗ Re ↘ Ni ↗ Sa	↘ Sa	↗ Sa	To Re	To Pa	Other
A (vil)	21	9		1		
A (drut)		6		3		
B (madhya)	5	10	5	1		1
C (madhya)	1	20		13	19	2
D (madhya)	5	14	1		1	
D (drut)	7	5		1	3	3
Subtotal	39	64	6	19	23	6
Subtotal		——→	109	19	23	6
Total						157

[19] KPM, 6:297.

Both in the approaches to the mukhṛā and in the mukhṛā of Rāg Desī, the pitch Sa is the most important final resting point. The vādī and saṁvādī are the only other pitches frequently used at these points.

The concept and use of the mukhṛā as both a beginning and an end provide a structural possibility for song-without-end. Conversely, any cadence could potentially be the final cadence of a portion of the performance or of the entire performance. In the vocal genre khyāl two compositions (with improvisation within each) are usually linked to form the complete performance: a longer slow or medium speed khyāl (baṛā khyāl) and a shorter fast speed khyāl (chhoṭā khyāl). An artist will end the first khyāl or the complete performance for practical and artistic reasons, for instance, when he becomes physically exhausted or when his imagination and inspiration begin to lag, for an audience will be able to tell when he has reached that point. And, of course, there is often a time limit imposed by a broadcasting schedule or a roster of artists on a performance program. A singer who plans to follow his baṛā khyāl with a chhoṭā khyāl must allot sufficient time and energy for that, as well.

Final cadences of baṛā khyāls transcribed from performance are shown in Example 8. The three cadences in Rāg Desī end with a descent to Sa, though the vādī Re occurs on sam in two of the three. The two cadences in Rāg Lālit end decisively on Ma. The Jaunpurī cadences emphasize Sa, a vādī, but resolve to Pa to end. All of these are mukhṛās and are not different from the mukhṛā as it appears in the internal cadences of the same performances.

Example 8. Final Cadences of Baṛā Khyāls that Lead to Chhoṭā Khyāls

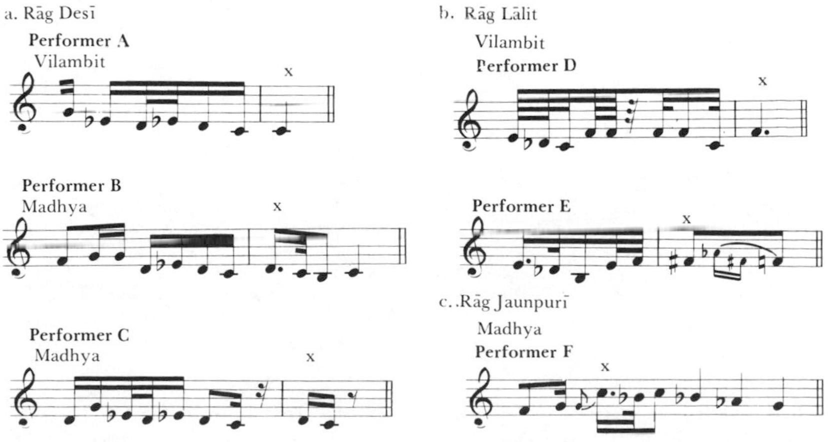

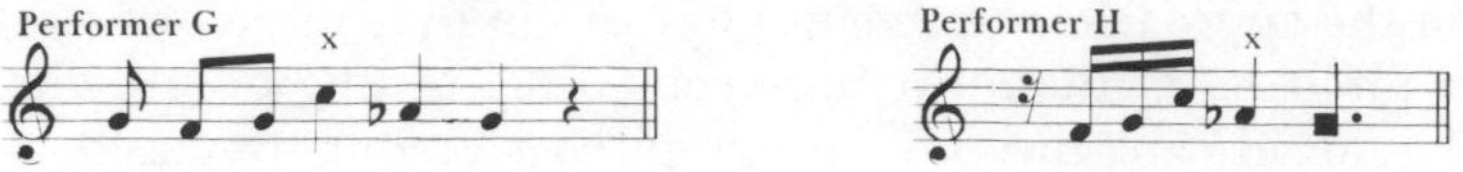

The cadence that concludes the entire performance, the end of the chhoṭā khyāl, is a telling cadential moment. The last tablā stroke falls on sam of the final mukhṛā, and the vocalist usually makes a ritard from that point. The practice in the performances transcribed in Example 9 is to have the final cadence orient to Sa to some extent, but not necessarily as the final resting place.

Example 9. Final Cadences of Chhoṭā Khyāl

In Rāg Lālit, an approach is made to Sa before settling back to Ma. In the first Rāg Jaunpurī cadence the vocalist reiterated Dha→Pa,

but the sāraṅgī accompanist continued the melody down to Sa. In the second Jaunpurī cadence shown in Example 9, Sa is only touched as a light ornament to Re. On the basis of these and a large number of other final cadences considered in this analysis two points are striking. An ascending shape is common in cadences even at the final moment of a performance. This is largely determined by the rāg. Furthermore, while pitch Sa frequently is the final resting point, even when it is not a prominent pitch in the rāg, that is not the case nearly as much as I expected it to be when this study was begun.

One further possible characteristic of cadence in khyāl is a type that emphasizes rhythm as much as melody: *tihāī*. Literally, a tihāī is a rhythmic (drumming) pattern repeated exactly three times in succession and calculated to end on sam; it can encompass few or many beats. In khyāl, the sung tihāī is not necessarily so exact, as Example 10 below shows. Some artists repeat only one word; other artists repeat a whole phrase. Example 10d is a textual tihāī, but with melodic and rhythmic extension. Tihāī occurs relatively infrequently in the many fast speed performances I have examined. I have heard repetition of the sthāyi first phrase three times in succession, but that phrase is repeated so often in any case that it does not have the same effect as a rhythmic tihāī.

Example 10. Tihāī

a. Ektāl Vilambit — Rāg Lālit

b. Ektāl Vilambit — Rāg Lālit

c. Tīntāl Madhya — Rāg Jaunpurī

d. Tīntāl Madhya — Rāg Desī

e. Tīntāl Drut · Rāg Desī

f. Tīntāl Drut · Rāg Todī

Summary

Cadence practice in the Hindustānī vocal form, khyāl, adheres to traditional ideas. The expectation that particular pitches in a rāg will occur at stopping points is carried out. The stopping points considered here were three: the ending of the melodic phrase immediately preceding the mukhṛā; the pitch on sam in the mukhṛā; and the final pitch of the mukhṛā phrase, if that extended beyond sam. The pitches occurring most frequently at these points were, as expected, vādī, saṁvādī, and Sa, but also other appropriate resting pitches. In Jaunpurī the vādīs Dha♭ and Ga♭, pitch Sa, and also Pa were stopping points, and artists tend to extend the mukhṛās beyond sam. In Lālit vādī Ma predominates over vādī Sa, but the progression Ma♯ to Ma♮ is frequently the resolution of the mukhṛā from sam to beyond it. In Desī, the saṁvādī Re is a more frequent resting pitch than vādī Pa, but Sa is most frequently the pitch to which phrases resolve, before the mukhṛā and beyond sam in the mukhṛā.

There is some thought today that pitch Sa is assuming a cadential role above and beyond its importance in particular rāgs. In the mukhṛās surveyed for this study there is no strong indication of that; the pitch associations at sam, particularly, are those of the particular rāg. Sa may be assuming a more important role in the closing of improvised melodic phrases before the mukhṛā, but that is a question for a study with considerable historical depth.

The approach to the cadence is treated in either of two ways: the improvised melody flows without disjuncture into the mukhṛā or that melodic phrase is completed, then followed by the mukhṛā. Pitches deemed proper for stopping points are used to close off the pre-mukhṛā melodic phrase.

The statement that a cadence consists of a certain pitch falling on count 1, sam, is only a partial statement. Cadences most often include an appropriate pitch on sam, but the resolution from that pitch to another in the counts immediately following is just as much a part of cadence practice in many rāgs as the designation of what happens on sam.

Terry E. Miller

Free-Reed Instruments in Asia: A Preliminary Classification

Musical instruments whose sounds are produced by reeds are common throughout the world. Classifications vary. Apel, in the *Harvard Dictionary of Music*, distinguishes two basic types: idiophonic ("a hard, heavy material, usually metal") and heterophonic ("a flexible, light material, usually cane") while making a further distinction between free reeds and beating reeds.[1] Sachs distinguishes three types: single beating reed (clarinets), double reed (oboes), and free reed.[2] Both the clarinet, whose reed beats against a slightly smaller opening, and the oboe, whose two reeds vibrate together, differ from free-reed instruments whose metal or cane reed, cut on three sides into a larger plate, passes back and forth through the slot. Free reeds will not sound unless the tube or air column is complete; thus a finger hole burned or bored into the midst of the column silences the reed by interrupting the acoustical coupling. Whether the player inhales or exhales, the same pitch sounds. Originally, at least, free-reed instruments were confined to East and Southeast Asia, but since the eighteenth century the free reed has migrated to the West, where it appears in the harmonica, harmonium, and accordion.

A study of Asian instruments invariably leads into the dense tangle of ethnic groups that makes this continent so colorful and complex. Concentrated study of one type of instrument, the free-reed in this case, depends heavily on descriptions of these cultures by anthropologists and explorers as well as the much rarer musical

[1]2nd ed., s. v. "Reed."

[2]Curt Sachs, *History of Musical Instruments* (New York: W.W. Norton and Co., 1940), p. 458.

study. Too many of these sources, however, appeared in the early days of anthropology, and the description of instruments was usually rather amateurish. Thus the researcher is faced with a plethora of ethnic groups as well as instruments but cannot always trust these to be correct. Thanks to two recent catalogues of Southeast Asian ethnic groups,[3] it is now possible to sort the ethnic groups into linguistic families and make further sense out of the earlier and less professional studies.

It could be argued that the jaw harp is the most basic form of the free reed. Although metal versions found in the West have narrow tongues in much larger frames, most of those found in Asia, where they probably originated, have tongues which pass through slots only slightly larger. The mouth acts as resonator in place of a bamboo tube, and thus the jaw harp is closely related to the free reed. Free-reed instruments proper manifest themselves in a variety of shapes with varying materials for windchests, number of pipes, and reed materials. The following classification seeks to organize Asian free-reed instruments according to simple logic—shape and number of pipes; an evolution is not implied although readers may detect a simple to complex pattern. It cannot be assumed, as so many writers have, that the most highly developed version, the Chinese *sheng*, is the form from which all others developed. Indeed, attempts to assign a time and place of origin would be futile until the prehistory of Asia is better understood. The seven categories are:

1. Free-reed horn
2. Free-reed pipe with finger holes
3. Free-reed pipe with finger holes and gourd windchest
4. Gourd windchest mouth organ
5. Miao mouth organ (*gaeng*)
6. Lao mouth organ (*kaen*)
7. Chinese mouth organ (*sheng*)

1. Free-reed Horn

Found over a wide area extending from Burma to Vietnam, the free-reed horn is merely the horn of a water buffalo or cow (or formerly an elephant tusk) hollowed out and fitted with a metal free-reed on the concave side (Figure 1).

[3]Frank M. Lebar, Gerald C. Hickey, and John K. Musgrave, *Ethnic Groups of Mainland Southeast Asia* (New Haven: Human Relations Area Files Press, 1964); and Frank M. Lebar, ed., *Ethnic Groups of Insular Southeast Asia* (New Haven: Human Relations Area Files Press, 1972).

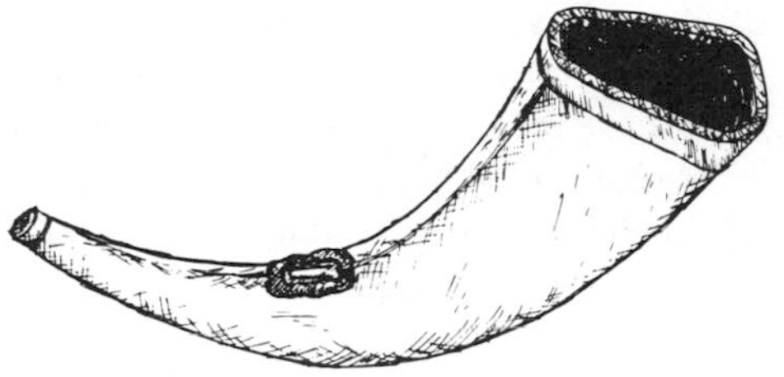

Figure 1. *Free-reed horn*

The reed, normally of brass or copper, is sealed into the rectangular hole with a black sticky substance resembling beeswax (Figure 2).

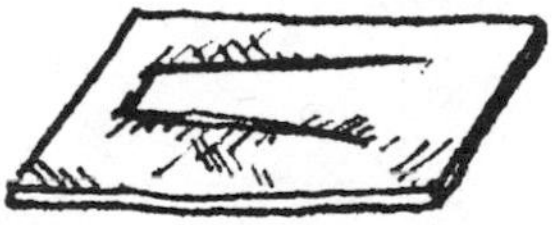

Figure 2. *Free reed*

According to Sachs the reeds are also tuned with small pieces of "tuning wax," probably the same black wax used to seal in the reed.[4] The player seals his mouth over the reed and either blows or sucks to produce one of three available pitches, first with both ends open, second with his hand closing the narrow end, and third with both ends closed.

Nine ethnic groups are known to use such an instrument, four of them being Karen subgroups. The Karen (or Kariang, Kayin, and Yang), numbering some one-and-a-half million, inhabit a vast portion of Burma from 11° north along the Thai border to 21° north near the city of Taunggyi. Two writers, Curt Sachs and Harry I. Marshall, have described Karen free-reed buffalo horns. The Brek-Karen, living in Kayah State near Loikaw, Burma, use such an instrument whose name Sachs gives as *gä*.[5]. In a similar entry Sachs describes a buffalo horn used by the Karen-ni (also

[4]Curt Sachs, *Die Musikinstrumente Birmas und Assams im K. Ethnographischen Museum zu München* (Munich: Verlag der Königlichen Bayerischen Akademie der Wissenschaften, 1917), p. 40.

[5]Ibid.

called Red Karen, Kayah, and Kayin-ni) living near Pekon whose name is given as *gů*.[6] Marshall, in his book *The Karen People of Burma*, describes the *kweh* as being made of either buffalo horn or ivory and fitted with a metal free reed.[7] Sachs lists an instrument called *kwāi* used by the Padaung, a Karen people living in Kayah State near Klobyaku.[8] In reference to the Padaung, he says they use *kwāi* in chorus to blow long, solemn chords.[9]

I have inspected two Karen horns purchased along the Thai-Burmese border near Chiang-mai in northern Thailand. The first, whose concave side measured 36 centimeters, had a reed 3 centimeters long placed 12 centimeters from the narrow end. Three pitches were produced: *a'* open, *g'* with narrow end closed, and an unidentified pitch with both ends closed. A second specimen produced *a♭'* open, *g'* with the small end closed, and *f'* with both ends closed. Such instruments may vary in length from 25 to 50 centimeters.

The Akha, a Tibeto-Burman speaking hill tribe living in north Thailand, Burma, Laos, and Yunnan province in south China, also use such an instrument but with a bamboo reed. According to Bernatzik, these instruments are played after game has been killed.[10] The free-reed horn is also found further east among the Lao in northeast Thailand, where it is used as a noise maker in festivals and called a *b̲ee-sanai*[11] and in Cambodia and Vietnam. The Saoch, an upland Mon-Khmer group in Cambodia, play free-reed horns with metal reeds at funerals while the lowland Khmer use a similar instrument with a bamboo reed called *sneng* in spirit ceremonies and elephant hunts.[12] The Jarai, an upland Cham group (Malayo-Polynesian linguistic family) living on the Darlac Plateau near Pleiku in Vietnam also play such an instrument having a wooden mouthpiece built above the reed.[13] Doubtless other

[6]Ibid.

[7]Harry I. Marshall, *The Karen People of Burma: A Study in Anthropology and Ethnology* (Columbus: Ohio State University, 1922), p. 167.

[8]*Musikinstrumente Birmas und Assams*, p. 40.

[9]It is uncertain if *gä*, *gů*, *kweh*, or *kwāi* are related to the Tai word *kwai* meaning "buffalo."

[10]Hugo A. Bernatzik, *Akha and Miao*, trans. Alois Nagler (New Haven: Human Relations Area Files Press, 1970), p. 205.

[11]*B̲ee-sanai* normally refers to a short Siamese oboe now nearly obsolete, the *b̲ee-chanai*. See Dhanit Yupho, *Thai Musical Instruments*, 2nd ed., trans. David Morton (Bangkok: Fine Arts Department, Silpakorn University, 1971), pp. 79-80.

[12]Commission de musique de l'Université royale des beaux-arts, *Musique Khmère* (Phnom Penh, n. p., n. d.), p. 77.

[13]Jacques Dournes, "La musique chez les Jörai," *Objets et Mondes* 5 (1965): 232.

ethnic groups possess them, but no other sources are known at this time.

2. Free-reed Pipes with Finger Holes

The free-reed pipe with finger holes, because it resembles an ordinary flute, might easily escape observation by non-musicians. From the few available references it is certain that the instrument is widely distributed, at least from Chittagong district (Bangla-desh) to Vietnam, and that it is used by both upland and lowland groups. Such instruments consist of a bamboo tube into the wall of which a free reed of copper and silver alloy or brass has been inserted. The reed, somewhat smaller than that of the free-reed horn, is placed at the "head" (upper end); the node at this end is left unpierced, but others must be removed. The player places his mouth over the end of the tube–including the reed–and blows or sucks holding the instrument at an angle (Figure 3).

Figure 3. *Free-reed pipe with finger holes*

Perhaps the best-known free-reed pipe is the northern Thai *b̲ee saw* (also called *b̲ee joom* and *b̲ee payup*) used in performing traditional music, especially in Lumbang, Lumpoon, Chiang-mai, and Chiang-rai provinces. Dhanit Yupho's *Thai Musical Instruments* provides a fairly detailed description of this instrument.[14] *B̲ee saw* may vary in length from 40 to 80 centimeters. There are seven finger holes cut along the tube which, including the open position, produce eight pitches. Dhanit also notes that *b̲ee saw*, which may be used in groups of three, five, or seven, come in three sizes called *b̲ee doi* (shortest), *b̲ee glang* (medium), and *b̲ee yai* (longest); Gerald Dyck, formerly of the Thailand Theological Society in Chiang-mai, reports, however, that they are used in groups of three, four, or five with four being usual. The four, from longest to shortest, are called *b̲ee mae* ("mother"), *b̲ee glang* ("medium"), *b̲ee goi* ("little finger"), and *b̲ee noi* ("small").[15]

[14]Pp. 74-76.
[15]Personal communication, August 1974.

The uses of the *b̲ee saw* are many. While played solo, usually to imitate a singer, they are customarily played in ensembles to accompany singing called *saw. Saw* is performed by alternating men and women singing about love as well as learned topics, a kind of musical repartee common in Southeast Asia. *B̲ee saw* may also accompany *joi*, a kind of flirting or love song sung by males and females at night in the villages. Dhanit Yupho further mentions that *b̲ee saw* accompany songs from the epic poem *Pralaw*, a history of the north written in *lilit* verse.[16]

An early description of the *b̲ee saw* by H. Warington Smyth written in 1898 refers to its use in Nan province bordering Lumbang and Chiang-rai provinces. Smyth says that this instrument, which he merely calls the "reed flute of Nan," is played in trio and that the pitches of the middle size were *a♭, b♭, c′, d♭′, e♭′, f′, g′*, and *a♭′*. Comparing its intonation to the better known Lao *kaen*, he says, "In the single reed of Nan, owing probably to the greater difficulty of adjusting the breath, the intervals are generally less satisfactory to the ear."[17]

While Smyth is probably referring to this instrument's use among the Thai, the Miao inhabiting the mountainous areas of the same region as well as Laos and southern China use the free-reed pipe. Bernatzik notes that their instruments come in various lengths and have five finger holes producing six pitches, "a simple minor scale."[18] The Poo-tai and Lao in northeast Thailand and southern Laos use such instruments called *look-b̲ee-kaen* (*look* means "child," *b̲ee* is "oboe," and *kaen* the Lao mouth organ), apparently expressing the idea that the free-reed pipe is like a single *kaen* tube, which indeed is called *look* or "child." In Cambodia lowland Khmer play the seven-hole *pey pork (pey pôk)* in spirit ceremonies and to accompany certain folk dances. Sisowath, however, also mentions a *pey-pôk* having five finger holes played among the Pear, a Mon-Khmer group nearly synonymous with the Samre, who live on the northern slopes of the Cardamon Mountains in Kampong Thom province and near Siem Reap. He further notes that their instrument has a gourd placed over the tube's end to increase resonance.[19]

How common free-reed pipes are in Vietnam is uncertain because few sources mention them. Hoang-Yen describes the *hoang* with

[16]*Thai Musical Instruments*, p. 75.

[17]H. Warington Smyth, *Five Years in Siam, from 1891-1896*, 2 vols. (London: J. Murray, 1898), 1:200.

[18]*Akha and Miao*, p. 201.

[19]Sisowath, *Musique du Cambodge* (Phnom Penh: Direction du Tourisme Khmer, n.d.), p. 17.

nine finger holes,[20] but Trần văn Khê, in his more extensive study, fails to mention them.[21] In his shorter study, *Viêt-Nam*, however, Trần văn Khê, in discussing the "instruments populaires," states that the Tai people (probably in the north) use a "chalumeau double" called *pidôi* composed of two bamboo tubes joined together, each having a free reed.[22] The people in question are probably the White, Red, or Black Tai. It may be worth noting that *pi* or *b̲ee* in Siamese means oboe, though it may also refer to free reeds as in the *b̲ee saw*, and that the smallest of the northern Thai instruments is called *b̲ee doi*, similar to *pidôi*.

The free-reed pipe is also found in modern Bangla-desh. According to Riebeck's 1885 study of the hill tribes in the Chittagong area, a tribe called the Chakmâs use a free-reed pipe. Two are illustrated, one having six holes, the other seven.[23] The Chakmâs, for whom no reference can be found in Lebar, live forty-five miles northeast of Chittagong near Kasalong according to Riebeck. Even less specific is a reference by Thomas C. Hodson regarding the use of such an instrument among the Tangkhuls, a Naga tribe living in Manipur province, India: "The Tangkhuls are expert buglers and use a simple piece of bamboo with a vibrating reed. They give the regimental calls with great accuracy."[24]

3. Free-reed Pipe with Finger Holes and Gourd Windchest

A hollow gourd placed over the reed end of a free-reed pipe would serve the same function as the mouth. Indeed, such instruments with or without drone pipes are found from north Burma to Cambodia among a great variety of peoples. Sachs' *Die Musikinstrumente Birmas und Assams*, a catalogue of selected instruments in Munich's Ethnographisches Museum, describes gourd pipes used among four groups;[25] the work of two other writers further augments the list.[26]

[20] "Le musique a Hué, don-nguyet et don-tranh," *Bulletin des Amis du Vieux Hué* 6 (1919; English ed. trans. Keith Botsford [New Haven: Human Relations Area Files Press, 1953]), p. 255.

[21] *La musique vietnamienne traditionnelle* (Paris: Presses Universitaires de France, 1962).

[22] (Paris: Buchet-Chastel, 1967), p. 113.

[23] Emil Riebeck, *The Chittagong Hill-Tribes*, trans. A. H. Keane (London: Asher and Company, 1885), pl. 15.

[24] Thomas C. Hodson, *The Naga Tribes of Manipur* (London: Macmillan & Co., 1911), p. 67.

[25] See below.

[26] Leslie Milne and Maurice Abadie; see below.

The Taungthu, a Karen minority (Pa-O group) living in north Burma near Loikaw, use a single pipe instrument with metal reed and seven finger holes in front and one in back.[27] Sachs also illustrates two such instruments from the Taungyo, a Tibeto-Burman people living in the Shan States near Kalaw and Yawnghwe[28] (Figure 4).

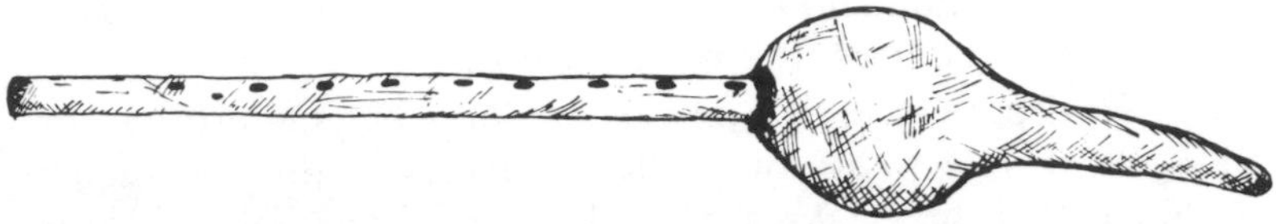

Figure 4. *Free-reed pipe with gourd*

In one case the tone is amplified by a second gourd attached to the lower end of the pipe. Both pipes measure under 40 centimeters, have metal reeds, and are sealed into the gourd windchests with strips of cloth. The Kachin, another Tibeto-Burman tribe living in north Burma, southwest Yunnan, and northeast Assam, use double pipes, one for the melody, the other as a drone. All have metal reeds, vary in length from 23 to 29 centimeters, and include a wooden stick which, according to Sachs, can be inserted to change the pitch. He cites three names for these instruments: *roizå, pībat*, and *magrī sumpī.*[29]

The Palaung, including the Kwanhai and Humai Palaung branches, are Mon-Khmer people living in the Shan States. Sachs illustrates eight instruments used by them, varying from a single pipe called *but seau* ("blow pipe") or *wao* to a double pipe called *kawö* to a triple pipe whose name is lacking.[30] All three have metal reeds, and at least one of them has a bamboo "quiver" over the end to alter the tone just as the lower gourd did in the Taungyo specimen. According to Sachs, these instruments, having six or seven finger holes in front and one in back, are used at marriage ceremonies.

Among the Shan the triple gourd pipe is associated with courting. The Shan or Tai-yai are one of the three major branches of the Tai, the Siamese and Lao being the others. Leslie Milne, who visited the Shan just after the turn of this century reported:

[27]Sachs, *Musikinstrumente Birmas und Assams*, p. 42.

[28]Ibid., pp. 41-42.

[29]Ibid., p. 43.

[30]Ibid., pp. 41-42.

> A young man does not compromise himself or the girl, if he comes to see her in her own home. He visits her quite openly, sometimes playing short tunes on a gourd flute outside the house before he enters. Often the tunes are in a minor key, and are very melancholy in their cadences. . . . If a young girl dies before marriage, having had no lover, the youths of the village in turn play sad little tunes to her, on their gourd flutes, as she lies dead.[31]

The pipe illustrated has six or seven finger holes in front and one in back.

4. Gourd Windchest Mouth Organs

The most widespread free-reed instrument in Southeast Asia, both on the continent and in the archipelago, consists of from one to ten bamboo pipes inserted into a gourd which acts as the windchest. The reeds, whether of metal or of a natural material such as cane, are fitted into the pipe walls at the lower ends inside the gourd. Pipes may be arranged in a bundle, in raft form, or obliquely. In some instruments the pipes protrude through the bottom of the gourd; in others they do not. Although at least twenty-five ethnic groups are known to use gourd mouth organs, there are probably other groups who also use them but whose instruments await description. The study of gourd mouth organs is further complicated by inadequate descriptions, probable confusion in terminology, and, in the case of Borneo, a poor understanding of the ethnic groups.

Sachs in his *Die Musikinstrumente Indiens und Indonesiens* states, "The original form is still found in Chittagong District in the East Bengal highlands among the Mro and Kumi."[32] The Mro and Kumi are members of the Tibeto-Burman Chin group living in present-day Bangla-desh. The "original form" to which Sachs refers is a gourd pierced by a single bamboo pipe nearly two meters long with a free-reed covering a hole in the wall of the pipe inside the gourd. Unlike free-reed pipes built into a gourd windchest, which are parallel to the mouthpiece (neck) and thus played like recorders, the pipes of the gourd mouth organ are perpendicular to the neck mouthpiece. Riebeck illustrates this instrument with a five-foot specimen from the Kumi people who live about sixty miles southeast of Chittagong.[33]

[31]Leslie Milne, *Shans at Home*, (London: John Murray, 1910), pp. 70-71.

[32]2nd ed. (Berlin: Walter de Gruyter and Co., 1923), p. 64. Author's translation.

[33]*Chittagong Hill-Tribes*, pl. 15.

Sachs was unaware that this instrument is also found in the highlands of Vietnam among the Jarai, an upland Cham people (Malayo-Polynesian) living on the Darlac Plateau. Their instrument is called the *dding-klut* or *dding-pi* and has three finger holes above the gourd. Dournes, who has provided a detailed drawing as well as photographs, adds that the instrument is now nearly obsolete and used mostly for ceremonial purposes but that it is still used by the Trung, presumably the Trung-cha, an eastern Tai group living on the border of Vietnam and China[34] (Figure 5).

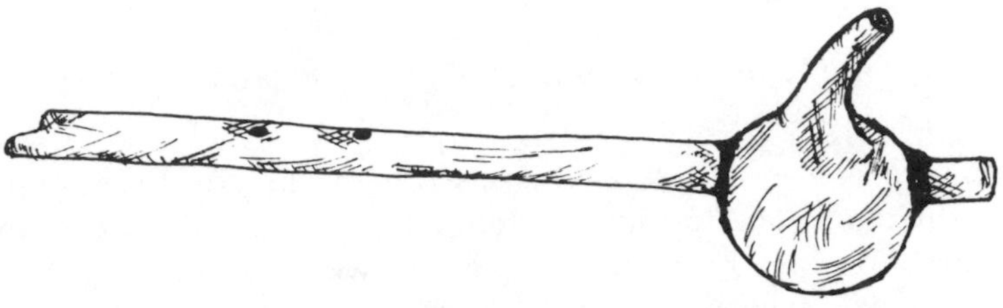

Figure 5. *Single-tubed gourd organ*

Abadie may be alluding to such an instrument when he says the Lolo in north Vietnam, a Tibeto-Burman people, use a single-tubed gourd flute.[35]

A more highly developed form of the gourd mouth organ is illustrated in Jaap Kunst's *Hindu-Javanese Musical Instruments*, where he shows a Lushan instrument having seven pipes in two oblique rows, the front having three, the rear four.[36] The Lushan, also a Chin subgroup in Assam, probably do not call their instrument *khen* as indicated by Kunst, however, for *khen* refers to the Lao instrument. Shakespear, in his study of the Lushei Kuki people in Manipur and Assam, describes an instrument called a "rotchem having nine pipes, one of them a mouthpiece." He glibly adds that the music is "dull and monotonous."[37] It appears that the pipes of these instruments all pierce the gourd's bottom and are set obliquely in two rows (Figure 6).

Riebeck illustrates a similar instrument with six pipes used by the Mrung, a Tibeto-Burman hill group living east of Chittagong. He adds that this organ is used for dancing and, "although mono-

[34]"Musique chez les Jörai," p. 234.

[35]Maurice Abadie, *Les races du Haut-Tonkin* (Paris: Société d'editions géographiques, maritimes et coloniales, 1924), p. 179.

[36]2nd ed. (The Hague: M. Nijhoff, 1968), fig. 100.

[37]J. Shakespear, *The Lushei Kuki Clans* (London: Macmillan & Co., 1912), p. 28.

tonous, its music is not unharmonious."[38] The Tibeto-Burman speaking Naga tribes living in India's Nagaland as well as in Manipur and across the border in Burma use an instrument of this type according to Hodson. Referring to a subgroup of the Naga, he says, "In a Chiru village near Thobal, in the valley, I saw men playing on a goshem (Lushai rotchem). This instrument is distinctly Kuki as opposed to Naga. I believe every Kuki clan uses it."[39]

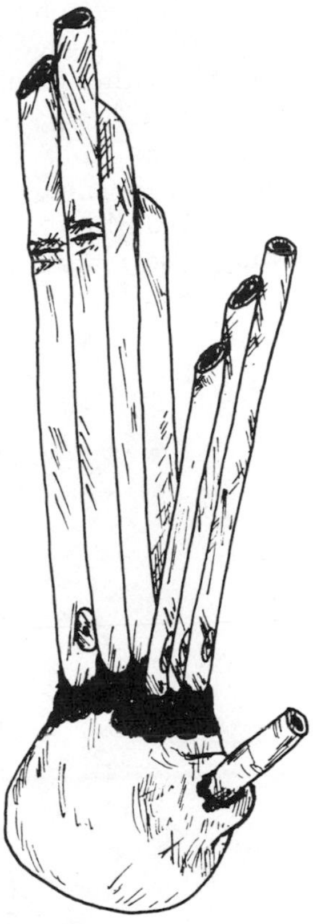

Figure 6. *Free-reed gourd organ from northeastern India*

The Karen people in Burma use a bamboo mouth organ. Marshall reports that either the Kerko or Paduang group (he is uncertain which) uses a mouth organ with five pipes,[40] but Sachs gives us a more detailed description. His specimen, obtained from the Black Karen in Kayah state near Taunggyi, has ten pipes with lengths varying from 34 to 122 centimeters, each with a metal reed. The pipes, which extend below the gourd, are sealed in place with wax and bundled together in circular fashion, unlike the oblique pipes found near Chittagong. There are, in addition, six bamboo cups fitted over the longest pipes and sometimes over shorter pipes as well to influence the tone color. These are similar in effect to the lower gourd used by the Taungyo and the "quiver" used by the Palaung.[41]

At least four tribes living in the so-called "golden triangle" area of Thailand, Burma, Laos, and Yunnan province use gourd mouth organs. The Akha, also known as Kaw or Ekaw, a Tibeto-Burman

[38] *Chittagong Hill-Tribes*, pl. 15.

[39] Hodson, *Naga Tribes*, p. 67.

[40] *Karen People*, p. 166.

[41] Sachs, *Musikinstruments Birmas und Assams*, pp. 40-41.

people, use an organ having five pipes which penetrate the bottom of the gourd only slightly. A specimen in the author's collection has a reed of either bamboo or palm leaf whose tongues have been tuned with tiny lumps of black wax, which also holds the reeds in place. According to a Thai professor in Bangkok (whose name I did not record) who owns two such instruments, they are called *la-yü* or *layübai*, but Boon Chuay calls them *naw.*[42] According to the owner, the player not only closes the finger hole above the gourd but may also close the bottom of the pipe (Figure 7).

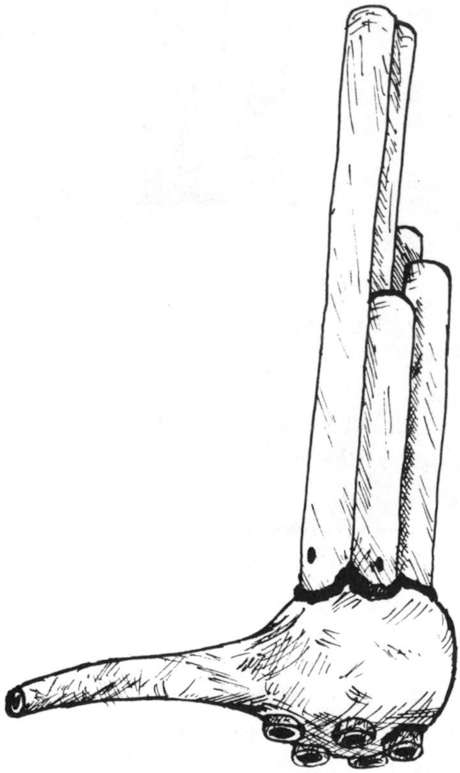

Figure 7. *Free-reed gourd organ from northern Thailand*

The Lahu, also called Mussuh or Musur, living in the same region use an instrument nearly identical to that of the Akha. Young also

[42]Boon Chuay Srisavasdi, *The Hill Tribes of Siam* (Bangkok: Khun Aroon, 1963), p. 22.

calls it a *naw*,[43] but Sachs gives its name as *fulū*.[44] As in the case of the Akha instrument, the five pipes are bundled and protrude slightly beneath the gourd. According to both Sachs' specimen and Woodthorpe's reference,[45] the reeds are of metal, but two instruments in the author's collection have reeds of cane or bamboo. Young, who adds that such instruments are used by the Lahu Nyi, Lahu Shelah, and Lahu Shi in north Thailand, indicates that women normally play the *naw* while both men and women dance in a circle. At night they play it to entice the boys from their homes and also to accompany "ballads," especially at New Year.[46]

The Lisu or Lisaw living in north Thailand use a similar instrument called *balileao*, which is, according to photographs in Young[47] and a specimen seen by the author, much longer than those of the Akha or Lahu. This instrument, whose bundled pipes may be capped with resonators, are often used in combination with a bowed lute to accompany dancing. Abadie alleges that the Lolo in north Vietnam, who are related to the Akha, Lisu, and Lahu, use a "great flute," called *sen*, which has six to eight pipes.[48]

Although Young does not mention the mouth organ as occurring among the Yao, a Sino-Tibetan people whose language is related to Miao, a tape in the author's collection from the Chiang-mai (Thailand) radio station includes an excerpt of Yao mouth-organ playing. Information regarding other tribes in the area is scant, and in the case of southern China there is only one known reference to a gourd mouth organ. Dodd, in his book *The Tai Race*, quotes a report written by T.S.A. Bourne in 1898 in which he describes a procession of Tung-chia people, a Tai group living in Kweichow province, China, in which two men played mouth organs:

> In front about thirty girls were walking in single file, stepping out briskly over the rocky path in black tunics, short petticoats and grass sandals; behind them also in single file, was a large party of men, and in the rear two musicians—with things like organ pipes of bamboo, stretching three or four feet over their heads, through which they blew by means of a horizontal mouthpiece: the music sounded fairly melodious. . . .[49]

[43]Oliver G. Young, *The Hilltribes of Northern Thailand* (Bangkok: The Government of Thailand and USOM, 1961), p. 22.

[44]*Musikinstrumente Birmas und Assams*, p. 41.

[45]R. G. Woodthorpe, "The Country of the Shans," *Geographical Journal* 7 (1896):598.

[46]Young, *Hilltribes of Northern Thailand*, pp. 12-33.

[47]Ibid., p. 42.

[48]*Races du Haut-Tonkin*, p. 179.

[49]William C. Dodd, *The Tai Race, Elder Brother of the Chinese* (Cedar Rapids: The Torch Press, 1923), p. 27.

The main difficulty with this reference is the "horizontal mouthpiece," for if literally correct it may indicate the use of the Miao mouth organ to be described below.

Information concerning gourd mouth organs from Cambodia is based primarily on Baradat and Sisowath apart from a uselessly vague reference in Sachs to an instrument called the *mbott* used among the *möi*, a word which merely means "savages."[50] Baradat, in his study of the songs and dances of the Samre and Pear, describes a seven-pipe organ called a *phloy* or *phlouy* which is made in two sizes, *phloy khun* ("female") and the more common *phloy khen* ("child").[51] The pipes, arranged in a bundle and protruding beneath the gourd, vary in length from 22 to 78 centimeters. Sisowath adds only that *phloy* may have as few as five pipes.[52]

Baradat further mentions the use of a five-pipe instrument among the Chong-khnang-phnom, a Mon-Khmer tribe living southwest of the Tonle Sap. Similarly, he claims that the Saoch, another Mon-Khmer tribe in Cambodia, use such an instrument but, not having seen it, could not describe it.[53] Sisowath also refers to a gourd mouth organ with oblique rather than bundled pipes used among the "Khmer-Loeu,"[54] a newly invented term for "upland Khmer" to replace the pejorative *möi*.

The borders between Laos, Cambodia, and south Vietnam are of little relevance to hill tribesmen, who avoid lowlanders as much as possible. The dominant hill tribes are southeast upland Mon-Khmer speakers such as the Ma, Mnong, and Stieng. Further east nearer the coast the dominant groups are upland Cham or Malayo-Polynesian speakers such as Jarai, Rhade, and Raglai. In Vietnam these people are collectively known as *möi, montagnards*, or, to use a non-pejorative term, *Dong Bau Thuong* ("upland compatriots"). Information regarding the use of mouth organs among these peoples is scarce.

The best source is Jacques Dournes, who describes in great detail the *dding-nam* ("six tubes") of the Jarai, upland Cham in Vietnam.[55] The six tubes, which pierce the bottom of the gourd, are arranged in two rows, each controlled by two fingers and thumb of one hand. Trần văn Khê only mentions the "*ding nam* (mouth

[50] *Musikinstrumente Indiens und Indonesiens*, p. 165.

[51] R. Baradat, "Les Sămrê ou Peăr, population primitive de l'ouest du Cambodge," *Bulletin de l'Ecole Française d'Extrême-Orient* 41 (1941):81.

[52] *Musique du Cambodge*, p. 19.

[53] Baradat, "Sămrê ou Peăr," p. 80.

[54] *Musique du Cambodge*, p. 18.

[55] "Musique chez les Jörai," p. 234.

organ with six tubes); *köm boat* (upper plateau of central Vietnam [*sic*]) or *mboat* or *nboat* (mouth organ with five or six tubes); [and] *ding teak*, mouth organ with thirteen tubes (Djörai, Bahnar)."[56] The Bahnar are Mon-Khmer speakers, but the terminology is obviously mixed among several languages. A French-made recording in the author's collection includes an excerpt played on a six-tubed gourd mouth organ called *komboat* by a member of the Ma or Cau Ma tribe, a Mon-Khmer group living near the Upper Donna River in south Vietnam. Gironcourt describes a six-tubed gourd organ called *m'buat* or *mboa* nearly 80 centimeters high used by the Bu-Neur in Kratie (Kracheh) province, Cambodia. The Bu-neur or Bu Nor are a subgroup of the Mnong, a Mon-Khmer hill tribe.[57]

The author's collection includes a mouth organ purchased in Saigon which came originally from the Vietnamese central highlands, but the tribal group to which it belonged is unknown. The six pipes are arranged in two oblique rows having four in front and two in back, protruding slightly below the gourd. The reed, measuring 1.2 centimeters by .5 centimeters, is made of a ragged piece of metal, and the tongue is tapered. A reddish substance covers the reed either to seal or preserve it. Four of the pipes, which vary in length from 39 to 63 centimeters, have finger holes in back, two in front, obviously to accommodate the hands. Although the specimen was purchased in early 1970 and had not been played for four years, the reeds functioned and produced the pitches indicated in Figure 8.

Pipe	Length	Open Pitch	Bottom Closed
1	63.2 cm.	c'	b
2	36.0 cm.	b'	a♭'
3	39.5 cm.	a♭'	g♭'
4	58.0 cm.	d'	c'
5	42.7 cm.	g'	f'
6	54.0 cm.	e♭'	d♭'/d'

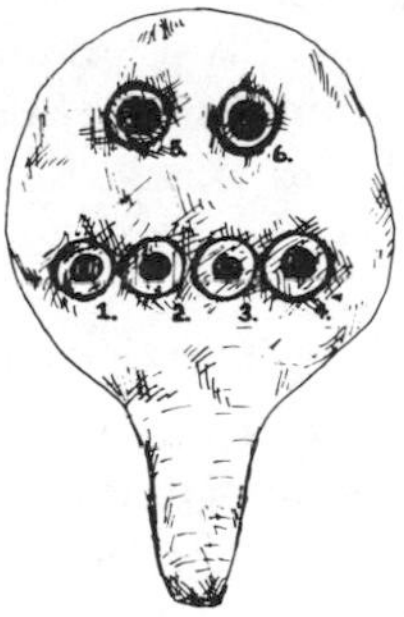

Figure 8. *Specifications of a gourd mouth organ from upland Vietnam*

[56] *Viêt-Nam*, p. 113. Author's translation.
[57] Georges de Gironcourt, "Recherches de géographie musicale en Indochine," *Bulletin de la Société des Etudes Indochinoises* 17 (1942; reprint ed., Saigon: Société des Imprimeries et Librairies Indochinoises, 1943):80, 84.

Although it is virtually certain that many other ethnic groups in mainland Southeast Asia have gourd mouth organs, no others are known at present. There remains one more area, however, where this instrument occurs, namely, in Borneo, including Sarawak and Sabah (formerly British North Borneo). Though anthropologists have gathered a great amount of detailed material on individual tribes living on Borneo, a comprehensive picture is yet to emerge. Linguists are still unable to classify many of the languages, and consequently it is difficult to group the tribes. Six tribal groups are associated with mouth organ instruments in the literature regarding Borneo, three of them tentatively classified as Malayic speakers, two as Austronesian speakers of the Idahan subgroup, and one as speakers of a type of West Indonesian language.

The tribe mentioned most often in that literature is the Dayak, a Malayic people living principally in the western half of Borneo. J.B. Avé describes this term as "a collective name for a great many predominantly non-Muslim ethnic and linguistic groups—e.g., Ngadju, Maanyan, Lawangan—who live along the banks of the larger river systems, growing rice on swiddens and collecting forest produce such as rattan, ironwood, rubber, resin, and skins."[58] Various writers have referred to their mouth organ as *enkerulai, kledi, engkruri, keluri*, and *garude*, the last quite possibly an error since an unrelated tribe also calls their instrument by this name.

According to available illustrations there are two slightly different designs. The *kledi* pictured in plate 99 by Kunst in *Hindu-Javanese Musical Instruments* has five or six pipes bundled in a circle into a gourd whose mouthpiece curves downward. Atop the longest pipe is a smaller gourd with a hole cut in the side, the probable function of which is to alter the tone color as the bamboo caps of the Black Karen instrument do. Krohn illustrates a *kledi* having five pipes sealed into the gourd with "gutta percha."[59] The longest pipe is topped by a short section of bamboo turned horizontally while the other pipes have bamboo cups placed over them. The gourd differs only slightly from that shown in Sachs.[60] Roth illustrates a "Dyak Engkruri" having seven tubes in two parallel rows fitted into a gourd whose neck turns sharply upwards[61] (Figure 9).

[58]Lebar, *Ethnic Groups of Insular Southeast Asia*, p. 185.

[59]William O. Krohn, *In Borneo Jungles* (Indianapolis: Bobbs-Merrill Co., 1927), p. 230.

[60]*Musikinstrumente Indiens und Indonesiens*, p. 165.

[61]Henry L. Roth, *The Natives of Sarawak and British North Borneo*, 2 vols. (London: Truslove and Hanson, 1896), 2:259.

While Kunst contradicts Hose and McDougall on the exact nature of the reed,[62] it is nevertheless clear that its material is vegetable fiber rather than metal. In reference to the *keluri* Hose and McDougall report:

> The artist blows through the neck of the gourd, and the air enters the base of each pipe by an oblong aperture which is filled by a vibrating tongue or reed; this is formed by shaving away the wall of the bamboo till it is very thin, and then cutting through it round three sides of the oblong; it is weighted with a piece of wax.[63]

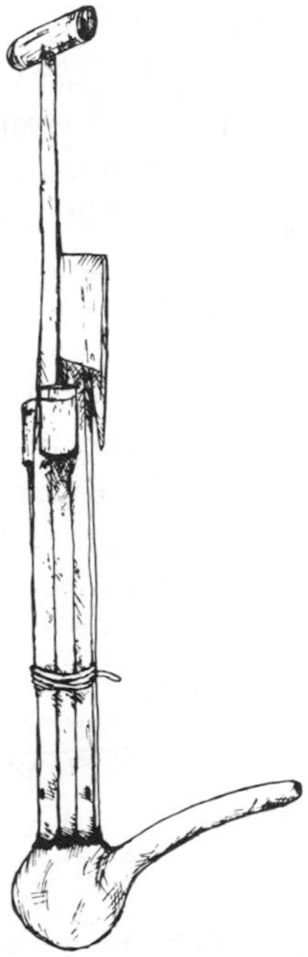

Figure 9. Kledi

Thc instrument illustrated there on page 167 has six pipes bundled with at least one covered with a quiver-like bamboo cup. Kunst, however, indicates that all Borneo mouth organs have separately cut reeds:

> Each of these tubes has a vibrating tongue made of palm wood (therefore, heteroglottal) which can sound only when the player, blowing the narrow end of the gourd, closes the hole in the tube he wants to hear. The lowest note is sounded continuously in the manner of the drone of the bagpipe or of the Indian instrumental music. With the other five (or seven) notes the player produces necessarily simple melodies.[64]

While the *kledi* caught the eye of most observers among the Dayak, only one writer, Krohn, gives us any information on its use: "The *kledi* is exclusively a man's musical instrument. Women adore the music it makes, but do not attempt to play it. This instrument is a great favorite and is played at the long house, in the field, at padi harvest, and is used to accompany songs at the weapon dance."[65] Only Kunst provides an illustration with a player. The male pictured holds the instrument near the gourd

[62]Kunst, *Hindu-Javanese Musical Instruments*, p. 27.

[63]Charles Hose and William McDougall, *The Pagan Tribes of Borneo*, 2 vols. (London: Macmillan & Co., 1912), 2:166.

[64]Kunst, *Hindu-Javanese Musical Instruments*, p. 27.

[65]Krohn, *In Borneo Jungles*, p. 232.

with his left hand and places his right hand and fingers around the pipes.[66]

Two related tribes, the Iban (or Sea Dyak) and Sibuyow (also spelled Sebuyau), have similar instruments. Sachs describes an organ called *Engkruri* or *Engkerurai* used by the Sea Dyak which is "smaller than the *keluri*" and has from six to eight pipes plus a bamboo cup to alter the tone of the longest pipe.[67] These "Proto-Malay riverine people, practicing shifting agriculture in the low hills behind the coast of Sarawak in western Borneo"[68] were head-hunters until the 1920s. The only available reference to a mouth organ among the Sibuyow is found in Roth's book where he quotes another writer: "Mr. Hornaday (p. 468) speaks of the 'pleasing clarionet-like notes of the numerous reeds, made like a shepherd's pipe, which the Sibuyow men, women, and children were so fond of playing upon in concert.' "[69] Little is known of this group except the statement by Lebar that "the Sebuyau appear to be a para-Malay people derived from the Iban."[70]

The Dusun and Murut, living in Sabah in the northern part of Borneo, are related linguistically as different branches (Dusunic and Murutic) within the Idahan family forming part of the Northern Indonesian branch of Austronesian. According to Sachs, the Dusun possess a gourd mouth organ called *garude,*[71] an instrument which is described in greater detail by Roth: "The Dusun pipes are formed of eight pipes, four short and equal in length, and four long and unequal. Reeds are cut at the lower end in all the pipes, but the fingering is performed on the ends of the four equal short pipes, there being no holes cut in the pipes for this purpose."[72]

Although contradictions among authors must be expected, given the nature of the problem, the Dayak *engkruri* pictured by Roth,[73] with its mouthpiece turned upward and which differs from those shown by Sachs, Kunst, and Krohn, appears again in Rutter's *The Pagans of North Borneo* but as the Murut *sumpotan*. The player appears to blow across the mouthpiece since the neck curves so far

[66] *Die Musik in Geschichte und Gegenwart*, s. v. "Indonesische Musik," col. 1191.

[67] Curt Sachs, *Real-Lexikon der Musikinstrumente* (Berlin, 1913; reprint ed., Hildesheim: Georg Olms, 1964), p. 129.

[68] Lebar, *Ethnic Groups of Insular Southeast Asia*, p. 180.

[69] *Natives*, 2:260.

[70] *Ethnic Groups of Insular Southeast Asia*, p. 180.

[71] *Musikinstrumente Indiens und Indonesiens*, p. 165.

[72] Roth, *Natives*, 2:260.

[73] Ibid., 2:259.

around that placing the mouth over it would be difficult. His right hand is shown holding the pipes near the top while the left grips the instrument just above the gourd. Rutter says:

> The *sumpotan* consists of eight bamboo pipes fitted vertically into the empty shell of a gourd, which functions as a windchest. One of the pipes is a dummy; the others produce, by "free" reeds, the notes of the pentatonic scale. Three of the pipes are stopped at their orifices by the fingers of the right hand; three others have small apertures at their base, which are stopped by the fingers of the left hand; while the remaining pipe is a drone. At times two or three of the pipes sound together, yet the effect is not unpleasant.[74]

It appears, then, that both Dusun and Murut organs must be similar since both have eight pipes, and only four of these have finger holes. Roth's reference to performing "on the ends of the four equal short pipes" then means stopping them at the top with the right hand. Rutter's illustration, however, is of the left side of the instrument; nothing can be seen of the right. Roth's "Dyak *engkruri*," however, has only seven pipes, but he does not mention finger holes. While it is possible that the Dayak do indeed use a similar instrument, Roth may have confused his tribes and inadvertently pictured a Murut or Dusun gourd organ.

Bliss Wiant of Delaware, Ohio, possesses a gourd mouth organ from Borneo purchased at the Jesselton (now Kota Kinabalu) airport in British North Borneo (now Sabah). Although he knew neither the tribe nor the instrument's name, it is apparent that he acquired a Murut *sumpotan*. As indicated in the chart below, there are eight pipes, each with the bottom ends closed (either with black wax or an unpierced node) fitted in two parallel rows (raft fashion) into a gourd, although the neck is not curved. Of these, three have finger holes (1, 4, and 8), each cut as two triangles: ⧗ . A fourth pipe is a dummy, but the remaining four speak unless the player closes the tops with his fingers. The drone referred to by Rutter is apparently pipe 3, and the player stops the tops of pipes 5-7 with his right hand. The reeds are of bamboo or palm leaf fitted over a slot and sealed with a black wax. The pipe tips, which do not pierce the gourd, are joined with wax into a solid block inside the gourd. The reeds measure 3 by .8 centimeters and the tongues 1.8 by .2 centimeters. The pitches indicated possibly may not be the original ones since the reeds, unused for many years, had warped and sounded only upon persuasion.

74Owen Rutter, *The Pagans of North Borneo* (London: Hutchinson and Co., 1929), p. 110.

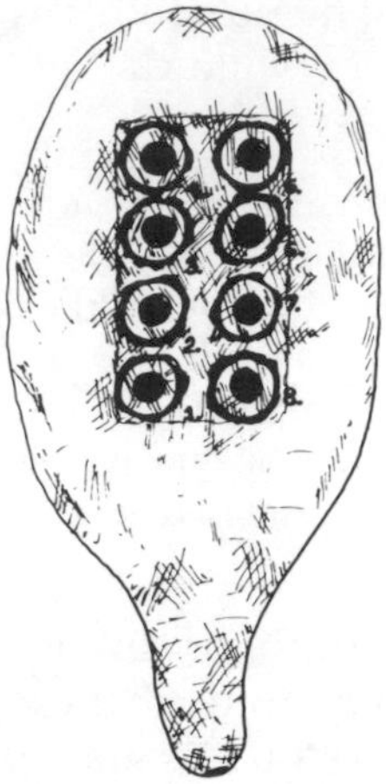

Pipe	Length	Pitch
1	42.1 cm.	d♯’
2	50.6 cm.	dummy
3	50.6 cm.	between c’ and d’
4	35.0 cm.	g’
5	27.6 cm.	g♯’
6	27.8 cm.	b’
7	27.2 cm.	d”
8	27.7 cm.	e”

Figure 10. *Specifications of a Murut* sumpotan

The Murut *sumpotan*, Dusun mouth organ, and Dayak *engkruri* are apparently related, unless Roth is mistaken in assigning his specimen to the Dayak. It would be odd that the Dayak possess instruments in two distinct forms, bundled and raft.

Throughout central Borneo lives a group of people known as Bahau or Kenyah-Kayan-Kajang. These terms “denote a culture complex which includes in addition to the well-known Kenyah and Kayan peoples a great many smaller riverine ‘tribes’ and long-house units in both Sarawak and Kalimantan.”[75] Furness describes their gourd organ best, calling it *kaluri, kaleeri*, or *kaludi*, terms which have been used in reference to the Dayak instrument as well:

> It consists of a bottle-shaped gourd with six hollow reed pipes set into the body of it; a finger-hole is cut in each pipe at such a place that the fingers of both hands while holding the instrument can cover all the holes. The middle reed is the longest, and is therefore the bass; it has no finger-hole, but its tone is subdued by a movable cap at the end.[76]

A *keluri* in the Stearns Collection of Musical Instruments at Ann Arbor, Michigan, has six tubes from 33 to 66 centimeters long inserted into the top of a gourd, but all have finger holes. The palm-leaf reed measures 3 by .9 centimeters.[77]

Roth describes a *keluri* from the Kayan on the Baram river

[75]Lebar, *Ethnic Groups of Insular Southeast Asia*, p. 168.

[76]William H. Furness, *The Home-Life of Borneo Head-Hunters* (Philadelphia: J. B. Lippincott, 1902), p. 6.

[77]Item no. 701.

having seven pipes, six arranged around a central drone. As in the specimen cited by Furness, this instrument also has a bamboo cap over the longest pipe. According to Roth the instrument measures 38½ inches in length and weighs only 10½ ounces. "Four pipes produce the chord F (F A C F, with upper and lower tonic). A fifth has a faint suspicion of a flattened ninth ♭G (of course from the lower tonic), while a sixth pipe adds the pluperfect fourth B. It is played by suction and is tuned by shortening the pipes."[78] Hedda Morrison, in her photographic essay *Sarawak*, illustrates a ceremony among the Kayan at Long Buroi in upper Tinjar in which a man is being healed through invocation of the spirits. Facing a tray covered with ceremonial objects, the sick man sits beside a second man playing a small *keluri*, which more closely resembles the mouth organ of the Akha and Lahu than those shown by Roth and Furness.[79]

5. Miao Mouth Organ

Differing significantly from that of other ethnic groups in Southeast Asia, the mouth organ of the Miao is, next to that of the Lao, the most advanced and highly finished free-reed instrument on the subcontinent. Lebar divides the Miao into three subgroups called South China Miao (or Hmong, Hmu, and Hmung), Indochina Meo (or Mlao and Mnong), and Thailand Meo (or H'moong, Meau, Mong).[80] Their total estimated population throughout the region is 2,700,000, of which less than 200,000 live outside southern China. The center of Miao culture in China is the Kweichow plateau extending into neighboring Yunnan, Szechwan, Hunan, and Kwangsi provinces. In northern Vietnam they are concentrated near the Chinese border in the Red and Black River basins, in Laos in Xieng Khouang province, and in Thailand in Nan, Chiang-mai, and Chiang-rai provinces.

Little is known of the origin or early movement of the Miao, but they were already known to the Chinese in the pre-Han period (before 202 B.C.) when they appeared on the lower middle Yangtze River. Later they began moving into the Yellow River region, but under Chinese pressure retreated into Kwangtung, Hunan, and Kwangsi provinces and later into Kweichow, the most impoverished province in southern China. The last three hundred years have seen not only additional Chinese pressure on the Miao but frequent

[78] Roth, *Natives*, 2:259.

[79] Hedda Morrison, *Sarawak* (Singapore: Donald Moore Press, 1965), p. 280.

[80] Lebar et al., *Ethnic Groups of Mainland Southeast Asia*, p. 63.

uprisings. In Laos they were recently employed by the United States Central Intelligence Agency (CIA) to fight the North Vietnamese and Pathet Lao. They also migrated into northern Thailand about sixty years ago and now number approximately 45,000 there. A few Miao have recently moved into other Thai provinces such as Pitsanulok and Loey and sometimes appear in Northeast Thai markets selling herbal medicines.

The Miao, because they are the largest of the "hill tribes" in China, have received more attention than other such groups. At least fifteen writers discuss the Miao mouth organ in varying degrees of detail. This instrument is known among the Miao as *gaeng* or *daeng* although Clarke calls it *Kĭ*,[81] and others refer to it by its Chinese designation *liu sheng*.[82] In its most usual form, the *gaeng* has six heavy bamboo tubes inserted into a long bulbous windchest made from two carved hardwood halves. Both the windchest and the long tapering mouthpiece are bound with straps of bark or, if the instrument is an expensive one, bands of silver. The reeds are cut into rather heavy metal, probably brass or an alloy of silver and copper. The right front pipe, which is shorter but of greater diameter than the others, is fitted with two or three such reeds and naturally sounds loudest. While the relative pitches remain the same on all instruments observed or described in writing, the length of the longest pipe may vary from 50 centimeters to nearly 2 meters (Figure 11).

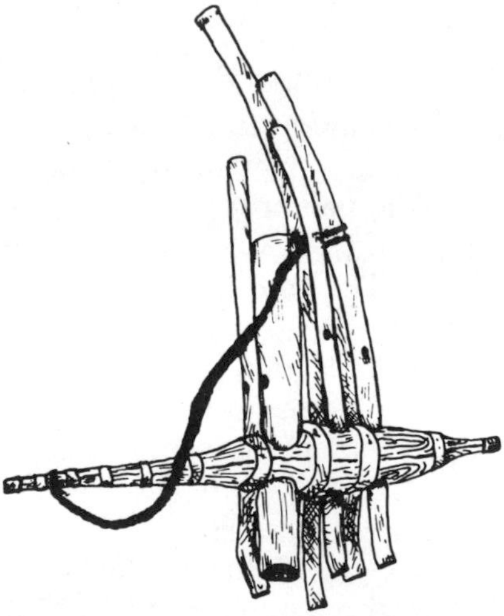

Figure 11. Gaeng

[81]Samuel R. Clarke, *Among the Tribes in South-West China* (London: China Inland Mission, 1911; reprint ed., Taipei: Ch'eng Wen Publishing Co., 1970), p. 64.

[82]See, e.g., R. Gordon Agnew, "The Music of the Ch'uan Miao," *Journal of the West China Border Research Society* 11 (1939):13ff.

Although *gaeng* may be as small as 54 centimeters long and 60 centimeters high, the most usual size is nearly double this. A specimen observed in a Luang Prabang (Laos) shop had pipes ranging from 47 to 91 centimeters while the windchest measured 68 centimeters overall. All reeds were similarly cut, but the three reeds of the shortest pipe measured 27 by 9 millimeters while those of the other five pipes measured 25 by 7.5 millimeters. Without information regarding modes in Miao music, it is impossible to describe the tonal arrangement in other than Western terms. If the shortest pipe having three reeds is considered the "tonic" (and it alone is duplicated at the octave), the scale is an anhemitonic pentatonic scale: C, D, F, G, A (Figure 12).

Pipe	Length	Pitch
1	47.0 cm.	f♯'
2	66.5 cm.	c♯'
3	73.4 cm.	b
4	62.5 cm.	d♯'
5	91.0 cm.	f♯
6	84.5 cm.	g♯

Figure 12. *Specifications of a Miao* gaeng

Regarding the craft of making *gaeng*, only Bernatzik gives us any details:

> The wooden body consists of two symmetrical halves, which are precisely fitted together and wound with bamboo strips, and the joints are smeared with buffalo fat. The holes for the pipes are burned into this wooden body, perpendicular to the joints, with a red-hot piece of metal. . . . For the manufacturing process, the length of the pipes, which, along with the diameter, determines the pitch, is always chosen so that their tone is somewhat lower than the one actually aimed for; finally the instrument is tuned by appropriately shortening the tubes.[83]

Both the instrument observed in Luang Prabang and a smaller specimen in the writer's collection have wooden stoppers inserted into the lower ends of certain pipes. It is possible that these tune the pipe by shortening its speaking length.

Compared to other hill tribes, the uses of the Miao mouth organ have been extensively described, especially by Bernatzik and

[83] Bernatzik, *Akha and Miao*, pp. 199-200.

Agnew.[84] The former reports that the *gaeng* is a sacral instrument whose tone is pleasing to the spirits whose worship is the heart of Miao religion. In ceremonies many *gaeng* may be played together, and their sound is said to echo across the mountain tops.

Maurice Abadie in his study of the hill tribes of upper Tonkin (northern Vietnam) rather inaccurately describes the Miao mouth organ as a *sen* having from six to eight tubes.[85] He notes, however, that two other ethnic groups use this instrument. The first is the Lolo, a Tibeto-Burman people mentioned earlier as having a single-tubed instrument. The second is the Man-ta-pan, a Chinese designation for a little understood tribal cluster designated Indochina Man by Lebar. Although found in small concentrations in northern Laos, the Man-ta-pan are mostly found in north Vietnam west of Cao Bang towards the Chinese border. Dodd's description of a mouth organ among the Tung-chia having a "horizontal mouthpiece"[86] may refer to the use of the Miao organ by Tai-speaking people in southern China. In recent years the Communist Chinese have urged ethnic minorities to improve their instruments, and one result is a fourteen-tubed Miao mouth organ. These, however, are of little interest at the present time.

Although the usual mouth organ among the Miao appears to be the *gaeng*, several writers, most notably Moule and Clarke, describe a mouth organ among the Heh Miao or Black Miao similar to the *gaeng* but with modifications and dimensions that are quite astonishing. Quoting from G.E. Bett's description of the Seventh Moon Festival in southwestern China, Moule offers the following note:

> There were thirty-six bands, six instruments to one band, and six sounds to one instrument. These instruments are constructed with bamboo pipes having brass reeds. The largest sized instrument is made of the trunk of a tree hollowed out. A bamboo pipe fourteen feet long with reed and mouth-piece is placed in the hollowed tree trunk.[87]

In reference to the *Kĭ*, apparently the same instrument as Moule described, Clarke provided a slightly clearer description than Moule:

> They are made in sets of different sizes, the smallest having pipes about three feet long, and the largest with pipes twelve or fourteen feet long. The lower end of the large pipe is put into a drum or cylinder three or four feet long, hollowed out of the trunk of a tree. These large reeds

[84]Ibid., p. 140ff.; and Agnew, "Music of the Ch'uan Miao," pp. 9-65.

[85]*Races du Haut-Tonkin*, p. 152.

[86]*Tai Race*, p. 28.

[87]A. C. Moule, "A List of the Musical and Other Sound-producing Instruments of the Chinese," *Journal of the North China Branch of the Royal Asiatic Society of Great Britain and Ireland* 39 (1908):95.

> give forth a very creepy sound, the lowest note, we believe, to which mortal ears are sensible. The tunes they play are very monotonous.[88]

The Heh Miao are concentrated in southeast Kweichow province but in recent decades have been migrating to neighboring provinces.

6. Lao Mouth Organ (*Kaen*)

Because modern political boundaries in Southeast Asia rarely reflect the actual distribution of ethnic groups, it is not surprising that the vast majority of Lao, a main subgroup of the Tai, live not in Laos but in Northeast Thailand. Laos is also home to many non-Lao ethnic groups, which constitute about fifty percent of the population. The Lao mouth organ, called *kaen*, flourishes throughout the region, but *kaen* making centers in Roi-et province, Thailand, and *kaen* playing is best in the provinces along the Chi River in Thailand from Kawn-gaen (Khon Kaen) in the west to Oobon (Ubon) in the southeast. *Kaen* playing in Laos centers in the southern provinces along the Maekong River.

Kaen are raft-form instruments whose tubes (*mai goo kaen*) are arranged in two parallel rows. Four sizes are known today: *kaen hok* ("six") with six tubes, *kaen jet* ("seven") with fourteen tubes, *kaen baet* ("eight") with sixteen tubes, and *kaen gao* ("nine") with eighteen tubes. Until recent years *kaen jet* was standard, but today *kaen baet* is the most common size. The *kaen hok* is considered a child's toy but, in fact, may show the *kaen* in its original size, while *kaen gao* are rarely seen or heard today. There being neither standard length nor pitch, *kaen* vary in length from about 80 to 130 centimeters. According to late nineteenth-century descriptions, *kaen* of the time often extended to as much as 4 meters in length,[89] but such dimensions are now impractical and no longer seen (Figure 13).

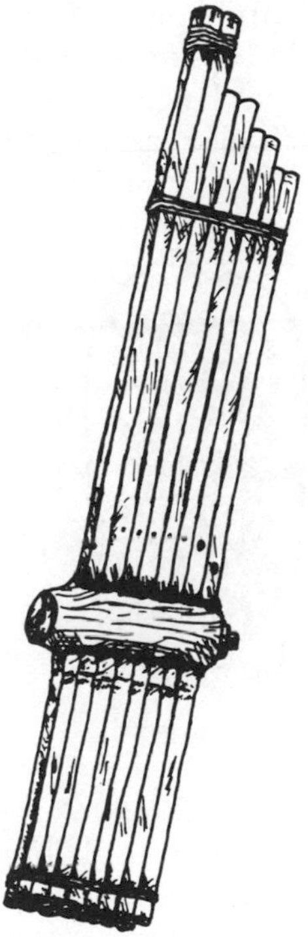

Figure 13. Kaen

[88]Clarke, *Tribes in South-West China*, pp. 64-65.

[89]See, e.g., Prince Henri d'Orléans, *Around Tonkin and Siam* (London: Chapman and Hall, Ltd., 1894), p. 371.

Kaen reeds are of metal, usually a mixture of copper and silver, and fitted into the pipe walls inside the hardwood windchest. The latter, called *dao*, which, interestingly, means "gourd" as well as "breast," is carved from hardwood roots, usually from the *mai-bradoo* but also from the *dakian* tree, which is called *kaen* tree in Lao. The pipes are sealed into the windchest with the same black beeswax used on other free-reed instruments, in Lao called *kisoot*. The stepwise arrangement of pipes, however, does not indicate relative pitch in all cases because speaking length is determined by pitch holes cut in the tube which are hidden from sight. The arrangement of pitches, furthermore, appears to make little sense. Because it is difficult to play three consecutive pipes, builders evolved a system whereby the pitches were rearranged to avoid this problem and also provide balance between the two sides. It could be said that the pitch arrangement of the *kaen* fits the Lao musical language just as the letter arrangement of the typewriter, which also appears illogical, fits the English language (Figure 14).

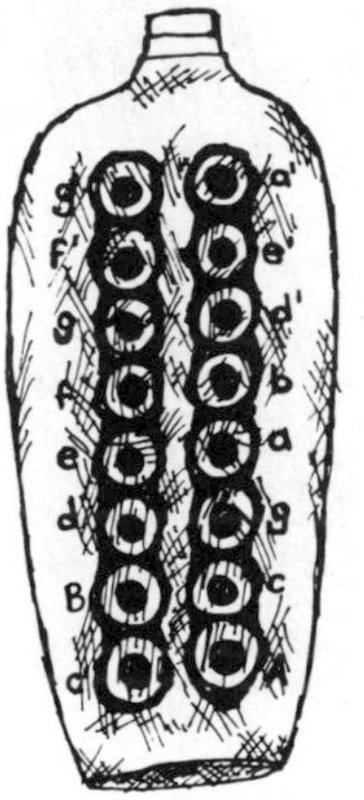

Figure 14. *Pitch arrangement on the* kaen

Kaen making takes place in village homes where craftsmen using a few simple tools build each instrument from start to finish. The materials are mostly produced locally—bamboo tubes from Kalasin province, *kisoot* from insect nests, *dao* windchests from local tree roots. The reed metal, however, derives from old Thai coins. Using a pattern handed down by generations involving both proportions and visual comparison, the maker tunes the pipes to a seven-note system using both semi- and whole-tones, the former approximately 100 cents, the latter 200 cents. The *kaen*'s total scale, thus, approximates the Western diatonic scale, a striking contrast to the seven equidistant steps of the Siamese scale used in nearby central Thailand.

From these seven pitches two pentatonic scales are derived: G, A, C, D, E and A, C, D, E, G. The first scale may be played in three positions or modes, beginning on theoretical G, C, or D, called *sootsanaen, bo-sai,* and *soi* respectively, while the second scale may be played in two positions, on A and D, called *yai* and *noi.* Each of these terms is preceded by the word *lai* (e.g., *lai sootsanaen*), which implies "improvisation" or, in the larger sense, mode. Each *lai* involves not just the melodic pitches but standardized drones (pipes stopped with bits of *kisoot*), "harmonic" combinations, and characteristic melodic and rhythmic motives.

Kaen may be played solo in private or for a circle of friends, but the normal function is to accompany traditional singing variously called *mawlum pün* (one singer; long, epic story), *mawlum glawn* (two singers, male and female), *mawlum moo* (serious theatre), and *mawlum plün* (lighter theatre). Old literature describes *kaen* being used in ensembles called *pinpat*, but ensembles involving *kaen* today are rather uncommon except in parts of southern Laos where ensembles including *kaen*, plucked lute, and percussion instruments accompany *mawlum*.

According to myth, the *kaen* was invented long ago to imitate the sounds of the *garawek* bird (the Indian cuckoo). Little is known of actual *kaen* history because most records of the Siamese were destroyed in 1767, and the Lao court was destroyed twice, once in the late eighteenth century, again in the 1820s. The earliest known illustration in the region is found on the bas relief front wall under the portico of Wut Mai in Luang-prabang, Laos, a building dated between 1796 and 1820. The instrument, however, is unclear in its details. The earliest written description of the use of *kaen* was by the English diplomat Sir John Bowring in 1857.[90]

While *kaen* are played primarily by Lao speakers, a few other ethnic groups have adopted the instrument. The Poo-tai, upland Tai living in both northeast Thailand and Laos, use the *kaen* to accompany their singing; little is known of the musical instruments of the Tai living in southern China and northern Vietnam. In Thai provinces bordering Cambodia the ethnic Khmer now use the *kaen* to accompany their traditional singing, called *jariang*. According to Baradat, the Chong, a Mon-Khmer group living in Thailand, use the *kaen*,[91] as do the Mon-Khmer Tau-oi in Sarawun (Saravane) province, Laos, according to researcher Carol Compton.[92] Stern and Stern have also described the *kaen*'s use among Pwo Karen in western Thailand who came into contact with Lao.[93]

[90] *The Kingdom and People of Siam*, 2 vols. (London, 1857; reprint ed., London: Oxford University Press, 1969), 2:324, 328.

[91] "Sămrê ou Peăr," p. 80.

[92] Personal communication, Ann Arbor, Michigan, November 1974.

[93] Theodore Stern and Theodore A. Stern, " 'I Pluck my harp': Musical Acculturation among the Karen of Western Thailand," *Ethnomusicology* 15 (1971): 186-219.

7. The Chinese Mouth Organ (*sheng*)

The most widely known and accessible Asian free-reed instrument is the Chinese *sheng (cheng, šeng, tcheng)*. Because the Chinese have a written tradition going back more than three thousand years, a great deal of historical material relating to the *sheng* is available. The Chinese Classics, particularly the *Shih Ching* [Classic of Songs or Book of Odes], refer frequently to the *sheng*:

> The dancers move with their flutes to the notes of the organ
> [sheng] and drum,
> While all the instruments perform in harmony.
> All this is done to please the meritorious ancestors,
> Along with the observance of all ceremonies.[94]

No less a man than Confucius (Kong Tse) (554-479 B.C.) is said to have played the *sheng*.[95] The antiquity of this instrument is undisputed.

The *sheng* known today consists of a bowl-shaped windchest into which seventeen bamboo pipes are placed in a circle. The windchest, called *sheng tou* ("chamber") or *p'ao* ("bottle gourd"), may be constructed of lacquered wood or pewter, the latter being usual since the later Ching dynasty. When metal is not employed, the windchest is of *wu-t'ung* wood scented with camphor, lacquered black, and shaped like a small mixing bowl with curved sides. The bottom is either perforated with several artistically shaped cutouts or a circular piece of carved ivory. In some specimens there is a horizontal partition just below the projecting mouthpiece onto which a circular drum is placed to restrict the air within a jacket around the inside of the bowl. On other specimens there is no horizontal partition, but the drum extends downward and meets the wall near the base. The top of the bowl is perforated with seventeen holes to receive the pipes.

The pipes (*huiu* or *kuan*) are of relatively heavy bamboo with closely spaced pierced nodes. The longest of them rarely exceeds 50 centimeters, but the shortest may be less than 15 centimeters. These are arranged in five symmetrical levels, four of which form into two separate semi-circles with the two tallest pipes in the middle of both the front and rear. The circle of tubes is braced with a thick band of cane. Because the pipe lengths do not reflect actual pitch relationships, tuning is accomplished, as in the *kaen*,

[94] *The Chinese Classics*, ed. James Legge, vol. 4, *The She King*, trans. James Legge (Hong Kong and London: n. p., 1871), pt. 2, bk. 6, ode 6, st. 2.

[95] Trần văn Khê, "Confucius, musicien et théoricien de la musique," *France-Asie* 185 (1966):316.

with slits cut in the pipe walls hidden within the circle. A careful maker will also cut the bamboo tubes so that the lowest nodes form a continuous line (Figure 15).

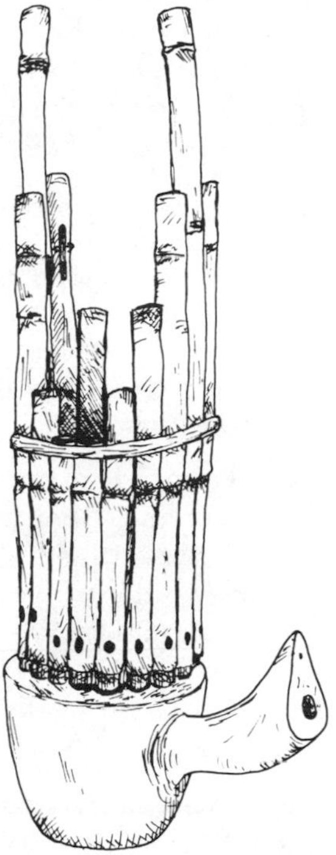

Figure 15. Sheng

About 1 centimeter above where the pipe enters the bowl the bamboo is cut off and a wooden foot inserted. The outer face of this 4-centimeter-long foot of the pipe is then cut away, exposing the hollow core of the tube. This opening is covered with a small sheet of metal (brass or copper-silver alloy) into which a tongue has been cut and then sealed carefully onto the foot with a substantial layer of wax. The reeds are then coated with a green substance derived from a stone to prevent deterioration from moisture, and the tongues tuned with tiny drops of red wax placed near the tips. These reeds are called *huang*; the plates measure approximately 3.5 by .5 centimeters while the tongues are approximately 13 to 15 millimeters long and 2 millimeters wide. On some specimens the finger holes are reinforced with tiny brass rings; the mouthpiece, *chou* ("mouth of a bird") or *tsui* ("mouth"), may be capped with ivory or a teapot spout-like extension added to the mouthpiece.

Most writers, including Moule,[96] Courant,[97] and Smith,[98] indicate that from two to four pipes are mutes, having neither reeds nor finger holes. Numbering the pipes from the left side of the gap in a clockwise pattern, pipes 1, 9, 16, and 17 are mutes in the charts published by Smith[99] and Van Aalst.[100] A specimen in the author's collection from Peking, however, has seventeen speaking pipes and includes all chromatic steps from *d''* to *d♭'''*.

In China *sheng* are now rarely seen or heard. Recordings of

[96]"List of the Musical and Other Sound-producing Instruments," p. 91.

[97]*Encyclopédie de la musique*, s. v. "Chine et Corée," by Maurice Courant.

[98]Herman Smith, *The World's Earliest Music* (London: William Reeves, n.d.), p. 202.

[99]Ibid.

[100]J. A. Van Aalst, *Chinese Music* (Shanghai: Statistical Department of the Inspectorate General of Customs, 1884), p. 82.

them are rather scarce, and some Chinese, even musicians, have never heard of the *sheng*, much less played one. The coming of the Maoists in 1949 spelled the end of many traditional ceremonies and the virtual closing of old temples. Van Aalst, writing in 1884, mentions the *sheng*'s position in the temple and processions:

> At the Confucian ceremonies there are six *sheng*, three on the east and three on the west side of the hall. They play exactly the same music and the same notes as the *ti-tzu*, or "flute." The *sheng* is never used in popular orchestras; at nuptial and funeral processions the *sheng* is sometimes seen, but it is there merely for form's sake, in accordance with the requirements of the rites, and the hired coolie who *carries* it simply simulates playing.[101]

Bliss Wiant, however, who spent many years in China teaching music, refutes this claim saying, "The funeral procession is often very long so that the *sheng* would not be played the entire time, neither would it be carried the entire time."[102]

F. Warrington Eastlake, who published a lengthy article on the *sheng* in the *China Review* (August, 1882) extensively quoted by Van Aalst, notes that *sheng* were suspected of causing medical problems in players:

> One very rarely hears the *sheng* nowadays, on account of a curious superstition. The Chinese say that a skillful performer on the *sheng* becomes so wedded to its music that he is ever playing; but the instrument is played by sucking in the breath, and a long continuance of this brings on inflammation of the bronchial tubes and diseases of the lungs. So no performer is ever known to live longer than forty years![103]

Living players, however, claim this is false and that blowing the *sheng* is good for the lungs. Furthermore, one inhales and exhales equally. As with the *kaen*, the *sheng* may also be sounded by blowing, but Moule also reports that suction is more usual than blowing. He adds, "It is said that men who play the *sheng* die early of consumption."[104] That these assertions are probably "old wives tales" is suggested by the fact that *kaen* players often perform all night many nights of the year and remain in good health into their sixties or longer, as with the rest of the population.

As with most instruments, the origin of the *sheng* is shrouded in a myth, according to which the female sovereign Nü Wa (Nyu-kwa

[101]Ibid.

[102]*The Music of China* (Hong Kong: Chung Chi Publications, Chung Chi College and the Chinese University of Hong Kong, 1965), p. 153.

[103]Van Aalst, *Chinese Music*, p. 82.

[104]Moule, "List of the Musical and Other Sound-producing Instruments," p. 95.

according to Sachs[105] and Nü-wo according to Van Aalst[106]) invented the instrument.[107] She is said to have succeeded Fu Hsi, the legendary inventor of music, who reigned from ca. 2852 B.C. Curt Sachs claims that the *sheng* is first mentioned in documents dating from 1100 B.C. but neglects to mention where.[108] References to the *sheng* occur frequently in the *Shih Ching*, the Classic of Songs. This earliest member of the five great Chinese Classics contains 305 songs dating from the tenth to seventh centuries B.C.[109]

Until 1972 the earliest known illustration was to be found on a stele dating from 551 A.D. in Philadelphia's University Museum,[110] but details of the instrument are unclear. In that year Chinese archaeologists excavating at Ma-wang-tui near Ch'ang-sha, Hunan province, in central China opened the tomb of a high ranking lady, possibly the wife of the first Marquis of Tai, who died of a heart attack in 186 B.C. Besides a perfectly preserved body and numerous pieces of cloth and pottery, the archaeologists discovered a remarkable collection of musical instruments, some still playable. In addition to a zither with twenty-five silk strings (*sê*) and a set of twelve *lü* pipes, they also found a *sheng*, called a *yü*. This *sheng* is of the greatest interest because it is so unlike those of today. Unfortunately the specimen was only a burial object and had no reeds. There are twenty-two pipes of various lengths arranged in two slightly curving rows which pierce the bottom of the wind-chest. The latter, though it appears to be a gourd, is actually lacquered wood. The instrument overall bears a closer resemblance to the raft-form *kaen* than the circular *sheng* but with the rows perpendicular to the mouthpiece rather than parallel.[111]

While the *sheng* is rarely heard in modern China, its sounds still permeate the *gagaku* orchestra of Japan. In Japan the *sheng* is called *sho* or *cho* while in Korea, where it has also been known, it was called *saign* or *saeng-hwang*. Sachs asserts that the *sheng* reached Japan about 1000 A.D.[112] while Reischauer and Fairbank state

[105] *History of Musical Instruments*, p. 184.

[106] *Chinese Music*, p. 81.

[107] *Grove's Dictionary of Music and Musicians*, 5th ed., s. v. "Chinese Music," by Laurence Picken.

[108] *History of Musical Instruments*, p. 184.

[109] Edwin O. Reischauer and John K. Fairbank, *East Asia: The Great Tradition* (Boston: Houghton Mifflin Co., 1960), p. 65.

[110] Illustrated in Sachs, *History of Musical Instruments*, pl. 10, item A.

[111] Fong Chow, "Han Dynasty Musicians and Instruments," *Journal of the American Musical Instrument Society* 1 (1975):113-25.

[112] *History of Musical Instruments*, p. 183.

that T'ang court music (618-906) has been preserved in Japan as *gagaku.*[113] Picken says, "In its turn Chinese music in the fifth century found its way to the Korean court and thence in the sixth century, to Japan."[114] Courant claims that the Korean *sheng*, which he called *hou lou cheng*, had a gourd windchest, but documentation is lacking.[115] Of the Korean instrument, Sŏng, Kyŏng-rin reports that the *saeng* were normally imported from China and that today they are nearly obsolete, playing but one piece, *chajin hanip*, a duet with flute (*tanso*).[116] Indeed, the Koreans have now lost the tradition entirely, and neither are instruments made there nor are players active.

Piggott, writing about Japanese music in 1909, describes the *sho* as having seventeen pipes, two of which are dummies, and a bowl of lacquered cherry or pine.[117] Malm, writing in 1959, concurs with Piggott's description and adds that the reeds are coated with a preservative and tuned with drops of wax, as was the case in China.[118] Players normally sit ,near a *hibachi* and periodically warm the bowl of the *sho* over the heat to prevent moisture from accumulating and to keep the wax pliable in order to maintain a good seal. The Vietnamese also used the *sheng*, called *sênh*, in times past. According to Trần vǎn Khê, the ancient *sênh* had a gourd windchest and thirteen to nineteen pipes in five lengths. It was used in the court orchestra *duong thuong chi nhac* during the Lê dynasty in the fifteenth century and in the *nhac huyên* in the nineteenth century. The pervasive influence of Sinitic culture on that of the Vietnamese imposed through centuries of domination is well known.[119]

Miscellaneous Free-reed Instruments

Moule alone mentions two Chinese free-reed instruments referred to as toys which are otherwise unknown:

> KU KUAI (KOU KOUAI). A toy which is sold or given every Spring to pilgrims to the *Mao Shan*, a hill south-east of Nanking. It consists of

[113] *East Asia*, p. 485.

[114] "Chinese Music."

[115] "Chine et Corée."

[116] "Korean Musical Instruments," in *Survey of Korean Arts, Traditional Music* (Seoul: National Academy of Arts of the Republic of Korea, 1973), p. 44.

[117] Francis Piggott, *The Music and Musical Instruments of Japan* (Yokohama, 1909; reprint ed., New York: Da Capo, 1971), p. 153.

[118] William P. Malm, *Japanese Music and Musical Instruments* (Rutland, Vermont and Tokyo: Charles E. Tuttle, 1959), p. 99.

[119] Trần, *Musique vietnamienne traditionnelle*, p. 116.

a drum of bamboo about 1.125 inch high and 1.75 inch in diameter. Both ends are covered with pieces of bamboo and there is a partition in the middle. In the centre of each end a small free reed tongue is cut. Two different notes are produced.

A similar thing called *Sheng tzü* is sold to pilgrims at T'ai An. Here the reeds are inserted into the sides of short bamboo pipes. Two pipes are fastened side by side, or the reeds are put at the two ends of a single longer pipe, which has a division in the middle. Each reed has a blowing tube, like those of the *Ku Kuai*, let into the side of the pipe.

These toys are interesting as preserving perhaps the original form of the free reed.[120]

The Stearns Collection of Musical Instruments in Ann Arbor, Michigan includes two tiny instruments of Japanese provenance listed as items no. 710 (*mitz-shio-shi*) and no. 711 (*sho-shi-buye*). The former consists of three lacquered tubes 6.6 centimeters long held together with a metal wire running through the mid-sections of each pipe, while the latter consists of six silver tubes measuring 7.7 centimeters in length and 4.5 centimeters in width. Inserted into each end of each tube is a tiny wedge-shaped wooden plug whose lower side has been cut away and covered with a tiny brass plate measuring 10 by 4 millimeters. A free reed is cut into each plate. Smith described a similar instrument having six lacquered pipes and called it "Japanese pitch pipes." He added that the reeds were carefully tuned since the tube length had nothing to do with pitch and the tips curled slightly upwards, forcing the player to inhale. Exhalation would cause moisture to form inside the tubes. Smith lists the approximate pitches as follows: D, E♭, E, F♯, G, G♯, A♭, A, B♭, B, C, C♯.[121]

The questions of when and where the free reed was invented may be unanswerable, even when more complete studies detailing distribution become available. Answers to these questions would require a more complete understanding of the prehistory of Asia, material that is slowly being uncovered only now. Assumptions that the *sheng* came first because Chinese culture is so pervasive in Asia simply will not do. Sachs' assertion that the single-tubed gourd mouth organ found among the Chin in Chittagong district is the "original form" of the *sheng* and *kaen* unjustifiably presupposes an evolution from simple to complex.[122]

Of the 156 separate ethnic groups in continental Southeast Asia listed by Lebar, only about twenty-eight are known to possess free-reed instruments. Of the four major language groups, half of these

[120]Moule, "List of the Musical and Other Sound-producing Instruments," pp. 88-89.

[121]*World's Earliest Music*, pp. 214-15.

[122]*Musikinstrumente Indiens und Indonesiens*, p. 64.

are among the Sino-Tibetan languages, and only three are among those speaking Malayo-Polynesian. Only seven of the seventy-six groups speaking Mon-Khmer languages, part of the larger Austro-asiatic family, are known to possess such instruments. We must assume that other groups probably possess them too, but present information is inadequate. It is interesting that, of the major cultures in Southeast Asia having political states, only the Lao have free-reed instruments, although some Khmer seem to have borrowed them from their upland neighbors and the Vietnamese used the Chinese *sheng* at one time. One wonders why the Lao and Shan among the Tai have them but not the Siamese further south. If all three originated in southern China and acquired free-reeds there, why would the Siamese have lost theirs? Free-reed instruments have not been described among the peoples of Malaysia or the Burmese. In the archipelago only Borneo is known to have gourd mouth organs, none being known from Sumatra, Java, Bali, Flores-banda, Halmahera, New Guinea, the Celebes, or the Philippines today.

Bronze drums from Southeast Asia first appeared at an exhibition in Paris in 1889 but attracted little or no attention until in 1902 archaeologists digging near Phú Lý about 55 kilometers south of Hanoi discovered a related drum. Yet another drum was found in 1903 in Ngoc-lu. Four theories of origin were offered:

1. J.D.E. Schmeltz suggested the drums were of Indian origin.
2. F. Hirth thought they were Chinese.
3. A.B. Beyer and M.F. Foy believed that they were from tribes related to the Cham in South Vietnam.
4. De Groot attributed them to the *man* in upper Indochina and south China.[123]

Victor Goloubew, who discovered the Dong-son bronze culture in north Vietnam, which flourished about two thousand years ago, found another drum near Hoang-ha in Ha-dong province in 1940.[124] Related to these drums in another now kept in the Museum für Völkerkunde in Vienna which had been in the possession of a Miao chief from Kaihwa in southeast Yunnan for an unknown number of years and reputed to be very old.[125] These drums are of significance to the question of mouth organ history because at least three of them picture mouth organ players. While their ages are uncertain, those unearthed in north Vietnam may date from the first years of the Christian era.

[123] Trần, *Musique vietnamienne traditionelle*, p. 13.

[124] "Le tambour métallique de Hoàng-ha," *Bulletin de l'Ecole Française d'Extrême-Orient* 40 (1940):383-409.

[125] See Bernatzik, *Akha and Miao*, p. 653.

The drum from Ngoc-lu shows a procession in which two figures dance and three play mouth organs whose gourd windchests are pierced with two or three pipes in a bundle.[126] Unlike the *kaen*, whose tallest pipes are closest to the player, the shortest pipes depicted on the drum are closest to the player. The Hoang-ha drum pictures a single mouth organ player with an instrument similar if not identical to that of Ngoc-lu. At Dong-son, four kilometers north of Thanh-hoa, Goloubew also unearthed a small bronze statue of a man carrying a mouth organ player on his back;[127] details of the instrument are unclear, however. The Miao drum also pictures mouth organ players wearing feather headdresses similar to those shown in the Dong-son specimens, and the four bundled pipes clearly pass through the windchest. The instrument is quite different from that used by contemporary Miao, and Bernatzik points out that many other features pictured on the drum, including clothing, headdresses, boats, and houses, are unlike those of the Miao. With further doubts that the Miao might have had an early period of bronze culture, he concludes that the drum is not of Miao origin.[128]

Another illustration occurs in central Java at Barabadur, a magnificent temple whose relief carvings date back to the end of the seventh and beginning of the eighth centuries. Jaap Kunst pictures a portion of a panel in which men are seen playing a Chinese wooden slit drum, begging cup with tinkling rods, wooden scraping stick, and two mouth organs.[129] The instruments obviously have gourd windchests and are bundled, but whether they penetrate the gourd cannot be determined. Kunst notes that such instruments may then have been widely known in Java but gradually began to disappear after the coming of the Hindus in the fifth century. Free-reed instruments are no longer found there.

The movement of the free reed west was a gradual process about which we know little. Farmer in his book *Islam* illustrates a relief from Ṭāq-i Bustān in Iran, four hundred kilometers southwest of Tehran near Kermānshāh, dated about 600 A.D.[130] as well as a post-Sassanian silver bowl from the sixth century which clearly show mouth organs with tubes fitted into bowl windchests. The instrument is known In Iranian as *mušta, muštaq,* or *mušta sīnī.*[131]

[126]Victor Goloubew, "L'âge du bronze au Tonkin et dans le Nord-Annam," *Bulletin de l'Ecole Française d'Extrême-Orient* 29 (1929): 29.

[127]Ibid., p. 30.

[128]Bernatzik, *Akha and Miao*, pp. 651-61.

[129]*Hindu-Javanese Musical Instruments*, fig. 5.

[130]Henry George Farmer, *Islam*, Musikgeschichte in Bildern, vol. 3, no. 2 (Leipzig: Deutscher Verlag für Musik, 1966), pl. 1 and p. 14.

[131]Ibid., p. 14.

Aurel Stein in 1921 published reproductions of silk paintings dating from 850-900 A.D. found in the cave-temples of Tun-huang located in Kansu province about one hundred kilometers southwest of Anhsi, almost to the border of Sinkiang province. These paintings show groups of Chinese musicians including *sheng* players but were apparently of Indian rather than Chinese origin. Tun-huang was located along the route connecting West and East.[132]

Curt Sachs in his *History of Musical Instruments* tells of the *sheng*'s influence on Western instruments in the late eighteenth century:

> A certain musician, Johann Wilde, known as the inventor of the nail violin, purchased or was given a *sheng* in St. Petersburg. . . . The physicist Kratzenstein from Copenhagen heard him, examined the free reed and suggested to the organ builder Kirschnik in St. Petersburg that he introduce the free reed into the organ. Kirschnik, however, made no organ with free reeds, but only organ-pianos. . . . A large family of reed instruments, such as mouth harmonicas, accordions, harmoniums, was created from 1800 on.[133]

In 1780 Joseph Marie Amiot published in Paris his *De la musique des Chinois, tant anciens que modernes*, which describes the *sheng* in some detail.[134] Even earlier, Filippe Bonanni's *Gabinetto armonico* (Rome, 1723) illustrated the "Tām kǐm̄," a crude representation of the *sheng.*[135] But the earliest known European mention of the free reed, though not by name, appears in Marin Mersennes's *Harmonie universelle* published in 1636 and 1637.[136] His "Proposition XXXV" describes and illustrates an "Indian" instrument (probably from Further India, as Southeast Asia used to be called) which appears to be an inside view without windchest of twelve *kaen* tubes, though many details are wrong.

In studying the distribution and types of free-reed instruments, one gets the impression he is trying to see a complete picture from only twenty-five percent of the parts. The need for professional descriptions of instruments in Asia, especially of those in the more remote areas, is obvious. While it is unlikely that archaeologists working in Southeast Asia, currently in Thailand especially, will

[132]Aurel Stein, *The Thousand Buddhas* (London: Bernard Quaritch, Ltd., 1921), pls. 4-8.

[133]Sachs, *History of Musical Instruments*, p. 184.

[134]*Mémoires concernant l'histoire, les sciences, les arts, les moeurs, les usages, Ec. des Chinois, par les missionnaires de Pekin*, vol. 6, pp. 78-84, 229-32.

[135](Reprint ed., New York: Dover Publications, 1964), pl. 138.

[136]2 vols. (Paris: S. Cramoisy). English trans. Roger E. Chapman (The Hague: M. Nijhoff, 1957).

unearth anything as fragile and perishable as a free-reed instrument, their work should provide some answers to the questions concerning prehistoric demography. With more complete information it may be possible to ascertain the approximate time and location of the origin of free-reed instruments, but until then we can only conjecture.[137]

[137]The drawings of the instruments included in this article were executed by Dean Calmer.

Lee, Hye-ku

Triple Meter and Its Prevalence in Korean Music*

Triple meter is common in Korean music, while it is rare in the music of her neighbors China and Japan.[1] Indeed, there is no Korean word for triple meter though music in that meter exists in abundance. The various drum patterns (*changdan*) used in folk and popular songs, such as *chung-mori, kutkori*, and *se-mach'i*, are all in triple time; they differ only in tempo and rhythm. For instance, the farmer's song, *Nongbu-ga*, begins with the *chung-mori* pattern and is followed by that of the fast *kutkori*, and the three movements *Todŭri, Yŏmbŭl*, and *T'aryŏng* from the suite *Yŏngsan hoesang* are all in triple meter, the tempos of which become successively faster.

In order to make its character clear, triple meter will be considered in relation to both quintuple and duple meter. To facilitate comparison of the three, music in quintuple and triple meter on the one hand and its rhythmic variation in triple and duple meter respectively on the other hand is required. Music that meets this requirement is conveniently found in the Korean *Yŏngsan hoesang*, a kind of suite for chamber ensemble consisting of twelve movements. The first four movements are all in quintuple meter, and from the first of these the following three are derived. The fifth movement, *Samhyŏn todŭri*, is in triple meter; its second and third rhythmic patterns are variations of rhythmic patterns two and

*The writer is grateful to Mr. Keith Pratt for revising the English text of this essay.

[1]See Curt Sachs, *The Wellsprings of Music*, ed. Jaap Kunst (The Hague: M. Nijhoff, 1962), p. 114: "All over East Asia two or four-beat rhythms are almost exclusive; man's two-foot stride might account for it. They rule supreme in the Far East; and only Korea uses three beats here and there."

three of the fourth section of movement three (Fast *[Chan] yŏngsan*), both patterns of which are, of course, in quintuple meter. *Yangch'ŏng*, the penultimate movement of the suite, is in duple meter; it is a rhythmic variation of one of its predecessors, the triple-metered *Chan todŭri*. It should be noted that, in order to avoid undue complexity, only music for the *kŏmŭngo* (Korean zither of six strings) from *Yŏngsan hoesang* will be considered in comparing these three kinds of meter.[2] In addition, the comparison will be supported by examples from the older *Yŏmil-lak* and *Huangha ch'ŏng* as well as the recent music for *kayagŭm* (Korean zither of twelve strings) *sanjo* (solo).

Triple Meter in Relation to Quintuple Meter

The first four movements of *Yŏngsan hoesang* are, as previously noted, in quintuple meter, and, like the three movements in triple meter already mentioned, they too become successively faster. The first of them, Slow *(Sang) yŏngsan* (♩. = 25), is the original music from which is derived the following movement, Moderate *(Chung) yŏngsan* (♩. = 30).[3] Both of these have rhythmic patterns extending to twenty beats, while the following two, Fast *(Chan) yŏngsan* (♩. = 45) and *Karak* ("figuration") *tŏli* ("eliminated") (♩. = 45)—which are rhythmic variations of the first two—each have patterns of ten beats (see Table 1; here one beat is represented by the quarter note, either dotted or undotted).

The drum patterns associated with these rhythms differ, however, in that they are not organized into measures of 6, 4, 6, 4 and 3, 2, 3, 2 respectively but, rather, into 6, 4, 4, 6 and 3, 2, 2, 3. These four divisions of the drum patterns may furthermore be grouped into two: into either 6, 4 and 4, 6 beats or 3, 2 and 2, 3 beats. It is to be noted that the pattern of the first half (6, 4 or 3, 2 beats) is different from that of the latter half (4, 6 or 2, 3 beats). However, in the masked dance used at court exorcisms, *Ch'ŏyong-mu*—which is performed to the accompaniment of Fast

[2]The transcription of *Yŏngsan hoesang* in *Minsok Akpo* [Anthology of Korean traditional music], vol. 2 (Seoul: Ministry of Education of the Republic of Korea, 1959) will be used for this study.

[3]For details concerning the variations of *Yŏngsan hoesang*, see the writer's "*Chung yŏngsan* as a Variation of *Sang yŏngsan*" [in Korean], in *Hanguk ŭmak nonch'ong* [Essays on Korean music] (Seoul: Sumundang, 1976), p. 110.

Table 1

Rhythmic Patterns of the *Kŏmŭngo* in Selected Movements from *Yŏngsan hoesang*

Quintuple meter in twenty-beat patterns

(a) Slow *(Sang) yŏngsan* ♩. = 25

(b) Moderate *(Chung) yŏngsan* ♩. = 30

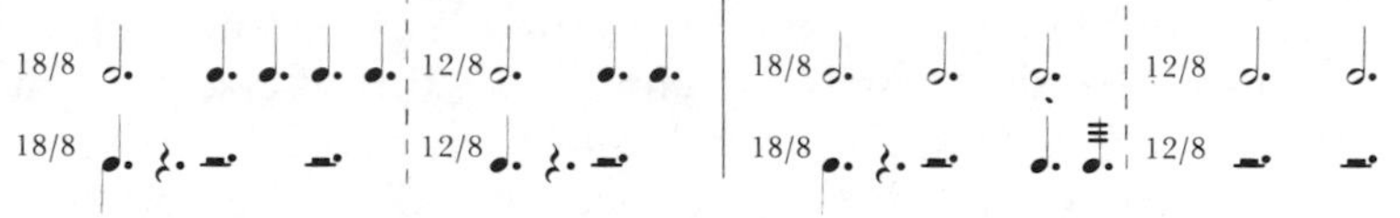

Quintuple meter in ten-beat patterns

(c) Fast *(Chan) yŏngsan* ♩. = 45

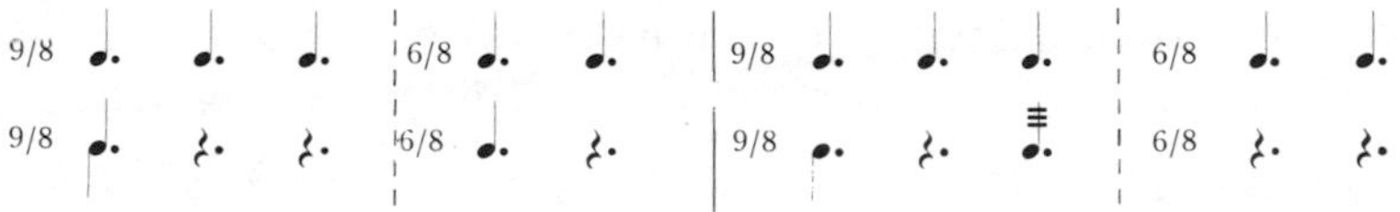

(d) *Kurak tŏli* ♩. = 45

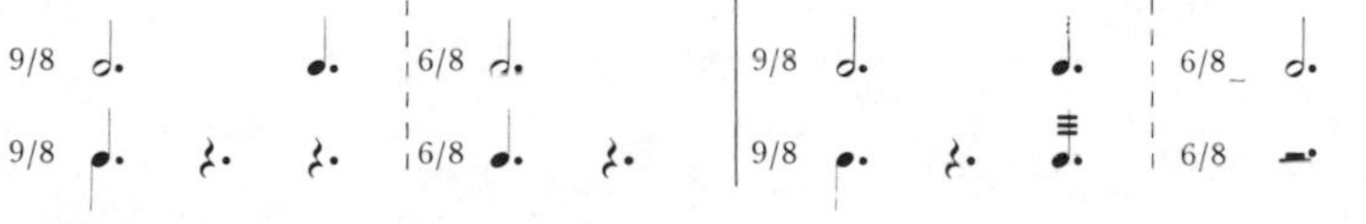

Triple meter in six-beat patterns

(e) *Samhyŏn todŭri* ♩. = 50

Duple meter in four-beat patterns

(f) *Yangch'ŏng* ♩ = 180

(Chan) yŏngsan with the drum pattern of ten beats–, the dancers take one step forward with their right foot in three beats and another step forward with their left foot in two beats, and these two steps are duplicated in the latter half of the drum pattern.[4] Especially in *Karak tŏli* and in the final three sections of *Huangha ch'ŏng* (five through seven), the rhythm of the first half (𝅗𝅥 ♩ 𝅗𝅥) is repeated in the second half. Thus, in these cases the drum pattern follows the metrical organization of the musical phrase (i.e., that of the *kŏmŭngo*).

The reason why the second half of the drum pattern (4, 6 or 2, 3 beats) differs from that of the first half (6, 4 or 3, 2 beats) is, presumably, to signal the approach of the end of the pattern. If the pattern of the first half were to be repeated in the second half, there would be no way of punctuating it. A parallel to the articulation of a musical phrase by employing the reverse rhythm is to be found in the drum pattern of *Samhyŏn todŭri*. The six beats there can be divided into two three-beat groups just as the ten beats of Fast *(Chan) yŏngsan* can be divided into two five-beat units. And in the case of the six-beat pattern the rhythm of the second half is the reverse of that of the first half, as it is with the ten-beat pattern (in the following example the pulse is represented by the quarter rather than dotted quarter note in order to indicate more clearly the total number of beats in the pattern):

6/4  (drum pattern of *Samhyŏn todŭri*)

10/4 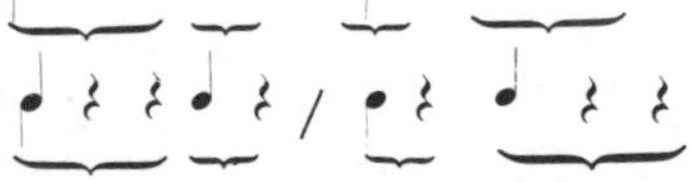 (drum pattern of Fast *[Chan] yŏngsan*)

Another parallel can be found in the drum pattern of *Chung-mori*, in 12/4 time:[5]

12/4 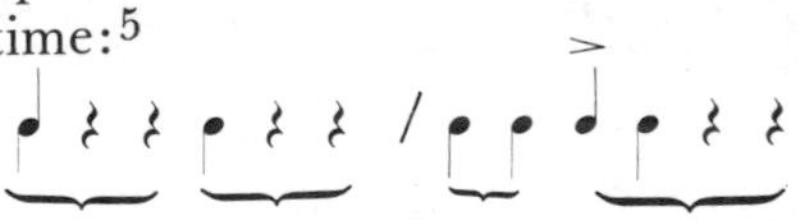

Here the third beat of the second half is stressed instead of the fourth, just as in Fast *(Chan) yŏngsan* the stroke falls on the third beat of the second half instead of on the fourth.

In *Yŏmil-lak* the opening three sections–all of which are slow (♩. = 24-28)–are also in twenty-beat patterns, and the following four sections–all of which are relatively fast (♩. = 41-84)–are in

[4]See Yi, Ae-ju, "A Study of the Historical Background and Transmission of the Ch'ŏyong Dance" [in Korean] (Master's thesis, Seoul National University, 1970), pp. 84, 94.

[5]For details concerning the drum pattern of *Chung-mori*, see Yi, Chae-suk, "Sanjo," in *Survey of Korean Arts, Traditional Music* (Seoul: National Academy of Arts of the Republic of Korea, 1973), pp. 203 and 219. The time signature of *Chung-mori* is either 12/4 or 12/8 (cf. ibid., pp. 203 and 219 respectively).

ten-beat patterns. The melodic lines of rhythmic patterns twenty-one through thirty-two of sections five and seven in a ten-beat pattern are rhythmic variations of the corresponding section (three) in a twenty-beat pattern, thus illustrating the way of converting music in a twenty-beat pattern into music in a ten-beat pattern.

In *Huangha ch'ŏng* as well, the first four sections—all of which are slow (♩. = 40-48)—are in twenty-beat patterns, and the following three sections—all of which are comparatively fast (♩. = 52-76) —are in ten-beat patterns. As already observed, in the last three sections the rhythmic figure of the first half of the musical phrase (𝅗𝅥 ♩ 𝅗𝅥) is repeated in the second half; consequently, the ten-beat pattern consists of the five-beat pattern stated twice or, in other words, of two measures in quintuple meter.

To sum up: one drum pattern or one musical phrase of ten beats is divisible into two equal parts or two quintuple measures, and the quintuple meter is a compound of three and two beats.

With regard to triple meter we note that the fourth movement of *Yŏngsan hoesang, Karak tŏli*—in a ten-beat pattern (♩. = 45)—, is immediately followed by *Samhyŏn todŭri*—in a six-beat pattern (♩. = 50). The second and third rhythmic patterns of *Samhyŏn todŭri* (♩. ♩. ♩. ♩. ♩. ♩.) are variations of the second and third rhythmic patterns of section four of Fast *(Chan) yŏngsan* (𝅗𝅥. ♩. 𝅗𝅥. 𝅗𝅥. ♩. 𝅗𝅥.).[6] Comparing these two pieces, we see that the ten-beat pattern of Fast *(Chan) yŏngsan* is converted into the six-beat pattern of *Samhyŏn todŭri* by the reduction of the longer note values. In other words, the ten-beat pattern is shortened to six by halving the dotted half notes while leaving the dotted quarters untouched.

As *Samhyŏn todŭri* is to Fast *(Chan) yŏngsan*, so *Mit todŭri* with its six-beat pattern (♩. = 70) is to *Huangha ch'ŏng* and its ten-beat pattern (♩. = 52-76).[7] As there, six beats (♩. ♩. ♩. ♩. ♩. ♩.) result from shortening the longer notes of the two quintuple measures (𝅗𝅥. ♩. 𝅗𝅥. 𝅗𝅥. ♩. 𝅗𝅥.). This method of reducing a longer note by half is also to be found in the classical lyric song *kagok*, the rhythmic pattern of which differs from those of ten and six beats as follows:

11/4 𝅗𝅥 ♩ 𝅗𝅥 ♩ 𝅗𝅥 𝅗𝅥 ♩ /5/4 𝅗𝅥 ♩ 𝅗𝅥 (drum pattern of *Ŏl-nong*)[8]

[6] Cf. *Minsok Akpo*, pp. 47-48 with p. 54.

[7] For details concerning the relationship between *Mit todŭri* and *Huangha ch'ŏng*, see Chang, Sa-hun, "Original Pohŏja and Its Various Modifications" [in Korean], in *Kugak Non'go* [Studies of Korean music] (Seoul: Seoul National University Press, 1966), p. 12.

[8] For details see Chang, Sa-hun, "The Relationship between Ŏl-nong and Ŏl-p'yŏn in Korean Classical Song" [in Korean], in *Essays in Ethnomusicology: A Birthday Offering for Lee, Hye-ku* (Seoul: Korean Musicological Society, 1969), p. 207.

(drum pattern of *P'yŏn*, a rhythmic variation of that of *Ŏl-nong*)

Since *Samhyŏn todŭri* and *Mit todŭri* are rhythmic variations of Fast *(Chan) yŏngsan* and *Huangha ch'ŏng* respectively, it can be seen that just as the ten-beat pattern is two quintuple measures—a compound of three and two beats—, so that of six beats is equivalent to two triple measures—a compound of two and one beats.

All in all, the fact that, in a series of movements that become faster, *Samhyŏn todŭri* in triple meter (♩. = 50) follows *Karak tŏli* in quintuple meter (♩. = 45) suggests that quintuple meter is limited to the slow movements, while triple meter occurs in those which are more animated. In addition to differences in tempo, we have seen that triple meter is a reduction of quintuple meter, the smaller number of beats (three as opposed to five) making the performance time much shorter. The convention that, in a series of movements which grow successively faster, movements in triple meter follow those in quintuple meter and the way in which quintuple meter is altered into triple meter by reducing the number of beats in a unit indicate that triple meter and quintuple meter have much to do with tempo. As far as Korean music is concerned, meter has little significance apart from tempo.

It is also to be noted that slow music in quintuple meter is only to be found in older music such as *Yŏngsan hoesang, Yŏmil-lak*, and *Huangha ch'ŏng*. The practice of reworking ancient music in quintuple meter into new, independent music such as *Mit todŭri* shows that triple meter appeared at a later date. Instead of slow music in quintuple meter, faster music in triple meter now prevails in both court and folk repertories.

Triple Meter in Relation to Duple Meter

Yangch'ŏng, in a rhythmic pattern of four beats (♩ = 180), is the penultimate movement of the suite *Yŏngsan hoesang*. Literally translated, *Yangch'ŏng* means two *(yang)* strokes of the first string *(ch'ŏng)* of the *kŏmŭngo* in every rhythmic pattern. The first string is always played open—never stopped—and is something like a drone, producing the pitch *E♭*. For instance, in the first rhythmic pattern, the two melodic notes *c'* and *b♭* are each preceded by the drone-like note *E♭ : E♭ , c', E♭ , b♭* . It is from these two recurring E-flats that this fast piece derives its name *Yangch'ŏng*.

As has already been seen, from *Huangha ch'ŏng* (in quintuple meter) is derived *Mit todŭri* (in ternary meter). By raising its melodic line an octave higher *Mit todŭri* gives rise, in turn, to *Chan todŭri*, which is therefore also in ternary meter. And from *Chan todŭri* (from the beginning to the fifty-fifth rhythmic pattern) is derived the four-beat pattern of *Yangch'ŏng.*[9] Thus, the tempos of *Huangha ch'ŏng* (in quintuple meter; ♩. = 45), *Chan todŭri* (in ternary meter; ♩. = 70) and *Yangch'ŏng* (in 4/4 time; ♩ = 180) become successively faster.

How the ternary meter of *Chan todŭri* is converted into the 4/4 time of *Yangch'ŏng* may be exemplified by the initial rhythmic patterns of these two pieces: the six notes of the beginning rhythmic pattern of *Chan todŭri (E♭ , c', c', / c', b♭ , b♭)* are reduced to four by suppressing one of the repeated notes in each group *(E♭ , c' / c', b♭)* similar to the manner in which quintuple meter is converted into ternary meter by reducing the long note values by half. Just as the ten- and six-beat patterns are two quintuple and ternary measures respectively, so the four-beat pattern is two duple measures.

The time unit or pulse of *Yangch'ŏng* has been notated by one scholar as the dotted quarter note in 12/8 time[10] instead of the quarter note in 4/4 time[11] (either ♩ or ♩. = 180). Consequently, the rhythmic pattern represented in 4/4 by the dotted rhythm (♪.♬) is there written as a triplet (♩ ³ ♪); this pattern, however, does not occur in the *kŏmŭngo* part but only in the wind instruments. These different interpretations betray the fact that in fast tempos the relative quantity of the two components of the dotted rhythm (♪.♬) and the triplet (♩ ³ ♪) as well as that of equal values (♫) cannot be accurately distinguished; only the stress is felt. It might be observed that, in fast tempos, when the stress felt on the first note is strongest the pattern should be notated as a dotted rhythm, when it is less strong, as a triplet, and when it is not conspicuously present, as two equal values. In other words, degrees of intensity are reflected in degrees of duration. The two different views regarding notation attest to the fact that in fast tempos quantity, or duration, is replaced by stress, or intensity.

In a similar way to *Yangch'ŏng* (♩ = 180), the *Tan-mori* move-

[9] For details see Chang, "Original Pohŏja," pp. 22-23.

[10] Ibid., p. 21; and idem, *Kugak Ch'ongnon* [Introduction to Korean music] (Seoul: Chŏngŭmsa, 1976), p. 394.

[11] *Minsok Akpo*, p. 111.

ment of *kayagŭm sanjo* (♩ = 168-208) is placed at the end of the suite,[12] the movements of which have, like those of *Yŏngsan hoesang*, become successively faster. This indicates the closeness of the relationship between duple time and fast tempos; in fact, duple meter is never encountered in slow tempos.

Yangch'ŏng is comparatively new, for it cannot be found in old music such as *Yuyeji* as edited by Sŏ, Yu-gu (1764-1845). This new music in duple time, which is fast and light, was presumably adopted at the end of *Yŏngsan hoesang* for the sheer joy of breaking away from old music in quintuple and triple meter, which was slow and heavy. Like *Yangch'ŏng, Tan-mori* is not performed by the Kang, Tae-hong school.[13] Furthermore, *sanjo* music in fast 4/4 time has various names: *Tan-mori, Sesanjosi*, or *Hui-mori*. In the case of *Hui-mori*, certain schools play it in 4/4 time,[14] others in 12/8.[15] The absence of *Tan-mori* in particular schools and the ambiguity of the terminology[16] indicate the recent origin of the duple-time movement.[17]

Comparing *Chan todŭri* with *Yangch'ŏng*, we see that triple meter is slower than duple time. Since the movements in triple meter precede those in duple time in *Yŏngsan hoesang*, triple meter is again regarded as being slower than duple time. From the five consecutive movements in triple meter in *Yŏngsan hoesang*—*Samhyŏn todŭri* (♩. = 50), *Yŏmbŭl* (♩. = 70), *T'aryŏng* (♩. = 90), *Kunag* (♩. = 120), and *Kyemyŏn karak todŭri* (♩ = 150)—it can be seen that the tempo of triple meter ranges from 50 to 150 beats per minute, while duple time begins at 180. Compared with music in duple time, which is rare and of recent origin, music in triple meter is prevalent and older.

[12] For details concerning *Tan-mori*, see Yi, Chae-suk, "Sanjo," in *Survey of Korean Arts, Traditional Music*, p. 204. There she gave the tempo of *Tan-mori* as the quarter note equaling 208-230, but recently she corrected it as shown here.

[13] Concerning the absence of *Tan-mori*, see Yi, Chae-suk, *Kayagŭm Sanjo* (Seoul: Korean Musicological Society, 1971), p. 78.

[14] E.g., the Pak, Sang-gŭn school. For an example of its music, see ibid., p. 172.

[15] E.g., the Kim, Pyŏng-ho and Kim, Yun-dŏk schools. For examples of their music, see ibid., pp. 99 and 139 respectively.

[16] This ambiguity of terminology is referred to by Yi in "Sanjo": "Since *hwimori* is simply *chajinmori* in a faster tempo, the two are sometimes considered one and called *chajinmori. Hwimori* is also on occasion called *tanmori*" (p. 204).

[17] In the preface to *Kayagŭm Sanjo*, Yi referred to the recent origin of *Tan-mori* without giving the date of its appearance (p. 3).

Summary

In a series of movements that become succesively faster, the ones in triple meter lie between those in quintuple and duple meter. From this sequence it may be deduced that triple meter was regarded as being faster than quintuple but slower than duple meter: in *Yŏngsan hoesang* the tempo of triple meter ranges from 50 to 150 beats per minute, that of quintuple meter from 25 to 45, while that of duple time begins at 180.

The time required for the performance of a rhythmic variation in a ten-beat pattern is as little as a quarter of that of its prototype in a twenty-beat pattern,[18] even when the metronome marking of the former is, say, 45 and that of the latter 50, i.e., when the difference in tempo is relatively slight. From this it is obvious that the performance time of a rhythmic variation in triple meter is less than that of the original in quintuple meter. The shorter time needed for the performance reinforces the impression of the faster tempo of the music. Thus, it might be said that the fewer the number of beats in a meter, the faster the tempo or, in other words, that meter has an innately close relationship with tempo.

We have seen that quintuple meter (compound of three and two beats), triple meter (compound of two and one beats) and duple meter (compound of one and one beats) are similar in that they are divisible into two different parts, the accented and the unaccented, be it a durational or an intensity accent. We have seen, further, that the compound of three and two beats is reduced to two and one and that in turn to the compound of one and one, the latter, however, allowing of no further reduction. In view of this fact we might say that those meters which allow a reduction in the number of their beats, i.e., quintuple and triple, have a quantitative, or durational, accent, while the one which allows of no further reduction (i.e., duple) has a qualitative, or intensity, accent. Thus, these three kinds of meter all have two different parts, the accented and the unaccented, which are either of a quantitative or a qualitative nature.

The reason why in slow music alone the durational accent (the ratio of three to two or of two to one beats) occurs may be understood from the following parallels: when one lifts a heavy weight, it takes more time than when one puts it down to its original place,

[18]The tape counter of the recorder read 52 and 41 respectively for sections two and three of Moderate *(Chung) yŏngsan*, while for their rhythmic variations (i.e., sections one and two of Fast *[Chan] yŏngsan*) it read 13 and 10. Thus, the performance time of the latter is a quarter of that of the former.

and when one raises or opens his arms widely, it takes more time than when one returns them to the previous position. On the contrary, in the case of lifting something light or moving one's arms less widely, the starting and returning movements take approximately the same amount of time. The longer note in slow music might be compared to the lifting of heavy weights and to wide arm movements, the shorter note, to the returning movements. It is said that *Sijo*, a slow Korean song, should be sung "heavily" (*mugŏpke*); thus, it can be seen that the durational or intensity accent also depends on the tempo.

Quintuple meter with slow tempo and durational accent is only to be found now in older music such as *Yŏngsan hoesang, Yŏmillak*, and *Huangha ch'ŏng*;[19] it is rare today. Duple meter with fast tempo and intensity accent is limited to music of recent origin such as *Yangch'ŏng* and *Tan-mori*; it is as rare as music in quintuple meter. On the other hand, triple meter—slower than quintuple but faster than duple—now prevails in both court and folk music.

[19]Kings Yŏngjo (1737 A.D.), Chŏngjo (1778) and Sunjo (1830) continuously prohibited fast music because they believed fast and florid music was hectic and unhealthy for humans (see *Chŭngbo Munhŏn Pigo* [Revised encyclopedia], vol. 94 [Seoul: Tongguk-munhua-sa, 1957], pp. 13,b, 16,a, 18,a). Such prohibitions suggest that tempos were already tending to become fast as early as the 18th century.

Bruno Nettl

Comments on the Persian Radif

My first acquaintance with Walter Kaufmann dates from the middle 1930s, when I was about four years old, and my first memory of him is a scene in the bathroom of my parents' apartment in Prague, a scene in which he, then a young student, expertly taught me to squirt water through my hands in order to drench the walls of the bathroom. It was about that time that I first heard, from or because of Walter, the words "Indian music," "raga," and "improvisation," words which were eventually, in various ways, to play such a significant role in both of our lives. I cannot maintain that I have been particularly a disciple of Walter Kaufmann; our studies of non-Western musical cultures have led us in entirely different directions, at completely different times. But just as he, in some of his major publications and through his long years in India, devoted himself to the delineation and description of the foundations for the performance of Oriental music, the ragas of India and the notation systems of Asian classical music, I have been increasingly fascinated by the material which constitutes the foundation of the composition and performance system of modern Iranian classical music, the radif. Kaufmann's devotion to the *art* music of Asia, and particularly to that of India, appears to me to stem from a belief that this music is the ideal of the entire population, that, while it is known and understood only by a relatively small number of musicians and a limited audience, it is the most truly representative music of these cultures, deriving from "strong relationship" to "the cosmos, magic, religion, philosophy . . . ."[1]

[1]Walter Kaufmann, *Musical Notations of the Orient* (Bloomington: Indiana University Press, 1967), p. 3.

My work in Iran leads me to suggest, similarly, that Persian classical music, even today, occupies a role of the musical ideal within the traditional culture and that this role is recognized by those who understand the music well but also by those who have only passing acquaintance, by those who love it because they wish to retain as much as possible of the traditional culture, as well as by those who disparage it as an undesirable symbol of an equally undesirable past. Like the raga system of Indian music, the radif occupies a central role in its society. Therefore, presumably like the ragas (for which a similar statement has not yet been developed), the radif in its very structure reflects various important aspects of Persian social behavior. And furthermore, the differences encountered today in the interpretation of the radif, in theory and performance among Iranian musicans and scholars, reflect some of the tensions found in present-day Iranian society.

The radif is discussed at length in a number of well-known publications by Iranian, European, and American scholars. It is described in various ways, as a "collection of melodies" by Ella Zonis[2] and a "collection of gusheha and pieces" by Tsuge[3], as an "unchangeable row of 12 equivalent modes" by Gerson-Kiwi[4] and as "style et procede d'arrangement et de composition d'un Avaz" by Caron and Safvate.[5] But, while the radif is indeed widely discussed, the term itself is not used extensively in a good deal of fundamental literature dealing with Persian classical music. The descriptions briefly mentioned here seem to me to indicate that the radif as a unit has been taken more or less for granted by musicians and that scholars use it, conceptually, as a way of organizing theoretically a number of actually more important, more primary, possibly more immediately practical, units of musical thought. This way of thinking may reflect the history of this material, for the components existed first and were later combined. It seems likely that at one time units of musical thought and practice equivalent to the dastgāhs and gushehs which make up the radif were coexisting in relative isolation but were eventually grouped and systematized into a body of material that came to be known as radif.[6] But a look at

[2]*Classical Persian Music, an Introduction* (Cambridge: Harvard University Press, 1973), p. 62.

[3]Gen'ichi Tsuge, "Avaz, a Study of the Rhythmic Aspects in Classical Iranian Music" (Ph.D. diss., Wesleyan University, 1974), p. 29.

[4]Edith Gerson-Kiwi, *The Persian Doctrine of Dastgah Composition* (Tel-Aviv: Israel Music Institute, 1963), p. 14.

[5]Neely Caron and Dariouche Safvate, *Iran: Les traditions musicales* (Paris: Buchet/Castel, 1966), p. 116.

[6]Khatschi Khatschi, in *Der Dastgah* (Regensburg: Bosse, 1962), describes this process in considerable detail. See particularly chap. 2.

the overall structure of the radif, something that is done in fewer publications, including those by Ella Zonis and by Caron and Safvate[7], indicates that a broad, complex structure, logical in some aspects, random in others, has developed. My purpose here is to comment on this structure and its relationship to Persian culture.

The impetus for giving attention to this grand design comes from my field research, especially from statements by Iranian musicians, particularly by older, authoritative figures, including my main teacher, Nour-Ali Boroumand. The general impression of the nature of the radif that may be gained from most literature is that it consists of a group of units which are at least potentially equal, twelve dastgāhs, each consisting of numerous gushehs, all of them equally capable of being the basis for improvisation and composition. The literature also indicates that gushehs differ in nature, in size, in kind and degree of "metricity" or rhythmic stability, and in the degree to which they are changed in the *typical* improvisation. But Persian musicians who teach the radif indicate much more definitively than do the publications that while, on the one hand, the radif is a "row" of musical equals, it is, on the other, much more a complex hierarchy of musical thought. It corresponds to the culture. In a sense, Muslim society consists of humans who are equal before God, but even brief residence in Iran makes clear the complex but definitely hierarchical system to which the human population is subject, a system that overrides the theory of equality.[8]

The concept of qualitative differences among components of the radif is discussed by Zonis, Khatschi, Farhat, and others, all of whom speak or imply the existence of relatively more and less important dastgāhs.[9] Similar distinctions among the gushehs within a dastgāh are made by musicians; and beyond that, at least some gushehs are composed of several distinct parts, some more and

[7]See Ella Zonis, *Classical Persian Music*, chap. 3; and Caron and Safvate, *Iran*, chaps. 4 and 5.

[8]See, for example, Reuben Levy, *The Social Structure of Islam*, 2nd ed. (Cambridge: At the University Press, 1965), chap. 1 and, particularly, p. 53; and Marvin Zonis, *The Political Elite of Iran* (Princeton: At the University Press, 1971), chap. 6, particularly pp. 134-35.

[9]Ella Zonis, *Classical Persian Music*, pp. 66, 67, 93; Khatschi, *Dastgah*, pp. 89, 100, 104, 107, 109, 113; and Hormoz Farhat, "The Dastgah Concept in Persian Music" (Ph.D. diss., University of California at Los Angeles, 1965), p. 45. The tension between equality and hierarchy is evident, for example, in the somewhat defensive statement about the importance of Nava in Caron and Safvate, *Iran*, p. 74. Personal interviews indicate the varying importance of the dastgāhs; Shur is readily admitted as most important. At the same time, the great authority of the radif is stressed through the statement, often repeated, that all parts are important, a statement denying the hierarchical relationship among the dastgāhs which is quite apparent in various aspects of musical behavior.

some less important. My teachers and informants expressed this view and, indeed, went considerably beyond it in a number of ways, exposing the radif as an extremely complex and sensitive organism, one of whose main characteristics is the relative value or importance of juxtaposed parts. There are three aspects of value which I should like to discuss briefly: 1) the perception of the radif as a series of parallel structures, all based upon the same principles, the largest encompassing the broad organizational features of the entire repertory, the smallest doing the same for the shortest components; 2) the question of value as related to departure from norms; and 3) the important role temporal considerations play as expressions of musical value (length and primacy being the key criteria). In these ways the radif (as a concept generally held and in manifestations realized as the individual radifs of various masters, none alike but all holding much in common) is best understood as something in which components are constantly compared and judged by the musician and listener, rather than as a series of parallel units treated equally. One might well state that any large musical creation or repertory is bound, in the view of its practitioners and users, to have components of varying importance and value. The point to be stressed, however, is the importance of this kind of comparison in Persian musical culture and the degree to which it is emphasized in the Persian musician's description and teaching of the radif.

This kind of comparison is also a major feature of other aspects of Persian culture. Decisions on value or importance in human society take place constantly, more so than is obvious in at least some other societies. For example, two Iranians doing anything together pay lip service to the concept of equality by engaging in *ta'arouf*, ceremonial politeness, but each of them knows his proper place, determined by various criteria—social class, wealth, education, age, status as host or guest, pupil or teacher, employer or servant—and readily expressed by forms of address, precedence in walking through a door, and many other verbal and non-verbal gestures in this extremely expressive culture. At the other extreme, the foreign tourist is asked to rank Iran and his home nation, the musicologist required to say whether he likes Persian music better than that of the West, the field worker expected to state a ranking of informant musicians. And the Persian musician or listener is quickly willing and able to decide the relative merits of musicians, composers, and performances. In other words, Iranians appear to concern themselves, more at least than some others, with the evaluative comparison of persons around them. Iranians do this despite a fundamental requirement to consider all men equal, and they behave similarly in their perception of their central musical artifact, the radif. It is no doubt this parallel between perception of society and of the radif which led my teacher, Boroumand, to say on occasion, "It is really something extraordinary, something wonderful, which we Persians have created. No other people have anything like it, and it fits and belongs precisely in and to Iran." Without engaging in elaborate analysis, he understood the relationship between culture and music, and he intuitively sensed the basic difference between the system of maqamat in Arabic practices, living in less organized and traditionally less hierarchical and less centralized societies, and the radif, a musical form reflecting the highly organized Persian social tradition, based on a concentric system of classes.

Now, by contrast, Persian social structure and behavior can also be seen as something lightly organized and individualistic, and, considering the importance of improvisation, most Persian music could also be viewed in this light. But the social ideal of traditional Iran, more than that of other middle Eastern cultures, is the empire with its rigid and complex social structure, based on federation of peoples under centralized leadership,[10] and my hypothesis is that the radif, which occupies quantitatively a small role in Persian music, known by few and not itself performed, a central governing musical principle used as teaching device and as a guide, occupies in the minds of tradition-minded Iranians a role in musical experience somewhat analogous to the idea of empire and its social structure, an ideal whose implications and intentions are only occasionally realized in life or in sound. It is against this background that we examine some aspects of the structure of the radif.

1) The organization as a series of parallel structures replicated at various levels is highly significant. It is a principle rather easily obscured by the many other aspects of organization underlying the radif, but it is clearly expressed in the traditional form of teaching.

The relationship within each dastgāh of the initial and dominating section, darāmad, and the other sections, gushehs, is well known. Darāmad is first in the radif of a dastgāh (or, rather, in that section of the radif belonging to a particular dastgāh), it is taught first, and it normally appears first in an improvised performance (Āvāz) or even in traditional compositions that are based particularly on the radif, such as pish-darāmads and tasnifs. In the radif itself, gushehs tend to use, as their endings, materials taken or derived from darāmad. And in longer radifs, such as those published by

[10]Marvin Zonis, *Political Elite*, pp. 8, 17; Seyyed Hossein Nasr, *Ideals and Realities of Islam* (London: Allen and Unwin, 1966), p. 166. Nasr also describes the character of Twelve-Imam Shi'ism, the state religion of Iran, as structurally more hierarchical than Sunnite Islam, which is more typical of Arabic nations.

Moussa Ma'aroufi,[11] darāmad tends to have the largest number of sections and to occupy the largest amount of time.

The relationship is microcosmically replicated in the gusheh. Many gushehs have several sections, and the first may actually be called "darāmad" by teachers. And within the gusheh this first section occupies a role similar to that of darāmad in the dastgāh, although it does so with only moderate frequency: the subsequent sections of a gusheh normally end with materials taken from the first, and improvised performances of the gusheh normally begin with it. And if one were to question a musician about the musical identity of a gusheh, he would normally sing the main motif of this first section, just as he would sing the main motif of darāmad in identifying a dastgāh.

A macrocosmic replication also presents itself, though more through the application of interpretive analysis than ethnographic reporting. The dastgāh of Shur occupies, within the entire radif, a role somewhat analogous to that of darāmad in the dastgāh. In the teaching of the radif it comes first. It occupies the largest amount of time in the radif, if one takes into account the four derivative dastgāhs (also called "Āvāz" or "mota'aleghat") traditionally related to Shur: Dashti, Afshāri, Abu-Atā, and Bayāt-e Tork. In a sense, these four derivative dastgāhs parallel the sections of darāmad —which may also be called "first" darāmad, "second" darāmad, etc., sometimes with special names added (e.g., "Zangouleh" in Chahārgāh)—in that each ends with material derived from Shur. Some musicians refer to this dastgāh as the "mother" of the dastgāhs, implying perhaps a relationship similar to that of darāmad to other gushehs. Thus, at three levels, we find the presentation of basic, fundamental, authoritative material (in the sense of further derivation) followed by dependent and less important material.

With further interpretation, one may even add to this regular structuring of the musical system the entire body of Persian classical music, for the radif itself occupies a role similar to darāmad in its relationship to the music based on it—both improvised and composed. While such a relationship is not (to my knowledge) thought to exist by musicians, the chronological order in a musician's education is also present here: the radif is learned first, it is followed by a career of performance based on the radif which, itself, is ideally studied again at various times and which provides most of the material for performance, occupying a role of musical authority in a sense parallel to the authority of Shur among the dastgāhs, of darāmad in the dastgāh, and of the mini-darāmad in certain gushehs.

[11]See Mehdi Barkechli, *La Musique traditionelle de l'Iran* (Tehran: Secretariat d'Etat aux Beaux-Arts, 1963).

2) Musicians and scholars indicate that certain parts of the radif are particularly important or prominent. Farhat, Ella Zonis, and Caron and Safvate all indicate the greater importance or prominence of certain dastgāhs over others, of certain gushehs over others in their dastgāhs.[12] No doubt a number of criteria determine this prominence. Among these appear to be length, number of parts, time occupied in the radif itself and in typical performances. The darāmad of each dastgāh, the dastgāh of Shur itself are examples. But another, possibly curious criterion of prominence seems to be departure from some kind of established norm or contrast with the main body of material of which the "important" component is a part. If one examines the gushehs in some of the dastgāhs that are said to be important, one finds a disproportionate number of these exhibiting departures from the scale of darāmad, using, as it were, "accidentals." In the case of Māhour, whose scale is more or less like that of the European major scale, the gushehs Delkash (scale: C, D, Eᴘ, F, G, Aᴘ, B♭, C) and Shekasté (scale: C, D, E, F, G, Aᴘ, B♭, C) are singled out; they are also among those performed most frequently, and they occupy considerable length in some of the radifs. (Note: ᴘ represents a pitch one-quarter tone flat.)

Now, it may be that it is the kind of musical independence which these gushehs exhibit that lends them prominence. When the radif is viewed diachronically, it appears to have grown in part by the tendency of certain prominent gushehs to develop into independent dastgāhs; this is said to have occurred in the case of the four dastgāhs related to Shur and to be in the process of occurring, for instance, in the case of one gusheh of Shur, Bayāt-e Kord, and one of Homāyoun, Shushtari.[13] On the other hand, gushehs which are regarded as less important are a) some of those which use the fundamental scale of a dastgāh and b) those which are metric and thus usually performed without much departure from the learned version, perhaps indicating that failure to depart from a norm lends low profile.

Many reasons for this particular characteristic of the hierarchical structure of the radif may be advanced. Let me suggest one, however: the value placed on innovation and the related theory that

[12]The notion of gushehs of varying degrees of importance is more widely encountered in the literature than is a qualitative distinction among dastgāhs. See Farhat, "Dastgah Concept," pp. 32, 50; Ella Zonis, *Classical Persian Music*, pp. 83, 85, and passim; and Caron and Safvate, *Iran*, p. 112. In the latter work the authors introduce the concept of *Shāh-gusheh*, a type of gusheh which itself has several separate sections and whose special elevated character is symbolized, as is that of many things in Iran, by the term *Shah*.

[13]Ella Zonis, *Classical Persian Music*, p. 104; Caron and Safvate, *Iran*, p. 62.

repetition is undesirable. In conversations with Nour-Ali Boroumand, the ideal of Persian music as something devoid of repetition was frequently emphasized. Boroumand cited, as a model, the singing of the nightingale, which in Persian musical folklore is thought never to repeat itself. In fact, of course, both nightingales and Persian musicians repeat themselves, but the ideal of non-repetition may be manifested in the greater prestige of material that is less obviously repetitive or that departs from a norm. The Āvāz, improvised, is more central, literally and conceptually, in a performance than are the composed pieces that precede and follow in a complete rendition of classical music. Gushehs with accidentals, which thus do not repeat the scale, tend to be prominent. Gushehs in which performers typically depart considerably from the radif, in which there is scope for departure because of the rhythmic freedom, are more "important." And dastgāhs which use substantial amounts of material also found in other dastgāhs may lack this importance. Thus, Rāst-Panjgāh and Navā, which repeat substantial materials from Māhour and Shur respectively, are less important and rarely performed.[14] Thus, I suggest that the secondary dastgāhs remain secondary (despite considerable popularity) in theory because of the redundancy of their scalar and thematic materials. Chahārgāh and Segāh, which have different scales but share much thematic material, are regarded as "brothers," and, in the typical terminology of some musicians interviewed, one of them (but *either* one) is regarded as important, the other one less so.

There exists, no doubt, a kind of tension between respect for authority and the expression of freedom and individuality in Persian society. Probably such tension is present in most, even all, societies. But it is particularly expressed in the radif, which, on the one hand, is itself authority and has built into it a hierarchy of musical authority and, on the other, rewards, as it were, departure from authority, from norms, by according prestige to improvisation and to materials which otherwise depart from a set standard, thus in a way symbolizing freedom.

3) Order in time is a major expression of relative importance. Things which are more important come first. As already stated, the main, characterizing section of a gusheh comes at its beginning. Darāmad, the characterizing and authoritative section of a dastgāh, appears in the radif at the beginning. In learning the radif, one is supposed to learn the dastgāhs in a fairly set order, and Shur is first. Less important gushehs in a dastgāh tend to appear near the end of its radif, although this is not invariably the case. But there is a correlation between the frequency with which a gusheh is selected for

[14]See Ella Zonis, *Classical Persian Music*, p. 93.

improvisation in a performance and its position in the radif—those most commonly played or sung are also near the beginning, and those that are near the end of the radif are in fact rarely performed. This is true also of dastgāhs—those learned last, usually Navā and Rast-Panjgāh, are also the least used, by far, in actual performance.

There is a curious contrast in Iranian social behavior between the temporal primacy of the prominent or important and the need for extensive introductory forms of behavior, illustrated by the ceremonial politeness in which one engages before, as it were, getting down to business, such as the use of intermediaries, the preliminary ceremonial on formal occasions. Of two persons going through a door, the more prominent must go first. The more formal the occasion, the more the two are likely to engage first in preliminary formalities, each asking the other to precede before the correct order is taken up. But in the structure of the radif, only one of these motivations, the precedence of the prominent, appears to be present.

Even so, it is possible to suggest parallels to the social behavior just mentioned. If we bear in mind the correlation between emphasis on preliminaries and formality of occasion, we may relate the structure of the radif alone to less formal behavior. It is, after all, not actually performed. It is the underlying basis for music but itself is only practiced and realized in teaching situations. When it is transferred to formal situations, that is, to actual performances such as concerts, the improvisatory material most related to it is preceded by other, less important pieces, the metric pish-darāmad and chahār mezrāb. And while these composed forms may be derived from the radif, its most ideal realization, the improvised Āvāz, appears only after these composed pieces. The more formal and complete a performance, the more likely a pish-darāmad *and* a chahār mezrāb are to be found. Thus, formality of performance requires introductory material of a less important sort; it is the counterpart of formulaic, ceremonially polite gestures and phrases, of the intermediary, of the assistant who speaks first in a business conference. By contrast, father and son, alone, do not require these extraneous gestures; the father is accorded immediate primacy, the relationship is informal and yet structured, a part of the skeleton of the social organization, as the radif is the skeleton of the musical system. While this interpretation is that of an outsider, never (to my knowledge) expressed by Persian musicians, it appears clearly to provide a heuristically valuable set of parallels between social behavior and musical structure.

These thoughts about the parallels are obviously tentative guesses. We have taken certain aspects of the radif and the performance based on it and pitted them against selected aspects of social behavior. Certainly other characteristics of musical structure contradicting these parallels are easily found. There are, for example, many types of performance of the Āvāz. In one typology we have identified four,[15] one in which darāmad is longest and successive gushehs decrease in length (here we find a parallel to the hierarchical structure of the radif); a second emphasizing two main gushehs, darāmad and one other, each of which is followed by briefer renditions of yet other gushehs; a third in which all gushehs are of approximately the same length; and a fourth in which darāmad dominates, appearing at the beginning and the end, while the performer touches only briefly on other gushehs in the middle of the piece. There are yet other types of performance, in some of which one cannot easily show that a section is dominated by a single gusheh and which are called, simply, "Āvāz-e Shur" or "Āvāz-e Segāh," indicating that a mixture of materials from several gushehs belonging to a dastgāh is moving past the listener in relatively undifferentiated fashion. There is the use of the "eshāreh," an extremely brief reference to a gusheh within a section of performance essentially devoted to another; there is the type of performance known as morakkab-khāni,[16] "in the style of the composer-singer," modulating from one dastgāh to another, now rarely heard. The types of performance listed in taxonomies of Iranian musicians include a distinction between simply playing the radif with minor changes and embellishments and playing a phantasy in which great but constructive liberties are taken.[17]

Obviously, departures from the mainstream of social structure occur, and departures from the mainstream of musical structure must also occur (for many reasons, musically and personally motivated), reflecting byways open to the connoisseur of the musical system. Nevertheless, my basic assumption is that social and musical structures must ultimately be, in all cultures, the result of a system of values deeply ingrained in a society and susceptible only to slow change. The fact that the radif and its resulting musical configurations are known to only a small proportion of Persian society but reflect, nevertheless, important aspects of the behavior of virtually all members of this society appears to me to make the radif, in Iran, the musical component of the "great tradition," in the sense of Redfield and Singer[18] (who developed the concept

[15]Bruno Nettl, "Aspects of Form in the Instrumental Performance of the Persian *Āvāz*," *Ethnomusicology* 18 (1974): 405-14.

[16]Caron and Safvate, *Iran*, p. 128.

[17]Ibid., p. 129.

[18]Robert Redfield and Milton Singer, "The Cultural Role of Cities," *Economic Development and Cultural Change* 3 (1954): 63: ". . . the Great Tradition

for Walter Kaufmann's India). The vast majority of Persians, when confronted with the question, may not recognize its special role, but it is the job of the ethnomusicologist to ask questions about music which may not have occurred to the practitioner.*

becomes the core culture of an indigenous civilization [and] describes a way of life and as such is a vehicle and standard for those who share it . . . as members of a common civilization." See also Singer, *When a Great Tradition Modernizes* (New York: Praeger, 1972), passim.

*This paper was written in 1977, and in its discussion of Iranian society does not mention the revolution of 1978-79; events since 1977 do not, however, appear to contradict what is said here.

Alan P. Merriam

African Musical Rhythm and Concepts of Time-reckoning*

The thesis of this paper is that most scholars—both Western and African—who have studied rhythm in African music have consistently made several unacknowledged basic assumptions which have shaped the nature both of the work done and the results achieved. The most fundamental of these assumptions concerns the nature of time-reckoning as it is usually conceived in the West, as opposed to the way it seems to be conceived in Africa. I am thus simultaneously concerned with the assumptions, the "facts" of African musical rhythm as they are broadly accepted by the scholarly community, and the possible results of applying different concepts of time-reckoning in analysis.

I have elsewhere called attention to the four most important of these assumptions, and thus need repeat them only briefly here.[1] The first is the assumption of an "equal pulse base," i.e., the Western conceptualization of time as a linear structure consisting of an infinite series of equally spaced pulses; it is this notion of time which will be the focus of this essay. The second derives from the first; that is, such a conception of time leads us easily to the further assumption of an implied steady musical beat which provides the framework upon which rhythm is built. This, in turn, suggests the notions of meter, measures with their accompanying

*Grateful acknowledgment is made to Ivan Karp and Jean E. Meeh Gosebrink for bibliographic assistance, to Judith Becker and Wyatt MacGaffey for permission to quote from their unpublished works, and to Valerie C. Merriam for her constructive criticism.

[1] "Traditional Music of Black Africa," in *Introduction to Africa*, ed. Patrick O'Meara and Phyllis Martin (Bloomington: Indiana University Press, 1977), pp. 243-58.

bar lines, accent, and downbeat, and all this leads, finally, to the notion of multiple, or simultaneous meters. The third assumption arises from the nature of African musical rhythm itself; given its undeniable complexity, scholars have made the assumption that a basic organizing principle must be present, either tangibly or intangibly, which holds together the various rhythmic streams and centralizes them into a single, regularly pulsating unit. And fourth, most of these assumptions demand that we be able to locate a specific starting point for rhythmic groupings—in other words, some concept of "beat one" must be present. All these conjectures depend in one way or another upon the first one, which is the view of time as a coordinate straight line of equal pulses.

Effective discussion of the problems involved depends upon some knowledge of one of the most basic and difficult problems of cross-cultural research, whether musical or not. This concerns the distinction between the insider's and the outsider's views of a particular phenomenon, for the two are by no means the same, and the researcher looks for, and reaches, different kinds of conclusions depending on whether he is approaching his problem from one or the other viewpoint, or from a combination of the two. The distinction has been expressed in many ways, ranging from Bohannan's "folk organization" and "analytical organization"[2] to the now widely used "emic-etic" dichotomy. Harris is primarily responsible for the transfer of the latter set of linguistic concepts to ethnology; he defined the two as follows:

> Emic statements refer to logico-empirical systems whose phenomenal distinctions or "things" are built up out of contrasts and discriminations significant, meaningful, real, accurate, or in some other fashion regarded as appropriate by the actors themselves.[3]
>
> Etic statements depend upon phenomenal distinctions judged appropriate by the community of scientific observers.[4]

In other words, the two kinds of statements proceed from different premises and arise from differing obligations. The "folk" or "emic" evaluation is the explanation and rationale given by the people themselves for their actions, while the "analytical" or "etic" evaluation is applied by the outsider and based upon his broad comparative prior knowledge. Thus, in simple terms, an African musician may visualize a certain type of music in his society as

[2]Paul Bohannan, *Social Anthropology* (New York: Holt, Rinehart, and Winston, 1963), pp. 10-11; see also Alan P. Merriam, *The Anthropology of Music* (Evanston: Northwestern University Press, 1964), pp. 31-32.

[3]Marvin Harris, *The Rise of Anthropological Theory: A History of Theories of Culture* (New York: Thomas Y. Crowell, 1968), p. 571.

[4]Ibid., p. 575.

existing for its entertainment value, while the analyst views it as contributing to the cohesion and stability of that particular group of people.

It is not difficult to see both that confusion of the two approaches can lead to disastrous results, and that each involves its own sets of problems. Emically, the investigator is faced with a wide variety of interpretations of phenomena into which he hopes to be able to insert some kind of etic order and understanding, but the latter is according to his own interpretation which, in turn, is based upon suppositions of his own culture. Further, cross-cultural definitions are often particularly difficult to achieve in connection with the arts,[5] thus compounding the problems. But it is the nature of the distinctions with which we are concerned here: on the one hand, we may be attempting to understand African musical rhythm from the Africans' point of view or, on the other, we may wish only to understand it as we perceive it from the outside. Both approaches have been used, and it is in these two contexts that I will discuss African musical rhythm and concepts of time-reckoning.

Time from the Western Point of View

The intricacies of understanding time as a conceptual, physical, and phenomenological entity in Western terms are legion, and I have no intention of attempting to deal with them here.[6] Rather, I wish to explore briefly the general nature of one aspect of time as we commonly view it in the West. Time for us is essentially linear; that is, it is viewed as a series of equally spaced pulses which are thought to extend infinitely both backward and forward from the particular time point at which we are thinking. Thus, as Evans-Pritchard has put it:

> European time is a continuum. Whatever point we start at, each succeeding generation increases the distance from that point. Our grandfathers were nearer to 1066 than our fathers and our fathers were nearer to 1066 than we are.[7]

[5]Alan P. Merriam, "Definitions of 'Comparative Musicology' and 'Ethnomusicology': An Historical-Theoretical Perspective," *Ethnomusicology* 21 (1977): 189-90.

[6]See, for example, Leonard W. Doob, *Patterning of Time* (New Haven: Yale University Press, 1971); Dale F. Eickelman, "Time in a Complex Society: A Moroccan Example," *Ethnology* 16 (1977): 39-55; Martin P. Nilsson, *Primitive Time-reckoning* (Lund: C.W.K. Gleerup, 1920); and David F. Pocock, "The Anthropology of Time-reckoning," in *Myth and Cosmos*, ed. John Middleton (Garden City, N.Y.: Natural History Press, 1967), pp. 303-14.

[7]E.E. Evans-Pritchard, "Nuer Time-reckoning," *Africa* 12 (1939): 212-13.

In his remark, Evans-Pritchard has noted not only the linear nature of our time-reckoning but also our conceptualization of it in terms of distance—events move "toward" and "away" from us in time. Furthermore, we think of time essentially in terms of repetition, and Leach has noted in this connection that "whenever we think about measuring time we concern ourselves with some kind of metronome; it may be the ticking of a clock or a pulse beat . . . but always there is something which repeats."[8] This repetition, in turn, is evenly divided into equal units, and this equality is important—a second is a second and precisely equal to any other second which has ever occurred or will ever occur. This is not true, of course, in the relativistic notion of time introduced by Einstein, but most Westerners do not understand the Einsteinian concept of time and do not use it. A further point to be noted is the infinite quality of time, which is what makes it linear—so far as we know, these equal pulses of time have always gone on, and they will always continue. Finally, returning to Leach's comment, we are accustomed to measuring time, as opposed to counting time. Bohannan has commented:

> We in Western Europe have elicited an idea, or a medium, which we call "time"—or better, "chronology"—and have calibrated it into a standard gauge against which we associate single events or a series of events. The presence of such a time gauge . . . means that . . . we measure time.
>
> A minute and a day are qualitatively as well as quantitatively different: the difference is that between measuring and counting. Days are natural events and can be counted without a special apparatus; minutes and hours are artificial events . . . and can be counted only with the aid of special apparatus.[9]

The special apparatus, of course, began with the general 17th-century introduction of clocks and watches into Western society and has moved steadily since then toward more and more complex devices. Two quantitative processes have been used to measure time. One is the concept of dynamical time which is based on the laws of motion and gravitation published by Isaac Newton in 1687, while the other, electromagnetic time, is based on the laws of electricity promulgated by James Clerk Maxwell in 1864. Dynamical time involves the motions of material bodies, whereas electromag-

[8]Edmund R. Leach, "Two Essays Concerning the Symbolic Representation of Time," in *Rethinking Anthropology*, London School of Economics Monographs on Social Anthropology no. 22, ed. Edmund R. Leach (London: Athlone Press, 1961), p. 125.

[9]Paul Bohannan, "Concepts of Time Among the Tiv of Nigeria," *Southwestern Journal of Anthropology* 9 (1953): 262.

netic time does not, but both are measurements of linear time.[10]

I am aware that other ways of contemplating time do exist in Western society, but the linear system which views time as a repetitive succession of equally spaced pulses which have no beginning and no end and which function as a device for measuring is the most common among the most people. And this is also the way we view rhythm in music: a time framework exists for us within which we cast meter, pulse, isometric forms, and so on, and against which we cast syncopation, offbeating, "irregular" rhythms, and heterometric forms. Indeed, without the concept of an equal pulse base, the latter terms could have no meaning.

African Musical Rhythm Viewed From the Western Time Concept

Given this conception of time, what can be said about Western analyses of African musical rhythm? In the first place, an exception must be made for music in free rhythm, the presence of which is admitted by all scholars. It must also be noted that when speaking of "Western" analysis, I am including those African scholars, such as Nketia, Eno Belinga, Bebey, Cudjoe, and others, whose approaches, insofar as time is concerned, do not vary significantly from those of their Western colleagues.

With all this in mind, the fact is that the Western analytic, etic, or outside time concept fits very well with African music as heard and described by virtually all researchers.

Almost everyone who has written about African musical rhythm speaks in one way or another of a steady time pulse. Thus Blacking notes an "underlying 'pulse'," and "almost metronomic tempo" in the music of two girls' initiation schools of the Venda,[11] and A.M. Jones speaks of the "absolute exactness of his [the African's] time-keeping."[12] This steady pulse is described by more than one author as strictly duple, and thus Ekwueme writes: "We can then say that the background of the bulk of most African musical rhythm is a duple statement or pulsation"[13] and that we can speak of an "inherent pulse," for ". . . behind each rhythm pattern, lies a regular steady duple pulse dividing the whole pattern in a binary balance, whether or not the initial points of both

[10] *Encyclopedia Britannica*, 15th ed., s. v "Time."

[11] John Blacking, "Tonal Organization in the Music of Two Venda Initiation Schools," *Ethnomusicology* 14 (1970): 5, 9.

[12] Arthur M. Jones, *Studies in African Music*, 2 vols. (London: Oxford University Press, 1959), 1:38.

[13] Laz E.N. Ekwueme, "Structural Levels of Rhythm and Form in African Music with Particular Reference to the West Coast," *African Music* 5, no. 4 (1975/76): 28.

halves are acoustically stressed."[14] Some years ago, Waterman introduced the concept of the metronome sense, which he explained as follows:

> From the point of view of the listener, it entails habits of conceiving any music as structured along a theoretical framework of beats regularly spaced in time and of co-operating in terms of overt or inhibited motor behavior with the pulses of this metric pattern whether or not the beats are expressed in actual melodic or percussion tones.[15]

Nketia has spoken of the "regulative beat"[16] and the "basic pulse,"[17] explaining that

> The listener or dancer must . . . be able to discover the regulative beat or basic pulse from the rhythmic structure that emerges in the performance.
>
> Because of the difficulty of keeping the subjective metronomic time in this manner, African traditions facilitate this process by externalizing the basic pulse . . . . The guideline which is related to the time span in this manner has come to be described as a *time line*.[18]

The "time line" is usually expressed by an instrument which has a penetrating or carrying tone, such as a gong, bell, small drum, or rattle, and as long ago as 1927, W.E. Ward spoke in such terms when he suggested that a single drum—the biggest if more than one were being used—played regularly in duple time: "This deep booming regular beat is the fundamental beat of the piece, and sets the time for all the other rhythms and instruments."[19] A.M. Jones pointed out handclapping, if present, as the indicator, and concluded that

> an African song which has a clap is constructed so that either 2 pulses or 3 pulses go to one clap right through the songs, irrespective of word division, word accent, or melodic accent. The claps do not indicate any sort of stress; their function is to act as an inexorable and mathematical background to the song.[20]

[14] Ibid., p. 30.

[15] Richard A. Waterman, "African Influence on the Music of the Americas," in *Acculturation in the Americas*, Proceedings of the 29th International Congress of Americanists, vol. 2, ed. Sol Tax (Chicago: University of Chicago Press, 1952), p. 211.

[16] J.H. Kwabena Nketia, *African Music in Ghana* (Evanston: Northwestern University Press, 1963), p. 64.

[17] *The Music of Africa* (New York: W.W. Norton and Co., 1974), p. 131.

[18] Ibid.

[19] William E. Ward, "Music in the Gold Coast," *Gold Coast Review* 3 (1927): 217.

[20] Arthur M. Jones, "African Rhythm," *Africa* 24 (1954): 28.

A considerable portion of the research on African musical rhythm has been carried out among peoples of the West African coastal area, particularly in the present country of Ghana, where a gong, usually identified as *gankogui*, "provides a background rhythm which keeps the whole orchestra in time."[21] The West African gong has also been described as "a common focal point,"[22] the "time keeper,"[23] and in other similar terms.

This assumption of a steady basic pulse is expressed in slightly different ways in tablature notation systems suggested for African musical rhythm by Serwadda and Pantaleoni,[24] as well as Koetting,[25] all of whom divide their graphs visually, and thus aurally, into segments of equal size which represent time. Koetting also makes the determination of "the fastest pulse" the keystone to his system,[26] and a "fastest pulse" requires a "steady pulse" for its conception: this idea has been picked up by a number of other writers such as Knight for use in their tablature systems.[27]

Pantaleoni has spoken of the basis of his notation system as the equal division of spans of time.

> Dividing a span of time may well be the fundamental orientation of the rhythmic process here transcribed. Certainly there is no evidence in our small sample to contradict such an interpretation . . . .
>
> To say we feel a pulse is to say we expect the equal spacing of a series of events to continue. It is not just a question of hearing or having heard such spacing; pulse involves the psychological state of anticipating its continuation. The play of *sogo* [a drum used among Ewe speakers of southeastern Ghana] . . . generated and sustained from beginning to end this kind of expectation.[28]

Only two writers seem to have deviated from this widespread endorsement of the presence of a steady and even pulse base, and in both cases the variations appear either to be minute or not to

[21]Jones, *Studies*, 1:53.

[22]Nketia, *African Music in Ghana*, p. 101.

[23]J.H. Kwabena Nketia, "Traditional Music of the Ga People," *African Music* 2, no. 1 (1958):21; and S.D. Cudjoe, "The Techniques of Ewe Drumming and the Social Importance of Music in Africa," *Phylon* 14 (1953):282.

[24]Moses Serwadda and Hewitt Pantaleoni, "A possible Notation for African Dance Drumming," *African Music* 4, no. 2 (1968):47-52.

[25]James Koetting, "Analysis and Notation of West African Drum Ensemble Music," *Selected Reports* 1, no. 3 (1970):116-46.

[26]Ibid., p. 125ff.

[27]Roderic Knight, "Towards a Notation and Tablature for the Kora and Its Application to Other Instruments," *African Music* 5, no. 1 (1971):31-32.

[28]Hewitt Pantaleoni, "Toward Understanding the Play of *Sogo* in *Atsīa*," *Ethnomusicology* 16 (1972):8, 9.

affect the pulse base itself. Thus Garfias, in transcribing a musical bow song of the San, used electronic aids to measure the rhythm of the bow beats; he found "many minute differences in spacing between these bow strokes," but they appeared to him to be of no significance.[29] More important was the time spacing of the overall six-beat pattern, in which the last two beats were separated from the first four by the factor of about 1/20th of a second.[30] However, Garfias gives no indication that this affected the overall length of the time span of each six beats, and, in fact, it was apparently the deviation from an assumed equal pulse base that drew his attention to the uneven rhythmic patterning.

Kubik also found small variations in the basic pulse when he transcribed "a large number" of films of African xylophone music. He reports:

> In general, one observes that tolerance of slight rhythmic unevenness on the part of the musician is greater than one would initially expect. . . . The distances between strokes which plainly ought to represent a beat or a regular basic pulse show considerable variation. While these strokes are clearly considered by the musicians as parts of a regular series of pulses, one cannot measure them with the regularity of a machine-made pulse.
>
> The listener's and the player's time perception "corrects" this physical irregularity and unconsciously bends the beats into a regular series. These deviations are only visible on the graph paper.[31]

Kubik's explanation of how the irregularities are resolved is reminiscent of Harwood's discussion of the theory of "chunking" used in information processing.[32] In any case, while he is careful to point out that some of the variation may be intentional and some unintentional, it is clear that the assumption of a steady pulse base is fundamental to Kubik's findings.

This assumption on the part of researchers is further emphasized by their concomitant assumption of meter. The tendency to group mechanically exact pulses is a well-known human phenomenon,[33] and thus it is perhaps no more surprising to find ascriptions of meter to African music than of an equal pulse base. Almost all students

[29] Robert Garfias, "Symposium on Transcription and Analysis: A Hukwe Song with Musical Bow. Transcription I," *Ethnomusicology* 8 (1964):240.

[30] Ibid.

[31] Gerhard Kubik, "Transcription of African Music from Silent Film: Theory and Methods," *African Music* 5, no. 2 (1972):33.

[32] Dane L. Harwood, "Universals in Music: A Perspective from Cognitive Psychology," *Ethnomusicology* 20 (1976):524.

[33] Daniel E. Berlyne, *Aesthetics and Psychobiology* (New York: Appleton-Century-Crofts, Meredith Corp., 1971), p. 238.

of African music assume metric organization, many without explanation or justification, such as Cudjoe,[34] Arom,[35] Knight,[36] and Nketia,[37] among others. Blacking points out that "for the Venda, the crucial difference between speech and song is that the words of a song are recited or sung to a regular metrical pattern,"[38] and Kolinski goes so far as to suggest that the African singer interprets what he is doing in specifically metric terms.[39] Only Eno Belinga seems to object, arguing that mensuration (which implies meter for him) is "hasardeux . . . parce qu'elle entraîne nécessairement l'existence de l'accent métrique dominant des temps faibles . . . ."[40]

The question of accent in conjunction with meter has apparently received little attention, although Blacking notes as a rule of the music of two Venda girls' initiation schools that "the basic tempo is expressed implicitly by accented performance or explicitly by a time-setter, such as the tenor drum."[41] For most students of music, accent and meter go hand in hand, but occasionally a definition of meter is proposed which eliminates accent as a necessary corollary. Such is the case of Kolinski's definition which was advanced in connection with a study of African music.

> *Rhythm is organized duration, meter is organized pulsation* functioning as a background for the rhythmic design. Contrary to the generally accepted concept which identifies meter with a more or less regular distribution of accents, it seems to me that neither accent nor stress represents a constituent element of meter.[42]

This definition makes the concept of meter slide almost imperceptibly into the concept of "pattern," a term which has frequently been used in connection with African musical rhythm and which functions as a successful explanatory principle. Once again, the concept seems clearly to fit the facts as perceived both by African

[34]"Ewe Drumming"; *An Approach to African Rhythm* (Legon: Institute of African Studies, 1971).

[35]Simha Arom, "The Use of Play-back Techniques in the Study of Oral Polyphonies," *Ethnomusicology* 20 (1976):486.

[36]"Notation and Tablature," p. 32.

[37]*African Music in Ghana*, p. 64ff.

[38]"Tonal Organization," p. 6.

[39]Mieczyslaw Kolinski, "Symposium on Transcription and Analysis: A Hukwe Song with Musical Bow. Transcription II," *Ethnomusicology* 8 (1964):251.

[40]Martin S. Eno Belinga, *Littérature et musique populaire en Afrique noire* (Paris: Editions Cujas, 1965), pp. 182-83.

[41]"Tonal Organization," p. 9.

[42]Kolinski, "Symposium," p. 249; see also idem, "A Cross-Cultural Approach to Metro-Rhythmic Patterns," *Ethnomusicology* 17 (1973):494-506.

and Western investigators. While no one has defined the term, it is consistently used in the sense of a set configuration of rhythmic pulses which is repeated either throughout a piece of music or through a significant portion of it.

Thus Cudjoe, for example, speaks of "rhythmic patterns appropriate to each dance" played by the gong,[43] and Jones writes that "what *Gankogui* plays is a rhythm-pattern. . . . There are several of these patterns whose length lies from 8 to 12 quavers."[44] Nketia speaks repeatedly of rhythm patterns of particular length and composition,[45] once again emphasizing the gong as the organizer of the ensemble, as in the following:

> Of the idiophones used in Ga society, gongs (*NoNo*) are the commonest. These are used both as "time keepers" and accompanying instruments. In the music of *Kple*, the principal cult of the Ga people, they may be used alone for providing the rhythmic basis of the mass stamping dance commonly called *obene Simo*.
>
> One or two gongs may be used, each one playing a different rhythm pattern.[46]

Koetting writes of the "twelve-unit pattern of the gankogui,"[47] Pantaleoni of the gong patterns among Ewe speakers in Ghana,[48] and many others have used the same language in describing African musical rhythm. Among the Basongye of Zaire, as among many other African peoples, mnemonic devices are used both to memorize and to retain rhythm patterns, as in the following, used by rattle players:

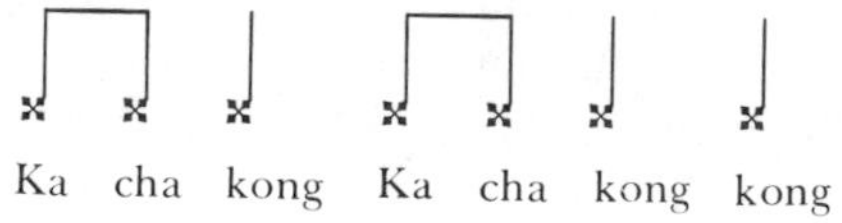
Ka cha kong Ka cha kong kong

Further, the "bass" xylophone of the two-xylophone ensemble plays a rhythmic-melodic ostinato which has clearly defined beginning and ending points and which forms the background against which more complex melodies are played on the "treble" xylophone. Other terms have been used for the same phenomenon; thus Blacking speaks of "a 'pulse' group equivalent to 12 quavers"

[43] "Ewe Drumming," p. 282.
[44] *Studies*, 1:53.
[45] *Music of Africa*, passim.
[46] Nketia, "Traditional Music," p. 21.
[47] "Analysis and Notation," p. 129.
[48] "Play of *Sogo*," p. 7, passim.

as being "a fundamental unit in many songs,"[49] as well as the fact that "Venda music consists of repetitions of basic patterns . . . ."[50]

The concept of pattern in African musical rhythm thus goes hand-in-hand with the assumption of a steady pulse base and a steady musical beat; it also accounts nicely for the suggested presence of meter, since a patterned unit can be taken as the equivalent of an (unaccented) measure, repeats itself consistently, and has a definable starting point. But most important to this discussion is the point that once a steady pulse base is assumed for African music (except in the case, always, of songs in free rhythm), a basic explanatory principle has been adduced which, when elaborated, accounts for, and explains, the organization of African rhythm as viewed by the outsider. In other words, the theory fits the facts as we perceive, and thus conceive, them.

Time from the African Point of View

Concepts of time in African societies have not been widely discussed in print, but what is available indicates patterns which differ from those of the West. It is useful to preface a brief review of the literature, however, by noting that even in the West, time is by no means always regarded as being strictly linear. Leach reminds us, for example, of two other kinds of time experience. The first is the notion of "non-repetition" by which is meant that "we are aware that all living things are born, grow old and die, and that this is an irreversible process."[51] Thus time in this sense, while still a gross unit and while still countable in the steady even pulse represented by the unit of a second, is not infinite so far as the individual is concerned, though we still presume that in the abstract sense it will go on forever. The second reminder given us by Leach is as follows:

> Our third experience of time concerns the rate at which time passes. This is tricky. There is good evidence that the biological individual ages at a pace that is ever slowing down in relation to the sequence of stellar time. The feeling that most of us have that the first ten years of childhood "lasted much longer" than the hectic decade 40-50 is no illusion. Biological processes, such as wound healing, operate much faster (in terms of stellar time) during childhood than in old age. . . .
>
> Such facts show us that the regularity of time is not an intrinsic part of nature; it is a man made notion which we have projected into our environment for our own particular purposes. Most primitive peoples

49"Tonal Organization," p. 9.

50John Blacking, *Venda Children's Songs* (Johannesburg: Witwatersrand University Press, 1967), p. 17.

51Leach, "Two Essays," p. 125.

> can have no feeling that the stars in their courses provide a fixed chronometer by which to measure all the affairs of life. On the contrary it is the year's round itself, the annual sequence of economic activities, which provides the measure of time.[52]

The same argument concerning the potential importance of phenomena of nature as time-reckoning devices has been echoed by Pocock, who objects to Nilsson's idea that time is based upon a small number of natural phenomena. While Nilsson suggested that such phenomena could be divided into those of the heavens and the phases of nature,[53] Pocock argued that ". . . it is by no means inevitable that a given society should find the movement of the heavenly bodies useful in ordering its affairs."[54]

Yet it has been primarily on bases such as these, as well as on social activities, that observers have focussed in discussing time in African societies. Thus Bohannan says that "when it is necessary to place an incident in time . . . Tiv do so by referring it to a natural or social activity or condition, using solar, lunar, seasonal, agricultural, meterological or other events."[55] He then enumerates Tiv divisions of years, months, the market-day week, and the day, but says of the last that "there is no notion of periods of the day which can be counted; nothing of which you can say that there are four or five between dawn and dusk."[56] Rigby speaks of the "reversal" of time which occurs during Gogo ritual,[57] and Evans-Pritchard summarizes Nuer time-reckoning as follows:

> . . . strictly speaking, the Nuer have no concept of time and, consequently, no developed abstract system of time-reckoning. . . . there is no equivalent expression in the Nuer language for our word "time", and . . . they cannot, therefore, as we can, speak of time as though it were something actual, which passes, can be wasted, can be saved, and so forth. Presumably they have in consequence a different perception of time to ours. Certainly they never experience the same feeling of fighting against time, of having to co-ordinate activities with an abstract passage of time. . . . There are no autonomous points of reference to which activities have to conform with precision.

52Ibid., pp. 132-33.

53*Primitive Time-reckoning*, p. 2.

54"Anthropology of Time-reckoning," p. 305.

55"Concepts of Time," p. 252.

56Ibid., p. 257.

57Peter Rigby, "Some Gogo Rituals of 'Purification': An Essay on Social and Moral Categories," in *Dialectic in Practical Religion*, Cambridge Papers in Social Anthropology no. 5, ed. Edmund R. Leach (Cambridge: At the University Press, 1968), pp. 172-73.

> Also the Nuer has . . . few, and not well-defined, units of time. . . . They think much more easily in terms of activities and of successions of activities . . . than they do in units of time.[58]

Beidelman speaks of time-reckoning among the Kaguru in very similar terms.

> Kaguru time is essentially a vague sliding scale focused on the near present in which the past and future are of relatively little concern. Time is expressed in terms of the occurrences of various natural and social phenomena, not in terms of any abstract units of measurement, such as are utilized in Western society. No single type of reference point for charting time is used by the Kaguru, so that attention tends to focus not upon points in a time continuum separated by clearly defined distances in experiences but, rather, to be fixed alternately upon a number of different types of points in time separated only by a vague sense of the passage of many or few intervening events. Although the Kaguru have at least two abstract terms for "time," they do not reify time in the Western sense in which it sometimes seems to take on the attributes of a substance or a commodity, at least in the conversation and thinking of ordinary persons.[59]

The Basongye also reckon time according to the seasons and other natural phenomena, but they apparently use fixed points of reference more frequently than the societies referred to above, and thus approach, at least, a linear concept of time.[60] Over the life cycle, however, time is conceived as circular, since the individual spirit is reincarnated, returning in a different body at least twice after its first existence. This concept of time has strong consequences for Basongye social life since, for example, it obviates the need for elaborate explanations of an afterworld, and since it explains in part the strong desire for children in whom the spirits of departed ancestors are reincarnated.[61]

MacGaffey speaks of the BaKongo concept of time as spiral in nature,[62] since it "allows for the occurrence of similar but non-repetitive events,"[63] and notes also that "BaKongo . . . do not

[58]Evans-Pritchard, "Nuer Time-reckoning," p. 208.

[59]Thomas O. Beidelman, "Kaguru Time Reckoning: An Aspect of the Cosmology of an East African People," *Southwestern Journal of Anthropology* 19 (1963):18.

[60]Alan P. Merriam, *An African World: The Basongye Village of Lupupa Ngye* (Bloomington: Indiana University Press, 1974), p. 40.

[61]Ibid.

[62]Wyatt MacGaffey, "African History, Anthropology, and the Rationality of Natives," (Unpublished ms., 1977), p. 16.

[63]Personal communication.

think of history as a record of linear progress in the accumulation of material and moral goods, and indeed do not appear to think historically at all."[64] A "mouvement circulaire ou spirale du Cycle de Vie" is also ascribed to the Luba-Kasai by Tiarko Fourche and Morlighem.[65] Writing in such a manner as to include African societies, Leach summarizes as follows:

> Indeed in some . . . societies it would seem that the time process is not experienced as a "succession of epochal durations" at all; there is no sense of going on and on in the same direction, or round and round the same wheel. On the contrary, time is experienced as something discontinuous, a repetition of repeated reversal, a sequence of oscillations between polar opposites: night and day, winter and summer, drought and flood, age and youth, life and death. In such a scheme the past has no "depth" to it, all past is equally past; it is simply the opposite of now.[66]

Finally, Mbiti, generalizing specifically for Africa, stresses that the linear concept of time "is practically foreign to African thinking," that Africans organize time primarily in terms of the past and the present but have "virtually no future" concept, and that "numerical calendars . . . do not exist in African traditional societies . . . ."[67]

These accounts of African time-reckoning, while showing a considerable variety and while representing a tiny fraction of the societies of Africa, seem to hold certain things in common. Time-reckoning is thought to be non-linear; instead, it can be reversed, discontinuous, a "sliding scale," circular, or spiral. Time-reckoning is carried on in terms of referral to natural phenomena or, most particularly, social activity. Time is not reckoned as distance, it is not epochal, and it is not measured with special apparatus.

Although it does not appear specifically in the passages cited above, one further, and most important, point must be noted, and this is that the smallest time divisions cited by the various authors are divisions of the day; this is also true of the many general ethnographies of African societies. These divisions are usually based on natural segments encompassing fairly large time periods, such as

[64] "The West in Congolese Experience," in *Africa and the West,* ed. Philip D. Curtin (Madison: University of Wisconsin Press, 1972), p. 60.

[65] J.-A. Tiarko Fourche and H. Morlighem, "Architecture et analogies des plans des mondes, d'après les conceptions des indigènes du Kasai et d'autres régions," *Institute Royal Colonial Belge, Bulletin des Séances* 9 (1938):658; see also pp. 652-53.

[66] Leach, "Two Essays," p. 126.

[67] John S. Mbiti, *African Religions and Philosophy*, chap. 3, "The Concept of Time" (Garden City, N.Y.: Doubleday Anchor Books, 1970), pp. 21, 24.

the Basongye idea of "sunrise"; the period "when people leave their fields," which centers loosely around noontime; "sunset"; and night, which is loosely subdivided.[68] It seems to be generally agreed, then, that the smallest period in African time-reckoning is the division of the day, but it must be remembered that the divisions may or may not be reckoned discontinuously, that they are not measured with special devices, and that they are quite probably non-linear.

Discussion and Conclusions

What kinds of problems emerge from this seemingly paradoxical situation, and what, if any, conclusions can be drawn from it? It is clear that from the etic-analytic-outsider's point of view, African music is organized in such a way that the assumption of an equal pulse base seems perfectly reasonable. It makes no difference whether the assumption is right or wrong so long as we keep it constant; that is, the analysis works, given the assumption. Both African and Western scholars have carried out their studies on this basis, although it is stated implicitly rather than explicitly.

The problem is that the assumption seems to contradict the African conception of time as understood by Western observers. That is, while from the Western standpoint, African musical rhythm appears to demand a linear concept of time as well as measurement of time in small units, the scanty knowledge we have of African time-reckoning seems to point to the exact opposite, i.e., a non-linear concept and no measurement of time in small units.

Several possible resolutions of this conflict are available to us. The first is that we may simply be wrong about African time-reckoning, but this does not seem likely given the unanimity of those who have focussed attention upon it, as well as the facts that chronometers are not a part of traditional African life and that observers report no time units smaller than the rough division of the day.

This, however, leads to a second possibility, which is that African societies, like our own, may use more than one system of time-reckoning, i.e., one in general social and cultural life as described in previous pages, and a second made up of small units which operates most specifically in connection with music (and presumably with dance as well). This suggestion might be supported by the fact that most ethnographers are not interested in music past the simple level of describing music instruments, if that, and, further, that ethnographers seem clearly to have been interested in

[68]Merriam, *An African World*, pp. 61-62.

gross, rather than fine, segments of time. Once again, however, the explanation does not seem likely in view of the fact that no one who has focussed on African musical rhythm, including trained ethnomusicologists—both African and Western—has found or suggested such a dual time-reckoning system. This does not mean the idea is impossible, however, and the problem clearly needs investigation.

A third resolution of the conflict is simply that some other system may be operating in connection with the small units required in musical time, and this appears to be a distinct possibility. Involved is what can be called "learning or comprehension by unit," an idea which has been suggested by several investigators, though in different terminology and not in nearly enough instances or depth.

Blacking, for example, in dealing with "the metrical structure of Venda children's songs and its relationship to the words," has formulated a rule which states, in part, that "each 'line' of a song is in itself a total pattern," thus suggesting that the unit is learned as an entity rather than in terms of separate, counted out, parts.[69] Much more specific is Cudjoe's description of children's games which are used in the learning process. He writes:

> Music starts at an early age in Eweland. There are many games designed not only for amusement, but also for developing a strong feeling for compound rhythms. In one such game, the child is held between two adults by the arms and legs and swung to and fro, gently at first and violently later, to the following accompaniment:
>
> Devi mase no do'o da ne,
> Wlaya wlaya do'o da ne.
>
> What is most interesting here is the use of three different rhythmic patterns in a short piece of this kind. The vocal portion of the game consists of two sentences each of which ends with the phrase "do'o da ne." The rhythmic basis of this common phrase is broad triplets, whereas the rest of each sentence is based respectively on short triplets and semi-quavers. Note also that the main 2/4 pulse is maintained in the swinging as a background to the sharply contrasting triplets.
>
> There is another simple game which children play after a bath in the sea. They sit in a circle, gather as much sand as they can into their laps, and with each hand playing a different rhythm, beat out 6/4 against 4/4 on the sand.[70]

Pantaleoni has made the most direct and detailed assertions concerning the matter of learning or comprehension by unit, a theme he has reasserted in several articles. For example, in connection

[69] *Venda Children's Songs*, p. 159.
[70] Cudjoe, "Ewe Drumming," pp. 280-81.

with his forwarding of a new tablature system for African rhythm, he wrote, with Serwadda:

> Unfortunately, one drawback of Western notation remains inherent in our tablature, and that is the unavoidable fractionating of the total ensemble into its component parts. For instructional purposes this is undeniably useful, but it is a Western instruction. The African learns the whole simultaneously with the parts, which is why he has never depended upon stress for rhythmical precision . . . . The Westerner taps his foot to give himself a regular stress on which to hang his part; the African taps his foot to mime the motion of the dancers, or any other part of the ensemble he wishes to add particularly strongly to his own.[71]

Four years later, Pantaleoni expressed the matter even more sharply.

> This paper discusses only the matter of timing in *Anlo* drumming. The source of timing is a high, soft voice that gives out a repeating, asymmetrical pattern. The process of timing one's part to this voice is a process of creating correct polyphony with it. The players neither follow a beat nor build additively upon a small, common unit of time; they simply play in duet with the steady cycling of the bell. This relationship gives them both the correct timing for their strokes and the correct location for their patterns in the flow of the ensemble. Performers may derive from the play of the bell a feeling of pulse suited to their individual rhythmic needs, but this feeling of pulse is not the primary source of timing.[72]

The suggestions, then, are that Africans are neither counting nor learning their parts individually; rather, the basic conception is an entity, a single unit made up of several parts which are envisaged as a totality.

Even this, however, does not *prove* that Africans do not measure or that they do not have a linear concept of time in connection with music. The facts that an individual bases his pattern on that of the gong, and that he hears the ensemble as an entity, may indicate learning or comprehension by unit, but the units themselves may be counted or heard as a linear sequence. The question, then, is not finally resolved, for we have no real proof in either direction.

It is at this point that the emic-etic distinction becomes clearest, for the Western view points one way, the traditional African another, and the interpretation of both is necessarily being made from the Western standpoint—even those Africans who have tackled the problem of African musical rhythm have done so from the

[71]Serwadda and Pantaleoni, "Notation for African Dance Drumming," p. 52.

[72]Hewitt Pantaleoni, "Three Principles of Timing in *Anlo* Dance Drumming," *African Music* 5, no. 2 (1972):62.

foundation of their Western training. It has been pointed out that the analyses carried out to date have accumulated an impressive body of structured information by holding as a constant the Western assumption of an equal pulse base. From the strictly analytic point of view, the use of this assumption makes no difference so long as it *is* held as a constant. But from the emic or internal point of view, it may make a great deal of difference, for in this case it is not a Western analysis which concerns us, but rather the understanding of African musical rhythm from the African standpoint. From the African's outlook, our notions may be entirely wrong, his concept of rhythm may be very different from ours because his concept of time is different, and where we see rhythm in African music as a form of linear propulsion, he may well see it as circular or spiral or in some other form.

This forces us to take a fresh look at the phenomenon, but, alas, our information is so scanty that little can yet be achieved. We may, however, pose the question of whether a circular conception of time-reckoning could help us to account for any aspects of the structure of African music, and the answer is in the affirmative. If it is correct to assume that repetitive pattern is at the basis of African music structure, then a cyclical view of time may be its basis. *Within* the pattern, linearality of some kind must be present, but the broader music structure is not necessarily so viewed. The same point can be applied to the formal structure of African song, which is so often couched in the repetitive call-and-response form of litany, for this, too, could clearly be cyclical rather than linear in conception. Finally, it is germane here to point out that Becker has reached much the same conclusion but in connection with the music of Java; she holds that the Javanese time concept is cyclical, that in certain cases it is divided into halves, halves into halves, and so forth, and that this process is repeated in music both rhythmically and melodically.[73] The point is important because it reinforces the suggestion that concepts of time-reckoning do differ from society to society, and that they almost certainly must affect music.

Finally, I wish to pose a question to which I have no answer, and this is whether music for all mankind must have a steady pulse base, no matter how it is conceptualized and expressed. Certainly it is this assumption that for Westerners makes what we call rhythm possible. Can we conceive of a music without it? Even when we create music with free rhythm or deliberately attempt to

[73]Judith Becker, "Time and Tune in Java," in *The Imagination of Reality: Essays in Southeast Asian Coherence Systems*, ed. A.L. Becker and Aram A. Yengoyan (Norwood, New Jersey: Ablex Publishing Corporation, 1979), pp. 197-210.

destroy a regular rhythmic base through computer randomization, our efforts seem almost necessarily projected against an equal pulse base. In other words, without order, can disorder exist?

Again the question is unanswerable cross-culturally because of the paucity of our information, but it has often been suggested that human beings relate their sense of time to tne regular heart beat which, for most of us in any case, is an equal pulse beat (with obvious exceptions, such as change of tempo resulting from exercise). Kubik has analyzed the timing pattern of mallet strokes in Ugandan xylophone playing and discovered patterning of which the players are completely unaware.

> Triple subdivision of the space of time between two strokes is frequently to be found in Africa, the lifting of the striking medium taking two basic pulses, and the downstroke one. This is also widespread in work situations, for example pounding maize and millet, or using a hammer or mallet. The rhythmic organization of blacksmiths working the bellows has already struck many observers.[74]

Why such fundamental underlying patterns of organization should exist, and whether they are common to the human species, we do not know, yet regularity of pulse underlies much of human activity. We in the West are echoing it when we apply a linear, measuring, concept of time to the analysis of all music. If we employ the equal pulse base as a constant for analytic purposes, we are on one kind of firm ground, so long as we realize we are being arbitrary. But if the search is for how Africans conceptualize and organizc their musical rhythms, and what it means to them, then we must also consider the organization, meaning, and application of time-reckoning in their cultural system.

[74]Kubik, "Transcription of African Music," p. 34.

Kurt Reinhard

Turkish Miniatures as Sources of Music History

It is widely known that research in Western art history has for a long time ignored Turkish painting, especially miniatures, although much attention has been given to the graphic arts of the Persians and, in part, also to those of the Arabians. Richard Ettinghausen, among others, has advanced some specific reasons for this situation.[1] As early as 1938 Peter Panoff published four colored drawings;[2] those figurines belong, however, to the realm of costume illustrations and thus are hardly to be regarded as miniatures. This collection has been kept in Germany, where it serves its purpose as a purely music-historical reference. A real interest in actual miniatures did not arise until the middle of this century when, for example, Süheyl Ünver singled out Levni as one of the most important older painters of Turkey.[3] It is interesting to observe how people who have occupied themselves with Turkish miniatures have often done so through an indirect route, as, for example, in the attempt to document other cultural and historical relationships, be it the history of the dance, of entertainment, or of the theater–as did Metin And[4]–or even music history–as did Mahmut R. Gazimihâl[5] and Henry Farmer.[6] The first allusions to actual Turkish

[1]See publication j, p. 5 ff. in the literature enumerated in Appendix II. Hereinafter all citations of publications similarly designated refer to works listed there.

[2]Publication a.

[3]Publication b.

[4]Publications f and h.

[5]Publications c and e.

[6]Publication d.

miniature painting and to its significance occurred in two publications which were supported by UNESCO.[7] Shortly thereafter Filiz Öğütmen prepared a brief catalogue of the 13,533 miniatures which belong to the Library of the Topkapı Seraglio Museum in Istanbul.[8]

We will not comment here on the art-historical significance of these miniatures, nor will we consider the historical events depicted in the paintings. The former has been dealt with in publications g and j; the latter has been treated in many other articles.[9] Rather, as in most other studies relating to music, we will focus upon types of instruments, the formation of ensembles, performance practice, and, of course, the direct context or function of the music.[10] We will deal with those miniatures which the author himself photographed in Istanbul in 1966 as well as with the paintings published elsewhere which were accessible to the author.[11] All told, there are 128 such illustrations, sixty of which are available only as photographs. Thirteen others have been reproduced in publications by the author; fifty-five in the publications of other scholars. With only a few exceptions,[12] non-Turkish miniatures have not been considered.[13] We have omitted an extensive source listing because it is of no particular relevance here except in regard to dating. In any event, these listings are to be found in the publications to which we have referred in the list of original sources (see Appendix I), though, even there, dates are occasionally missing. Thus, we have been forced to do without the dates of these sources, as well as without the dates of those lacking commentary which can no longer be examined. It must also be mentioned that in the explanations which appear in Appendix I—and which save us lengthy

[7]Publications g and j.

[8]Publication k.

[9]E.g., publications l, s, t, w, and y.

[10]Compare publications i, m, n, o, p, q, r, u, x, z, and, in part, v. One would also have expected such illustrations in Henry George Farmer, *Islam*, Musikgeschichte in Bildern, vol. 3, no. 2 (Leipzig: Deutscher Verlag für Musik, 1966), but no Turkish miniatures are included therein. Only the book of instruments entitled "Kaşf al-ġumūm va'l-kurab fī şarḥ ālat aṭ-ṭarab," of Egyptian provenance but now residing in the Library of the Topkapı Seraglio Museum in Istanbul (shelf number A 3465), is considered (as illustrations 92-97). Although the author has also photographed this work, it is not discussed in the present article.

[11]See Appendix II. The miniatures available to the author are designated by Arabic numerals (see Appendix III), by which means they are cited throughout. (The original sources—listed in Appendix I—are identified by Roman numerals.)

[12]E.g., miniature No. 89.

[13]E.g., the Egyptian manuscript mentioned in n. 10.

references in the text—the names of the authors of the original manuscripts are not mentioned; the names which do appear there are generally those of the painters.

In many of the miniatures it is difficult to distinguish construction and shape of the instruments, the number of strings on chordophones, the number of finger holes on aerophones, or other specifics. It is possible that the particular painter did not intend an accurate reproduction of all the details. But perhaps the individual illustrations of instruments and musicians do give us precise information,[14] since the obvious purpose of the paintings was to inform. Of special interest in this connection are the illustrations in a manuscript presumably from the 17th century which is preserved in Berlin (XX) and which has been discussed extensively by Campbell.[15] In addition to the ud, three other lute types—the kopuz, the bozuk, and the şeştar—are nowhere else so accurately represented, which makes an exact comparison difficult. The ud is here pictured in an exceptional way (very short neck and purely oval body. The spike fiddle ıklığ, which Gazimihâl considers important in the historical evolutionary process,[16] has only been documented by that author. However, many rebabs found in other miniatures should also be regarded as such, but, because of the frequently imprecise illustrations, they will not be so considered in the present work.[17] Only in the book of instruments (XXVI) are two types of ıklığ distinguishable: the two-stringed (77) and the three-stringed (64). But Gazimihâl has also found the ıklığ with three strings (89).

The fact that the book of instruments includes a number of European types (gamba: 65, organ: 70, cittern: 71, cymbals: 72, gusle: 76) proves to a certain extent that these instruments were in use, or at least were known, in Turkey around the middle of the 18th century. The masterly painting by the famous Levni depicting four women musicians (61) shows how accurate illustrations of musical instruments could be in certain cases. For example, the twenty pipes of the panpipe (mıskal) are precisely represented. This instrument is held in such a way that the lower pipes—as seen in the perspective of the player—are located on the right side. This

[14]Compare in particular miniatures 32-37 from manuscript XX (discussed in detail in publication x) and miniatures 63-77 from manuscript XXVI as well as Nos. 93-96 in the "costume book" (XXI), the female musicians in miniatures 61, 78, and 79, and the women dancers in Nos. 89 and 111-114.

[15]Publication x.

[16]Publication e.

[17]In only one case (104) was the drawing sufficiently clear to justify the use of the term ıklığ.

Figure 1. *Scene in the sultan's courtyard with two groups of musicians. Upper left: four players from the Janizary band (mehter), with oboe (zurna), pair of large timpani (kös), and two pairs of small timpani (nakkare). Lower right: harp (çeng) and frame drum (def). Source: Navā'ī, Alī şir, Divān, Hérat (16th century); Istanbul, University Library, T 5470.*

seems to have been the usual custom with this instrument (which today is no longer played), for ten other miniatures present the same posture, with only two (25, 26) showing the reverse. The border decoration on the face of the long lute tanbur is also clearly distinguishable in Levni's painting. All other miniatures have this same type of decoration, though on modern instruments it is no longer used. Here and in certain other examples the face of the tanbur is not exactly round—in contrast to today's instruments—but merges into the neck in small interlocking curves.

Among the harps the most common type is the angular harp, which is surely derived from the archaic oriental instrument. Its slightly curved sound box stands erect and extends into a spike at the bottom on which the instruments rests. The string holder runs vertically, and there is no pillar. The çeng is held and played by both hands. The number of its strings is difficult to determine. In miniature 1 (reproduced as Figure 1) nineteen strings are visible, but a painting will hardly be reliable in this respect. In addition to this type of harp, which one repeatedly encounters in scenes depicting musical activities, the book of instruments (XXVI, page 70) includes a more European version whose shape is reminiscent of the Gothic harp. Its upwards slanting body is indirectly visible and closes like a frame harp into a triangular shape, much like the Greek trigon. The instrument described by Öztuna,[18] apparently also taken from a miniature, is constructed in a similar way. The çeng in the Berlin manuscript (XX, page 35) is, however, totally different. As R. G. Campbell also maintains,[19] it has been drawn with considerable artistic license. It is interesting to observe that the angular harp is apparently not always supported by the spike (as, for example, in miniature 7) and that it is sometimes even carried while marching (31).

Because of the small dimensions and the resulting inaccurate representations of the scenes featuring instruments, one often gets the impression from certain miniatures (20, 23, 24 and 29, among others) that the principal auditor, who is probably the sultan himself, is in the company of another man who appears to play a wind instrument (mey?). In reality he is probably not a musician at all but, rather, a servant who is holding some other object for his master.

The trumpet boru appears in its three forms: as a straight tube, as one curving into an S-shape towards the end, and–what is most common–in a spiral form. The straight and S-shaped types were probably in use only in the 16th century (13, 86-88 and 4, 5), though the later spiral type was already in existence as early as 1575 (107).[20]

Most of the female dancers depicted in the miniatures hold percussion sticks in their hands. Whether these dancers are actually females or are, in fact, boys dressed in women's clothing–the so-called köçek–remains an open question. The percussion sticks are known by the ambiguous term "çarpare," which, nevertheless, is probably the most appropriate name, for these rhythm instruments are neither the popular wooden spoons (kaşık) nor the small finger

[18]*Türk Musikisi Ansiklopedisi*, s.v."çeng."

[19]Publication x, p. 35f.

[20]For additional illustrations of the spiral trumpet type from the last quarter of the 16th century, see miniatures 9-11, 14-16, 18, 19, 22, 24, 27, and 29.

cymbals (parmak zili) nor even castanets (kastanyet). One would expect at least an occasional illustration of one of these three in the miniatures, but everywhere the same scene is pictured: dancing females holding in each hand a pair of crudely shaped sticks held slightly apart from each other. Little has been written about these instruments, but even less about another rhythm instrument that has a decorated bar onto which are fastened three medium-sized pairs of cymbals which are "rattled" together. On the basis of a literary passage Metin And concluded that the proper name of this instrument is "çegane,"[21] and that term has been adopted here. The çegane is played by female dancers in the same way as the çarpare. It is depicted in six of our miniatures; in one case it is merely lying on the table of a circus performer (120), in another it is of especially large dimensions (119).

In representations of the frame drum one is often unable to determine whether the type without (def) or with a built -in pair of cymbals (zilli def) is depicted. It is the dimensions, however, which vary the most. Many instruments are very large and should actually be called mazhar. Sometimes, though, they contain cymbals, which are not characteristic of the mazhar. Here, again, either the artists did not reproduce the instrument accurately or it was impossible to separate those different types of frame drums as neatly as is done in books on musical instruments. The double-felted cylindrical drum called the "Turkish drum" or davul, which found its way to Europe along with other instruments, was formerly made with a much higher frame. This contradicts Sachs's statement that the early Turkish drums were rather shallow.[22] Our miniatures show drums similar to Western ones used by 16th-century mercenaries. On the other hand, the Turkish davul of today, which has been employed almost exclusively in folk music ever since the dissolution of the Janizary bands, is usually of lesser height than the diameter of its skin.[23]

Before considering questions regarding performance practice and music life in general, we present below an overview of the instruments represented in our miniatures, excluding those few which are of European origin.[24] The Turkish names, which hardly ever occur with the paintings, are based on findings of the author in works on instruments or are taken from other secondary sources.

[21]See publication f, p. 47.

[22]Curt Sachs, *Handbuch der Musikinstrumentenkunde* (Leipzig: Breitkopf & Härtel, 1920), p. 110.

[23]The Janizary bands (mehter) of today, which have been revived along historical lines, also use this apparently younger davul type.

[24]Miniatures 65, 70-73, 76, and 79.

Flutes

ney: open vertical flute with finger holes, used in art music
kaval: open vertical flute with finger holes, used in folk music
düdük: internal-duct flute with crescentic windway
mıskal: panpipes

Reed Instruments

zurna: conical oboe
mey: short oboe, without bell (probably not depicted in the miniatures)

Trumpets

boru: (1) straight, (2) S-shaped, or (3) spiral trumpet
nefir: horn made of natural material

Bowed Lutes

ıklığ: spike fiddle, older type
rebab: spike fiddle, younger type
kemençe rumi: fiddle, half pear-shaped

Plucked Lutes

kopuz: short lute, older type
ud: short lute (which has also reached Europe)
bağlama, also called saz, which actually means "musical instrument": long lute, used in folk music
bozuk: bağlama (saz) of medium size
tanbur: long lute, used in art music
şeştar: long lute, Persian type

Zithers

kanun: plucked zither
santur: zither struck with small stick

Harps

çeng

Idiophones

çarpare: unconnected percussion sticks, one pair in each hand
zil, known as halile in religious music: cymbals of various sizes
çegane: three medium-large zil fastened onto a bar

Drums

mazhar: large frame drum without jingles
def: small frame drum without jingles
zilli def: frame drum with zil pairs inserted into the frame
deblek (darabuka in Arabic): goblet-shaped drum with one head, used in folk music
davul: large two-headed cylindrical drum, the "Turkish drum"
kös: large kettle drum
nakkare, known as kudüm in religious music: small kettle drum

In attempting to relate the situations depicted in the miniatures to specific ways of employing instruments, one discovers that the clearest and most characteristic pattern emerges from those scenes concerning the military and combat. There one finds only those instruments which belong to the mehter, the so-called Janizary band. The crescent (çağana), which is mentioned in many literary sources—especially later ones—and which was adapted by Europe, appears in none of the miniatures. But the other five instruments (zurna, boru, zil, davul, and nakkare) occur in varying combinations. Often the pair of large kettle drums known as kös are depicted, of which only a single pair are ever encountered, even in the full band. A full band, which consists of fifty-five musicians, never occurs in any miniature.[25] Thus, it is to be assumed that, where a mehter ensemble appeared outside of Turkey while representing their country, only a portion of the complete group was present. One should keep this in mind when considering the question where European composers (Mozart, for example) might have heard Janizary bands before conceiving their Turkish operas or Turkish marches.

In our miniatures alone we can identify fourteen different ensembles, not all of which, however, will be discussed here. Occasionally only a single instrument is portrayed, as, for example, an oboe (12, 17) or a trumpet (5, 86-88). In the latter case we can surely assume that the instrument merely served a signaling function. In eighteen of the total of twenty-four mehter scenes oboes are involved. This corresponds to historical findings, for the zurna, together with the davul, formed the nucleus of Turkish military music from the very outset. These two instruments, which today—as in former times—constitute the most important representatives of professionally executed instrumental folk music, are shown alone in only two miniatures, strangely enough in two which do not have an exclusively military character: in a depiction of a festive procession (92) and in a funeral ceremony (106). The largest groupings, with five or even six different types of instruments, are seen in miniatures 10, 14, 22, 29, and 38. The most impressive one is a painting by Levni (57), which has already been published several times. It portrays a six- or eightfold grouping, with the musicians riding on horses and camels. For some reason, though, no oboes are represented.

After consideration of many of the remaining miniatures, it

[25]Each of the six instrumental groups comprising the ensemble prior to its dissolution in 1826 (oboes, trumpets, crescents, cymbals, large drums, and small timpani) consisted of nine musicians, exclusive of the large timpani (kös). The entire group was only employed, however, on special occasions.

Figure 2. *Lady with long-neck lute (bağlama or saz) used principally in folk music. Source: 'Abd Allāh al-Buḫārī ["Album de portraits"] (18th century); Istanbul, University Library, T 9364.*

becomes apparent that two long-accepted statements regarding the history of Turkish music require slight revision: first, the assumption that the ensemble in art music differs totally from that in folk music; second, the corallary idea that prior to the so-called time of the tulips (lâle devri), between the years 1718-1730, the court had never listened to folk music.[26] In a manuscript from the 18th century (XXVII), for instance, one finds two separate figurines, each showing a lady from the nobility, one with a European gamba (which belongs, without a doubt, to art music), the other with a bağlama. The santur and the kanun occur only rarely,[27] but other instruments belonging to the realm of art music are found quite often, such as the ney, rebab, tanbur, panpipes, and frame drums.

[26]It is believed today that it was during that time that the court musicians first came into contact with folk singers and other folk musicians who—according to the custom of the day—were admitted to festivities in the sultan's tulip gardens.

[27]The dulcimer santur appears twice (39, 44) in the same manuscript (XXII/XXIII, from ca. 1711) while the zither kanun (67) occurs only in the book of instruments (XXVI).

Similarly, the folk instruments nefir (21) and deblek (30, 37) occur very rarely while the zurna appears relatively often.

It is impossible to list here all the instruments that occur singly or in ensembles, nor can we discuss the composition of all those ensembles. Appendix III provides precise information regarding such matters. Of importance, though, is the realization that there were apparently no strict conventions concerning the make-up of ensembles. Nearly all the scenes are set at court or, at least, in the homes of noblemen, thus, in the same social milieu. Differences regarding the musical situation can therefore only be determined from the musical function. But no fixed rules seem to have existed. Some performances are purely instrumental; others—and these are more common—involve male or female dancers. At the court celebrations, which were apparently quite numerous, circus performers and animal trainers are usually pictured. Here the frame drum was the dominant instrument, as it still is today with Gypsy bear trainers. It is not surprising that circus performances were accompanied mainly by wind and percussion instruments—there is a total of twenty-three miniatures depicting jugglers, animal trainers, etc.—, though sometimes also the rebab (7, 62), the ud (22, 25), or the çeng (23, 25) are involved. It may be added that most of these scenes are to be found in the albums of Murad III (VI and VIII), who was born in 1546 and reigned from 1574 to 1595.

It is uncertain whether those scenes which are recorded in only a single miniature give an accurate account of the customary musical practice, for there exists no corroborating evidence. It is therefore surprising that the dancing boy—or is it a female dancer?—in the tavern (80) is accompanied by only two stringed instruments and not by a percussion instrument, provided in this case we are not dealing with a singer. By comparison, the ladies' social gathering (104) stands out because its two female dancers are accompanied by a rich body of instruments. The same is also true of the masked dances, which are depicted rather frequently (30, 84, 100, 116, 117). These are always accompanied by drums which are enriched by an ensemble of string instruments rather than of winds.

Problematic is the question whether singers participated in those court performances in which dancers were involved. Quite often one sees seated adjacent to the instrumentalists individuals, or even entire groups, who might well be soloists or choruses. In all probability they are singers because the so-called fasıl (i.e., song cycles), which were enframed by instrumental music, were already performed in the 16th century. In this regard the oft-stated thesis that ensembles were typically small must be corrected: many groups were rather large; thus, a court concert is not to be pictured by only a small body of instrumentalists and a single vocal soloist.

This fact somewhat legitimizes contemporary performances of older classical Turkish music in which various instrumental groups as well as choruses participate.

Purely instrumental performances are encountered in only a few miniatures: Nos. 2, 3, 82, the upper portion of 30, and the bottom half of No. 1 (the top half of which depicts several mehter musicians). It is striking that all of these–which, significantly, are among the oldest paintings–portray chamber combinations in which the melody instruments (ney and ud, ney and çeng, ud and çeng, or ney or çeng alone) are always accompanied by the frame drum. Ensembles in which the instruments appear twice or more are not found until the two collections of Levni's paintings (XXII and XXIII) from the year 1711. In these collections numerous representations of the same event are found, namely, the festival of two weeks' duration on the occasion of the circumcision of four of the sons of Sultan Ahmed III. The festivities took place partly at the firing range (okmeydan), partly in and around the palace at the seaside.[28] Other entertainment included concerts, ballets, and circus acts. Sometimes single instruments were involved, at others a variety of different instrumental combinations, including, on occasion, large ensembles of varied composition. Of the thirty miniatures recording this event which are available to us, only seven do not show evidence of a frame drum, proving that this instrument was virtually mandatory for festive occasions at court. In one case (41) only two davul and four zurna, held by musicians in a boat, are depicted. Such is understandable because the occasion represented here is an aquatic procession. In other cases as well one encounters combinations of instruments belonging to the mehter, provided we accept as such the frame drum, which always seems to replace the davul. Other ensembles are even more reminiscent of Janizary bands, such as those with trumpets, as, for example, miniature 53, with four zurna, two boru, and four davul, or miniature 103, with five zurna, three boru and six davul. This group of fourteen musicians is, however, by no means the largest pictured. Apart from those ensembles with nineteen, twenty-four, or even twenty-six players seen in mehter portraits (38, 57, 14), there is one with eighteen performers illustrated in miniature 62 upon the occasion of a large court festival in which three ney, two mıskal, two rebab, two tanbur, one def, five zilli def, and three davul can be identified, an ensemble consisting therefore of five or six different types of instruments. With the exception of several mehter scenes, similar variety in the composition of instrumental

[28] In Appendix III the abbreviation "court festivity at the seaside" is employed.

ensembles is otherwise found only in those groups pictured in miniatures 25, 44, 49 and 110 or in those playing Janizary instruments for the entertainment of the court (24, 27). Likewise differentiated is the group of female musicians seen at the ladies' social gathering in No. 104.

An exceptional case is illustrated in No. 39, where four shrill zurna are accompanied by, among other instruments, the much softer dulcimer (santur). It is possible, though, that these instruments were played alternately here. Of historical interest is the fact that already as early as 1711 harps no longer appear to have been employed, as evidenced by the paintings of Levni. However, it should be noted that Levni also failed to picture the ud, although that instrument, unlike the çeng, was still in use in the 18th century.

The foregoing observations regarding an admittedly small selection of Turkish miniatures illustrating instruments and musical activities cannot, of course, clarify all the questions concerning Osmanic music history. But it should point out the fact that here we have found a new and promising avenue for research. One needs now to examine all the miniatures in a systematic manner—either the originals themselves or the reproductions already published—to determine their relation to music and to compare them with one another as well as with written documents.

Appendix I

The Original Sources, Listed in an Approximately Chronological Order

References in brackets are to literature (see Appendix II) in which commentaries on the respective sources are to be found while numbers within parentheses refer to the miniatures as catalogued by the author in Appendix III which are discussed in the text of the present article. The names following "by . . ." refer to the painters of the miniatures, not to the authors of the sources.

I) Navā ı, Alī şir, Divān. Hérat, 16th century; Istanbul, University Library, T 5470. (1-4)

II) Süleyman-nâme, by Ali b. Emir Beyk Şirvani, 1557; Istanbul, Library of the Topkapı Seraglio Museum, H. 1517. [k, p. 26] (12, 13)

III) Nüzhet (el-esrar) ül-Ahbar der Sefer-i Sigetvar, 1568/69; Istanbul, Library of the Topkapı Seraglio Museum, H. 1339. (106 [same miniature in IV])

IV) Kanuni Sultan Süleyman'ın Tarih; Dublin, Chester Beatty Library, 414.
[j, p. 19] (106 [same miniature in III])

V) Tabakaat-el-Memâlik ve Derecât-el-Mesâlik, 1575; Vienna, Nationalbibliothek. (107)

VI) Sur-nâme-i hümayun, by Nakkaş Osman, ca. 1582; Istanbul, Library of the Topkapı Seraglio Museum, H. 1344. Also known as "III. Murat Albümü."
[k, p. 30] (98, 99, 116-119, 121, 123, 124, 126)

VII) Hünername (2 vols.), by Nakkaş Osman, 1584 and 1588; Istanbul, Library of the Topkapı Seraglio Museum, H. 1523/1524.
[g, p. 23; j, p. 17; k, p. 28] (9, 101, 102)

VIII) Şehinşahnâme-i Murad III, by students of Nakkaş Osman, 1592; Istanbul, Library of the Topkapı Seraglio Museum, B. 200.
[g, p. 23; j, p. 28; k, p. 30] (10, 11, 14-29)

IX) Sultan Ahmed I Albümü, end of the 16th century; Istanbul, Library of the Topkapı Seraglio Museum, B. 408. [k, p. 36] (30, 100, 114)

X) Iskender nâme; Library of the Türk ve Islam Eserleri Müzesi, T. 1921. (82)

XI) Teskerey-i evliya; Library of the Türk ve Islam Eserleri Müzesi, T. 1966. (83)

XII) Aczibul mahlukat; Library of the Türk ve Islam Eserleri Müzesi, T. 2013. (84)

XIII) Külliyatı Sadi; Library of the Türk ve Islam Eserleri Müzesi, T. 1963. (85)

XIV) Eseri ahi Cinsayî kebir; Library of the Türk ve Islam Eserleri Müzesi, T. 1968. (86-88)

XV) Vekayinâme, by Celâlzade. (97)

XVI) Venice, Museo Civico Correr, Ms. Cicogna 1971. (104)

XVII) Şemail nâme-i Âl-i Osman veya Taliki-zâde Şehnâmesi, ca. 1600; Istanbul, Library of the Topkapı Seraglio Museum, III. A. 3592. [k, p. 30] (31)

XVIII) Ca. 1620; London, British Museum, Sloane No. 5258 (263). (111, 112)

IXX) Divan-ı Nadirî (the painter Nadirî lived between 1573 and 1626/27); Istanbul, Library of the Topkapı Seraglio Museum, H. 889. [k, p. 32] (5-8)

XX) Mağmūa-i-musiki, presumably 17th century; Berlin, Staatsbibliothek Preussischer Kulturbesitz, Orient-Abt., Or. Fol. 3370. [x, p. 31ff.] (32-37)

XXI) "Turkish Costume Book," 1650; Berlin, Lipperheidesche Kostümbibliothek. (93-96)

XXII) Surname-i Vehbi, by Abdülcelil Çelebi (Levni), ca. 1711; Istanbul, Library of the Topkapı Seraglio Museum, III. A. 3593. [g, p. 26; j, p. 22, k, p. 36] (57-60, 62, 91, 92, 103, 108-110, 115, 120, 122)

XXIII) According to Filiz Öğütmen (see publication k), parallel manuscript to the preceding source (XXII), which has, however, not been listed in the catalogue; Istanbul, Library of the Topkapı Seraglio Museum, III. A. 3594. (38-56, possibly also 105)

XXIV) 17th/18th century; Vienna, Nationalbibliothek, Cod. 8562-8564. (113)

XXV) Levninin kadın figürleri, first third of the 18th century; Istanbul, Library of the Topkapı Seraglio Museum, H. 2164. [b] (61)

XXVI) Tefhim el-makamat fi tevlid en-nagamat (manuscript of the composer Kemânî Hızır Ağa concerning makams and musical instruments), 1749; Istanbul, Library of the Topkapı Seraglio Museum, H. 1793. (63-77)

XXVII) 'Abd Allāh al-Buḫārī, 18th century; Istanbul, University Library, T 9364. (78, 79)

XXVIII) Ḫubān-name ve zenan-name, 1771/92; Istanbul, University Library, T 5502. (80, 81)

IXXX) Unspecified, European miniature, 18th century. (89)

XXX) Unspecified, Turkish miniature, 18th century. (90)

Appendix II

List of Publications Containing Turkish Miniatures Illustrating Musical Activities or Instruments

The numbers in parentheses refer to the miniatures catalogued in Appendix III which are presently available to the author. The miniatures for which no numbers are given have not yet been published, though they have been photographed by the author.

a) Peter Panoff. "Das musikalische Erbe der Janitscharen." *Atlantis* 10 (1938):634-39. (93-96)

b) Süheyl Ünver. *Levni.* Istanbul: Milli Eğitim Basımevi, 1951. (61, 62)

c) Mahmut R. Gazimihâl. *Türk askerî muzıkaları tarihi.* Istanbul: Maarif Basımevi, 1955. (93-97)

d) Henry George Farmer. "Janitscharenmusik." In *Die Musik in Geschichte und Gegenwart* (1957). (93-96)

e) Mahmut R. Gazimihâl. *Asya ve Anadolu Kaynaklarında Iklığ.* Ankara: Ses ve Tel Yayınları, 1958. (62, 89, 90)

f) Metin And. *Kırk gün, kırk gece, Eski donanma ve şenliklerde seyirlik oyunları*. Istanbul: Taç, 1959. (58, 59, 62, 98, 100, 103, 108, 109)

g) M. S. Ipşiroğlu and S. Eyuboğlu, with a foreword by R. Ettinghausen. *Türkei: Frühe Miniaturen*. Paris: UNESCO, 1961. (9-11, 30, 57, 59, 60)

h) Metin And. *A History of Theatre and Popular Entertainment in Turkey*. Ankara: Forum Yayınları, 1963/64. (39, 40, 45, 46, 48, 49, 54, 60, 80, 98, 99-102, 104)

i) Vural Sözer. *Müzik ve Müzisyenler Ansiklopedisi* (1964). (57, 58)

j) Richard Ettinghausen. *Türkische Miniaturen vom 13. bis zum 18. Jahrhundert*. Milan: Amilcare Pizzi S.p.A., 1965. (9-11, 30, 57, 59, 60)

k) Filiz Öğütmen. *XII-XVIII. Yüzyıllar Arasında Minyatür Sanatından Ornekler.* Istanbul: Güzel Sanatlar Matbassı, 1966. English edition with the same illustrations but partially different descriptions: *Miniature Art from the XIIth to the XVIIIth Century*. Istanbul: Güzel Sanatlar Matbassı, 1966. (13)

l) T. Yılmaz Öztuna. *Başlangıcından Zamanımıza Kadar Türkiye Tarihi*, vol. 10, *1683-1703 yılları*. Istanbul: Hayat Yayınları, 1966. (43)

m) Hans Hickmann. "Trommeln und Pauken (B)." In *Die Musik in Geschichte und Gegenwart* (1966). (57)

n) Karl Signell. "Mozart and the Mehter," *The Consort*, no. 24 (1967):310-22. (38)

o) Hüseyin Sadettin Arel. *Türk Musikisi Kimindir*. Istanbul: Milli Eğitim Basımevi, 1969. (105)

p) Kurt and Ursula Reinhard. *Turquie*, Les traditions musicales, vol. 4. Paris: Buchet-Chastel, 1969. (38, 42, 44, 61)

q) Kurt Reinhard. "Klassische türkische Musik" (sound recording with commentary, located in Museum für Völkerkunde, Berlin [shelf number KM 0002], 1961). (44)

r) Haluk Tarcan. "Anadolu etnik müziğinin tarih içindeki kökleri." *Türkiyemiz* 2(1970):28ff. (91)

s) Nurhan Atasoy. "Topkapı Sarayındakı Papuç ve Çizme Hazinesi." *Türkiyemiz* 5 (1971):12ff. (92)

t) Géza Feher. "Türk Minyatürlerinde Macar Tarihi." *Türkiyemiz* 7 (1972):2ff. (9, 12)

u) Krister Malm. "Turkisk musik" (sound recording with commentary, located in Gymnasiematerial från Rikskonsetter, Stockholm [shelf number RIKS LPX 6], 1973). (44, 57)

v) Cevdet Kudret. *Ortaoyunu*. Ankara: Türkiye ve Bankası Kultur Yayınları, 1973. (59, 60)
w) Géza Feher. "Türk Vekayinamerlerinde Zigetvar." *Türkiyemiz* 13 (1974):11ff. (106)
x) Richard G. Campbell. "Instrumentenkundliche Notizen zu sechs türkischen Miniaturen." *Baessler-Archiv*, n.s. 23 ("Festschrift Kurt Reinhard zum 60. Geburtstag," 1975):31-37. (32-37)
y) Géza Feher. "Mohaç Savaşının yayınlanmamış bir Minyatürü." *Türkiyemiz* 18 (1976):15ff. (107)
z) Reşat Ekrem Koçu and Sabahattin Doras. *Mehterhane*. Ankara (?): Türkiye Turing ve Otomobil Kurumu (Apa Ofset Basimevı), n. d. (57)
aa) T. Yılmaz Öztuna. "Tanbur." In *Türk Musikisi Ansiklopedisi* (1976). (62)
bb) T. Yılmaz Öztuna. *Türk Bestecileri Ansiklopedisi* (1969). (57, 62, 108, 122)[29]

Appendix III

List of the Miniatures[30]

(SR = photographs from the collection of Reinhard [Sammlung Reinhard])

Miniature No.	Original source	Photo and/or publication	Subject	Instruments,[31] singers, dancers
1	I	SR: 10, 5	court concert and mehter	singer (?), çeng, def, zurna, 2 nakkare, kös
2	I	SR: 10, 6	court concert	singer (?), ney, ud, zilli def
3	I	SR: 10, 7	court concert	singer (?), ney, çeng, zilli def

[29]In this publication of Öztuna there are four additional miniatures for which no specific sources are given (125-128). For the sake of completeness, however, they are included in the list in Appendix III.

[30]The numbering does not correspond to the dates of origin of the miniatures nor do those miniatures occurring in the same source necessarily follow in sequence due to the fact that the publications were not available to the author at the same time, thereby creating, at the outset, many identification problems. The indulgence of the reader is kindly requested.

[31]Where çarpare, zil, nakkare and kös are listed in this column, it is understood that the reference is to the respective pair of instruments.

4	I	SR: 10, 8	tournament	boru (2), def, kös, nakkare
5	IXX	SR: 4, 8	battle	boru (2)
6	IXX	SR: 4, 9	battle	boru (3), kös (separated)
7	IXX	SR: 4, 10 and 4, 11	royal circus performers	ney, rebab, çeng, zilli def
8	IXX	SR: 4, 12	battle	zurna, boru (3), davul
9	VII	g, pl. 18 j, pl. 14 (section without instruments) t, p. 3	battle	top right: 3 zurna, 3 davul center right: 2 boru (3)
10	VIII	g, pl. 19 j, pl. 15	victory march of the army	3 zurna, 2 boru (3), 2 zil, 2 davul, nakkare
11	VIII	g, pl. 20 j, pl. 16 (section)	military campaign	three groups: 1) 3 zurna, 3 boru (3) 2) 2 zurna, 4 boru (3) 3) 2 zurna, 2 boru (3)
12	II	t, p. 5	battle	2 zurna
13	II	k, p. 27	death of a general in war	zurna, boru (1), nakkare
14	VIII	SR: 7, 11	mehter in court-yard of the seraglio	6 zurna, 4 boru (3), zil (?), 3 davul, 4 kös, 8 nakkare
15	VIII	SR: 7, 12	camp	4 zurna, 3 boru (3), 2 davul, nakkare
16	VIII	SR: 8, 1	military expedi-tion	3 zurna, 2 boru (3), 3 davul
17	VIII	SR: 8, 2	battle	6 zurna
18	VIII	SR: 8, 3	battle	4 zurna, 3 boru (3), 2 davul
19	VIII	SR: 8, 4	camp	3 zurna, boru (3), 2 davul
20	VIII	SR: 8, 5	royal circus performers	3 mazhar, 3 nakkare
21	VIII	SR: 8, 6	royal circus performers	nefir, mazhar

22	VIII	SR: 8, 7	entry into the seraglio plus circus performers	two groups: 1) 4 zurna, boru (3), zil, 2 davul, nakkare 2) 2 ud, zilli def, dancing female with çarpare
23	VIII	SR: 8, 8	entry into the seraglio plus circus performers	çeng, çegane, zilli def, dancing female with çarpare
24	VIII	SR: 8, 9	royal circus performers	2 zurna, 2 boru (3), zil, 2 davul, 3 kös
25	VIII	SR: 8, 10	royal circus performers	mıskal, ud, çeng, çegane, zilli def, 2 dancing females with çarpare
26	VIII	SR: 8, 11 and 8, 12	royal circus performers	mıskal, zilli def, 4 dancing females with çarpare
27	VIII	SR: 9, 1	royal circus performers	2 zurna, boru (3), zil, 2 davul, 3 kös
28	VIII	SR: 9, 2	royal circus performers	mıskal, zilli def, 3 dancing females with çarpare
29	VIII	SR: 9, 3	military parade	2 zurna, 2 boru (3), zil, 2 davul, 2 kös
30	IX, p. 19a	SR: 4, 5 and 4, 6 g, pl. 26 h, fig. 26 (only upper half) j, pl. 22 v, color ill. 2	upper portion: chamber music bottom portion: masked dance	above: ud, çeng, zilli def, 2 girls with çarpare below: çeng, 2 zilli def, deblek
31	XVII	SR: 1, 1 and 1, 2	march	3 ney, 3 ud, 3 çeng
32	XX	x, ill. 1	musicians	ud, mazhar
33	XX	x, ill. 2	musicians	ney, kopuz, kanun
34	XX	x, ill. 3	musicians	3 kopuz
35	XX	x, ill. 4	musicians	bozuk, çeng, mazhar
36	XX	x, ill. 5	musicians	ney, single kudüm
37	XX	x, ill. 6	musicians	şeştar, deblek

38	XXIII	SR: 6, 3 n, p. 312 p, photo 2	mehter on horseback	7 zurna, 5 boru (3), 2 zil, 3 kös, 2 nakkare
39	XXIII	SR: 6, 4 and 6, 5 h, fig. 23 (black and white, with sides reversed)	court festivity at the seaside	4 zurna, santur, 4 zilli def, 2 nakkare
40	XXIII	SR: 6, 6 h, fig. 30	court festivity at the seaside	4 zilli def, 2 nakkare, 3 dancing females with çarpare
41	XXIII	SR: 6, 7	court festivity at the seaside	4 zurna, 2 davul
42	XXIII	SR: 6, 8 p, photo 3b	court festivity at the seaside	4 zurna, 4 zilli def, 2 nakkare, 4 dancing females with çarpare
43	XXIII	SR: 6, 9 L, pl. 6 (sides reversed)	court festivity at the seaside	4 zurna, 4 zilli def, 2 nakkare, 4 dancing females with çarpare
44	XXIII	SR: 6, 10 p, photo 5 q, cover u	court festivity at the seaside	3 ney, rebab, tanbur, santur, 2 zilli def, chorus (?)
45	XXIII	SR: 6, 11 h, fig. 7	court festivity at the seaside	5 zurna, 6 zilli def
46	XXIII	SR: 6, 12 h, fig. 12	court festivity at the seaside	zilli def
47	XXIII	SR: 7, 1	court festivity at the seaside	2 zurna, 4 zilli def, 2 nakkare, 4 dancing females with çarpare
48	XXIII	SR: 7, 2 h, fig. 13	court festivity at the seaside	3 davul
49	XXIII	SR: 7, 3 h, fig. 9	court festivity at the seaside	2 ney, 2 mıskal, rebab, 2 tanbur, 4 zilli def
50	XXIII	SR: 7, 4	court festivity at the seaside	3 zurna, 3 zilli def, 4 dancing females
51	XXIII	SR: 7, 5	court festivity at the seaside	4 zurna, 2 nakkare

52	XXIII	SR: 7, 6	court festivity at the seaside	4 zurna, 5 zilli def, 6 dancing females with çarpare
53	XXIII	SR: 7, 7	court festivity at the seaside	4 zurna, 2 boru (3), 4 davul
54	XXIII	SR: 7, 8 h, fig. 31	court festivity at the seaside	3 zurna, 4 zilli def, 2 nakkare, 5 dancing females with çarpare
55	XXIII	SR: 7, 9	court festivity at the seaside	2 zilli def, 2 dancing females with carpare
56	XXIII	SR: 7, 10	court festivity at the seaside	boru (3), 3 other musicians with ?
57	XXII	g, pl. 29 i, cover j, pl. 25 m, pl. 27 u z, (section) bb, p. 141 (section)	mehter on horse- and camel back	6 boru (3), 6 zil, 6 davul, 6 kös
58	XXII	f, ill. 24 i, cover	court concert with ballet	2 ney, 2 tanbur, 4 zilli def, 8 dancing females with çarpare
59	XXII	f, ill. 27 g, pl. 28 j, pl. 24 and cover v, color ill. 1	ballet and circus performers	2 zurna, 3 zilli def, nakkare, 5 dancing females with çarpare
60	XXII	g, pl. 32 h, fig. 24 (section) j, pl. 28 v, cover (section)	court concert, circus performers	2 zurna, 4 zilli def, 3 nakkare
61	XXV	SR: 4, 7 b, color ill. 5 p, photo 1	female musicians	mıskal, zurna, tanbur, zilli def
62	XXII	b, ill. 6 (black and white) e, p. 37 f, ill. 31 aa, p. 300 bb, p. 73 (section)	court concert, circus performers	3 ney, 2 mıskal, 2 rebab, 2 tanbur, def, 5 zilli def, 3 davul

63	XXVI	SR: 1, 3	musicians	tanbur
64	XXVI	SR: 1, 4	instrument	rebab with bow
65	XXVI	SR: 1, 5	instruments	gamba with bow, bağlama
66	XXVI	SR: 1, 6	instruments	santur with percussion sticks
67	XXVI	SR: 1, 7	instrument	kanun
68	XXVI	SR: 1, 7	instrument	ud
69	XXVI	SR: 1, 8	instrument	çeng
70	XXVI	SR: 1, 9	instrument	organ
71	XXVI	SR: 1, 10	instrument	cittern
72	XXVI	SR: 1, 11	instrument	cymbal
73	XXVI	SR: 1, 12	instrument	European lute
74	XXVI	SR: 2, 1	instruments	2 zurna, düdük, kaval, beak flute
75	XXVI	SR: 2, 2	instrument	nakkare
76	XXVI	SR: 2, 3	instrument	gusle with bow
77	XXVI	SR: 2, 4	instrument	rebab with bow
78	XXVII	SR: 9, 8	female musician	bağlama
79	XXVII	SR: 9, 9	female musician	viola with bow
80	XXVIII	SR: 9, 6 h, fig. 33	dancing boy in tavern	kemençe rumi, ud
81	XXVIII	SR: 9, 7	dancing bear	zilli def
82	X	SR: 5, 7	domestic concert	ney, zilli def
83	XI	SR: 5, 11	men's dance	def, zilli def, 2 dancers
84	XII	SR: 5, 12	masked dance	above: çeng center: ney, zilli def
85	XIII	SR: 6, 1	dance in front of entrance gate	2 zilli def, people clapping hands, dancers
86	XIV	SR: 5, 8	reception by the sultan	2 boru (1), separated

87	XIV	SR: 5, 9	battle	boru (1)
88	XIV	SR: 5, 10	war counsel	2 boru (1)
89	IXXX	e, p. 25	dancing woman	ıklığ
90	XXX	e, p. 30	women's social gathering	ıklığ
91	XXII (?)	r, p. 31	court ballet	mıskal, zurna, 4 zilli def
92	XXII	s, p. 14	festive procession	2 zurna, 2 davul
93	XXI	a, p. 635 c, p. 17 d, pl. 72	musician	davul
94	XXI	a, p. 635 c, p. 16 d, pl. 72	musician	boru (3)
95	XXI	a, p. 635 c, p. 17 d, pl. 72	musician	zil, nakkare
96	XXI	a, p. 635 c, p. 16 d, pl. 72	musician	kös
97	XV	c, p. 27	mehter in the field	3 zurna, 2 boru (3), 2 zil, 2 davul
98	VI	h, fig. 3 f, ill. 3	circus performers in the seraglio	zilli def
99	VI	h, fig. 47 f, ill. 4	marionettes in the hippodrome	mıskal, zilli def, dancing female with çarpare
100	IX	h, fig. 25 f, ill. 13	masked dance	mıskal, zilli def
101	VII, vol. 2	h, fig. 4	circus performers in the hippodrome	2 zurna
102	VII, vol. 2	h, fig. 5	circus performers in the hippodrome	2 zurna, 2 davul (?)
103	XXII	f, ill. 77	court festivity	5 zurna, 3 boru (3), 6 davul
104	XVI	h, fig. 38	ladies' social gathering	mıskal, ıklığ, çeng, 2 zilli def, nakkare, 2 dancing females with çarpare

105	XXII or XXIII (?)	o, cover (section)	court concert (?)	2 ney, mıskal, 2 tanbur, 4 zilli def
106	IV and V	w, ill. 7	funeral ceremony	4 zurna, 2 davul
107	V	y, p. 16	mehter in battle	3 zurna, 2 boru (3), 2 zil, 2 davul
108	XXII	f, ill. 6 bb, p. 76 (section)	court festivity with circus performers	2 mıskal, tanbur, 4 zilli def
109	XXII	f, ill. 7	court festivity at the seaside	2 mıskal, 2 zurna, 5 zilli def
110	XXII	f, ill. 9	court festivity at the seaside	mıskal, 4 zurna, 3 boru (?), 4 zilli def, 3 davul, 2 dan-ing females with çarpare
111	XVIII	f, ill. 14	dancing woman	çarpare
112	XVIII	f, ill. 15	dancing woman	çegane
113	XXIV	f, ill. 16	dancing woman	çarpare
114	IX	f, ill. 17	dancing woman	çarpare
115	XXII	f, ill. 19	court ballet	mıskal, 2 zurna, 6 zilli def, 4 dancing females with çarpare
116	VI	f, ill. 20	masked dance at court	ud, 3 mazhar, 4 dancers with çarpare
117	VI	f, ill. 23	masked dance and circus performers	3 zilli def
118	VI	f, ill. 33	circus performers at court	3 zilli def, çegane
119	VI	f, ill. 34	circus performers	3 zilli def, large çegane
120	XXII	f, ill. 35 (section)	circus performers	zilli def, çegane (lying on table)
121	VI	f, ill. 36	circus performers	2 zilli def
122	XXII	f, ill. 46 (section) bb, p. 128	court festivity at the seaside	6 zurna, 5 zilli def, 6 dancing females with çarpare
123	VI	f, ill. 58	circus performers with animals	2 zilli def or def

124	VI	f, ill. 60	circus performers at court	2 zilli def
125	?	bb, p. 65	mehter at boxing match (güreş)	7 zurna, 4 boru (3), 5 kös, 4 nakkare
126	? (beginning of 18th c.)	bb, p. 68	fireworks and band on raft	2 mıskal, 2 tanbur, 4 zilli def
127	? (painter: Levni)	bb, p. 80 bb, p. 70 (black and white only, with sides reversed)	mehter at fireworks	5 zurna, 5 boru (3), 3 zil, 6 davul
128	? (painter: Levni)	bb, p. 149	mehter on horseback on the march	8 zurna, 5 nakkare

Translated by Karen Sahu

Ralph T. Daniel

The Wanley Partbooks

In the Bodleian Library at Oxford University are three manuscripts bearing the call numbers "Bodl. Mus. Sch. e. 420-422," which are the survivors of an original set of four partbooks containing church music in English. The tenor book is missing, leaving the first contratenor, second contratenor and bass parts.

Their provenance is unknown, but their plain, scarred leather binding indicates that they were not intended for the Royal Chapel. Because of their small size, rectangular shape and evidence of much wear and tear, it is likely that they were prepared for use in the private chapel of some wealthy patron and/or lesser nobleman. The several references to King Edward VI (reigned 1547-1553) establish the possible time period. The fact that several Services follow the wording of the first *Book of Common Prayer* (1549) further limits the time period, but one can reasonably assign their origin to no earlier than ca. 1550 since it is unlikely that a collection so vast could have been assembled in less than one year.

One might assume that most, if not all, of the texts were drawn from a few sources in common usage at the time, but it was found that such was not the case. A survey of all of the Primers and Bibles published before and during Edward's reign reveals a great diversity of wording. The texts in the partbooks indicate that many sources were used, that the scribes relied too much on faulty memory, that they felt free to alter the texts, or that they were simply careless. For example, this writer was greatly encouraged when he found the phrase "suffered under Ponce Pilate" in the first *Prayer Book* and in the first Service in the Wanley Books. "Ponce" is to be sung to one note, so there is no doubt that it is a one-syllable word. I have found no instance of earlier usage than the first Edwardian *Book of Common Prayer.*

An unjustified confidence is created by this departure from the norm of the earlier Primers, for that confidence is shattered by other departures from the authorized wording of the Creed (Apostles' rather than Nicene) in the same *Book of Common Prayer.* This sort of departure from the text in known sources seems to be the rule rather than the exception and reflects the lack of concern for conformity (note the number of ways that Shakespeare spelled his own name) by writers and composers of the Renaissance. Butterworth has found fourteen versions of the phrase "Thy will be done on earth as it is in heaven" in pre-Edwardian sources.[1]

The singing of the Service or portions of the Service in English was practiced occasionally before the coronation of Edward, of course. It is well known that Compline was sung in English in the Royal Chapel in April 1547 and that English versions of the Service had been printed in Marshall's *Goodly Prymer* (1535), Hilsey's *Manual of Prayer* (1539), and King Henry VIII's *Primer* of 1545. Henry VIII had already ordered an English version of the Litany in 1544. In April 1547 the Service was sung and said completely in English at both St. Paul's Cathedral and Westminster Abbey, providing a precedent for other cathedrals and parish churches for the use of the vernacular. It was not until June 9, 1549, that the official change from the Roman Mass to the English Service was decreed, the culmination of a gradual process that established the English version, which was used until it was suppressed by Queen Mary in 1553. When Queen Elizabeth I was enthroned in 1558 the *Book of Common Prayer* became the official Service book, with provision made for the Latin model in some private chapels and collegiate churches.

The three manuscripts under scrutiny are informally referred to as "The Wanley Books" or "The Wanley Partbooks" because of the inscription "Liber Humphrdi Wanley, 18 Nov. 1715" which appears on the title page of each book. Humphrey Wanley (1672-1726) was an indefatigable bibliophile who spent most of his adult life scouring Great Britain for treasures for the Bodleian Library as well as for private collectors.[2] Although he identified many of his acquisitions by means of his signature, his name is most closely associated in musical circles with the set with which this essay is concerned.

[1]Charles C. Butterworth, *The English Primers (1529-1545)* (Philadelphia: University of Pennsylvania Press, 1953), pp. 301-2.

[2]Biographical information is based mainly on the article about Wanley in the *Dictionary of National Biography*.

The original scribes divided the contents into three "books," with all three books bound together for each voice part. This apparently arbitrary division is justified only by the fact that the second book appears to have been copied by a different scribe; the first and third seem to be in the same calligraphy. It would be interesting to know if the two (or possibly more) scribes were working simultaneously and, if so, how they decided on the division and distribution of labor. The writer(s) of the first and third books was obviously the most energetic—or had more time at his command. Both (or all) are to be commended for the small number of errors in notation.

Determining the number of works in the collection depends on whether one counts a Service as one or as five items. The latter practice produces 137 separate works; counting the composite works as one, there are ninety-two—a monumental collection for its period and genre. Limitations of space and time prevent the remainder of this essay from being more than an inventory of the works with occasional annotations which would be of immediate interest to the reader. For example, no composers are named in the Wanley Books, but some have been identified through concordant sources.

Book I

1. Kyrie: Lord, have mercy upon us. Christ, have mercy. . . .
2. Communion:[3] . . . . [John? Heath]
   a. Kyrie—Lord, have mercy upon us. . . .
   b. Gloria—Glory be to God on high. . . .
   c. Credo—I believe in one God. . . .
   d. Sanctus—Holy, holy, holy, Lord God of hosts. . . .
   e. Agnus Dei—O lamb of God. . . .

   Heath is named as the composer of a somewhat modified version of the same work in John Day's *Certaine notes* (1560). In both the manuscript and printed sources an unusual notation obviously related in some ways to medieval practice is used. The following example from John Merbecke's *The Book of Common Praier Noted* (1550), page 197, is typical:

[3]Hereinafter the five items of the Ordinary of the Mass and the Service will be abbreviated K, G, C, S, and A.

The Offertories.
1
Let your light so shyne before
men, that they may se your good workes and
glorifie your father which is in heauen.

3. Magnificat: My soul doth magnify the Lord. . . .
4. Nunc dimittis: Lord, now lettest Thou Thy servant. . . .
5. Domine secundum actum: In judgment Lord. . . .
6. Magnificat . . . . [Christopher Tye]
7. Nunc dimittis . . . . [Christopher Tye]

   Attributed to Tye in Brit. Mus. Add. mss. 30480–84. Since the two canticles for Evensong were usually composed as a pair, it seems likely that the above Magnificat (number 6) was written by the same composer, especially in view of the similarity of style in the two works.
8. Anthem: I give you a new commandment. . . . . [John? Shepherd]

   Attributed to Shepherd in numerous manuscript sources, to Tallis in one. See Ralph T. Daniel and Peter G. Le Huray, *The Sources of English Church Music 1549-1660*, Early English Church Music, supplementary vol. 1 (London: Stainer and Bell, 1972).
9. Anthem: O praise the Lord, for it is a good thing. . . .
10. Post-communion: Happy are those servants. . . .
11. Anthem: In no kind of creature. . . .
12. Communion: G, C, S, A.
13. Offertory: Charge them that are rich. . . .

14. Post-communion: The night is past. . . .
15. At the burial:
    a. I am the resurrection. . . .
    b. I know that my Redeemer liveth. . . .
    c. We brought nothing into this world. . . .
    d. Man that is born of woman. . . .
    e. In the midst of life. . . .
    The first appearance of this Service in the 1549 *Book of Common Prayer* suggests its date of composition.
16. I heard a voice from heaven. . . .
    Properly part of the foregoing Burial Service, but separated from the other items in the Wanley Books.
17. Anthem: Make ye melody unto the Lord. . . .
18. Anthem: I am the true vine. . . .
19. Anthem: Submit yourselves one to another . . . [Shepherd]
    Attributed to [John?] Shepherd in Day, *Certaine notes* (1560), and numerous manuscript sources. See Daniel and Le Huray, *Sources.*
20. Anthem: Happy is the people. . . .
21. Christus resurgens: Christ rising again. . . .
    Christ is risen. . . .
    The unusual black notation referred to in the note for number 2 is used for these two selections.
22. Anthem: O most merciful Jesu Christ. . . .
    Contains a reference to "King Edward the Sixth," which helps in dating the manuscript.
23. Anthem: Lord, Jesu Christ, Son of the living God. . . .
24. Benedictus: Blessed be the Lord God of Israel. . . .
25. Anthem: This is my commandment . . . . [Tallis]
    Attributed to different composers (R. Johnson, J. Mundy, W. Mundy and T. Tallis) in various sources. See Daniel and Le Huray, *Sources.*
26. Weddings: Blessed art thou that fearest God. . . .
27. Usquequo Domine: How long wilt Thou forgive me. . . .
28. Deus in adjutorium: Haste Thee, O God, to deliver me. . . .
29. Anthem: Hear the voice and prayer. . . . . [Tallis]
    Attributed to Tallis in Day, *Certaine notes* (1560). See also *Thomas Tallis: English Sacred Music* I, Early English Church Music, vol. 12, ed. Leonard Ellinwood (London: Stainer and Bell, 1971).
30. Anthem: Praise we the Father. . . . . [Okeland]
    Attributed to [Robert?] Okeland in Day, *Certaine notes* (1560).
31. Te Deum: We praise Thee, O God. . . .
32. Post-communion: I am the voice of a crier. . . .

Book II

33. Magnificat
34. Nunc dimittis
35. Te Deum
36. Benedictus
37. Magnificat
38. Nunc dimittis
39. Te Deum
40. Benedictus
41. Venite
42. Anthem: Let all the congregation . . . . [Caustun]
    Attributed to [Thomas?] Caustun in Day, *Certaine notes* (1560).
43. Anthem: All people hearken and give ear. . . .
44. Anthem: Praise be to God . . . . Come Thou holy ghost . . . .
45. Anthem: The spirit of the Lord. . . .
46. Benedicite: O all ye works of the Lord. . . .
47. Anthem: O clap your hands. . . .
48. Anthem: O eternal God, almighty . . . . [Johnson]
    Attributed to [Robert?] Johnson in Day, *Certaine notes* (1560).
49. Anthem: Remember not, O Lord, our old iniquities. . . .
50. Anthem: If ye love me . . . . [Thomas Tallis]
    Attributed to Tallis in Day, *Certaine notes* (1560), and numerous manuscript sources. See Daniel and Le Huray, *Sources*.
51. Anthem: Verily I say unto you. . . .
52. Anthem: Praise the Lord, O our souls . . . [Robert Okeland]
    Attributed to Okeland in Day, *Certaine notes* (1560).
53. Christus resurgens: Christ rising again. . . .
    Christ is risen. . . .
54. Anthem: O Lord, the maker of all things. . . .
55. Anthem: We praise thee now. . . .
56. The Litany: O God, the Father of heaven. . . .
57. The Lord's Prayer
58. The Lord's Prayer . . . . [Stone]
    Attributed to Stone in Day, *Certaine notes* (1560).
59. Communion: K, G, C, S, A.
60. Post-communion: Christ, our paschal lamb. . . .
61. Communion: K, G, C, S, A.
62. Communion: K, G, C, S, A.
63. Post-communion: Christ, our paschal Lamb . . . [Shepherd]
    Attributed to Shepherd in Brit. Mus. Add. ms. 15166.

64. Anthem: O God, be merciful. . . . . [Taverner]
    According to Peter Le Huray an adaptation of Taverner's *Missa Mater Christi*. In five parts, including two treble parts.
65. [Textless chordal chant, with a fermata at the end of each of five phrases.]
66. Offertory: Let your light so shine before men. . . .

Book III

67. Communion: K, G, C, S, A.
68. Anthem: O Lord of hosts, Thou God of Israel . [Shepherd]
    Attributed to Shepherd in Day, *The Whole Psalms* (1563), and to Tye in some manuscript sources. See Daniel and Le Huray, *Sources*.
69. After the communion received: O almighty God the Father. . . .
70. Anthem: Praise the Lord, O ye servants. . . .
71. Anthem: O God in whose hands. . . .
    A prayer for Edward VI.
72. Venite
73. Te Deum
74. Benedictus
75. The Procession [Litany] : O God, the Father. . . .
    Another medius part is given in the bass partbook resulting in a five-part setting for men.
76. The Lord's Prayer
    Another medius part is given in the bass partbook resulting in a five-part setting for men.
77. Anthem: I have not my hope. . . .
    Another medius part is given in the bass partbook resulting in a five-part setting for men.
78. Communion: K, G, C, Offertory (Lay not up for yourselves . . . .), S, A, Post-communion (If any man will follow me . . . .).
    Another medius part is included in the bass partbook resulting in a five-part setting.
79. Magnificat . . . . [Whitbroke]
    Attributed to Whitbroke in Day, *Certaine notes* (1560), and manuscript sources. See Daniel and Le Huray, *Sources*.
80. Christus resurgens: Christ rising again. . . .
    Christ is risen. . . .

81. For Ash Wednesday: Turn Thou us, good Lord. . . .
    An additional medius part is given in the bass partbook resulting in a five-part setting.
82. Magnificat
83. Nunc dimittis
84. Anthem: Walk while ye have light. . . .
85. Offertory: Do ye not know. . . .
86. Post-communion: If any man will follow me. . . .
87. Anthem: If a man say I love God. . . .
88. Communion: K, G, C, S, A.
    An extra contratenor part is given in the bass partbook resulting in a five-part setting.
89. Communion: G, C, S, A.
    Adapted from Taverner's *Missa Sine Nomine*. Extra contratenor and medius parts produce a six-part setting.
90. Communion: G, C, S, A.
    Adapted from Taverner's *Missa Small Devotion*.
91. Venite
92. Responses to the Ten Commandments.

The scribes of these manuscripts were obviously mature and knowledgeable musicians. The composers represented are the leaders of their generation, and as their identities are gradually discovered (hopefully) the inestimable value of this collection will be confirmed.

Willi Apel

Punto intenso contra remisso

One of the most important sources of Spanish organ music of the 17th century is the *Libro de tientos . . . intitulado Facultad Orgánica* by Correa de Arauxo, which appeared in 1626. First of all, it is important because the compositions contained therein represent a step between those by Peraza and Aguilera from the beginning of the century on the one hand and those by Cabanilles from about 1680 on the other. It is also of great interest because it contains extended explanatory remarks called *advertencias*, in which Correa calls attention to the many *curiosidades* and *cosas nuevas* which the reader is going to find in the publication. One of these curiosities is the *medios registros* which had been introduced by Peraza and which played an important role in the later development of Spanish organ music. This was a device of organ building which consisted in dividing the stops into two independent halves so that the upper and the lower parts of the keyboard could be played with different registrations. It is interesting to notice that present-day organ builders want to introduce this device again. In another *advertencia* Correa deals with *proporciones*, that is, with the use of figurations consisting not of four, eight or sixteen but of five, seven, nine and eleven notes, figurations that actually occur in some of his tientos. In yet another *advertencia* he describes the *falsas y licencias* of which he says that at first they don't seem to be good music but that the benevolent reader will nevertheless admire and enjoy them. *Falsas* are what the Italians at the same time called *durezze e ligature*: pieces in which the composer deliberately exploits the then novel idiom of harmonic dissonance in violation of the rules of 16th-century counterpoint. There exists a number of Italian compositions entitled *Durezze e ligature*, e.g., by Giovanni

Macque, Ercole Pasquini, Giovanni Maria Trabaci, and Girolamo Frescobaldi, as well as Spanish compositions entitled *Tiento de falsas*, e.g., by Aguilera de Heredia (ca. 1600), Pablo Bruna (ca. 1650), and Juan Cabanilles (ca. 1680). The last *advertencia* to which Correa de Arauxo calls the reader's attention also deals with dissonances, but with a very special and unusual one which he calls *una nueva falsa de punto intenso contra remisso.* This designation, which could be translated: a novel dissonance of the raised note against the low note, actually means the simultaneous occurrence of a degree and its chromatic alteration, e.g., of B-flat against B-natural or of C against C-sharp. Correa uses this dissonance in some of his tientos, and in defense of this novel and daring practice names some earlier works in which it occurs: a treatise by Francisco de Montanos; a five-part cancion *Ay me qui voldra* by Nicolas Gombert which "Hernandez de Cabezon has glossed and published in the works of his father;" Gombert's motet *O gloriosa Dei genitrix*; and a three-part *Pleni sunt* by Josquin, the *autor antiguo e grave*, as he calls him. The example from a Mass by Josquin he actually reproduces in that peculiar system of Spanish keyboard notation in which the tones of the diatonic scale from *f* to *e'* are indicated by the numbers 1 to 7. Transcribed into modern notation it is as follows:

Example 1.

In Correa's own compositions there are three passages in which the *punto intenso contra remisso* occurs; they are reproduced below:

Example 2.

A comparison of Josquin's example with those by Correa shows that, although they all involve the clash between a note and its chromatic alteration, there is an important difference. In Josquin's example the *punto intenso* (B-natural) occurs shortly after the *punto remisso* and on a weak beat, a situation that probably also existed in the examples by Gombert, which Correa mentions in order to justify his *falsa nueva*. In Correa's examples, on the other hand, both *punto intenso* and *remisso* enter simultaneously and on a strong beat, thus forming indeed a *falsa nueva*, a new kind of dissonance which neither Josquin nor Gombert would ever have admitted. Needless to say, all the examples are entirely correct from the point of view of contrapuntal voice movement; in fact, they could not be written without the dissonant clash of B-natural and B-flat or of C and C-sharp.

It should be noticed that the effect produced by such passages if played on a modern pianoforte is somewhat misleading because of its well-tempered tuning. What kind of temperament was used in vocal performance of the 16th century—in a motet by Gombert or in a Mass by Josquin—is a question which cannot be answered with certainty. In the case of keyboard instruments, however, there can be hardly any doubt that in the 16th as well as in the 17th century organs and harpsichords were tuned in the mean-tone temperament described by Arnolt Schlick and others. Now, in this temperament the difference between C and C-sharp is only about one-half of what it is in equal temperament, namely, 56 rather than 100 cents. Thus, the two pitches in question were not a half-tone but only a quarter-tone apart from one another. Does this make them more strikingly dissonant or less so?

Instead of dealing with this question, the answer to which is bound to depend to a large extent on personal preference, I should like to raise another question: are Correa's examples of *punto intenso contra remisso* unique or can we find additional examples in other sources? The answer is that many other composers of 16th- and 17th-century keyboard music have written passages involving exactly the same dissonance, that is, the simultaneous sounding of a note and its chromatic alteration. Example 3 shows a small but representative selection, arranged in chronlogical order.

Example 3.

There follow some explanatory remarks about each example.

a. This example, dating from ca. 1520, is by Johannes Kotter, who was born in 1485 in Strassburg, was organist in Freiburg (Switzerland) and Bern, and died in 1541. It is found in a manuscript probably compiled by him and therefore known as the "Kotter Tablature." This manuscript is written in the so-called old German organ tablature notation in which the upper part is notated on a staff while the tones of all the lower parts are represented by letters. In this letter notation chromatic alterations are unequivocally indicated by a loop attached to the letter, which clearly marks them as *cis, fis, dis*, etc. B-natural and B-flat are distinguished as *h* and *b* respectively. This is one of numerous examples in which the dissonant clash of F-sharp against F-natural is caused by the logic of voice movement: the soprano moves upward with the *punto intenso* (*e''-fis''-g''*) while the tenor moves downward with the *punto remisso (g'-f'-e')*.

b. This example (ca. 1520) is by Leonhard Kleber (ca. 1490-1556), born in Göppingen. Like Kotter, he compiled a collection of organ compositions which is known as the "Kleber Tablature" and which employs the same notation as the Kotter Tablature. As in Example 3a, one voice part (here the tenor) moves upward with the *punto intenso (a-h-c')* while another (here the soprano) moves downward with the *punto remisso (c''-b'-a')*.

c. This example is of English origin, being written by Thomas Tallis, who was born ca. 1505. Until about 1537 he was organist at the abbey of the Holy Cross in Waltham, then member and finally organist of the Chapel Royal in London. He died in 1585. Most of his organ compositions are preserved in the so-called Mulliner Book, which was compiled about 1560. Our example dates from the middle of the 16th century. Here the *punto intenso contra remisso* results from the simultaneous occurrence of the leading tone (F-sharp) and the minor seventh (F-natural), the latter forming the turning point of a melodic motion. This kind of seventh is so frequent in English music (especially by William Byrd) that it has been termed "English seventh."

d. This example is of Spanish origin. It is found in a *Pange lingua* by Johannes Urreda (fl. second half of 15th century) which Hernando de Cabezón included in the famous publication containing the works of his father, Antonio de Cabezón (1500-1566): *Obras de musica para tecla arpa y vihuela, de Antonio de Cabeçon,* which appeared in 1578. The musical situation is the same as that in Example 3c, the dissonance resulting from the simultaneous sounding of the leading tone and the "English seventh."

e. This example is by Elias Nicolaus Ammerbach, who was born ca. 1530 in Naumburg and died in 1597 in Leipzig. He was one of the earliest organists at the St. Thomas Church of Leipzig, more than 150 years before Bach. In 1571 he published a book entitled *Orgel oder Instrument Tabulatur*, a second edition of which appeared in 1583. In this publication he employs the so-called new German organ tablature system of notation, which differs from the old German organ tablature system (Examples 3a and 3b) in that letters are used for all the voice parts. The F-sharp in the descending scale, sounding in a dissonant clash against the F-major chord of the lower parts, is somewhat arbitrary but is clearly indicated by the *-is* loop attached to the letter *f'*.

f. This example dates from the end of the 16th century, being taken from a manuscript *Tabulaturbuch auff dem Instrumente* (1591) by Augustus Nörmiger, who was active at the court of Saxony (Dresden). Nörmiger employs the same notation as Ammerbach. Like Ammerbach, he writes an F-sharp against an F-major chord, but in a more logical manner because the *f-sharp"* leads upward to *g"* and also prepares for the F-sharp in the D-major chord of the following measure.

g. With this example we move into the 17th century. It is by the Spanish organ master Sebastian Aguilera de Heredia, who was born about 1565. From 1583 to 1623 he was active as organist at the cathedral of Huesca (Aragonia), then went to Saragossa where he is mentioned in the archives as *Portionarius* and *organis praeceptor*. He is known to us through seventeen organ compositions, most of which are preserved in a manuscript of the El Escorial monastery near Madrid. Our example is found in a composition entitled *Falsas de 6º tono*. As previously explained, *falsa* is the Spanish equivalent of what in Italy was named *durezze e ligature*, i.e., a composition in which the novel idiom of the *stile moderno* with all its daring harmonies and dissonances was deliberately exploited. No wonder that Aguilera's *Falsa* includes an example of the *punto intenso contra remisso*, one, in fact, very similar to those given ten or twenty years later by Correa de Arauxo.

h. This example is by Hieronymus Praetorius, who may be said to stand at the beginning of the grandiose development that organ music was to take in North Germany during the 17th century. He was born in 1560 in Hamburg where, in 1582, he succeeded to the post of organist at St. Jacob's upon the death of his father. He died in that city in 1629. As an organ composer he is known to us through a complete cycle of Magnificats (*primi* to *octavi toni*) which is preserved in the so-called Petri Tablature of 1611. Our example, from the *Magnificat Secundi toni, 2. Versus im Discanto*, shows in the first measure the clash between B-natural and B-flat, in the second that between E-flat and E-natural. It may be noticed that the Petri Tablature is notated in the same system of new German organ tablature employed by Ammerbach (Example 3e) and Nörmiger (Example 3f), in which chromatic alterations are unequivocally indicated by the *-is* loop, E-flat (*es*) being written as D-sharp (*dis*).

i. While many examples of the *punto intenso contra remisso* can be found in Spanish, English, and German sources, they occur rarely and relatively late in Italy. Our example is by Bernardo Storace, who was *vice maestro di cappella* in Messina. In 1664 he published a collection of keyboard compositions entitled *Selva di varie compositioni d'intavolatura per cimbalo ed organo* which, among others, includes several *Passagagli* that, taken together, contain more than 300 variations of the famous theme of the descending tetrachord. Our example shows a measure in which the bass has the *G* required by the ostinato, while the right hand plays *g-sharp'* followed by *a-sharp'* and *b-natural'* instead of *g'-a'-b'*, which would be possible and more natural, but less interesting.

j. This example was written by the North-German organ master Adam Reincken, who was born in 1623 and who, in 1663, became organist at St. Catharine's Church in Hamburg as the successor of Scheidemann. He died in 1722, almost 100 years old. Among his organ compositions is an extended fantasy based on the chorale *Was kann uns kommen an für Not*, from which our example is taken. Here the right hand plays line three of the chorale: / 𝄽 D D D / C A B G / F-sharp with sixteenth-note figurations in the second measure, while the left hand plays a contrapuntal line with a *c-sharp'* sounding simultaneously with the *c'* of the chorale melody.

k. Our last example comes from France, where the *punto intenso contra remisso* is even rarer than in Italy. It is found in a composition by Nicolas de Grigny, who was born in 1672 in Reims. In 1693 he became organist at St. Denis of Paris but a few years later returned to Reims, accepting the position of the organist at the cathedral, a position that he held until his early death in 1703. In 1699 he published a *Premier livre d'orgue* containing an organ Mass, five hymns and, as a conclusion, a *Point d'orgue sur les grands jeux*. The last-named composition is based on an extended pedal point, first on *A*, then on *E*, above which the hands of the organist play a long series of most interesting and unusual formations, among them those shown in our example.

***

In 1936 I published a book entited *Accidentien und Tonalität in den Musikdenkmälern des 15. und 16. Jahrhunderts*[1] in which I took a strong stand against the widespread practice of adding editorial accidentals, maintaining that they often amount to a falsification of old music, to a misinterpretation of its special tonal language which, with the application of editorial accidentals, is wrongly translated into an 18th/19th-century major or minor. During my investigations of the various types of idiomatic usages I happened upon two or three examples which I described as follows: "so kommen wir nun auf jene andere Gruppe von Erscheinungen zu sprechen, bei denen die Diskrepanz zwischen dem harmonischen und dem melodischen Tonbereich sich in viel auffallenderer Weise, nämlich gleichzeitig auswirkt" (p. 35). At that time only a few examples of the "gleichzeitige Auswirkung" (i.e., the simultaneous occurrence of a note and its chromatic variant) were known to me, and I was unaware of the extremely important information provided by Correa de Arauxo. Of course, it is possible to disregard his *advertencia* completely and to eliminate the entire problem of *punto intenso contra remisso* by the addition of editorial accidentals. I am quite certain that as recently as twenty or thirty years ago most editors would have used this radical remedy. However, there are signs of a change of heart and of mind. In the article "Editionstechnik" in *Die Musik in Geschichte und Gegenwart* the question is raised "ob in der ndl. Polyphonie . . . Reibungen wie die übermässige Oktave vorkommen." My answer is that they undoubtedly occur in the vocal music of Dufay, Ockeghem, Obrecht, Josquin and later masters to the same extent as they do in the keyboard music of the 16th and 17th centuries. That does not mean to say that every case of an "übermässige Oktave" should be accepted at its face value. Many cases undoubtedly require emendation, but not all of them. The decision depends, not on the requirements of harmony, but on the logic of voice movements, as it does in all the examples quoted and discussed in the present article.

[1]Strasbourg; reprint ed., enl., Baden-Baden: V. Koerner, 1972.

Chappell White

First-Movement Form in the Violin Concerto from Vivaldi to Viotti

The questions surrounding first-movement form in the solo concerto have centered on its relation to sonata form, viewed as standardized and conventionalized in the symphony, the sonata, and chamber music. As early as 1902, Tovey faced some of the crucial issues squarely, in one of his most famous and valuable essays; but he was dealing with only a handful of pieces from a large repertory, focusing on Mozart with Bach as a predecessor and Beethoven and Brahms as successors. And Tovey's conclusion, that scarcely thirty examples show the form well treated, is hardly one to satisfy the interest of modern historians.[1]

Long after Tovey's perceptive effort, research by William Newman and Leonard Ratner cleared away the basic 19th-century misconceptions, and a number of other scholars, most notably Edwin Simon, took up the question of sonata form directly from the view of the concerto.[2] The recent, laudable tendency to consider

[1]Donald Francis Tovey, *Essays in Musical Analysis*, vol. 3, *Concertos* (London: Oxford University Press, 1936), pp. 3-27.

[2]William Newman, "The Recognition of Sonata Form by Theorists of the 18th and 19th Centuries," *Papers of the American Musicological Society*, Annual Meeting, 1941 (1946):21-29; see also idem, *The Sonata in the Classic Era*, 2nd ed. (New York: W.W. Norton and Co., 1972), pp. 19-42 and 142-58. Leonard Ratner, "Harmonic Aspects of Classic Form," *Journal of the American Musicological Society* 2 (1949):159-68; and "18th-Century Theories of Musical Period Structure," *Musical Quarterly* 41 (1956):439-54. Of special interest to this study are Edwin J. Simon, "The Double Exposition in the Classic Concerto," *Journal of the American Musicological Society* 10 (1957): 111-18; and Jane R. Stevens, "An 18th-Century Description of Concerto First-Movement Form," *Journal of the American Musicological Society* 24 (1971):85-95.

sonata form, not in terms of a rigid design, but in terms of principles, has removed still other obstacles to understanding.

Nevertheless, inconsistency and ambiguity remain. In *Die Musik in Geschichte und Gegenwart*, Hans Engel still speaks in the old manner of "the new bithematic sonata form, which is modified in the concerto."[3] In the entry "Sonata Form," the *Harvard Dictionary of Music* neatly sidesteps the issue of whether concerto movements are or are not in sonata form; but, in "Concerto," it retains, like Engel, the old, conventional approach: "The first movement is written in a modified sonata form in which the exposition . . . is written out twice. . . ."[4] James Webster, in the forthcoming (sixth) edition of *Grove's Dictionary of Music and Musicians*, specifically separates concerto movements from sonata form, a decision that is probably wise; but in discussing the concerto as a "related form," he necessarily makes use of sonata-form terminology.[5] Most introductory books, even those by scholars unquestionably aware of the most recent research, still discuss sonata form as seen in the concerto.

The questions actually hinge not only on the relation of the concerto to other Classical genres but also on the relation of Classical form to the older ritornello form. This essay, while making no pretense of solving all disputes, aims to present a selective survey of the form in one type of concerto through the years of stylistic change and thus to shed some light on how sonata-form principles actually acted on the old, well-established form of the Baroque concerto and what the conventions of form thus became.[6]

The most popular pattern of the ritornello form in which most late Baroque violin concertos are constructed is that established (and probably in large part developed) by Vivaldi.[7] Vivaldi's favorite design involves four ritornelli played by the tutti and three episodes played by the solo. Most commonly, the second ritornello is in the dominant and the third in the relative minor, but one finds considerable variety in key arrangement and even in the number of ritornelli. The lack of a firmly set key design is especially signifi-

[3] S. v. "Konzert."

[4] 2nd ed.

[5] I wish to thank Prof. Webster, Cornell University, for kindly sending me a copy of his article previous to publication.

[6] This essay is based on the study of some 250 violin concertos, not including those of Vivaldi and Viotti. This is, of course, only a small portion of the violin concertos in existence from the period.

[7] For a concise discussion of Vivaldi's ritornello form, see Walter Kolneder, *Antonio Vivaldi: His Life and Works*, trans. Bill Hopkins (Berkeley and Los Angeles: University of California Press, 1970), pp. 54-59.

cant, for it results from the lack of emphasis on any single contrasting key. With the exception of the first tonic statement, all ritornelli may be created equal.

As might be expected, thematic contrast plays little part in the structure. The episodes may repeat the ritornello material, and, with Vivaldi's younger contemporaries, this practice becomes almost standard, in the first episode at least. When the ritornello theme is not repeated in the episode, the new material is continuing rather than dramatically contrasting. Thematic and motivic repetition may be a subtle unifying element in the form, but thematic contrast is almost never an articulating force in the form.

Alternation in medium of performance and in texture, on the other hand, certainly helps define the form; indeed, it may appear as the most important of the articulating forces, since it is the most obvious. But alternation in the texture, even when marked as clearly as it is in most solo violin concertos, is not the most fundamental element of formal articulation. The basic difference between ritornello and episode in the solo concerto is one of character and function.

The ritornelli are compact, thematically decisive, and tonally stable. The episodes are expansive, figurative, and modulating.[8] The additional, obvious contrast of texture and medium re-enforces the essential contrast of character and thus bends a common Baroque method of procedure to the particular nature of the concerto.[9] The role of the ritornello is not merely to introduce and close the solo; it serves as a stable point of reference and a source of energy, a "springboard" from which the episode propels itself and to which it returns for fresh energy. This is the functional relationship that allows Bach to play so effectively with changes in the alternation scheme—to present ritornello material by the tutti within the episodes or to present a solo statement of the ritornello itself—without suggesting to the listener that the fundamental form has been made ambiguous.

Whether one regards the relationship of tutti and solo as combative or cooperative is a moot question, but the relationship is certainly one of mutual dependency. The ritornello controls the form, but neither ritornello nor episode exhibits any degree of structural self-sufficiency.

The most important violinist and composer of violin concertos

[8]Ritornelli that modulate occur occasionally, but the stable character is usually maintained for at least a defining phrase or two, with the modulation occurring quickly at the end of the passage.

[9]Kolneder, among others, has commented on the similarity of ritornello form to episodic fugal form.

in Italy during the middle years of the 18th century was Giuseppe Tartini. The lack of firm chronological information prevents us from tracing his stylistic development with certainty, but it is nevertheless clear, both from internal and external evidence, that the new *galant* style concerned him specifically.[10] He may be regarded, tentatively at least, as the first important composer to come to terms with the new style in the form of the violin concerto. Lesser composers, some of Tartini's pupils among them, adopted the simpler texture and the shorter melodic phrases of the *galant*, but often they found no way to modify the ritornello form and no method of procedure other than by sequence. A concerto by Pasqualino Bini, one of Tartini's favorite pupils, is typical (Figure 1).

Figure 1.

Bini: Concerto [No. 2] in F major (Ms. 95, Paganelli Collection, University of California, Berkeley)[11]

Texture*	T	S	T	S	T	S	T	S	T end of
Material	A	A	A	A	A	B	A	C	A
Key	I	I - V	V	V - vi	vi	vi - I	I	I	I

*T = tutti; S = solo throughout all figures.

The form is completely conventional, but the propulsive flow of Vivaldi's characteristic motives has been lost. Continuous sequential development does not flow logically from Bini's choppy melodies.

Tartini himself faced the situation with more perception, as the two characteristic and easily available concertos in the Smith College series will show.[12] The one in F major (D. 67) is of a type that Dounias finds common in the second period of Tartini's creative career, 1735 to 1750; it represents a combination of the binary form found in dance movements with ritornello form using tutti-solo alternation (Figure 2).

10For a hypothesis of the chronology of Tartini's concertos, see Minos Dounias, *Die Violinkonzerte Giuseppe Tartinis* (1935; reprint ed., Zurich: Moseler Verlag Wolfenbüttel, 1966). Charles Burney mentions Tartini's change of style; see *A General History of Music*, ed. Frank Mercer, 2 vols. (New York: Harcourt, Brace and Co., 1935), 2:446.

11Scored by Jane Troy; my thanks to her and to the librarians of the Music Library of the University of California, Berkeley, for allowing photographs to be made.

12*Smith College Music Archives* no. 9, ed. Gilbert Ross (Northampton, Mass.: Smith College, 1947).

Figure 2.
Tartini: Concerto in F major (D. 67)

Texture	:T	S :	:T	S	T :
					end of
Material	: A	A :	: A	A A	A :
Key	: I(V)I	I-V :	: V(ii)V	V-vi-V-iii-I	I :

The movement contains no contrasting thematic material whatever; even the contrast between decisive ritornello motives and expanding passage-work is to a large extent lacking here. Its place is taken by short phrases and clear cadences, which naturally produce a more sectional type of structure.

The A-minor concerto (D. 115) is one of only thirteen (out of 125) which Dounias places in Tartini's last, longest, and least productive period, 1750-70. The overall form is similar to that of the F-major, the movement lacking only the decisive delineation of the double bar (Figure 3).

Figure 3.

Tartini: Concerto in A minor (D. 115)

Texture	T	S	T	S	T
				end of	end of
Material	A B	A B A B	B	A B	B
Key	i	i - V v	v	III - i	i

The greatest difference between the two is the striking contrast of motives, a contrast both of rhythmic movement and tempo, in the A-minor. But the contrast has nothing to do with tutti vs. solo; it thus introduces into the concerto a principle of contrast that does not involve the characteristic concerto alternation.

Among other Italian violinists of the crucial 1750s and 1760s, when the concerto was declining in the face of increasing popularity of the symphony, none appears to be in a more important position than Gaetano Pugnani (1731-98) in Turin. He was the teacher of both Borghi and Viotti, and he traveled widely enough to have come in contact with all styles. Unfortunately, only one of his violin concertos survives, and it appears to be an early work, dating, according to Elsa Zschinsky-Troxler, from about 1754.[13] Cast in a three-ritornello form, it emphasizes an almost ternary structure by the use of a *da capo* back to the first tutti (Figure 4).

[13] *Gaetano Pugnani, 1731-1798* (Berlin: Atlantis-Verlag, 1939), p. 169.

Figure 4.

Pugnani: Concerto in E-flat (Ms. Litt. T, No. 12.220, Bibliothèque du Conservatoire Royal de Musique, Brussels)

Texture	T	S	T end of	S	*da capo* of first tutti
Material	A	A	A	A	
Key	I	I - V	V	V - vi	

The form reflects the new style in its clearly marked sections and its decisive, limited modulations, which significantly place paramount emphasis on the dominant. The movement is monothematic, however.

A more decisive advance into early Classical style and form is shown in the concertos of Felice Giardini (1716-96), another Turinese violinist, who published six concertos in London about 1770 or possibly the late 1760s.[14] The ritornello still clearly controls the form with its three statements of the main theme (Figure 5).

Figure 5.

Giardini: Concerto in B-flat, Op. 15, No. 1 (London: Welcker)

Texture	T	S	T	S	T	S	T end of
Material	A B A	A C	A	D	A	E	A
Key	I VI	I V	V	V-iii-vi-I	I	I	I

The solo, however, presents new melodic material at two of its three entrances, and the principle of thematic contrast enters the first tutti as well. Despite some brilliance in the solo passage-work, tutti-solo contrast here is not so much a matter of style and function as it is a matter of thematic difference. To modern ears, the form seems as close to a modulating rondo as to the old ritornello.

A somewhat similar structure but with less control given to the tutti and with more thematic repetition is seen in a representative concerto by Maddalena Lombardini Sirmen, one of Tartini's most brilliant students and the recipient of the famous letter that was published by Burney. Sirmen's six concertos published as Opus 3

[14]The six concertos, issued as Opus 15, are catalogued in the Breitkopf Supplement of 1774 (see *The Breitkopf Thematic Catalogue*, ed. Barry S. Brook [New York: Dover Publications, 1966], p. 537), but it is likely that they appeared earlier, probably in connection with Giardini's return to performance and teaching in 1766.

in London in 1769 reflect much of the simplicity of late Tartini, and the tendency toward binary form is clearer than in Giardini (Figure 6).

Figure 6.

Sirmen: Concerto in B-flat, Op. 3, No. 1 (London: William Napier)

Texture	T			S		T		S				T
Material	A	B	C	A	D	A	C	A	A	D	C	C
Key	I	V	I	I	V	V	V	V-vi	I	I		I

The simplicity is a limiting factor, however, and it had evidently progressed too far for many of the younger virtuosi to imitate. This type of almost pure binary movement, although not limited geographically, is encountered only occasionally.

Insofar as they have been investigated, the violin concertos of Johann Stamitz show a stylistic and formal conservatism compared with his symphonies and chamber music. A concerto attributed to Stamitz's pupil and successor Christian Cannabich presents a rather different picture. The ms. in Paris in which the concerto is preserved carries no date, but the style of the work seems to place it early in Cannabich's long career (if it is, indeed, by Cannabich). It is clearly based on Vivaldi's four-ritornello design; but there are two distinct themes, the second more lyrical than the first, in the opening tutti, and both are repeated in the solo (Figure 7).

Figure 7.

Cannabich: Concerto in D major (Ms. 2.2736, Bibliothèque du Conservatoire, Paris)

Texture	T			S			T	S	T	S			T
Material	A	B	k	A	B	k	Ak	A	A	--	B	k	k
Key	I			I	V		V	V - vi	vi	I	I		I

In addition, another figure (indicated by "k" in Figure 7), less melodic but still distinct, closes three of the four tutti passages and two of the three solos. These distinctions represent examples in the violin concerto of the tendency toward association of thematic character with structural function which plays such an important role in the articulation of Classical form.

In France, the six concertos of Gaviniés were the first French works (or at least the first in print) in this form since Leclair. Gaviniés used the four-tutti structure, with less thematic repetition than is found in the concertos of the Tartini school (Figure 8).

Figure 8.

Gaviniés: Concerto in D major, Op. 4, No. 3 (Paris: Sieber)

Texture	T	S	T	S	T	S	T
			end of		motives from		end of
Material	A	A'B	A	A'	A	C	A
Key	I-V-I	I V	V	V-v-ii	vi	vi-I	I

A tendency toward binary form results from the emphasis on the dominant, but the design is less clearly delineated than it is in Tartini or even Sirmen, and thematic contrasts, which occur only in the solo, are not so decisive. The situation at the return of the tonic key is of some significance: there is only new passagework at this point, without any thematic emphasis, much less thematic repetition.

The decline of the concerto vis-à-vis the symphony is quite evident among Austrian composers; indeed, the relatively small number of Austrian examples is one of the difficulties faced in tracing the development.[15] Even composers who were noted violinists were likely to be more productive in other areas. A typical example, undated but probably from the 1760s or early 1770s, comes from Vanhal, a Bohemian violinist resident in Vienna and composer of more than a hundred symphonies. The movement almost matches the simplicity of Lombardini Sirmen, and its design is similar. Vanhal spent time in Italy, and in any case Tartini's influence was wide (Figure 9).

Figure 9.

Vanhal: Concerto in A major (Ms. T. 5845, Bibliothèque du Conservatoire Royal de Musique, Brussels)

Texture	T	S	T	S	T	S	T
Material	A B C	A B	A B	A	--	A B	-
Key	I V I	I V	V(I)V	V		I	I

A more sophisticated state of the violin concerto in Austria in the 1760s may be seen in Haydn's three examples, despite some survivals of Baroque style. The concertos in C (Hob. VIIa: 1) and in G (Hob. VIIa: 4) were listed in the Breitkopf Supplement for 1769, but they probably date from a few years earlier. In the

[15] See Herbert Neurath, "Das Violinkonzert in der Wiener klassischen Schule," *Studien zur Musikwissenschaft* 14 (1927):125 ff.

C-major, the first of the four tutti sections has three distinct tonal areas, like the first tutti plan in Giardini and Gaviniés; and there is a clear, if subordinate, motive for each area (Figure 10).

Figure 10.

Haydn: Concerto in C major, Hob. VIIa:1

Texture	T	S	T	S	T	S	T
Material	A B C	A D	-- B C	A B B	--	A	B C
Key	I V I	I V	V	V ii iv-vi	- V	I	I

The second tutti, entering on the cadence of the first solo with material only vaguely related to the ritornello, moves quickly to the last portion of the first tutti. The third tutti is short and prepares the final tonic return, while the fourth again repeats the last portion of the opening. The solos tend toward a completeness of design that only the first of the tutti sections approaches. The second theme in the first solo is clearly contrasting, and the dominant extension that follows is relatively long. It is the second solo —not the second tutti—that restates the opening motive as if beginning the second part of binary form, and it is the third solo that re-establishes the tonic.

Overall, the movement may be considered a longer and thematically richer version of Tartini's "rounded binary" concerto form, with the roles of the tutti and solo changed somewhat. Since the second tutti does not repeat the opening theme, the tutti thus loses the role of stressing the most important thematic material and assumes at that point the role of providing a closing section for the first solo. The third tutti also sounds, not like a ritornello (that is, not like a point of arrival and a springboard for expansion) but like a closing section of the preceding unstable tonal area and a preparation for the following solo—in short, like the preparation for a recapitulation. The emphasis is on the final return in the solo.

This movement is not especially unusual for the 1760s. Both Michael Haydn and Carl Ditters von Dittersdorf have similar concerto movements perhaps as early; and the two Italian concertos close to this time included here are related, if somewhat smaller, forms. What the movement represents relative to others in this survey up to this point is the clearest composite form, an incorporation into the older ritornello form of features characteristic of sonata-form principles: thematic contrast, stable tonal areas, decisive repetition at the return of the final tonic section, and the articulation of structure by thematic repetition. It is of some significance that Haydn has handled these elements so as to place more emphasis on the solo and less on the tutti.

Haydn's G-major concerto (Hob. VIIa: 4) has a very similar design, except that the second and third tutti sections present the opening theme once more. Because themes are an important means of defining form in the Classical style, such repetitions appear to increase the formal importance of the tutti sections and thus to relate the form more closely to the older ritornello form. The presence of such a formal difference in two Haydn concertos of approximately the same period simply indicates that the development of the form does not follow a straight, logical road to a predetermined end. Even in a composer as perceptive to formal questions and as generally progressive as Haydn, we may find the choice falling at times on a procedure that is backward-looking. Progress does not come through inevitable, step-by-step discovery but by a process of selection. The selection is individual; only gradually, and to a limited extent, does one convention become generally prevalent.

Nevertheless, over the years and through numerous places the process of selection often follows a general direction; and, although it never stops, it reaches a point at which certain elements are more often than not controlled by convention. Such a point was rapidly reached in first-movement concerto form in Paris in the 1770s.

Figure 11 shows four different concertos by composers of three different nationalities; all four concertos appeared in Paris in the 1770s. The supply of concertos at this historical stage is much larger and more accessible than previously, not only because of an upsurge in the creation of solo concertos but also because of the numerous Parisian publications. Chronology, although still a problem, can be approximated more easily through the dating of prints (see Figure 11, following page).

The type shown in Figure 11 is not exclusively Parisian—it is, obviously, similar to the Haydn example—but there is little doubt that the form crystallized in Paris. In addition, the form seems more decisively controlled by the themes and less by the alternation. The basic outline includes these elements:

First, an initial tutti that contains contrasting themes—at least two, sometimes three. One of these themes is often in the dominant (there is no use talking about the relative major; violin concertos in the minor are virtually unheard of in the 1760s, 1770s, and early 1780s, up to Viotti's Concerto No. 14 in A minor, ca. 1788).

Second, a long solo, also featuring contrasting themes and this time contrasting key as well (always). The number of themes is not usually less than two but otherwise is not a matter of strict convention, nor is the thematic relation to

Figure 11.

St.-Georges: Concerto in G major, Op. 2, No. 1 (Paris: Bailleux)

Texture	T	S	T	S	T	S	T
Material	A B	A B	--	C D		A B	D end of B
Key	I (V) I	I V	V	V - vi	V	I	I

Simon Le Duc: Concerto in C major, Op. posth., No. 2 (Paris: Le Duc le jeune)

Texture	T	S	T	S	T
Material	A B	A C	A	D E B	A
Key	I	I V	V	V - vi i I	I

Borghi: Concerto in E-flat, Op. 2, No. 2 (Berlin: Hummel)

Texture	T	S	T	S	T	S	T
Material	A B C	A' D B	--	E (B)	-- C	A B	--
Key	I V I	I V	V	V vi	vi-I	I	I

A. Stamitz: Concerto in A major, No. 4 (Vienna: Durieu)

Texture	T	S	T	S	T	S	T
Material	A B C	A D	--	E F	G	D	end of C
Key	I V I	I V	V	V vi	vi	I	I

the opening tutti, except that the first theme is the same, varied according to the needs of the virtuoso.

Third, a second tutti entering on the cadence of the first solo. Its material usually comes from the first tutti, but the practicc of bringing back the first theme (as in the Giardini and Haydn's G-major) is fading. By the late 1770s it is definitely old-fashioned.

Fourth, a second solo, beginning in the dominant (occasionally, the relative minor) and moving to a slightly more distant key, usually in a contrasting mode—the relative minor or the relative of the dominant. The nature of the thematic material in the second solo is one matter on which convention had not settled. Often there are two new themes, one for each key area; only occasionally is a theme from the earlier sections of the movement used.

Fifth, the final solo. It is much less conventionalized than the first solo; with the exception of the tonic key, nothing seems quite settled.

Sixth, the final tutti. It usually relates closely to the second tutti; use of the opening theme is even rarer than in the second tutti.

Sometimes there is another element, a tutti between the second solo and the final tonic solo, thus preserving the remnant of Vivaldi's four-tutti plan. But this is by no means an essential element. When it is present, it may serve as a closing section, cadencing in the tonic; it may re-establish the tonic with the opening theme; or it may accomplish both of these things.

We may now attempt to understand how this form relates to the sonata-form principles and what remains of the ritornello form. First of all, there are two sections that bear at least some resemblance to the sonata-form exposition. The second of these, featuring the solo, unquestionably qualifies as an exposition in every respect. The first, the opening tutti, reflects the characteristic principle of thematic contrast and in many examples presents contrast of tonality as well. Tovey made a great point of the fact that Mozart did not modulate in the (so-called) first exposition, and this feature has usually been accepted as characteristic of the Classical concerto. With the violinists, however, the modulation takes place in considerably more than half of all examples (to estimate conservatively).[16] What distinguishes the first tutti from a true exposition is the return to the tonic. This effectively closes the section, and it also effectively renders it an introduction. The first tutti sets the stage for the solo but does not, as in the case of the old ritornello, seem to be an essential point of departure for it. If the return to the tonic renders the term "first exposition" inaccurate, it would seem that the similarities of design, as well as differences from the old ritornello, would make "introductory exposition" an acceptable compromise.

An indication of the introductory character of the first tutti may be seen in the procedure adopted by Giornovichi, one of the most significant violinists of his generation, when he arranged a concerto as a keyboard sonata. The first tutti is simply eliminated, and the form of the sonata works perfectly well without it.[17] The solo is no longer dependent on the tutti.

[16]All of Giornovichi's seventeen surviving concertos and twenty-seven of Viotti's twenty-nine concertos contain the modulation in the first tutti.

[17]The concerto, No. 10 in F major, was first published by Hummel about 1782; the sonata appeared in the 1790s as the first of "Two Violin Concertos composed and arranged . . . for the pianoforte with a violin accompaniment by Mr. Giornovichi . . . . Printed for the author . . . by Longman & Broderip, London." For a detailed account of the opposite procedure at an earlier date, see Edwin J. Simon, "Sonata into Concerto, a Study of Mozart's First Seven Concertos," *Acta Musicologica* 31 (1959):170-85.

As to the historical element, it is important to confirm that no relation whatsoever has been revealed between this introductory exposition and the repeat of the first section in binary form. Indeed, the presence of both the initial tutti and the repeat sign in Tartini's concertos seems specific evidence against such a derivation.

The second tutti, like the first, has no exact parallel in the sonata-form structure, and its source also is obviously the old ritornello. But it functions as a closing section. Together, the first and second tutti sections act as a frame for the essential, self-contained solo. If the composer should choose to restate the principal theme in the second tutti, then, because of the importance of themes in articulating structure in this style, the section begins to achieve the importance of the old ritornello; this is the reason the practice is abandoned. Sonata-form principles call for a closing section at this point, not for a climactic structural repetition.

The second solo occupies the position and performs a parallel function to the development section, although it almost never assumes a really developmental character in the symphonic sense. That it may on occasion begin with the opening theme, as in Tartini's binary design, is an indication that the binary aspect of sonata form has its influence in the concerto; that it usually does not begin with the opening material but with a new melody is an indication that the thematic limitation of Baroque binary form has given way, as in other genres, before the appetite of the new style for fresh melodies. That the section is usually made up entirely of new material emphasizes this point and suggests further that perhaps the direct influence of the symphony on the concerto form is less pervasive than analysts have thought who have concentrated on the piano concertos of Mozart. The violin concerto writers, focusing more on the cleverness of the performer than the cleverness of the composer, capitalize on freshness and variety of melody rather than conciseness or learnedness; they create, therefore, a somewhat looser form—but one based on the same principles.

Whatever else one wants to say of sonata form in relation to binary and ternary structures, it is certain that some kind of recapitulation—a "double return," to use James Webster's term, of theme and key—is one element that distinguishes sonata form from its ancestors and helps define its dramatic nature. It is exactly at this point of return that the violin concerto previous to Viotti exhibits the most variety, the point at which conventional principles seem least firmly established. In more than half of the seventeen concertos of Giornovichi, for example (some perhaps written as late as 1795), the tonic key is firmly re-established well before the restatement of the opening theme, thus losing the climactic effect of the coincidence of theme and tonality. Both of the

Stamitz sons, Karl and Anton, usually omit the opening theme altogether in the recapitulation and restate only the less decisive second theme. Sometimes, as in a Neapolitan concerto by the otherwise unidentified Filipo Colle, of value primarily because it is dated 1779, there is no reference to old material in the final tonic section, a procedure recalling Gaviniés in the mid-1760s. Even in the concertos of Viotti himself, whose pre-eminence among violin composers is as clear today as it was to his contemporaries, the first five examples (published between 1781 and 1783) show some variation at this point. Thereafter, Viotti reflects an increased perception of the structural importance of the recapitulation. From his sixth concerto on, there is never any doubt as to where that point is; it is always emphasized by both tonal return and decisive restatement of the memorable opening thematic material. There is evidence also that Viotti begins thinking in terms of recapitulating previous material, for he develops an individual formula: he recapitulates the opening theme and then follows it, still in the tonic key, with the passage-work that originally came after the second theme. He thus achieves a recapitulation of the most important theme and a transposition of the dominant-key passage-work, while accomplishing considerable saving in time.

It is thus well into the 1780s before this final principle of sonata form becomes the usual convention in the violin concerto. The relatively late date may have resulted, in part, from the small attention paid to violin concertos by the greatest of composers. As we have seen, Haydn's violin concertos are very close to the fully developed form, despite occasional backward-looking details, but Haydn gave the genre scant attention. Mozart's five examples, which I have purposely and perhaps willfully omitted up to now, actually present the first-movement form in a state that the conventions did not reach for another decade. But Mozart also stopped writing violin concertos, and those he wrote were not widely circulated. While we are left with precious examples of the art and still more illustrations of Mozart's superb understanding of formal needs, his violin concertos are scarcely typical and are probably of limited influence.

But the difference in the development of first-movement form in the violin concerto and the development of that form in other genres also resulted from historical reasons. The symphony has its roots in Italian opera, intertwined with the deepest roots of the early Classical style. The keyboard sonata was a rarity before the advent of the *galant* style, and its development is closely associated with the popularity of that style. As for chamber music, it cannot even exist in the Classical sense until the Baroque practice of basso continuo is no longer obligatory. The violin concerto was part of the old era. It thus provides us with an example of the old form transformed by the new style; that the form differs in some ways from the form developed simultaneously in newer genres is hardly surprising.

It is important, however, to recognize not only the differences but the similarities of form and to preserve at least those essential parts of terminology that give us the basis for comparisons and which reflect the essential unity of Classical formal principles. The development of first-movement form in the violin concerto provides striking evidence of the strength of sonata-form principles as these gradually transformed the old structure and finally relegated the ritornello itself, the very basis of the old design, to a different and much less fundamental function.

Erwin R. Jacobi

Giuseppe Tartini's *Regola per bene accordare il Violino*

The translation of Tartini's treatise which follows has been made from ms. IX-33956 of the library of the Gesellschaft der Musikfreunde in Vienna.

Rule for Tuning the Violin

The most important string of the violin is the G string. Therefore, to tune the violin one begins with the G, afterwards tuning the other strings in fifths from the G. The D is tuned with the G, as the G has precedence over the D; the A is tuned with the D, as the D has precedence over the A; finally, the E is tuned with the A, as the A has precedence over the E. This is how the violin should be tuned.

The foregoing rule applies only to solo playing and is of no use for orchestral playing. If the G string were tuned first, it would be impossible to tune accurately because the copper-wound G string is not true. It therefore cannot be tuned in unison with any other instrument, as it does not produce a pure note. For orchestral playing the D string should be tuned first by being brought into unison with the D of the organ or harpsichord. Once the D string is in tune, the G is tuned a fifth below it, after which the A and E are tuned. Many violinists tune the A first, but this method is bad for two reasons: if one tunes the upper strings first, the notes cannot be heard clearly. Secondly, one cannot begin with the upper strings because the bass notes, which are the more important, must be tuned first. Anyone aiming at greater distinction as a violinist will bear in mind that the violin scale begins in the bass, not in the treble. If one begins with the lower strings, any doubts about the correctness of the views expressed above will disappear.

To tune the violin with the greatest precision, one should listen for the consonance an octave below the note of the lower string .

For correct intonation of any note, it must be tuned with one of the four open strings, which can be relied on.

Reliable strings: 

Once the violin is tuned, we have four reliable strings for intonation purposes, namely, the four open strings.

To tune perfectly any note which is not an open string, we must tune it with one of the four open strings. For this purpose we choose the one that is nearest and most convenient.

This dyad should be one of the following intervals, using the nearest and most convenient open string: octave, unison, major or minor third, major or minor sixth, or fourth.

If, however, there is no open string available giving any of the above intervals, a reliable stopped note must first be found which has been tested against an open string. This stopped note is then combined with the note it is desired to tune. The following examples will make this clear.

Intonation Table

The note G  is perfectly tuned, being, of course, an open string. There is no doubt about its intonation, as it is an open string and, hence, reliable.

The D  is also an open string, but it will only be in tune if it has first been accurately tuned a fifth above the open string  .

Similarly, the A  , also an open string, will only be correct if it has been tuned a fifth above the open D string  .

The E  , again an open string, will only be correct if it has been tuned a fifth above the open A string  .

For perfect intonation of the A 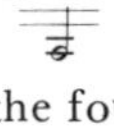 , which is not an open string, it must first be tuned with one of the four reliable open strings. Of the four open strings the nearest is the D  . We therefore combine this with the A to give the interval of a fourth  , thus tuning the A  . This is the most convenient dyad, but it is possible to tune the note in other ways in order to master the basic technique on the violin. This is very necessary for those who aspire to be really good players. Thus, to tune the A by various methods, we proceed as shown in the following examples:

It can be tuned a fifth below E on the D string  . To relate it to an open string, the E must first be tuned a fourth below the open A string . The E is then combined with A on the G string, giving the dyad , so that the A is perfectly in tune.

It can be tuned a minor sixth below F on the D string . To relate it to an open string, the F must first be tuned a major third below the open A string . When the F is in tune, it is combined with A on the G string, giving the dyad , so that the A is in tune.

It can also be tuned as a major sixth . The F-sharp is first tuned as a minor third , then we combine with , giving the dyad . The A is thus in tune.

Again, it may be tuned an octave below A on the D string . But, since this note is not an open string, it must first be brought into unison with the open A string: . We then combine and , giving the dyad , so that the A is perfectly in tune.

For perfect intonation of the B , which is certainly not an open string, we can tune it with the open D string, giving a minor third ; it is at once perfectly tuned. Various other ways of tuning it are shown by the following examples.

It can be tuned a fourth below E on the D string . To relate it to an open string, the E must first be tuned a fourth below the open A string . The E is then combined with B on the G string, giving the dyad , so that the B is perfectly in tune.

It can also be tuned a fifth below F-sharp on the D string . To relate it to an open string, we first tune the F-sharp a minor third below the open A string . The F-sharp and the B are then combined, giving the dyad , so that the B is perfectly in tune.

It can be tuned a minor sixth below G on the D string . To relate it to an open string, we first tune the G an octave above the open G string . The G and the B are then combined, giving the dyad , so that the B is perfectly in tune.

For perfect intonation of the C , which is not an open string, we can tune it with E on the D string, giving a major third . To relate it to the nearest convenient open string, we first tune the E a major sixth above the open G string 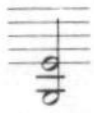 and then combine the E and the C , so that the C  is perfectly in tune.

It can also be done by the method just described, but with the E on the D string tuned a fourth below the open A string . We then combine the E with the C on the G string , so that the C  is perfectly in tune.

It can be tuned a fourth below F on the D string . To relate it to an open string, we first tune the F a major third below the open A string . We then combine the F and the C , so that the C  is in tune.

It can be tuned a fifth below G on the D string . To relate it to an open string, we first tune the G an octave above the open G string . The G and the C are then combined , so that the C  is in tune.*

For perfect intonation of the E , which is certainly not an open string, it may be tuned with an adjacent open string, namely, the A, giving the interval of a fourth ; it is at once perfectly tuned. Alternative methods are as follows:

It can be tuned a fifth below B on the A string . To relate it to an open string, we first tune the B a fourth below the open E string . The B is then combined with E on the D string, giving the dyad , so that the E  is perfectly in tune.

It can also be tuned a minor sixth below C on the A string . To relate it to an open string, we first tune the C with the open E string, giving a major third . The C is then combined with E on the D string, giving the dyad , so that the E  is in tune.

It can be tuned an octave below E on the A string . To relate it to an open string, the E must first be brought into unison with the

*In the original Italian text there is the following remark beginning at the foot of the page and continuing at the foot of the next page: "There are also other possible ways of tuning this C."

open E string. Then by playing the dyad  , the E  is tuned.

For perfect intonation of the F  , which is not an open string, it may be tuned with an adjacent open string, namely, the A, giving a major third  . Thus, it is immediately tuned. Alternative methods are described below.

It can be tuned an augmented fourth below B on the A string  . To relate it to an open string, we first tune the B with the open D string  , giving a major sixth  . The B is then combined with F on the D string, giving the dyad  , so that the F  is perfectly in tune.

It can also be tuned a fifth below C on the A string  . To relate it to an open string, we first tune the C a major third below the open E string  . The C is then combined with F on the D string, giving the dyad  , so that the F  is perfectly in tune.

It can be tuned a major sixth below D on the A string  . To relate it to an open string, we first tune the D on the A string an octave above the open D string  . The D is then combined with the F  , so that the F  is perfectly in tune.

Postface[1]

Tartini's *Regola* has hitherto never been published and is therefore largely unknown. The only available source consists of a contemporary copy of it which is to be found in the library of the Gesellschaft der Musikfreunde in Vienna and which was originally part of the collection of Count Viktor von Wimpffen (1834-97). The hand in which the manuscript is written is unknown. However, on the left-hand side near the title on the first page there is the note "Aut. Originale Tartini." This note is in the hand of Giulio Meneghini, Tartini's pupil and successor in the office of concertmaster of the Cappella del Santo in Padua, as the Tartini scholar and biographer Pierluigi Petrobelli has ascertained (see his letter to

[1]Translated from the German by David A. Scrase.

the administration of the archives of the Gesellschaft der Musikfreunde in Vienna of November 22, 1962). In spite of Meneghini's note, this is not one of Tartini's original manuscripts, as paleographic tests have shown—even though there is a certain resemblance between Tartini's hand and that of the author of the manuscript. It was this fact that led Paul Brainard to question Tartini's authorship in his article on Tartini in *Die Musik in Geschichte und Gegenwart*. (Brainard is probably the first and, up till now, the only person to have referred to the *Regola*. This he did in his doctoral dissertation entitled "Die Violin-Sonaten Giuseppe Tartinis," [University of Göttingen, 1959], p. 218.) But, since the contents of this manuscript are nonetheless described as deriving from Tartini, it may be assumed that this *Regola*, even if it is not actually his own, does indeed come from someone close to Tartini and expresses the composer's own personal theory. For this reason alone its publication would seem to be justified. But the fact that very little is now generally known about the tuning of the violin in the 18th century—although it was considerably more refined than our own standardized method and varied remarkably from it (this will doubtless come as a surprise to many people)—is an additional reason why it should be published.

The Viennese manuscript consists of four sheets with eight pages of music paper filled with writing. Each page contains ten printed staves and measures 30.5 x 23 centimeters. The text, written in the same hand throughout, is usually to be found over the staves but to some extent also between the two bottom-most lines. While the music examples on the first six pages are given in half notes, on the last two pages they appear as quarter notes without any reason for the change being apparent. It is possible that these last two pages were written at a different time from the first six. The writer may well have come from Venetia, since there are numerous Venetian dialect forms in the text.

The following is intended to be a summary of the most important contemporary theoretical and reference works which contain information concerning the tuning of the violin. This account does not, however, lay any claim to completeness. The sources noted are intended only to show how seriously the question of correct violin tuning was taken in the Baroque age as compared to today.

There are tuning methods dating from as early as the 17th century which deviate from today's practice. Accordingly, we find Michael Praetorius writing at the end of the sixth chapter in Volume III of his *Syntagma musicum* (Wolfenbüttel, 1619) that violinists generally tune their instruments from *g*, proceeding to *d'*, thence to *a'* and finally going up to *e''*.[2] Marin Mersenne, in Volume III of his *Harmonie universelle contenant la théorie et la pratique de la musique* (Paris, 1636), "Proposition II" of Book 4, entitled "Des instruments à chordes," likewise starts from *g*.[3] We may therefore consider this starting point (rather than today's *a'*) in violin tuning to have been a kind of norm from about 100 years before the time of Tartini. This clearly demonstrates that tuning from *g* was not an innovation on the part of Tartini. It is, perhaps, interesting to note in this connection that Jean Rousseau, in his *Traité de la viole* (Paris, 1687), in Chapter 4 of Part I ("La manière d'accorder la viole"), distinguishes expressly between two different ways of tuning the viola da gamba: if the gamba player does not have to conform to other instruments, he should begin with the C string (in the middle of the seven-stringed French gamba). If, however, he is playing in concert with other instruments and has to conform with them, he should normally (according to Rousseau) begin with the A string (the second from the top).

Of prime interest among the works of the 18th century is Johann Gottfried Walther's *Musicalisches Lexikon* (Leipzig, 1732), in which we can read under the entry "Violino" that the four strings of the violin are tuned from high to low, i.e., from *e''* to *a'*, then to *d'* and from there to *g*. In paragraphs 17, 21 and 22 of Chapter 26 in Part III of his *Vollkommener Capellmeister* (Hamburg, 1739), Johann Mattheson talks in no uncertain terms and at length about the importance of correct tuning technique for the orchestral violinist. He gives only one method, namely, starting from the G string and going from *g* to *d'*, from there to *a'* and finally to *e''*. Here Mattheson lists three points to be considered before beginning a musical performance, namely: "the number and choice of persons, singers, instrumentalists and instruments; the perfect tuning of the latter; and the rehearsals."[4]

In his treatise *The Modern Musick-Master or, the Universal Musician* (which appeared anonymously in London in 1731), Peter Prelleur demands that the violin be tuned in pure fifths from *g* up or, if this should prove to be impossible for the player (a beginner), from *e''* down with the aid in each case of the fourth finger on the

[2]P. 151 in the facsimile edition, ed. Willibald Gurlitt (Kassel: Bärenreiter-Verlag, 1958).

[3]P. 181 in the facsimile edition, ed. François Lesure (Paris: Centre national de la recherche scientifique, 1963).

[4]Pp. 482-83 in the facsimile edition, ed. Margarete Reimann (Kassel: Bärenreiter-Verlag, 1954).

lower string, after one has previously drawn a line across the precise place on the finger-board. Francesco Geminiani gives exactly the same direction in his *Compleat Instructions for the Violin* (p. 2), which appeared in London about a decade later.

Johann Joachim Quantz, in Chapter 17, section 7, paragraph 4 of his *Versuch einer Anweisung die Flöte traversiere zu spielen* (Berlin, 1752),[5] recommends for perfection in violin tuning the procedure "which has to be observed in the tuning of the keyboard instrument," that is to say, one should not tune in pure fifths (as was usual, according to Quantz), but the fifths should be somewhat diminished so that they correspond to those of the keyboard instrument. Otherwise, only *one* of the four strings would be in tune with the keyboard instrument. According to Quantz, one should, after tuning the A string in pure unison with the keyboard instrument, tune *e"* diminished a little to *a'*; *d'* should be raised a little to *a'*, and, likewise, *g* to *d'*. Quantz did not put forward this opinion to establish a rule, however, but, as he himself stressed, simply to provoke further thought. His recommendation applies to the accompanying instrumentalists in the orchestra. In Chapter 12, paragraph 6 of his *Versuch einer gründlichen Violin-Schule* (Augsburg, 1756),[6] Leopold Mozart writes that some players tune the A string first whereas others tune the D string first; he recognizes both methods as equally justified. In the same section he goes on to say that the violinist, when performing with the organ or the harpsichord, must adjust to the tuning of the keyboard instrument, which probably means with regard to all *four* strings and not just one. In the same way the violinist should tune according to the wind instruments if no keyboard instrument is available. These rules apply to orchestral players.

Even as late as 1790 we find Johann Georg Albrechtsberger writing in his *Gründliche Anweisung zur Composition* (Leipzig, 1790) that the violin is tuned "by means of three pure fifths, even though it should not perhaps be tuned quite to perfection on account of the unequal temperament of the organs and percussion instruments . . ." (p. 419).

Other contemporary quotations concerning violin tuning technique can be found in Aristide Wirsta's "Écoles de violon au XVIIIme siècle d'après les ouvrages didactiques,"[7] which is

[5]English translation by Edward R. Reilly, *On Playing the Flute* (London: Faber & Faber, 1966).

[6]English translation by Editha Knocker, *A Treatise on the Fundamental Principles of Violin Playing* (London: Oxford University Press, 1948; 2d ed., 1951).

[7]Thèse de Doctorat, University of Paris, 1955.

arranged according to the various national schools (France, Italy, Germany, England, and Russia). See also the same author's "L'Enseignement du violon au XIXème siècle,"[8] where the same arrangement by national schools has been adhered to. Neither work has until now appeared in print.

Finally, attention should be drawn to the sentence just prior to the first music example. This sentence gives in an accurate form the well-known *Terzo suono* (resultant tone), as opposed to the erroneous definition in Tartini's famous *Trattato di musica seconda la vera scienza dell'armonia* (Padua, 1754), where, on page 14, one can read: "Data la sesquialtera, o sia praticamente quinta, risulta il terzo suono *unisono* [my italics] alla nota grava della quinta. E il più difficile a distinguersi di tutti, perchè unisono; una si distingue abbastanza. 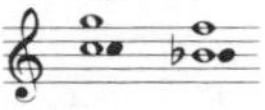 " In his later theoretical work *De' Principj dell'Armonia Musicale contenuta nel Diatonico Genere* (Padua, 1767), Tartini defines *Terzo suono* of the fifth correctly when he writes (p. 5): ". . . La forma della sesquialtera, o sia quinta è 2, 3. Moltiplicato 2 per 3, il prodotto 6 è il terzo suono, che risulta sudduplo al dato suono 3. . . ." By comparing these quotations from the two most important theoretical works by Tartini, we can conclude that the *Regola* was written, in all probability, between 1754 and 1767.

[8]Thèse pour le doctorat ès-lettres, University of Paris, 1971.

Richard D. Leppert

Johann Georg Plazer: Music and Visual Allegory

Johann Georg Plazer (1704-61) was an Austrian painter from the Tyrol active in Vienna from 1728 until sometime after the middle of the century.[1] His work is interesting to music historians because he often depicted musical events. Indeed, chamber music concerts and dance scenes involving persons of the upper middle class and nobility abound in his pictures. Moreover, he was a popular painter with the Viennese nobility, who as a class were certainly among the most ardent, musically minded *amateurs* in Europe. (The art patron and diplomat Albrecht von Sebisch bought no fewer than fourteen of his pictures within two years of Plazer's arrival in the city.) Accordingly, one might expect that Plazer's musical pictures

[1]Plazer's education in art is only sketchily known. His first training came through his stepfather and then his uncle, Johann Christoph Plazer, painter to the Elector's court at Passau. Once in Vienna he studied at the Akademie. Plazer's style is eclectic to an extreme. His love of *objets* is in keeping with the German tradition of the eighteenth century, but the roots of his assemblages of objects go back to the Dutch and Flemish masters of the seventeenth century. Like the followers of the Flemish Franckens and Jan Bruegel and his followers, Plazer liked to paint in miniature (the pictures to be discussed are within a forty-by-sixty cm. format). On the other hand, the visual opulence of his work also owes a great deal to the rococo style imported to Austria from France—Plazer himself learned it at the Vienna Akademie. The basic study on the painter is the dissertation by Gottard Agath, *Johann Georg Plazer, ein Gesellschaftsmaler des Wiener Barock (1704-1761)* (University of Breslau, 1923). See also his small monograph *Johann Georg Plazer: ein Gesellschaftsmaler des Wiener Rokoko (1704-1761)* (Dresden: VEB Verlag der Kunst, 1955). Agath has catalogued a total of fifty-six works by the painter but has not been successful in establishing a chronology of production. Few of Plazer's pictures are dated, and few are signed.

Figure 1. *Johann Georg Plazer,* Musical Entertainment (ca. *1740), Oil on wood, 36.4 x 48.4 cm., Innsbruck, Tiroler Landesmuseum, inv. no. 210.*

would reflect the practices and tastes of private music making in eighteenth-century Vienna. Yet that does not seem to be the case. Curiously enough, in fact, a number of his musical scenes reproduce ensembles of a very different place and time—specifically, *northern* Europe in the *seventeenth* century. Beyond that, the very paintings Plazer is thought to have produced for the Viennese market reflect an oddly ambivalent attitude toward music, if not an outright criticism of the practice of the art. What is particularly interesting about these pictures, then, is that, while they do not tell us very much about Viennese musical life in the second quarter of the eighteenth century, they do seem to reveal an attitude toward music which we might not expect.

What can be described as the underlying problem with these pictures is evident in a *Musical Entertainment* (Figure 1) dated about 1740. In the foreground a bit of *Hausmusik* occurs; the ensemble consists of singers (a man directing the ensemble at the left, and a woman and child reading from music held in hand) and instrumentalists (a male flutist, a female harpsichordist, and a young male "cellist"). None of the music they perform is decipherable.

To begin with, the picture does not represent a portrait. These people are too sketchily drawn to be convincing as anything more than types; they have no personality of their own. Instead, they serve only to contribute to some overriding theme or subject, the treatment of which constitutes the picture's *raison d'être*. Furthermore, the cavalier manner with which the musical instruments are treated suggests Plazer's interest is somewhere other than in replicating a musical event.

The harpsichord in particular is sketchy. It has only enough keys for a two-octave compass. The keys are clearly too large, leaving room for fewer of them than there ought to be. The instrument apparently rests on a table; the match between the two is rather awkward. The flute is keyed, but beyond that not much can be discerned. The "violoncello" is the most curious of the instruments. Its fingerboard is short, its neck both short and thick. The corpus, on the other hand, is narrow, delicate looking, and small. The player uses the old-fashioned convex bow, holding it in the characteristic "underhand" position of viol playing. The instrument is not held between the legs, as became customary in cello playing, but rather half to one side of the body and half across the lap, more in the manner used for playing the smaller members of the viol family.[2] Thus, while the ensemble is perfectly plausible for an eighteenth-century concert, the instruments themselves are both carelessly drawn and even—in the case of the "violoncello"—perhaps a bit anachronistic.

Now if the picture does not exist to preserve for posterity the faces of particular sitters and if the musical scene which dominates the picture space is itself rather sketchily handled, what is the point of the piece? Its functions are classical and twofold—to entertain and to instruct. The entertainment function is fulfilled by the visual opulence of the piece, its decorativeness, and its clutter of objects and events that conspire to leave hardly a square centimeter of picture space unadorned. Here is reflected Plazer's love of the old seventeenth-century Flemish masters of genre scenes, happily coupled with the elegance of the eighteenth-century French and German rococo.

The instructional function is more complex; it is also more revealing as far as the history of music is concerned. In essence, on this level the work represents a kind of morality play in which

[2]Cf. Paolo Veronese's *Marriage at Cana* (Paris, Musée du Louvre), where two musicians hold their viols across their laps at a similar angle. The painting dates from 1562-63. A good reproduction of this detail appears in an article by A.P. de Mirimonde, "Le sablier, la musique et la danse dans les *Noces de Cana* de Paul Véronèse," *Gazette des Beaux-Arts*, ser. 6, vol. 88 (1976): 131, fig. 3.

music serves less as a reflection of upper class refinement and taste than as a metaphor for time ill-spent in worldly pleasures. In a real sense the painting resembles the *vanitas* paintings produced by Dutch and Flemish artists during the seventeenth century.

Vanitas pictures were intended to deliver to the viewer the message that worldly knowledge, the arts, the pleasures, as well as wealth and power were all transient and that the single-minded pursuit of them was foolhardy–*memento mori* or *mors omnia vincit* were among the somber captions often appearing in these pictures. This message, while simple in its basic form, was visually handled with considerable symbolic complexity. The paintings were in fact riddles, whose full range of meanings the viewer was supposed to seek through pondering. Ideally, this meditative act would be morally uplifting. (It was somber Calvinist scholars at Leyden who specified in detail the significance of individual objects depicted in these works.)[3]

The symbolic content in Plazer's *Musical Entertainment* is revealed through an examination of the individual objects and events depicted, all of which come together into a coherent, if surprising, whole. Like the viewers of northern *vanitas* pieces, the Viennese nobility must have enjoyed unraveling the mysteries. Plazer possessed a sophisticated knowledge of mythology, the Bible, history, and legend; visual references to this knowledge dominate much of his work. They constitute the basis for the inclusion of most of the otherwise merely decorative aspects of the painting under consideration.

The most obvious "decorative" feature in this picture is the large painting within the painting filling nearly the entire back wall of the room. It is so large that it cannot be ignored, and its subject is so curious, so seemingly inappropriate, that it signals us that it serves as more than mere decoration. It depicts the story of the goddess Diana and her nymph Callisto (told by Ovid both in the *Metamorphoses* [2:376-495] and in the *Fasti* [2:155-92]).

Jove, roaming Arcady, caught sight of an Arcadian girl named Callisto who served in the company of fair Diana the chaste huntress. While Callisto rested from the hunt, Jove disguised himself as Diana, came to Callisto, and eventually took her by force once she recognized him as an imposter. Nine months later, after a hot and tiring chase, Diana invited her followers to refresh themselves with

[3]See further the study by Ingvar Bergström, *Dutch Still-Life Painting in the Seventeenth Century*, trans. Christina Hedström and Gerald Taylor (London: Faber and Faber, 1956), pp. 154-90; and A.P. de Mirimonde, "Musique et symbolisme chez Jan-Davidszoon de Heem, Cornelis-Janszoon et Jan II Janszoon de Heem," *Jaarboek*, Koninklijk Museum voor Schone Kunsten, Antwerp (1970): 241-96.

her in a pool. Callisto, not wishing to disrobe and hence expose her pregnancy, held back. But the others stripped her and thus betrayed her secret. In a rage at the sight of the defiled Callisto, Diana turned the unfortunate nymph into a bear to be hunted down.

The scene Plazer gives us is the usual one, the moment at which Callisto's condition is revealed. Diana, clearly identifiable by the small crescent moon (her conventional attribute) at the top of her forehead, is restrained by a nymph as she points to Callisto below her. Callisto, her quiver of arrows at her side, wretchedly and too late pulls up her garment of disguise.[4]

The classical gods and goddesses were commonly used as personifications of the virtues in Western art from the Renaissance on, and in this regard Diana was one of the usual personifications of Chastity. In Plazer's painting she seems to function as something of a model of sexual virtue. At the same time, other details in the picture provide abundant contrast to this theme by making oblique references to carnal love through Venus, goddess of love. These references include the putti forming part of a sculpted urn at the left[5] and Venus's shell motif forming part of the rococo wall sconce near the putti. The woman at the keyboard is adorned with Venus's pearls, both on her wrists and around her neck. In art, the *Venus Vulgaris*, who represented the Earthly Venus (as opposed to the *Venus Coelestis*) to Renaissance humanists, is "richly clad and may wear jewels, symbols of earthly vanities."[6] Venus's apples stand in the compote on the table at the right. They are to be served along with grapes, attribute of licentious Bacchus, whose excessive behavior is known to all. The wine from the grapes stands in a carafe being chilled in the wine cooler on the floor beside the table. And a besotted satyr, crony of Bacchus, seems to be depicted in the partially visible picture within the picture at the top right.[7]

The dog in the scene more or less slinks under a chair at the right; his pose does not suggest that he finds these events pleasurable. His precise function is difficult to discern, but it produces no

[4]The male figure at the far right holding a spear (?) probably represents Jove, although the character is rather difficult to discern. Jove's attribute of the thunderbolt was generally represented as a pronged and barbed fork. The spear may substitute here for that object.

[5]Aside from being merely decorative, putti play one of two roles in art, depending, as always, on context. They are either angelic spirits or the harbingers of profane love. See James Hall, *Dictionary of Subjects and Symbols in Art* (London: J. Murray, 1974), p. 256.

[6]Ibid., p. 319.

[7]On the apple as an attribute of Venus, and the grapes as an attribute of Bacchus, see Guy de Tervarent, *Attributs et symboles dans l'art profane, 1450-1600* (Geneva: E. Droz, 1958-64), cols. 311-12 and 318, respectively.

jarring split in my interpretation to suggest that he may refer to vigilance (in the sense of his being suspicious) and also to Diana the chaste huntress—numerous representations connect dogs with this goddess. Dogs are also common attributes of fidelity, but in such cases they are normally shown lying at their master's feet or sitting in his lap. In this sense dogs also serve as attributes of love, particularly in marriage portraits. But none of that fits here.[8]

The question arises, what do these allusions have to do with a concert scene? The essential controlling theme for the painting may come close to the old one that music is the food of love, with the added footnote that the artist has in mind *immoderate* love. That is suggested, I think, by the curious print which hangs on the back wall near the doorway through which a richly attired lady enters. The print represents a jester, specifically a fool dressed in the usual hooded costume with ass's ears. His sceptor is topped with a carved head, the image of the fool himself. He rules this kingdom—this is his *Vaterland*, as the inscription at the bottom of the print makes clear. In this respect, it is worth pointing out that in old pictorial allegories of the virtues and the vices, Jest is the companion of Cupid: folly, that is to say, is linked with love. The combat between the virtues and the vices is a very old one in both Western literature and art. Most famous is the fourth-century *Psychomachia*, by the Spanish poet Prudentius, in which individual combats between Faith and Idolatry, Chastity and Lust, etc. are described. Virtue, of course, always triumphs. As for the vices, the Church singled out especially Lust and Avarice for condemnation. Both can be said to hang around the edges—if not actually to inhabit—Plazer's scene.[9] Plazer's jester makes the gesture of holding his nose. He is not offended by any smell, obviously, except that ultimate stench, vice. This room is something like a stateroom in a ship of fools, sailing toward a bad end through a false sea of pleasures.[10]

There is a splendid painting in the Virginia Museum of Fine Arts, Richmond, by the seventeenth-century Dutch master Jan Miense Molenaer representing an *Allegory of Fidelity in Marriage*. It contains a musical group among whom is a woman keeping time—or *mesure*—with one hand. P.J.J. van Thiel, in a detailed analysis of the symbolism of this painting,[11] convincingly shows that the

[8]On the dog as an attribute, see ibid., cols. 93-96.

[9]See further Hall, *Dictionary*, pp. 336-37.

[10]See further ibid., pp. 169, 281-82.

[11]"Marriage Symbolism in a Musical Party by Jan Miense Molenaer," *Simiolus* 2, no. 2 (1967-68): 90-99.

woman's precise function is to refer to the virtue of Temperance or Moderation (along with a number of similarly allusive objects and events depicted therein). Plazer, too, uses a "conductor"—the man in the left foreground who beats time in an obvious manner. But in the context of this painting, I suspect that the man is used ironically, to suggest not moderation but its opposite. The key to this interpretation is the fact that he is dressed as a soldier of fortune (and his costume belongs to the seventeenth century rather than to the eighteenth). In traveling garb, his sword at his waist, he is certainly not attired like the typical nobleman attending to the refinements of chamber music. He may be more the servant of Mars than of the Muse.[12]

This picture, like the two others to be discussed, is fundamentally an image-laden conceit. It is partly entertainment—visual stimulation—and partly didacticism. Baltasar Gracián, in his *Agudeza y Arte de Ingenio*, published in 1649, describes the function of this sort of artistic construction:

> Understanding without Wit or Conceit is a Sun without light or rays. . . . This need for the conceit is common to prose and verse. What would Augustine be without his subtleties, and Ambrose without his ponderings? Martial without his salt and Horace without his maxims? . . . If perceiving Wit gives one the reputation of being an Eagle, producing it will make one into an Angel: for the latter is an office of Cherubs, and an exaltation of mankind, which elevates us to an extravagant Hierarchy. . . . *What beauty is to the eyes and harmony is to the ears, the Conceit is to the understanding* [my italics].

In further defining the conceit—and also describing the genre of Plazer's painting—Gracián later notes that "It is an act of the understanding which expresses the correspondence which is found between objects."[13]

It is perhaps best at this point to look at a *Vanitas* painting (Figure 2)—in this case by an unknown northern artist from the seventeenth century—in order to establish more clearly the relation between this genre and Plazer's work. Most of the objects in the *Vanitas* remind us that we spend our lives in the pursuit of worldly things. And what could be more mundane than the central event, the weighing of gold, which engages the man at the right? The table he sits at is overflowing with allusions to wealth and power

[12]There are two details in the picture that I cannot account for, the equestrian portrait and the oval town view on the back wall at the far right.

[13]The quotations appear on pp. 3-4 and 7 of the *Agudeza*, respectively. They are quoted from the study by Mario Praz, *Studies in Seventeenth-Century Imagery*, 2nd ed. enlarged (Rome: Edizioni di storia e letteratura, 1964), pp. 22, 29.

Figure 2. *Anonymous Seventeenth-Century Dutch or Flemish School,* Vanitas, *Private Coll. (Copyright A. C. L., Bruxelles).*

(the gold coins and the sealed legal document), the arts and sciences (the books in the left background, the small sculpture, and the print),[14] and to the tastes and pleasures (the playing cards, the smoking pipes, and the wine goblet all at the left, as well as—most notably—the musical instruments). But these pursuits, we are plainly reminded, are vain.

In this regard, the significance of the musical instruments is multi-leveled. At the right we see an instrument associated exclusively with art music. At first glance it appears to be a bass viola da gamba, with its characteristic high ribs and "C" holes (the height of the ribs is, if anything, greater than usual on viols). It is unfortunate that little of the neck is visible. The shoulders of the instrument appear more rounded than one might expect for viols. But the most surprising feature is that there are only four strings (one of which is symbolically broken in allusion to the impending decay of all things) instead of the customary six or seven. The instrument

[14]The print is a portrait of the Dutch-Flemish painter Jan Lievens (1607-74), who produced Biblical, historical, and genre pictures, as well as landscapes. See further the entry in Alfred von Wurzbach, *Niederländisches Künstler-Lexikon* (1907-11; reprint ed., Amsterdam: B.M. Israël, 1963), 2:44-51; and the monograph by H. Schneider, *J. Lievens* (Haarlem: F. Bohn, 1932). The *Vanitas* was most likely painted after Lievens' death; see the text, below.

would appear to be a hybrid, if we can assume the artist was not merely careless in painting the strings.

The two remaining instruments refer to other kinds of music. The violin in seventeenth-century northern Europe was essentially an instrument of the dance, a form of entertainment frowned upon by the Dutch Calvinists. As the Dutch poet Jan van der Veen noted:

> De VEDEL of FIOOL die wert God betert, meer
> Gebruyckt tot ydelheyt, als tot Godts lof en eer"

("The fiddle or violin is alas used more in the service of vanity than in the praise and glory of God").[15] The shawm which is partly visible beneath the violin is more overtly suspicious. While the instrument was commonly used in professional civic bands in the seventeenth century, its symbolic potential in art seems to have revolved around its less noble ancestry. It is a double reed instrument, like the Dionysian aulos of the ancients, the instrument of bacchanals. In this sense, it has been pointed out that in *vanitas* allegories, "music is often performed by the person representing lust. . . ."[16] In other words, music of virtually every kind, whether art or popular in genre, refined or frenzied in character, seems to be condemned. Thus "musical instruments were not regarded only as symbols of an art, but primarily as a warning against a lazy and sinful life."[17]

It is worth noting that it is the musical instruments which entirely surround the most obvious reference to death in the painting, the skull. And perhaps as though to clarify the sense of all this, the artist has perched a music partbook atop the violin and next to the skull. The text of its title page is partly decipherable. It reads approximately as follows:

De Ten Aards
XEDE VEERSE VAN DE YDELHEYT
en
unstantvastigheyd tes werelds
BASSUS

("Concerning the World
MORAL SONGS OF THE VANITY
and
instability of the world").

[15]Bergström, *Dutch Still-Life Painting*, p. 156. This statement represents the thirty-second riddle in van der Veen's *Zinne-Beelden oft Adams Appel . . .* (Amsterdam, 1659).

[16]Ibid.

[17]Ibid.

The last line, very difficult to see, seems to read "f. Amsterdam 16." The title of the first piece is visible. It appears to be "Aen mijn Here" ("To my Lord"). The choice of the particular partbook was not arbitrary, for it allows the artist to make a clever pun on the word *bassus*; the activity symbolized by these instruments–indeed, by all the wordly pursuits evident in the painting–is *base*.[18]

The inherent transience of the activities and pursuits these objects refer to is proclaimed not only by the skull but also by the yearly almanac (dated 1683–perhaps the painting's date of execution) in front of it,[19] and most explicitly by the skeletal figure of Death, who attracts the attention of the money weigher with an hour glass, whose sand has nearly all run into the bottom.[20]

A cleverly constructed visual conceit centering on a *vanitas* theme controls another *Musical Entertainment* by Plazer (Figure 3), although this picture looks much more like a portrait than does the previous example. Here the care lavished on the portrayal of each individual is obvious. In this case, however, both the setting and the costumes are closer to those of northern Europe in the seventeenth century than Austria in the eighteenth. The same can be said about the musical ensemble (violin, lute, flute, violoncello, and possibly one or two singers),[21] at least as far as the presence of the lute is concerned, since the popularity of the instrument declined by the end of the seventeenth century.

[18]I have not been successful in my attempts to identify fully this collection. It is not to be found in *RISM* (to date) nor in any of the following: Alphonse Goovaerts, *Histoire et bibliographie de la typographie musicale dans les Pays-Bas* (Antwerp: P. Kockx, 1880); D.F. Scheurleer, *Nederlandsche liedboeken: lijst der in Nederland tot het jaar 1800 uitgegeven liedboeken* (The Hague: M. Nijhoff, 1912); Robert Eitner, *Bibliographie der Musik-Sammelwerke der XVI. und XVII. Jahrhunderts* (1877; reprint ed., Hildesheim: G. Olms, 1963); W. Barclay Squire, *Catalogue of Printed Music Published between 1487 and 1800 now in the British Museum* (London: For the Trustees, 1912); and *The British Union-Catalogue of Early Music Printed before the Year 1801*, ed. Edith B. Schnapper (London: Butterworths Scientific Publications, 1951). The song text "Aen mijn Here" (if I have deciphered it correctly) does not appear in Florimond van Duyse's *Het oude Nederlandsche lied* (1903-08; reprint ed., Hilversum: F.A.M. Knuf, 1965).

[19]The almanac carries the coat of arms of Amsterdam.

[20]No details are evident on the globe in the background, but often globes were zodiacal spheres stopped at the point where the Lion replaces Cancer, thus marking the decline of the year.

[21]The violoncello closely resembles the instrument in the first Plazer painting, although here its floor spike is evident. The playing position more closely approximates modern practice. The bow is still convex, and it is held in the "underhand" manner. The player's grip, in front of the well-defined frog, helps tighten the bow hairs.

Figure 3. *Johann Georg Plazer,* Musical Entertainment, *Oil on copper, 40.6 x 58.7 cm., Prague, Národní Galerie v Praze, inv. no. 0 91.*

A number of objects in this painting are the same as those in the other picture by Plazer—the wine, grapes, and apples, for example, which probably function symbolically. Both pictures share a similar degree of general clutter, overdecoration, and overdress. The relation of all this to the vanity of human pursuits is obvious. Besides the six pictures on the walls, which as far as I can identify them seem to speak to this same theme, there are several other details present here but not in the first picture whose symbolic potential is worth studying. To begin with, there is the matter of the gesture of the man behind the violin player; he is fondling the breast of a woman—further evidence that this is no portrait, for such behavior would be inappropriate in such a genre. In addition, the fruit compote on the table at the right contains not only apples and grapes but also a pomegranate. The symbolic potential of this fruit is rich. In Greek mythology, the pomegranate was said to have sprouted from the blood of Dionysius when he was torn apart as a child by the Titans. But it is also an attribute of Persephone, who personifies both the birth and death of vegetation.[22] From this myth the pomegranate was taken over into Christian iconography as a symbol of resurrection.[23] In the context of Plazer's picture, this fruit may serve as a subtle reminder of the hope of resurrection and as a reminder of the task before man in order to achieve it. This same kind of mixing of visual allusion to the hope for resurrection and immortality alongside the usual vanities was customary in northern still lifes. Thus in the previously discussed painting, ripe wheat straw ironically wound around the skull also makes reference to resurrection, though here the ultimate source resides in the gospel of St. John (12:24) and not in a pagan myth.[24]

It is the paintings within the painting, however, which most obviously confirm that there is more to this music party. Some of these paintings are more clearly seen than others; some I have not been able to decipher with certainty. But I am quite sure that most are intended to serve as reminders of the vanity of the behavior of the people present in the room. By analogy these little vignettes obliquely reinforce—in a morally critical way—the notion that music is the food of carnal love.

The still life of flowers and fruit at the upper right is most likely inspired by Flemish masters of this genre like Jan "Flower" Bruegel (1568-1625), son of Pieter Bruegel the Elder. As Ingvar Bergström has pointed out, "the bouquet of a seventeenth-century flower-piece generally means Transience."[25] Taken as a whole, flowers remind us of a verse from Job (14:1-2): "Man that is born of a woman is of few days, and full of trouble. He cometh forth like a flower, and is cut down: he fleeth also as a shadow, and continueth not."

[22]Ovid, *Metamorphoses*, 5:372-569. Persephone was taken by force into the underworld by a love-struck Pluto. Demeter, her mother, in grief over Persephone's loss took away the fertility of the earth. Jove then allowed Persephone to return to her mother, but only on the condition that she eat nothing in the underworld. But Pluto tricked her into eating some pomegranate seeds (Ovid says seven). For that reason, she was made to spend an equivalent number of months a year with Pluto. As a goddess of fertility, her annual return to earth assured a season of growth. See further E.S. Whittlesey, *Symbols and Legends in Western Art: A Museum Guide* (New York: Scribner, 1972), pp. 275-76, 284.

[23]Hall, *Dictionary*, p. 249.

[24]"Verily, verily, I say unto you, except a corn of wheat fall into the ground and die, it abideth alone; but if it die, it bringeth forth much fruit." See further George Ferguson, *Signs and Symbols in Christian Art* (London: Oxford University Press, 1954), p. 31.

[25]"Disguised Symbolism in 'Madonna' Pictures and Still Life: II," *Burlington Magazine* 97 (1955): 342; and also idem, *Dutch Still-Life Painting*, pp. 161, 218. He devotes an entire chapter to flower and fruit paintings; see pp. 42-97.

Individual types of flowers, however, often had more specific significance within this larger context. In Plazer's painting, roses and (probably) peonies seem easiest to identify. According to seventeenth-century emblem books, both make specific allusion to the brevity of life.[26] Beyond this, the rose is, of course, the attribute of Venus,[27] as is the apple, and two apples appear at the bottom of the picture. (Venus received the golden apple from Paris after bribing him to judge her fairer than Juno and Minerva.) But this fruit was used by artists to refer to more than the pagan goddess of love. Notably, the apple was frequently treated as the fruit picked by Adam and Eve from the forbidden Tree of Knowledge in the Garden of Eden. In Latin, after all, the word for apple is *malum*, the same word which means evil.[28] The apple is thus a perfect object for a *vanitas* piece since its image can stir up a rich complex of meanings.

Since the vignette is so small, I cannot identify with certainty the rest of the flowers present, but there seem to be some narcissus and anemones as well. The former is naturally a symbol of self-love, from the story of the flower's namesake. Anemones in pagan mythology were symbols of sorrow and death, based on the story of Adonis, who died on a bed of anemones and whose blood turned the white flowers red (cf. Ovid, *Metamorphoses*, 10:708-39). Adonis was loved immoderately by Venus.

In the right foreground a painting leans against a little stool on which rests a basket of apples. The picture represents the *Punishment of Cupid*. The little god's wings seem to flutter helplessly as he is beaten for the mischief caused by his arrows (his quiver lies at his feet). He is probably being whipped by Venus, judging from the basket of apples and the woman's nudity, although chaste Diana also laid hands on him (in Gothic church windows and in Renaissance paintings, Diana is used as a personification of Chastity in allegories of Chastity versus Lust).[29] In the context of Plazer's

[26]See J. Camerarius, *Symbolorum ac emblematum ethico-politicorum Centuriae quattuor* . . . (Moguntiae, 1697), cited by Bergström, "Disguised Symbolism," p. 345, n. 29.

[27]"The rose, sacred to Venus, was originally a white flower but, according to tradition, while Venus was hastening to help the dying Adonis a thorn pierced her foot and the drops of blood fell on the white petals, staining them red." "The Renaissance likened the rose to Venus because of its beauty and fragrance, comparing the pricking of its thorns to the wounds of love." Hall, *Dictionary*, pp. 320 and 268, respectively.

[28]In some contexts the apple could also stand for Christ, as the new Adam. In art, when held by Adam it symbolizes sin; when held by Christ, salvation. See further Ferguson, *Signs and Symbols*, pp. 27-28.

[29]Hall, *Dictionary*, p. 102.

picture, this vignette probably serves as a rather good-humored commentary on love's folly.

The other painting on a specifically identifiable subject is the curious piece at the far left, below the oval portrait of the burgher-like gentleman. It shows an old man, unclothed, hands bound behind his back nursing from the breast of a woman. The picture represents the so-called *Caritas Romana* (Roman Charity). It is based on a story from antiquity, told by Valerius Maximus, according to which an aged man named Cimon was in prison awaiting execution. Because of his impending death he was given no food. But the man's daughter Pero came to the cell and nourished him. This subject was popular in Italian and northern art from the sixteenth to the eighteenth centuries. It was usually taken as an example of filial piety, but in the Baroque, "examples are often a simple allegory of youth and age, frequently with a sexual emphasis."[30]

In my view the matter of youth and age is particularly relevant to Plazer's picture: a logical case can be made for interpreting it in part as an illustration of the Ages of Man, a rather popular subject closely connected to the *vanitas* theme, in that it too emphasizes the transience of human life. Often only three "ages" are represented, and that seems to be the case here. The two extremes of youth and old age are shown at the far right, where a girl child with flowers in her hair sits on the lap of a mature woman. Next to her is a greybeard drinking wine, the product of the autumn harvest (the Ages of Man subject was sometimes linked to the seasons). The oval portrait hanging above the *Caritas Romana* bears real resemblance to the old man, though it was obviously painted when he was much younger. It may serve as a reminder of the brevity of life—as does the candle which stands amid all the fancy tableware (symbols of worldliness) just behind the old man and right below the flower piece. The candle has burned down; little of it remains. Furthermore, as close scrutiny will reveal, it has just gone out—its wick is still smoking. The identical vignette appears in the anonymous *Vanitas* discussed earlier. In each, the candle stands as a metaphor of life itself which, like smoke, disappears without a trace. (The textual roots for this notion are found in Scripture—the

[30]Ibid., p. 267. A version of this subject by the Netherlandish painter Jan Janssens (1590-after 1650) is reproduced in the exhibition catalogue *Caravaggio y el naturalismo español* (Seville, September-October, 1973), no. 43; see also Walter Friedlaender, *Caravaggio Studies* (Princeton: At the University Press, 1955), p. 209, fig. 114, for a version by Pierino del Vega. See pp. 207-9 for a discussion of Caravaggio's own use of this subject as an illustration of two of the seven works of mercy (Matthew 23:35-36), the feeding of the hungry and the visiting of the prisoner.

favorite source for *vanitas* scholars–, specifically, Psalm 102:3: "For my days are consumed like smoke. . . .") The middle age, life in full flower, is surely represented in Plazer's painting by the two lovers enjoying the music and each other.

All of this connects with the musical theme itself on several levels. I have already pointed to the connection between music and carnal love in the discussion of the *vanitas* still life. In this sense Plazer's picture illustrates the *vita voluptuaria*. More subtle is the reminder that the vitality of love–profoundest of human emotions, the emotion which assures the continuation of life itself–is like a musical sound: nothing decays so quickly. We are reminded that music is an art existing with time and dying with it. Music provides Plazer with an ultimate metaphor for transience. Within the context of a *vanitas* piece, music does not come off as time well spent.

I can offer at least tentative interpretations of the remaining three pictures in the center, the bottom two of which are difficult to identify with certainty due to their small size. At the top is an *Atelier-Bild*, a picture of an artist's studio (and a genre Plazer liked to paint). It is the largest of all the pictures, and it is placed in a prominent location. The scene is basically a lesson, with the old bearded artist instructing an adolescent in his art. I can think of two ways of viewing this piece. Plazer may be taking ironic aim at his own field of endeavor, showing how "useless" information is passed down from one generation to the next (in Calvinistic terms, the youth could spend his time more effectively with a Bible). Alternatively, Plazer may be suggesting that just as the painter teaches the student, Plazer instructs us in the fine art of living a good life. He reminds us of the pleasures of the world in large format, just as in the decorative details he whispers to us about temptation and the necessity of the pilgrim's progress. I suspect the former interpretation may come closer to his intention.

The remaining two paintings on the back wall just below the *Atelier-Bild* may provide additional reinforcement for the moral message. The one on the left may show the *Baptism of Christ*. If so, it would recall to the viewer the necessity of being reborn in Christ (see John 1:1-18 and Mark 1:1-11). The other may represent the *Return of the Prodigal Son* (Luke 15:18-21). After his debauch, during which he squandered his spiritual substance, the prodigal achieved a new awareness. "I will arise and go to my father," he says, "and will say to him, Father, I have sinned against heaven and before thee. . . ." His father–our Father, according to medieval exegesis–welcomed him back into his house (Heaven). In the tiny painting Plazer provides, we see a man traveling on a road (his posture shows that he is walking). He moves toward another man in long robes, a conventional way of depicting Biblical characters, who gestures toward a castle on a hill. Surely he is inviting him home. Similar vignettes bearing the same basic compositional character occur in Flemish renditions of this Scriptural tale.[31]

In summary, what seems at first glance little more than a somewhat cluttered genre scene with music turns out in the end to be a complex allegory of pleasure and morality, death and afterlife. In light of this, it bears restating that this essentially didactic work was produced at a time, in a place, and for an audience which—particularly with respect to its musical contents—we might find surprising. In the most musical of cities, in the socially gayest of times, there is found an apparent taste for a kind of art which in subject is utterly antithetical to that which we would expect to find.

[31]See two such examples, by Frans Pourbus the Elder and Frans Francken the Younger, reproduced in my study "The Prodigal Son: Teniers and Ghezzi," *Minneapolis Institute of Arts Bulletin* 61 (1974): 80 (fig. 1) and 82 (fig. 2).

David A. Sheldon

Exchange, Anticipation, and Ellipsis: Analytical Definitions of the *Galant* Style

The word *galant* is French in origin, traced by scholars back to the thirteenth century in its literary usage. By the seventeenth century the word was associated with the artistic life of fashionable salons and had become synonymous with wit, amorous conversation, elegant dress, *bon goût*, and a pleasing, polite social manner.[1] Although the word does have musical associations in French culture at this time, one must look to Germany for definitions of *galant* in a musical sense; for it is only in the writings of eighteenth-century German theorists that *galant* is used frequently enough to provide us with a musical definition. To be sure, the original, broader meanings of *galant*, and also *Galanterie*, continue to be in evidence among such German writers on music. For example, in a review of Ernst Wilhelm Wolff's *Sechs Sonaten für das Klavier* (1781) and other sonatas of that year by composers such as C.P.E. Bach, G. Benda and Haydn, Johann Friedrich Reichardt writes:

> To me, these are among the most important keyboard pieces of recent years. Bach and Benda distinguish themselves by means of a great and noble style, in jest and seriousness, Haydn through an original masculine mood, Wolff through wit and *Galanterie*, [J.G.] Vierling and [N.G.] Gruner through diligence and variety. . . . In the Wolff sonatas, one would not have recognized the otherwise serious composer, who already appears to carry the stamp of an artful classical composer, if his name were not affixed to them and if it were not already for his beloved small clavier sonatas (1779). Jest, wit, and *galant* expression [*Wendung*] are really more in evidence in the small sonatas than in these larger ones; at least one notices here only occasionally the attempt to be *galant*. In

[1] Vauglais was its chief literary theorist, Voiture its chief practitioner.

> some movements, however, there is an almost incomparably elegant, or rather polite sensitivity and witty refinement of taste, as in the second movement of the first sonata and the first movement of the fourth.[2]

The importation of the word *galant* and the French mannerisms associated with it was part of the culture craze for things new and fashionable that Germany experienced beginning in the seventeenth century, a phenomenon that peaked around 1700. The aspiring German middle class eagerly snatched up French words and mannerisms to acquire the semblance of social sophistication; serious social reformers, such as Christian Thomasius, tried to give *galant* modishness and urbanity a degree of moderation, respectability, and didactic purpose. Through the efforts of such writers as Benjamin Neukirch and Friedrich Christian Hunold there arose new literary genres: the *galant* novel, *galant* poetry, and the *galantes Lehrbuch*. The new and fashionable quickly acquired musical connotations in Germany. In the writings of Johann Mattheson in particular, beginning with his *Das neu-eröffnete Orchestre . . .* (Hamburg, 1713), one finds his idealized musical amateur referred to as a *galant homme* and associations of *galant* with musical embellishment and expressive nuance as well as operatic and keyboard music.[3] Mattheson, however, never really spoke of a "*galant* style." It was not until mid-century, long after the *galant* literary and social movement in Germany was spent, that *galant* was raised to the status of a theoretically recognized and defined musical style, the *galant* or free style as opposed to the *gearbeitet* (elaborate, contrapuntal, church) or *gebunden* (strict, bound) style. Although texture and embellishment are important factors here, the most frequently cited distinctions made by writers of the period have to do with dissonance treatment, a fact not surprising in view of the *gebunden* vs. *ungebunden* categorization as well as the predominantly harmonic concern of the figured-bass era.

It was actually Mattheson who provided the first harmonic associations with the word *galant*. Most of these have to do with the fourth. However, it was during the next generation of writers, with Marpurg, Quantz, C.P.E. Bach and others, that *galant* was associated with the actual preparation and resolution of dissonance and that

[2]Johann Friedrich Reichardt, *Musikalisches Kunstmagazin* 1 (Berlin, 1782): 87.

[3]The complete title of *Das neu-eröffnete Orchestre* is revealing: "The newly-inaugurated orchestra, or universal and fundamental instruction as to how a *galant homme* can achieve a perfect conception of the grandeur and dignity of the noble music, form his taste accordingly, understand the technical terms, and be able to reason capably concerning this excellent science." For a more complete discussion of the early musical associations with *galant* in Germany see David A. Sheldon, "The Galant Style Revisited and Re-evaluated," *Acta Musicologica* 47 (1975): 240-70.

the harmonic fourth was allowed not to be prepared in the "*galant* style."[4] Marpurg even states that such a fourth can resolve upwards as well as downwards, and Koch, admitting much the same thing, even gives an example of the fourth resolving downward in parallel motion to the augmented fourth of a $^{4}_{2}$ chord.[5] The greatest concern of Marpurg's generation, though, was for the free handling of seventh-chord dissonance. In his *Handbuch*, Marpurg not only conceded but also attempted to explain the lack of preparation for most seventh chords in the *galant* style.[6] This effort was made possible for Marpurg by several important new ideas in Johann David Heinichen's *Der General-Bass in der Composition* (Dresden, 1728). Heinichen's interpretations concerning the free handling of dissonance in the theatrical style, particularly in the recitative, provided Marpurg and later theorists with the conceptualization and terminology for their explanations of modern harmonic practice, explanations which provide us with a cohesive, eighteenth-century definition of the "*galant* style."[7]

[4] See especially Friedrich Wilhelm Marpurg, *Handbuch bey dem Generalbasse und der Composition* (Berlin, 1755-60), p. 152. C.P.E. Bach, in his *Versuch über die wahre Art das Clavier zu spielen*, Vol. 2 (facsimile reprint of the 1762 ed., Leipzig: Breitkopf & Härtel, 1957), pp. 164, 171, associates the unprepared fourth in the $^{9}_{4}$ and $^{5}_{4}$ chords with the *galant* style. See also Johann Caspar Heck, *The Art of Playing Thorough Bass* (London, [ca. 1777]), p. 64, for an association between the unprepared fourth and the *galant* ("elegant") style.

[5] Friedrich Wilhelm Marpurg, *Georg Andreas Sorgens Anleitung zum Generalbass und zur Composition* (Berlin, 1760), pp. 106-7, 131. Heinrich Christoph Koch, *Versuch einer Anleitung zur Composition*, Vol. 1 (Leipzig, 1782), pp. 160-61. Actually, this progression given by Koch had already been associated with the *frei* (as opposed to the *eingeschränkt*) style by Joseph Riepel, *Erläuterung der betrüglichen Tonordnung* (Augsburg, 1765), p. 45.

[6] P. 152. See ibid., pp. 120-129, 136, for other intervals exempted from preparation. It might be mentioned here that the most complete form of preparation for accented dissonance is when the note in question is tied over (*gebunden*) as a consonance from the preceding unaccented beat and that both Johann Philipp Kirnberger (*Die Kunst des reinen Satzes in der Musik*, Vol. 1 [facsimile reprint of the 1776-79 ed., Hildesheim: G. Olms, 1968], p. 81) and Koch (*Versuch*, 1:156) indicate that the mere absence of a tie in such a situation, with the now-dissonant note struck anew, constitutes a freedom of the *galant* style.

[7] See George J. Buelow, "Heinichen's Treatment of Dissonance," *Journal of Music Theory* 6 (1962): 216-76 for a translated summary of pt. 2, chap. 1 (*Von theatralischen Resolutionibus der Dissonantien).* Georg Andreas Sorge (*Vorgemach der musicalischen Composition* [Lobenstein, 1745-47], pp. 408-12) and Meinrad Spiess (*Tractatus musicus compositorio-practicus* [Augsburg, 1746], pp. 203-14) seem to be the first to deal extensively with Heinichen's ideas in this regard, but still without reference to a *galant* or free style.

Heinichen not only recognized the right of dissonance in the theatrical style to change position within a chord before resolution, but he also acknowledged that dissonance could be approached without preparation. This acknowledgement, however, seems contingent upon his interpretation of unprepared dissonance as actually being an *anticipatio transitus (per ellipsis)*, or anticipated passing tone.[8] Based on the fact that unaccented passing dissonance was traditionally acceptable if approached and left by step in the same direction, the interpretation here was the imagined omission or ellipsis of the preceding accented consonance, with the following passing dissonance now receiving the accent. Although Heinichen gives several examples of his concept of the anticipated passing tone, or *Vorausnahme einer durchgehenden Note* as it was commonly designated during the second half of the century, Marpurg seems to be the first to have illustrated this concept in the context of a series of dominant-seventh chords, as in Example 1.[9]

Example 1.

explained as:

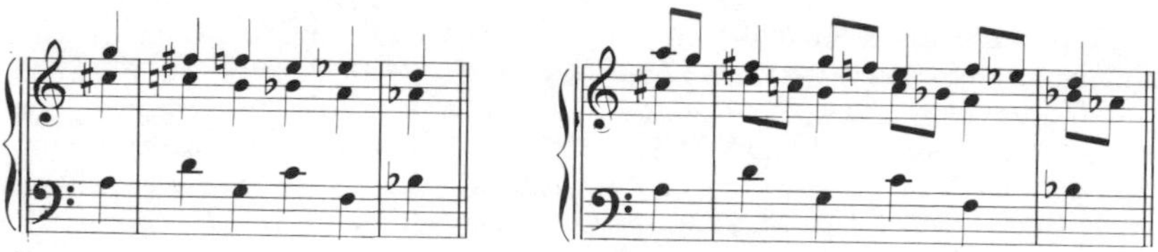

While obviously indebted to Heinichen, Marpurg also added to this general discussion of dissonance treatment a classification of dissonance in terms of chord quality and function: namely, in addition to diminished sevenths, the minor seventh of the chords of the dominant, the leading tone in major, and the supertonic and raised submediant in minor need not be prepared in the *galant* style. The dissonance may be either accented or unaccented, the chord in root position or inverted.[10] It might be pointed out that

[8]Heinichen, *Der General-Bass*, pp. 602-5, 613-18.

[9]Marpurg, *Handbuch*, table viii of sec. 2, figs. 42-43. Cf. ibid., pp. 134-35, Friedrich Wilhelm Marpurg, *Die Kunst das Clavier zu spielen* (Berlin, 1762), pp. 43-44, and Koch, *Versuch*, 1:192-93. David Kellner, in his *Treulicher Unterricht im General Bass* (Hamburg, 1737), p. 94, is perhaps the first to illustrate such a progression and to associate it with "the modern way of the resolution of dissonance." Neither this reference nor the succession of dominant-seventh chords, however, is explained; nor does Kellner mention, here or elsewhere in this source, a free or *galant* style.

[10]In other words, all dominant, diminished, and half-diminished seventh chords. See Marpurg, *Handbuch*, pp. 8, 152; Marpurg, *Die Kunst*, pp. 42-43;

Joseph Riepel, in his *Gründliche Erklärung der Tonordnung* of 1757, states that "in free compositions, as symphonies, concertos, etc., diminished sevenths and minor sevenths may be unprepared."[11] Also, Matthew Shirlaw has pointed out that Sorge in his *Vorgemach* had already exempted from preparation the dominant seventh and ninth, as well as other sevenths, and that even earlier Rameau had permitted unprepared dominant dissonance.[12] However, it might actually have been d'Alembert's exemption of the dissonance of the dominant-seventh chord and the subdominant with added sixth from preparation which had the most direct influence on Marpurg in this regard.[13] In addition to this evidence of Marpurg's openness to new ideas, though, one can also detect his moderation, a moderation to be expected in his transfer of stylistic insight from the situation of operatic recitative to that of modern music generally. When dealing with inverted seventh chords, for example, Marpurg introduces the notion of root preparation. He explains this as something between ordinary preparation and no preparation at all; quite simply, the root of the dissonant chord is tied over from the preceding consonant chord, and its seventh (or ninth, or eleventh) is freely introduced.[14]

Another feature of the free handling of dissonance in the *galant* style also occurs in situations where voices are handled freely in rather normal chord progressions. In these situations, however, the irregularities involve two parts rather than just one. Again, Heinichen was the first to identify and explain this particular phenomenon found in the theatrical style. He defined it as an exchange (*Verwechselung*) of the voices in the resolution itself, as distinguished from the more common change of position of pitches within a chord before an actual resolution.[15] Example 2 is one of Heinichen's illustrations of the exchanged resolution, a resolution which always involves the bass in his two-part examples.[16]

---

and Friedrich Wilhelm Marpurg, *Kritische Briefe über die Tonkunst*, Vol. 2 (Berlin, 1761-63), p. 187.

[11](Frankfurt-Leipzig), p. 36.

[12]*The Theory of Harmony* (De Kalb, Illinois: B. Coar, 1955), pp. 306-8.

[13]See Jean Le Rond d'Alembert, *Systematische Einleitung in die musicalische Setzkunst* (Leipzig, 1757), pp. 134-35. This is a translation with commentary by Marpurg of d'Alembert's *Elements de musique* (Paris, 1752).

[14]Marpurg, *Handbuch*, pp. 154-55. Koch (*Versuch*, 1:215) adds root-position chords to the discussion.

[15]Heinichen, *Der General-Bass*, pp. 662-85. This brings to mind discussions in which unprepared dissonance is interpreted as actually having been prepared in another part. See ibid., pp. 604-8; Marpurg, *Handbuch*, pp. 152-53; and Koch, *Versuch*, 1:214.

[16]*Der General-Bass*, pp. 668-69.

Example 2.

or: instead of:

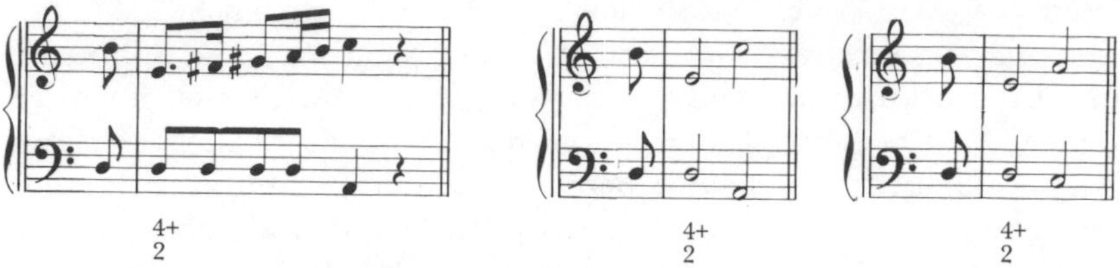

Even greater freedom is shown by such exchanged or inverted resolutions where only one of the two parts seems actually to participate in the exchange. Heinichen gives several illustrations of both kinds of this unilateral, or "irregular," exchange of the resolution. One illustration (Example 3a) shows the bass taking over the resolution of the upper part, with the upper part "seeking a new pitch." An illustration of the other kind of irregular exchange, given in Example 3b, shows the upper part taking over the resolution of the bass, with the bass seeking the new pitch.[17]

Example 3a.

or: instead of:

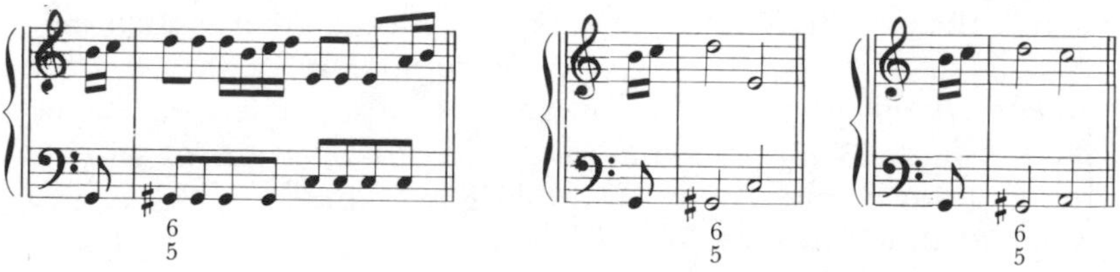

Example 3b.

or: instead of:

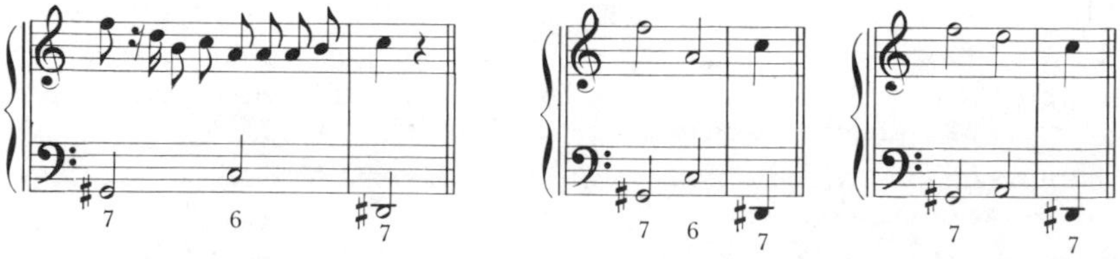

[17] Ibid., pp. 675-76.

Marpurg's moderation regarding this particular subject is apparent from the fact that where he speaks of three kinds of exchanged resolution in the *galant* style, the third of which "a *galant* composer would not use frivolously," in his examples the exchange mostly takes place before the seventh chord actually resolves.[18] Elsewhere in the *Handbuch*, however, several examples of truly exchanged resolutions are given. At one such point Marpurg states that "in the chord of the diminished fifth, the bass can, by means of the exchange of voices, rise a fourth in an extraordinary manner." He adds, though, that this exchange (*Verwechselung*), illustrated by letters in Example 4, is used really only in recitative.[19] It might be added, too, that this Marpurg example is not really an exchange in Heinichen's sense of the term, for here the bass is the only voice which moves irregularly.

Example 4.

c	b
a	g
d	d
F♯	B

On the subject of the elliptical resolution of dissonance, or dissonance apparently resolving to dissonance (in the same voice), Heinichen again provided the initial explanation in his discussion of the theatrical style and was followed by a more temperate recognition of it by Marpurg and others concerning its use in the *galant* style. Indeed, this freedom in the handling of dissonance assumed paramount importance among the theorists of the *galant* style, for their attention was occupied as much by the lack of preparation for the second dissonance as by the irregular handling of the first. Heinichen's interpretations all assume an alteration of the bass part

[18]Marpurg, *Handbuch*, pp. 148-50. A direct theoretical link between the "theatrical style" and the "*galant* style" is provided by Georg Andreas Sorge, *Compendium harmonicum, oder kurzer Begriff der Lehre von der Harmonie* (Lobenstein, [1760]), pp. 101-2, who quotes, using letter notation, many of Heinichen's examples of exchange resolution of the former style as harmonic freedoms of the latter. Sorge's examples are all exchanges to which a seventh (or diminished fifth) has been added to the chord of resolution. Cf. Heinichen, *Der General-Bass*, pp. 683-85.

[19]Marpurg, *Handbuch*, p. 96.

and are associated with the *anticipatio transitus* concept.[20] Firstly, a freely-approached $^{4+}_{2}$ chord is explained as the result of an anticipated passing tone in the bass, the explanation illustrated essentially in Example 1 but involving the lowest voice.[21] (In this circumstance, of course, the dissonance of the $^{4+}_{2}$ chord may or may not be preceded by an initial dissonance.) Secondly, the bass involved with an initial dissonance anticipates the second dissonance by omitting either part or all of its assumed (i.e., proper) value. Example 5, provided by Heinichen, illustrates both possibilities of this second category. In Example 5a the bass note *e* loses part of its assumed value;[22] in Example 5b it loses all of it.[23]

Example 5a.

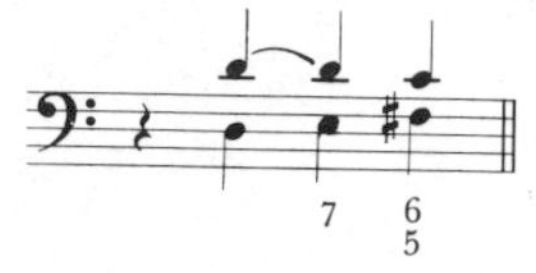

explained as:

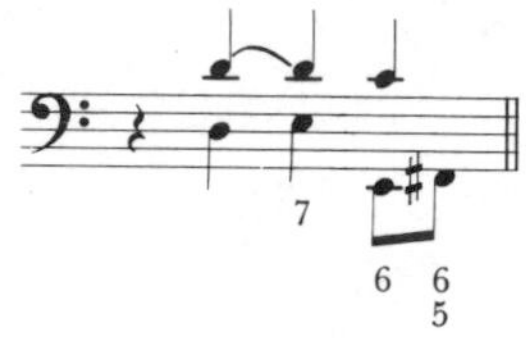

Example 5b.

explained as:

[20]*Der General-Bass*, pp. 685-95.

[21]Marpurg uses this expanation for a seventh resolving to the augmented fourth of a $^{4}_{2}$ chord (*Handbuch*, table iv of sec. 2, figs. 19-20). Both Sorge (*Compendium*, p. 32) and Koch (*Versuch*, 1:189-90) repeat Marpurg's explanation and example. Koch (ibid., pp. 201-2) uses the same means to explain a ninth resolving to a seventh.

[22]Heinichen, *Der General-Bass*, pp. 691-92. This and other examples quoted on p. 691 are also given by Sorge (*Compendium*, p. 103), are termed *transitum anticipatus*, and are discussed in the context of "ellipsis"; Sorge, however, does not specifically mention the *galant* style here.

[23]Heinichen, *Der General-Bass*, pp. 693-94. The example has been transposed down a minor third. From Heinichen's discussion and other examples it seems apparent that he regarded the essential melodic progression here to be from *a* to *g*, i.e., from dissonance to dissonance.

In both these examples the lack of resolution of the first dissonance and the subsequent lack of preparation for the second obviously cannot be explained readily by means of an assumed consonant passing tone, and Heinichen is careful not to speak of *transitus* in these two situations.[24] The explanation of Example 5a is certainly a bass anticipation with regard to assumed rhythmic displacement. What is perhaps uncertain from Heinichen's two-part examples, though, is the assumed movement of the inner parts. For instance, in Example 5a, is not the explanation more a matter of assumed retardation of the dissonant melodic part than the assumed anticipation of the bass? Is not the dissonant melodic part more harmonically free than the bass, which is tied rhythmically to the motion of the inner parts? With a slight rhythmic alteration, Heinichen's explanation becomes an assumed 7-6 melodic suspension. My harmonic realizations of Heinichen's explanation of Example 5a, given in Example 6, reveal this fact as well as the fact that if the bass is interpreted as an assumed anticipation of what should take place, so too must the inner parts be interpreted.

Example 6.

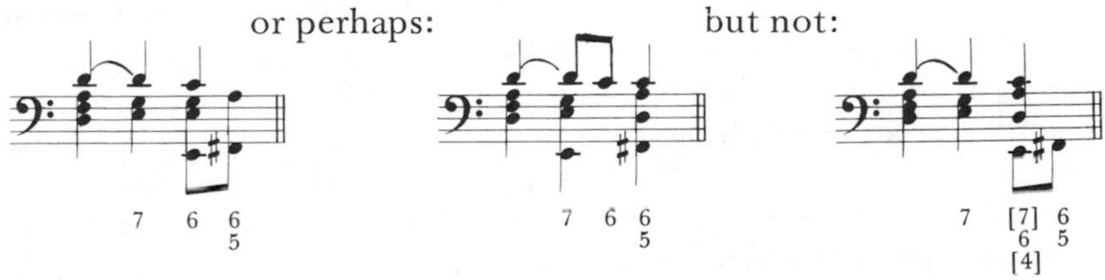

It is perhaps important to note here that Marpurg uses merely the word *Anticipation* to describe several situations where the bass part is clearly assumed to be moving in rhythmic (and harmonic) independence of the upper parts. One such full-voice explanation, clearly associated by Marpurg with the *galant* style and involving

[24]Marpurg is not as careful. In the *Handbuch* (pp. 151-52), *Vorausnahme einer durchgehenden Note*, equated by Marpurg with *anticipatio transitus*, is associated with the resolution of dissonance to dissonance in general. With one exception (see n. 21, above), the basses of Marpurg's examples in the *Handbuch* all move downward by step from one dissonance to another, suggesting merely an assumed rhythmic anticipation, i.e., the assumed partial loss of the value of the bass note associated with the first dissonance, somewhat the same as in Heinichen's Example 5a. See also ibid., pp. 102 and 134, as well as Marpurg's examples (*Handbuch*, table iv of sec. 2, figs. 16-18, 28, 31, and table vi of sec. 2, fig. 33).

the resolution of one second to another, is given in Example 7.[25]

Example 7.

explained as:

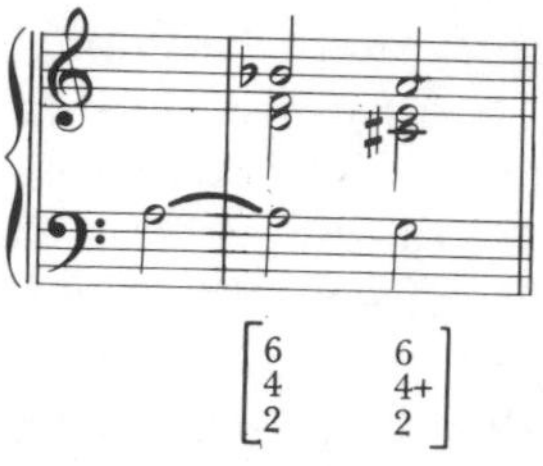

But most of Marpurg's examples and explanations in the *Handbuch* of dissonance resolving to dissonance deal with sevenths as the initial dissonance—tied over from the preceding measure. Of these, most attention is given to sevenths resolving to sevenths, the bass parts descending a second.[26] Marpurg provides, however, only a single two-part, unfigured example to illustrate his explanation for a series of such progressions. The explanatory example creates a 7-6 resolution of the initial seventh by assuming that the bass has anticipated its downward motion. The full harmonic realization of this example which Koch provides in his *Versuch* indicates the implicit melodic-harmonic retardation of the initial seventh, although clearly the main emphasis here is on the rhythmic anticipation by the three lower parts. Koch states specifically that the initial seventh is assumed to resolve to a sixth, after which it becomes part of a passing seventh chord. His full-voice illustration, given in Example 8, makes this clear.[27]

[25] *Handbuch*, p. 116 and table v of sec. 2, figs. 24-25. See also p. 134 and table vi of sec. 2, fig. 36.

[26] In other words, a root-position version of the essential progression in Example 7. Apparently Heinichen does not use such a progression of two root-position seventh chords in his examples. Riepel (*Erläuterung*, p. 45) illustrates such a progression (but without the initial seventh prepared) and associates it with unresolving dissonance of the free style. Neither this, nor the unresolving-fourth progression (see n. 5, above), nor the V^{4}_{2}-I progression which he gives, however, is granted any further explanation.

[27] Koch, *Versuch*, 1:190-91. An explanation of this progression in terms of assumed bass anticipation would be, of course, the same rhythmically as Example 7. Cf. Marpurg, *Handbuch*, table iv of sec. 2, figs. 16-17. Marpurg's examples are also given by Sorge (*Compendium*, pp. 31-32) but are not associated specifically with a free or *galant* style.

Example 8.

explained as:

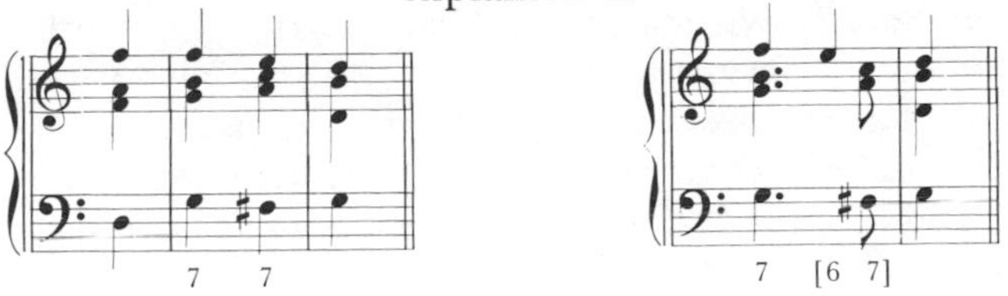

Interestingly, in his *Die Kunst das Clavier zu spielen*, Marpurg does provide for a similar situation an explanation simply in terms of an assumed 7-6 melodic suspension. In a discussion of dissonance resolving to dissonance in the *galant* style, a discussion parallel to that in the *Handbuch*, Marpurg illustrates in letter notation (Example 9) a seventh resolving to an augmented fourth.[28]

Example 9.

explained as:

c -	c	b	c		c –	c	b	b	c
	a	g	g			a		g	g
	f	d	c			f		d	c
	d	f	e			d		f	e

The top part now seems clearly to be an assumed retardation, rhythmically as well as melodically and harmonically. What was hinted at in Heinichen's example (Example 5a) and implied in Koch's (Example 8) is here explicit. In this instance Marpurg speaks of the seventh descending as a falling *Nachschlag* to a sixth; importantly, though, he does not refer to *Vorausnahme* or *Anticipation* in this discussion but rather to the suppression (*Verbeissung*) or omission (*Anlassung*) of a *durchgehende Note*.[29] Daniel Türk, in

28*Die Kunst*, p. 42. Marpurg could well have explained the progression by applying the *anticipatio transitus* concept to the bass, with this part interpreted as: *d g f e*. See n. 21, above.

29*Die Kunst*, p. 42. It might be pointed out, too, that Christoph Gottlieb Schröter's discussion of dissonance resolving to dissonance (*Deutliche Anweisung zum General-Bass* [Halberstadt, 1772], p. 126) features examples which all begin with prepared perfect fourths resolving downward by step on the next beat—all explained as nothing more than delayed (*aufgehalten*) thirds.

his *Anweisung zum Generalbassspielen*, summed up very well the interpretive possibilities of assumed bass anticipation and upper-part retardation regarding the resolution of dissonance to dissonance in the *galant* style. With a series of explanatory examples dealing with only one progression, he clearly illustrated both of the possibilities of Heinichen's second category (the assumed bass anticipation of Examples 5a and 5b) as well as the assumed upper-part retardation of Marpurg (Example 9). Türk's illustrations are given in Example 10.[30]

Example 10.

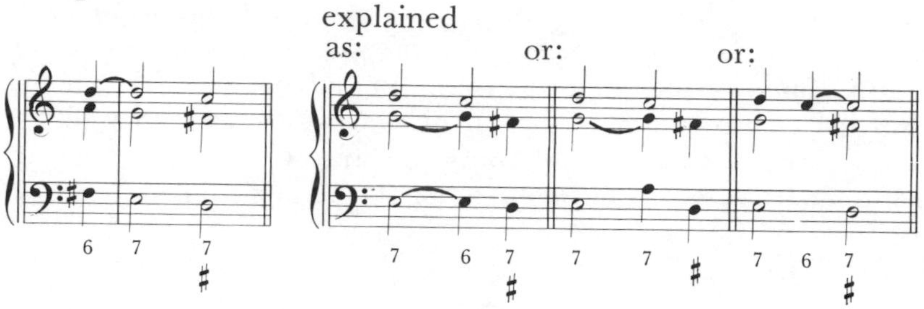

Türk's third solution, that of the assumed 7-6 suspension, also suggests the explanation given by Christoph Gottlieb Schröter of a progression in his *Deutliche Anweisung zum General-Bass*, a work actually completed by 1752 but not published until 1772. As so often occurs in Marpurg's examples of harmonic irregularity, the progression given by Schröter involves two successive seventh chords in root position. Here, however, their basses are a third apart; the bass of the first chord moves down a third, and its seventh resolves upward to the third of the second chord. Thus, seventh does not resolve to seventh in the same voice part, and Schröter's main concern here seems to be with the upward motion of the initial seventh. Frank T. Arnold's realization of Schröter's verbal explanation does indeed involve an assumed 7-6 resolution of the first seventh, but with a complete ellipsis of the intended note of resolution as in Heinichen's Example 5b.[31] Similar also to Heinichen's example is the skip *from* the assumed note of resolution. Again, it is obvious why neither Heinichen nor Schröter uses the *anticipatio transitus* concept to explain these situations.

[30]Daniel Gottlob Türk, *Anweisung zum Generalbassspielen* (Halle, 1824), pp. 102-3.

[31]Schröter, *Deutliche Anweisung*, p. 77 and Frank T. Arnold, *The Art of Accompaniment from a Thorough-Bass* (London: Oxford University Press, 1931; reprint ed., London: Holland Press, 1961), p. 847.

The discussion of such elliptical resolution, resolution which cannot be explained by means of anticipated or omitted passing tones, is taken up by Johann Philipp Kirnberger, who provides not only an explicit explanation but who also seems to be the first to associate it directly with the *galant* or free style. Kirnberger, in his *Die Kunst des reinen Satzes in der Musik* (Vol. 1, 1776-79), clearly states that in passing over the resolution of a seventh the consonant chord which would have resulted from the resolution may be omitted and another dissonant chord taken at once, the dissonance of which would have been prepared by the omitted chord. His illustration of this is given in Example 11.[32] As in the Schröter example discussed above, the first seventh, now in the bass, appears to resolve upward. All parts, however, proceed stepwise here, and the assumed omission, as Kirnberger points out, obviously would have prepared the dissonant diminished fifth of measure two as well as properly resolved the augmented fourth of measure one. Nevertheless, Kirnberger does not speak of *Voraus-nahme*, for it is very apparent that he has in mind the omission of an entire chord, with assumed contrary and oblique motion as well as anticipation among the individual voice parts.[33] The omitted C-major chord has two pitches foreign to the preceding seventh chord, and two foreign to the following one. The assumed resolution and preparation are accomplished conjointly by the various parts.

Example 11.

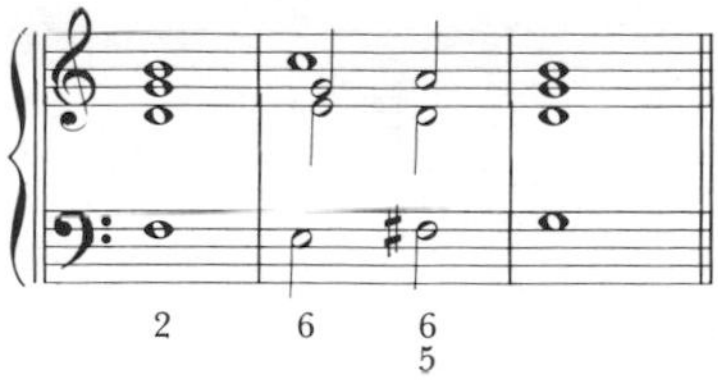

may become:

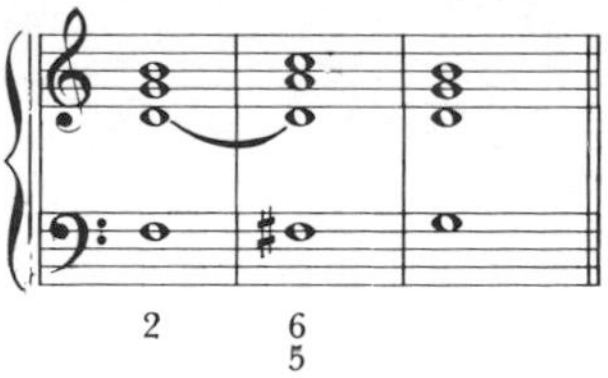

[32]Kirnberger, *Die Kunst*, 1:85.

[33]Certainly Kirnberger's erroneous conception of Rameau's fundamental bass is a factor here. See Johann Philipp Kirnberger, *Die wahren Grundsätze zum Gebrauch der Harmonie* (Berlin-Königsberg, 1773), pp. 41-45. See also Joyce Mekel, "The Harmonic Theories of Kirnberger and Marpurg," *Journal of Music Theory* 4 (1960): 184-86, 191 for a discussion of how Kirnberger's explanations of *Übergänge der Resolution* result from an attempt to render irregular progressions "more natural" and how these explanations relate to his conception of essential and non-essential dissonance.

Türk gives several examples of unresolving rising sevenths, also clearly associated with the *galant* style and also merely explained as elliptical or "catachrestic" resolutions. One progression, given in Example 12a,[34] is reminiscent of that given by Kirnberger. Another progression, Example 12b,[35] involves a diminished-seventh chord and is drawn supposedly from the music of J.S. Bach. A third progression, Example 12c,[36] deals with only one seventh chord; it resolves irregularly to a first-inversion diminished triad, the second dissonance being here an augmented fourth between the upper parts. Also, in this instance the assumed bass is approached and left by skip.

Example 12a.

explained as:

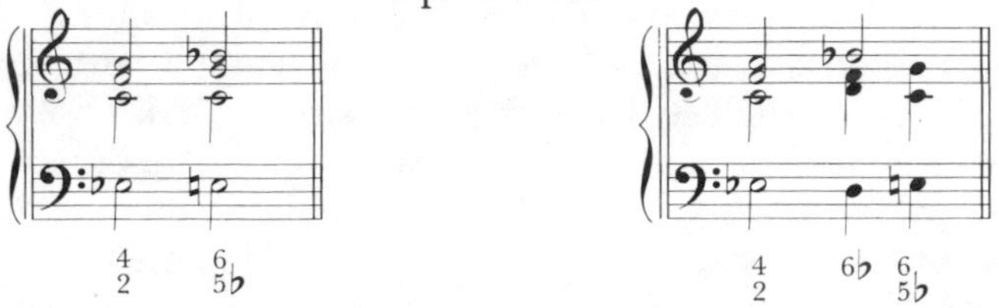

Example 12b.

explained as:

Example 12c.

explained as:

[34]Daniel Gottlob Türk, *Kurze Anweisung zum Generalbassspielen* (Halle, 1791), p. 67.

[35]Türk, *Anweisung*, p. 227; see also p. 104.

[36]Ibid., p. 64. See also Example 10, above.

It seems quite apparent that the *galant* style, formulated as it was mainly on freer dissonance treatment, represents more of a theoretical antithesis to the rule of tradition than an actual style. In reality, exchange, anticipation, and ellipsis, topics which figure so importantly in eighteenth-century German definitions of the *galant* in music, tell us as much about the attitudes and values of the *galant* theorists as about their *galant* style.[37] For it was the concern of these German theorists for the rampant modernity of their day which caused them to analyze and rationalize its harmonic freedoms; their moderate modernity, their respect for the past as well as interest in the present caused them to formulate the stylistic dichotomy of the strict style on the one hand and the *galant* or free style on the other. Their stylistic and aesthetic preferences were somewhere between the extremes which they postulated. On the subject of preparation, for example, Kirnberger provides several gradations of approach and taste at one point in his writings. In a first example (Example 13), a minor sixth and diminished octave are suspended as non-essential dissonances resolving to a seventh chord; as such they are well prepared. The notes of resolution, the *c*'' and *e*'', are explained as the seventh and ninth of a dominant chord with *d* as supposed root; therefore, according to *galant* theory, they do not require preparation.[38]

Example 13.

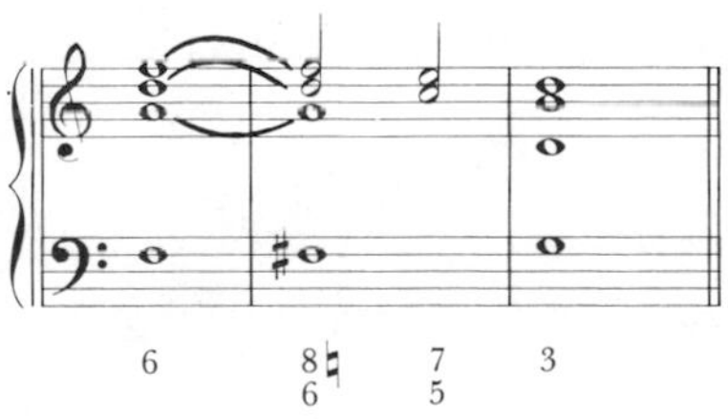

In a following example the ties are omitted and the notes *d*'' and *f*'' are struck anew as appoggiaturas.[39] This apparently still represents for Kirnberger a sufficient degree of preparation for the diminished octave. But, he continues, "when these appoggiaturas are intro-

[37]It should be pointed out that in addition to harmonic irregularities, the *galant* style suggested to eighteenth-century German writers a free texture inclining toward homophony. See especially Marpurg, *Kritische Briefe*, 2: 73 and Heinrich Christoph Koch, *Musikalisches Lexikon* (Frankfurt, 1802), col. 1453.

[38]Kirnberger, *Die wahren Grundsätze*, p. 31. The author is actually J.A.P. Schulz.

[39]Ibid., p. 32. See n. 6, above.

duced in our new compositions without any preparation and are treated as an essential chord [*Hauptaccord*] in the following manner:

Example 14.

and are further delayed by other appoggiaturas [as in the following example],

Example 15.

which are occasionally as little prepared as here:

Example 16.

the composers themselves might be able to justify it. We [, however,] cannot answer for the style of the unharmonic foreigners and for those who imitate them."[40]

A more positive, moderating attitude regarding the new music is shown by Johann Adam Hiller's definition of the free style:

[40] Ibid., pp. 33-34. Throughout the eighteenth-century theoretical literature, the *galant* style itself is not associated directly with any particular nation or national style.

> Moreover, we know from experience and from the history of music that much of what sounded horrible to our forefathers gives charming pleasure to our ears, so that it is unjust when one discards everything which sounds perhaps new and unfamiliar. . . . Genius dares to depart from rules, and what in the first instance does not succeed, becomes perhaps tolerable in the second, and beautiful in the third.[41]

The conception of the eighteenth-century German theorists of a *galant* style must be noted by modern music scholars, for it is the only one which the eighteenth century has clearly provided. Unfortunately, the many and diverse modern definitions of the *galant* style fail for the most part to acknowledge this contribution of eighteenth-century musical thought, which, in the opinion of this writer, can and should provide the essential and unifying basis for twentieth-century definitions. Perhaps Türk's somewhat reproachful definition, with its emphasis on harmonic eccentricity, can best serve as a model for the present-day writer of the eighteenth-century theoretical attitude regarding the *galant* style:

> In the free or *galant* style the composer does not always follow the grammatical rules so strictly. He allows, for example, certain dissonances to enter unprepared; he transfers their resolutions to other voices, or omits the resolutions altogether. He gives to dissonances a longer duration than to the following consonances, something which does not take place in the strict style. Moreover, he modulates excessively, allows various kinds of embellishments, and adds diverse passing tones. In short, he composes more for the ear and, if I might say so, appears less as a learned composer.[42]

[41]Johann Adam Hiller, *Anweisung zum musikalisch-richtigen Gesänge* (Leipzig, 1774), p. 211.

[42]Türk, *Anweisung*, p. 70.

A. Peter Brown

An Introduction to the Life and Works of Carlo d'Ordonez*

Much has been written about Haydn, Mozart, and Beethoven, whose works are the crowning achievements of the so-called Classic era. Yet little attention has been afforded to the 18th-century Viennese composers of lesser accomplishments who were enthusiastically patronized and are today recognized as historically significant for the development of the mid-century style. In addition to the composers directly associated with the imperial court, a group of dilettantes enriched the Viennese musical environment: Christoph Sonnleithner, a lawyer who wrote many church and chamber works as well as a few symphonies; Karl Kohaut, a government official—k. k. Hofsekretär—who participated in Van Swieten's musical enterprises and was considered one of the finest performers on the lute in his time; and, perhaps the most prolific, Carlo d'Ordonez,[1] Sekretär (or Registrant) of the k. k. niederösterreichisches Landrecht and violinist.

Except for a small amount of biographical data gleaned from contemporary newspapers, lexicons, and almanachs, and the *Sperrs-Relation*[2] for his death, very little is known about Ordonez; a potentially major source of biographical information, the Archiv des Landmarschallischen Gerichts—named the Niederösterreiches

*The author gratefully acknowledges the receipt of an American Council of Learned Societies fellowship which made this study possible.

[1]Although a number of variants appear in the sources (e.g., Ordonitz, Ordonnez), the author believes that the spelling used here—without the tilde—is the most satisfactory solution.

[2]"Sperrs-Relation. Toden-Fall. Carlo Ordonitz. September 6, 1786." Archiv der Stadt Wien.

Landrecht after 1764—was for the most part destroyed in the 1927 fire at the Justizpalast. Junker's (?) *Musikalisches Almanach für Deutschland*[3] gives 19 April as Ordonez's day of birth, and a notice in the *Wiener-Zeitung*[4] states that he died on 6 September 1786 at the age of 52. Count Karl von Zinzendorf reports in his diary that Ordonez was the "fils naturel de Mr. de Buquoy"[5]—probably either Karl Graf Buquoy (1705-59) or Franz Leopold Graf Buquoy (1703-67)—and it seems likely that his mother was Spanish and may have come to Vienna with the court of Charles VI.

Although we have no records relating to his musical education, three of his earliest works became a part of the collection at Stift Göttweig in the 1750s: the copies of two symphonies and a three-act ballet are dated 1756, 1759, and 1758 respectively. During this same period some of his works were also apparently distributed into Bohemia: a number of Ordonez symphonies in the Waldstein collection from Doksy[6] are also of a very early origin. During the 1760s his works were sold in Stockholm (1763),[7] and one or two symphonies (1764 and 1769) and a "Gassatione" (1768) were published by Vénier and Mlle Vendôme. It is in this decade that we have the first documentation of his activities in Vienna. He is included as a violinist in a 1766 listing of Viennese musicians in Hiller's *Nachrichten*[8] and is mentioned in the following excerpt from an article on Viennese musical taste in an issue of the *Wienerisches Diarium* of the same year:

> Wir haben noch Hrn. Zechner, weltlichen Priester, dessen Styl alla Capella; Hrn. von Ordoniz; Hrn. Starzer and Hrn. Gassmann, deren ersterer in Sinfonien, Cassationen, Quatri und letztere zum Theater recht schöne Stücke beygetragen haben.[9]

Perhaps as a result of new contacts offered by the formation of the Tonkünstler Societät in 1771[10] and the Masonic Lodge "Zu

[3]Freiburg, 1782.

[4]1786, no. 73.

[5]Entry for April 23, 1775. His *Tagebücher* are located in Vienna's Haus-, Hof- und Staatsarchiv.

[6]Now in the Národní Múzeum, Prague.

[7]According to an auction list in the Kungliga Biblioteket, Stockholm (OKAT. Bokaukt).

[8]J.A. Hiller, *Wöchentliche Nachrichten und Anmerkungen*, September 23, 1766, p. 99.

[9]1766, *Anhang* to no. 84.

[10]See C.F. Pohl, *Denkschrift aus Anlass des 100 jähr. Bestehens der Tonkünstler-Societät* (Vienna: Carl Gerold's Sohn, 1871), p. 122.

den drei Adlern" in 1773,[11] the number of Ordonez's recorded musical activities increases markedly. In 1771 the professional Viennese copyist Simon Haschke advertised his works,[12] and in 1777 two issues—the six quartets known as Opus 1 and a Symphony in C—were sold by the short-lived publishing house Guera of Lyon. Count Zinzendorf heard Ordonez perform with Starzer and Seuby (?) at Count Thun's in 1775,[13] while two years earlier Charles Burney wrote the following enthusiastic account:

> Between the vocal parts of this delightful concert, we had some exquisite quartets, by Haydn, executed in the utmost perfection; the first violin by M. Startzler [*sic*], who played the *Adagios* with uncommon feeling and expression; the second violin by M. Ordonetz; count Brühl played the tenor, and M. Weigel, an excellent performer on the violoncello, the base. All who had any share in this concert, finding the company attentive, and in a disposition to be pleased, were animated to that true pitch of enthusiasm, which, from the ardor of the fire within them, is communicated to others, and sets all around in a blaze; so that the contention between the performers and hearers, was only who should please, and who should applaud the most![14]

The announcement for the Tonkünstler Societät's Academy on 17 March 1777 listed "Eine neue, grosse Sinfonie von der Erfindung des Herrn von Ordonez." However, it is not clear if C.F. Pohl was correct when he reported that another Ordonez symphony was performed at a 1777 December Academy;[15] it may very well be that Pohl's reference was to a broadside in the Gesellschaft der Musikfreunde in Vienna which announces "Eine von einer hohen Standesperson verfertigte neue grosse Sinphonie" performed in December of the following year. The music for the fireworks display "Das Denkmal des Friedens" executed at the Prater on 25 June 1779 has unfortunately not been located. From an announcement in the *Wienerisches Diarium,*[16] we know that "die grosse Serenade" was scored for thirty-one wind instruments in two choirs, each with a conductor. The *Pressburger Zeitung* for 3 July published the following review:

[11] See Ludwig Abalfi, *Geschichte der Freimaurerei in Österreich-Ungarn* (Budapest: Aigner, 1890-93), vol. 2, pp. 181, 189; vol. 3, p. 219; vol. 4, pp. 242, 265, 270.

[12] See Hannelore Gericke, *Der Wiener Musikalienhandl von 1700 bis 1778* (Graz: Hermann Böhlaus, 1960), p. 104.

[13] See supra, n. 5.

[14] Charles Burney, *The Present State of Music in Germany*, vol. 1 (London, 1773), p. 290.

[15] See Pohl, *Denkschrift*, p. 58.

[16] 1779, *Anhang* to no. 49.

> . . . vorher eine vortreffliche sehr grosse Serenade einzig von blasenden Instrumenten, durch 31 der berühmtesten Tonkünstler Wiens aufführen: die von dem k. k. nied. österreichischen Land-Rechts-Sekretair Hrn. Karl v. Ordamoz hiezu neu componirt worden, und der Erwartung vollkommen entsprach, welche von den allgemein beliebten musikalischen Talente dieses grossen und Wien als seiner Vaterstadt Ehre manchenden Dilletantens zum voraus fassen konnte. Nach der kenner Urtheile herrschten in der ganzen Kompositionen leichter und edler Gesang: die übrigen aber waren so neu als hinreissend, kurz, man kann in diesem Fache nichts reissenders hören.[17]

It was also during the 1770s that Ordonez composed his only known works with voices: the two German operas *Alceste* and *Diesmal hat der Mann den Willen* and the cantata *Der alte wienerische Tandelmarkt*. Unfortunately, the libretto of the cantata—whose text is related to that of the well-known *Wienerischer Tandlmarkt* from ca. 1750 by Gregor Joseph Werner—survives without the music; it does, however, give the date of composition as 1779.[18] Ordonez's parody opera *Alceste* was first performed at the marionette theater in Esterháza on 30 August 1775 for the visit of Archduke Ferdinand and Maria Beatrice. In July of 1777 it was repeated at Schönbrunn by the Esterházy company in honor of Clemens Wenzel, Elector of Treves, at which time Maria Theresa—according to the *Wienerisches Diarium*—gave the work her "gnädigen Beyfall."[19] Perhaps most astonishing is the fact that between the years 1783 and 1795 forty-nine performances of *Alceste* were given at the theater in Leopoldstadt.[20] Apparently because its popularity was so great, in 1806 the theater's indefatigable musical director, Wenzel Müller, composed a parody of the parody, *Die neue Alzeste: Ein Karrikatur Oper*, which continued in the repertory until 1821.

Alceste provides the only link between Ordonez and Joseph Haydn that can be corroborated by external evidence. Haydn inserted a minuet from *Alceste* into his *Philemon und Baucis* (Hob. XXIXa: 1), and a score to *Alceste* is listed in the catalogues of Haydn's library and estate. In their excellent book *Haydn als Opernkapellmeister*, Bartha and Somfai wonder why Haydn's score to *Alceste* has none of the changes found in his other scores of

[17] 1779, no. 53.

[18] Stadtbibliothek, Vienna (Mc55305).

[19] See H.C. Robbins Landon, "Haydn's Marionette Operas and the Repertoire of the Marionette Theatre at Esterház Castle," *Haydn Yearbook* 1 (1962):190.

[20] See Franz Hadamowsky, *Das Theater in der Wiener Leopoldstadt 1781-1860* (Vienna: O. Höfles' Witwe, 1934).

operas performed at Esterháza.[21] H.C. Robbins Landon's explanation is that Ordonez himself went to Esterháza to conduct the première in 1775.[22] A comparison of Haydn's score—now in the National Széchényi Library[23]—with the librettos now in the Stadtbibliothek[24] and Nationalbibliothek[25] in Vienna used for the Esterháza and Leopoldstadt performances reveals that it matches neither libretto completely. However, as the discrepancies between the Esterháza libretto and Haydn's score involve only large dimension alterations probably caused by insertions, it must be assumed that the extant score was for the version performed at Esterháza during 1775.

Diesmal hat der Mann den Willen opened the second season of the old Burgtheater in 1778. Today, the Singspiel only survives in an abbreviated version; the libretto by Kommissionsrat J. F. Schmidt shows twenty numbers, whereas the surviving score and parts contain only seven consecutively numbered pieces.[26] Apparently this work, like *Alceste*, is a parody: according to Count Zinzendorf, it is an imitation of Grétry's [*recte:* Monsigny's] *opéra comique Le maître en droit* with libretto by Le Monnier, which played in Vienna in 1763. Zinzendorf also commented that "... la musique de Ordoñez est trop difficile, trop peu chantante ...."[27] The review in the 25 April 1778 *Wienerisches Diarium* unfortunately only is concerned with the Singspiel debut of a Madam Lange.

In contrast to the previous decade, for the 1780s little material concerning Ordonez has been uncovered. In 1780 his wife Johanna died, leaving behind two children; four years later he was the principal second violinist at a performance of Haydn's oratorio *Il Ritorno di Tobia* (Hob. XXI: 1) given by the Tonkünstler Societät and, for unknown reasons, subsequently closed his membership with this association.[28] At the time of his death on 6 September

[21]Dénes Bartha and László Somfai, *Haydn als Opernkapellmeister: Die Haydn-Dokumente der Esterházy-Opernsammlung* (Budapest: Verlag der Ungarischen Akademie der Wissenschaft, 1960), p. 391.

[22]Landon, "Marionette Operas," pp. 189-90.

[23]OE 65.

[24]A 140046.

[25]6.41.433-A.

[26]Österreichische Nationalbibliothek (SM 16148, 15632, and 641.433 AMS).

[27]*Tagebücher*, April 22, 1778.

[28]See Otto Biba, "Beispiele für die Besetzungsverhältnisse bei Aufführungen von Haydns Oratorien in Wien zwischen 1784 und 1808," *Haydn Studien* 4 (1978):94-95 and Pohl, *Denkschrift*, p. 104.

1786 he was pensioned from his official position and, according to the *Sperrs-Relation*, was a man of little means.

* * *

From information derived from the copies and 18th-century catalogues, it can be determined that Ordonez's musical productivity probably spanned the years between 1750 and 1780. A list of authentic extant works includes 68 symphonies, 12 minuets for orchestra, 1 violin concerto, 27 string quartets, 21 string trios, 2 sonatas for violin and bass, 6 divertimenti, 2 operas, and 1 ballet.[29] During the 18th century Ordonez's works were apparently distributed not only in the Austro-Hungarian empire but as far north as Stockholm and west as London.

The symphony is the genre to which Ordonez contributed the largest number of works. Besides the normal three- and four-movement sequences, here we find seven cycles with an extended introduction or an initial slow movement,[30] two in two movements,[31] and one in seven movements.[32] According to the *Wiener Theater Almanach*,

> Nebst den grossen Meistern, deren Berufsgeschäft die Kirchencomposizion war, gab es auch mehrere Männer, die bloss zum Vergnügen setzen, und auch vieles für die Kirche arbeiteten. Hr. Ordonnez schrieb vortreffliche Composizionen.[33]

As there is no documentation that Ordonez wrote Masses or other liturgical vocal works, the writer was apparently referring to instrumental works. Three Ordonez symphonies survive with liturgical indications: the seven-movement symphony is entitled *Sinfonia Solenne*, another is entitled *Partitta Solenne,*[34] and a third is inscribed *In Festo 3 Regum.*[35] According to Stephan Bonta, it is

[29] A complete thematic catalogue by the author has been published by Information Coordinators (Detroit, 1978). All subsequent references to the works in footnotes are by the numbers assigned in the catalogue.

[30] I: C1, E-flat 1, E-flat 3, E1, F8, F9, and B-flat 4. Symphonies I: C1 and B-flat 4 together with F11, A8, C9, C14, and G1 have been edited by the author and are published in *The Symphony 1720-1840,* ed. Barry S. Brook (New York: Garland, 1979-).

[31] I: E-flat 1 and E-flat 3. E-flat 1 also exists in a three-movement version. The two-movement cycle is probably secondary to the three-movement setting.

[32] I: D5.

[33] "Ueber den Stand der Musik in Wien," *Wiener Theater Almanach* (Vienna: [Kurzböck], 1794), p. 178.

[34] I: C3.

[35] I: C9.

possible that such a seven-movement work was used in the Mass,[36] as follows:

Free Instrumental Pieces Used in the Mass	*Sinfonia Solenne* in D (Brown I: D5)
Before the Mass	Adagio 3/4-Vivace 4/4, D major, ritornello form
Introit	Andante cantabile 3/4, G major, sonata form
Gradual	Intermezzo: Allegro Scherzante 2/4, D major, sonata form
Offertory	Menuetto and Trio 3/4, D major
Elevation	Andantino. Siciliano un poco lento 6/8, A major, concertante sonata form
Communion	Menuetto and Trio 3/4, D major
Deo Gratias	Finale: Allegro ¢, D major, fugue

As the two-movement and a few of the three- and four-movement symphonies begin with a slow movement—a characteristic of the *sonata da chiesa*—these works may also have been intended for liturgical use.

Two symphonies, in C[37] and D major,[38] with two pairs of trumpets were also probably used in the church. The C-major work, one of his most widely distributed compositions, was written for three instrumental groups: an orchestra of 2 oboes, 2 horns, and strings, and 2 antiphonal choirs of 2 clarini and timpani. This disposition of instrumental forces and trumpet color are part of a long tradition in Viennese music from Fux to Beethoven. The most original aspect of this symphony is the use of double stops in the timpani (Example 1), a precursor of the technique Berlioz employed so effectively.

[36]"The Uses of the *Sonata da Chiesa*," *Journal of the American Musicological Society* 22 (1969):72-73.

[37]I: C10. Modern edition by H.C. Robbins Landon, *Sinfonia per tre cori* (Mainz: Universal Edition, 1972).

[38]I: D7 exists in copies at Stift Lambach (73) and the Musikwissenschaftliches Institut der Universität Wien with four clarini, but the other extant copies indicate two clarini and two horns. Clarini, however, in some respects seem more idiomatic.

Example 1. Ordonez, Symphony in C (Brown I: C10), Mvt. I

Most of the symphonies require pairs of oboes and horns, while others add the trumpet and timpani; a pair of flutes and bassoons are only indicated in a single movement.[39] With a few exceptions, Ordonez's concept of the wind group is to support the strings. While a large number of the symphonies seem to lack a feeling for orchestral effect, one can point to instances of remarkable sophistication. In the seven-movement symphony, the contrast of winds and strings and the effective use of pizzicato in the bass in the slow introduction (Example 2) and the combination of sonority, rhythmic activity, and counterpoint in the finale (Example 3) are rarely equaled in the works of other *Kleinmeister*.

Example 2. Ordonez, Symphony in D (Brown I: D5), Mvt. I

[39]The slow movement of I: D1.

Example 3. Ordonez, Symphony in D (Brown I: D5), Mvt. VII

Orchestration is also effectively utilized to underline structural points, as in the transition of the second movement of Ordonez's Symphony in C minor (Example 4); in the finale of this same work, the initial thematic material of the recapitulation is reorchestrated and the dynamic level reduced to *pianissimo* (Example 5).

Example 4. Ordonez, Symphony in C minor (Brown I: C14), Mvt. II

Example 5. Ordonez, Symphony in C minor (Brown I: C14), Mvt. IV

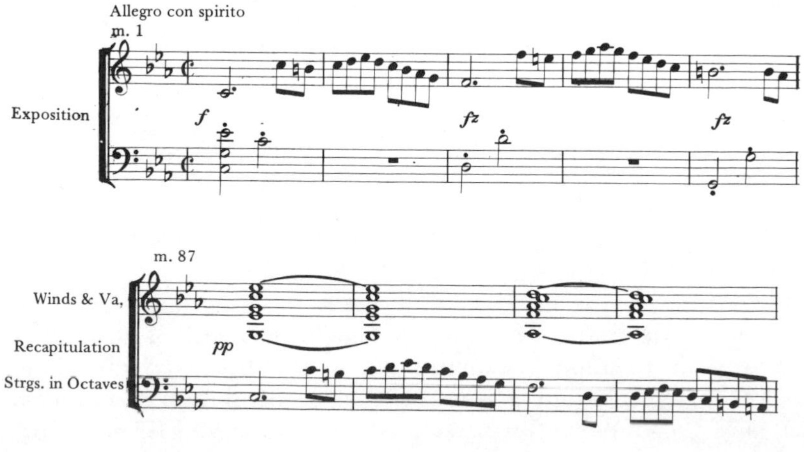

The viola, an instrument Ordonez himself may have played, is at times used beyond what is considered normal for the 18th century: in addition to soloistic viola lines in some chamber works, a number of symphonies require two violas, and in one case the highest positions are demanded in a soloistic role (Example 6).

Example 6. Ordonez, Symphony in B-flat (Brown I: B-flat 6), Mvt. II

Among Ordonez's chamber music, the string quartets hold a particularly important place in not only his own output but also the development of the genre. Here one can observe the influence of the *sonata da chiesa* and the divertimento. As in the former, the majority of these works begin with a slow movement and have a fugue for the second or fourth movement. Those that begin in quick tempo often conclude with a fugue and contain a *cantilena* slow movement so frequently encountered in the divertimento forms. Imitative beginnings, the build-up of sonority, and pedal points are not uncharacteristic of several of the sonata-form movements. Perhaps one of the more remarkable aspects of Ordonez's quartets is thematic unification of the cycle in several of the quartets from his published Opus 1.[40] In one instance, the recurring material functions differently in a manner not unlike that found in 19th-century cyclic structures (Example 7).

Example 7. Ordonez, Quartet in C minor, Op. 1, No. 3 (Brown IV: C4), Mvts. II, III, and IV

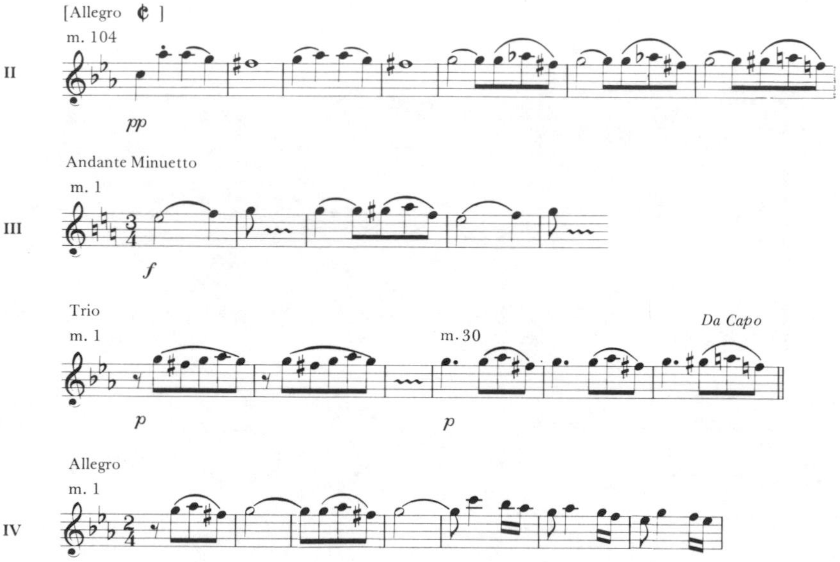

The trio sonata is the only other chamber music medium to which Ordonez contributed a substantial number of works. Somewhat surprising is the fact that the cyclic structures of the trios owe less to the functional Baroque styles than those of the quartets, although the individual movements tend to reflect the influence of the suite. While the trios emphasize a mid-century orientation, the quintets, sextet, and octet are distinctive in Ordonez's output for their finales in a primitive rondo form. In contrast to the trios, the works for five or more instruments also contain some felicitous coloristic effects: the soloistic passages for a pair of horns in works with string trio and quartet,[41] the scoring for pairs of oboes, English horns, bassoons, and horns in the wind octet,[42] and the opposition of the two violins and violas in the string quintet.[43]

[40]An edition by the author was published in 1980 by A-R Editions of Madison, Wisconsin.

[41]IIIb: F1, IIIc: F1 and F2.

[42]IIIa: F1.

[43]IIIc: E-flat 2.

Four chamber works have been attributed to both Haydn and Ordonez. On the basis of external evidence, the following divertimenti listed in Hoboken's Haydn *Verzeichnis* are probably by Ordonez: Hob. II: Es9, F5, F6. Although no copy or catalogue entry survives under Ordonez's name for Hob. II: F4, this divertimento is also probably from his pen. However, the Trio Sonata Hob. V: G4 attributed to Haydn in two sources and to Ordonez in a copy at the Gesellschaft der Musikfreunde in Vienna[44] is without question by Haydn: in the Gesellschaft source the copyist wrote Haydn's name on the underfold of the cover, while "Ordonez" was added to the front of the cover in pencil by a different hand.[45]

Ordonez's instrumental works in general are marked by the employment of a trill with a notated preparation (Example 8), sequences coupled with suspensions (Example 9), and a cadential rhythmic formula in triple-metered movements (Example 10).

Example 8. a. Ordonez, Symphony in D (Brown I: D6)
b. Ordonez, Symphony in G (Brown I: G5)
c. Ordonez, Symphony in A (Brown I: A2)

Example 9. Ordonez, Quartet in F minor (Brown IV: F5), Mvt. II

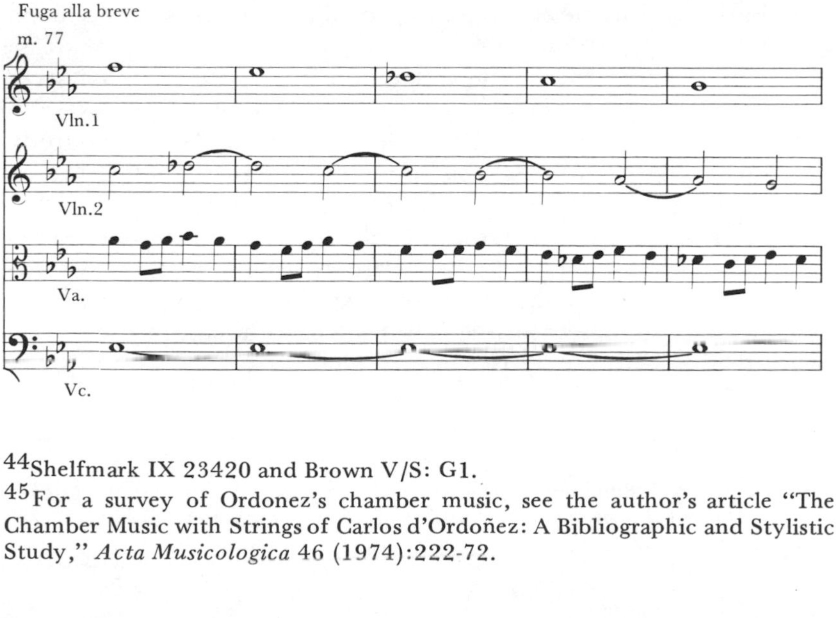

[44]Shelfmark IX 23420 and Brown V/S: G1.

[45]For a survey of Ordonez's chamber music, see the author's article "The Chamber Music with Strings of Carlos d'Ordoñez: A Bibliographic and Stylistic Study," *Acta Musicologica* 46 (1974):222-72.

Example 10. Ordonez, Symphony in G minor (Brown I: G7), Mvt. I

Although his phrases are often structured with care, Ordonez was a composer of limited melodic inspiration: stylized melodies—particularly the *siciliana*—are favored in slow movements, and the musical ideas in fast movements tend to be homogeneous. Lyrical melodies sophisticatedly controlled as in Example 4 are found only in a few of the later works. While harmony is at times treated coloristically in the small dimension, a large-dimension tonal drive is not fully realized. In the main, Ordonez's musical shapes are propelled by insistent rhythms and contrapuntal textures.

In his early years, Ordonez wrote only one work for the stage: a three-act *Pantomima*, which survives in a copy acquired by Göttweig Abbey in 1758. Consisting of thirty-four short numbers, the work is a compendium of both dances and "characteristic" styles (e.g., the storm and the underworld). In addition to being a precursor of some of Gluck's ballets—such as his *Don Juan* of 1761—one can see the influence of the late Italian Baroque/early Classic style in the motoristic rhythms and the dialoguing first and second violins.

Of Ordonez's three late vocal compositions, all of which seem to be based on the principle of parody, his German opera *Alceste* is the only work that can be compared with its model. This parody encompasses both the text and the music of the Gluck-Calzabigi original, printed in 1769. The librettist, Joseph Karl von Pauersbach[46]—a colleague of Ordonez in the Niederösterreichisches Landrecht, was praised in a *Wienerisches Diarium* review of the August 1775 performance at Esterháza for his "gute Laune."[47] This is readily apparent in the following comparison of Calzabigi's elevated style with the "localisms" of Pauersbach:

[46]See Klaus M. Pollheimer, "Karl Michael (Joseph) von Pauersbach (1737-1802)," *Jahrbuch für österreichische Kulturgeschichte* 3 (1973):34-78.

[47]No. 74.

Calzabigi, *Alceste* (1767)	Pauersbach, *Alceste* (1775 [1783?])
Act I, Scene ii–Aria of Alceste	*Act I, Scene ii–Aria of Alceste*
Io non chiedo, eterni Dei	Ich fordre nicht, ihr Ewige Götter,
Tutto il ciel per me sereno.	Im Jänner eine Schlittenbahn;
Ma il mio duol consoli almeno	Im Monath Maj heit'res Wetter,
Qualche raggio di pietà.	Dass ich im Duhof [Prater] fahren kann.
Act II, Scene i–Aria of Ismene	*Act II, Scene i–Aria of Ismene*
Parto . . . Ma senti . . . Oh Dio!	Ich geh! Doch, o Götter, sag
Di te che mai sarà!	Was wird mit dir geschehen?
Alceste, ah, per pietà,	Antworte mir, erst auf die Frag',
Parla . . . rispondi!	Dann will ich gerne gehen.
Mi fa tremar il core	Mein Herz sagt mir nichts Gutes vor;
Quel che non sai celar;	Halb schmeck ich schon den Lunden.
Ma più mi fa tremar	Entreisse mir den Zweifels Flor,
Quel che m'ascondi.	O Königin von Gmunden!

Although Ordonez does not follow Gluck's reform style in the Sinfonia to *Alceste*, he adopts the choral refrain pattern and aria structure of Gluck, as seen in the following diagram:

Ordonez, *Alceste*

Act I, Scenes iv-vii
Clarino Fanfare
Chorus–Moderato 6/8, C major
Recitative of Oracle–Andante ¢, F minor
Orchestral Interlude–Allegro C, F minor
Chorus–Allegro 3/8, F major/C major
Aria of Alceste–Adagio 4/4 (declamatory)
Un poco Allegro 2/4 (cantabile)
Adagio 4/4 (declamatory)
Un poco Allegro 2/4 (cantabile)
} C major
Chorus–Allegro 3/8, G major
[*Da capo* of Act I, Scene iv]

In addition to structural parody, the music of the first chorus of Gluck's Act I, Scene iv, is quoted in the first chorus of Act I, Scene ii of Ordonez's parody. A satirical mood is further underlined with the statement of a portion of the tune "God Save the Queen" in a chorus with the text "Weine O Vaterland! . . . Die Königinn ist pfutsch." More subtle is Ordonez's imitation of that distinctive yet simple melodic style which became a Gluckian hallmark during the 1760s and 1770s: in Example 11 the uncomplicated rhythms, easily negotiated melodies, and short phrases are uncharacteristic of the opera seria.

Example 11. Ordonez, *Alceste*, Aria of Alceste [No. 3]

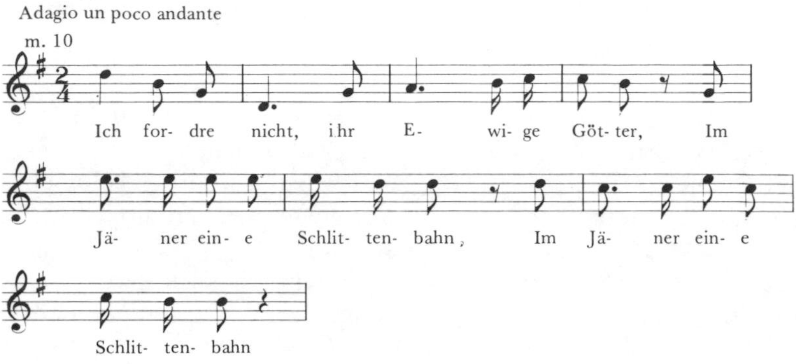

Lest there be any doubt of Ordonez's and Pauersbach's admiration of Gluck, the final chorus is seemingly a veiled tribute:

> Herrsch' über uns im besten Glück,
> Herrsch' über dieses grosse Reich,
> Der auf dem Throne keine gleich,
> Du einer Frauen Meisterstück!
> Schönheit, Keuschheit, Weisheit, Stärke,
> Und dein englischer Verstand
> Sind der milden Götter Werke,
> Die im engesten Verband
> Mit noch tausend andern Gaben
> Sie dir eingehauchet haben.

While in some respects Ordonez can be characterized as forward-looking and occasionally experimental, he properly belongs with the more conservative composers of his day who favored contrapuntal devices (e.g., Albrechtsberger, Gassmann, and Christoph Sonnleithner). An issue of greater interest, however, is whether or not Ordonez influenced or was influenced by Mozart and Haydn. With regard to the former, one can point to similarities between the first movement of the third quartet of Ordonez's Opus 1 from the 1760s and the second movement of Mozart's K. 168, which was composed in Vienna in 1773 (Example 12).

Example 12.

a. Ordonez, Quartet in C minor, Op. 1, No. 3 (Brown IV: C4), Mvt. I

Andante

m. 1

b. Mozart, Quartet in F (K. 168), Mvt. II

Andante

m. 1

The latter may be the result of Mozart's effort to gain a position at the imperial court by imitating the style of a composer already favored. As for Haydn, it is possible to find some melodic similarities (see Example 13), but these are for the most part rather tenuous.

Example 13.

a. Ordonez, Symphony in G minor (Brown I: G7), Mvt. III

Allegro non troppo con garbo

m. 1

b. Haydn, Symphony in E minor (Hob. I: 44), Mvt. I

Allegro con brio

m. 1

H.C. Robbins Landon

A New, Authentic Manuscript Source for Beethoven's Wind-Band Sextetto, Op. 71

Johann Nepomuk Hummel, composer and since 1804 *Konzertmeister* to Prince Nicolaus Esterházy, was an intelligent, difficult and often tactless man. Haydn had recommended Hummel (as the latter informs us in his autobiographical sketch of 22 May 1826) "to the reigning Prince Esterházy, his [Haydn's] patron, as *Concertmeister*, to assist him, as he became increasingly weak in his old age, in his duties. . . ." Hummel's rude behavior at Eisenstadt caused him to be dismissed in 1811, not least because he wrote in an official letter to the Esterházy administration that Prince Nicolaus "is no connoisseur of music . . ." (October 1811). Hummel was also a friend of Beethoven's, though relations between the two men had their ups and downs; but when Beethoven lay dying, Hummel was a welcome visitor.[1]

Hummel was something of an amateur collector of autographs. When he died, most of his collection remained intact, but a certain portion of the Haydn sources (autographs and authentic copies) eventually found their way, via a Leipzig antiquarian dealer, in 1883 to the British Museum. Now it develops that these Haydn compositions were all part of Haydn's legacy which went *en bloc* to Prince Nicolaus Esterházy and which (with the exception of the Hummel mss. and a few other items) is now the most cherished

[1] For Hummel's engagement at Eisenstadt, see H.C. Robbins Landon, *Haydn: Chronicle and Works*, vol. 4, *Haydn: The Years of 'The Creation' 1796-1800* (Bloomington: Indiana University Press, 1977), p. 48, n. 1, and vol. 5, *Haydn: The Late Years 1801-1809* (Bloomington: Indiana University Press, 1977), p. 280. Hummel's biography (including documents of his relationship with Beethoven) is best summarized in Karl Benyovszky, *Johann Nepomuk Hummel, der Mensch und Künstler* (Pressburg: Eos-Verlag, 1934).

part of the Esterházy Archives in Budapest and Eisenstadt. When he was in the service of Prince Nicolaus Esterházy, Hummel took charge of the musical archives and prepared a catalog (one copy is in the Hummel Archives, Florence, another in the Esterházy Archives), which is dated 1806. In the process of preparing this catalog, Hummel went through a considerable number of fragments in the (then abandoned) Castle of Eszterháza, and he appears to have begun his musical autograph collection with some odds and ends by Haydn that he found there. When Haydn died in 1809, Hummel was asked by Prince Nicolaus to attend the auction of the composer's effects, and it was Hummel who arranged for the Haydn legacy of music to be transferred to Eisenstadt—minus, it would seem, the items that eventually landed in the British Museum.

Among the most interesting mss. in the Hummel Archives at Florence is a hitherto unknown set of manuscript parts of Beethoven's *Sextetto* for wind-band, Op. 71. It is signed on the title page of "Clarinetto 1mo" by the composer: "Sextetto / da LvBthvn," and the parts contain an enormous number of holograph additions and corrections. In the absence of the autograph and any other authentic source, the Hummel ms. assumes considerable textual importance. Before we continue with a description of the Beethoven ms., however, we may wonder for a moment how Hummel came into possession of the source in the first place. The most obvious explanation is again connected with Hummel's position as *Konzertmeister* for Prince Nicolaus Esterházy.[2]

Although some kind of a catalog was drawn up in 1806, vast amounts of music are missing. We know from contemporary documents that there were balls with music many times each season at Eisenstadt; yet there is practically no dance music (and none by Haydn, for instance) listed. Similarly, the only substantial collection of wind-band music is the series of arrangements of contemporary operas: these are mostly still extant and are in the

[2] For the Haydn mss. from Hummel's effects which are now in the British Museum, see Jens Peter Larsen, *Die Haydn-Überlieferung* (Copenhagen: E. Munksgaard, 1939), p. 39f. We received valuable information from the late Mrs. Maria Hummel, in whose hospitable Florentine villa we spent many delightful hours and who kindly allowed us to study and photograph many of her treasures. Her ancestor Johann Nepomuk also had a valuable portrait collection, including unpublished portraits of Hummel (one is published in *Haydn: Chronicle and Works*, vol. 3, *Haydn in England 1791-1795* [Bloomington: Indiana University Press, 1976], the artist's signature identified by my wife), Gluck (*Haydn*, vol. 1, *Haydn: The Early Years 1732-1765* [forthcoming]), Mozart (*Haydn*, vol. 2, *Haydn at Eszterháza 1766-1790* [1978]), as well as Haydn's walking-stick and the picture of Haydn's house owned by Beethoven and given to him shortly before he died (to be published in *Haydn*, vol. 1).

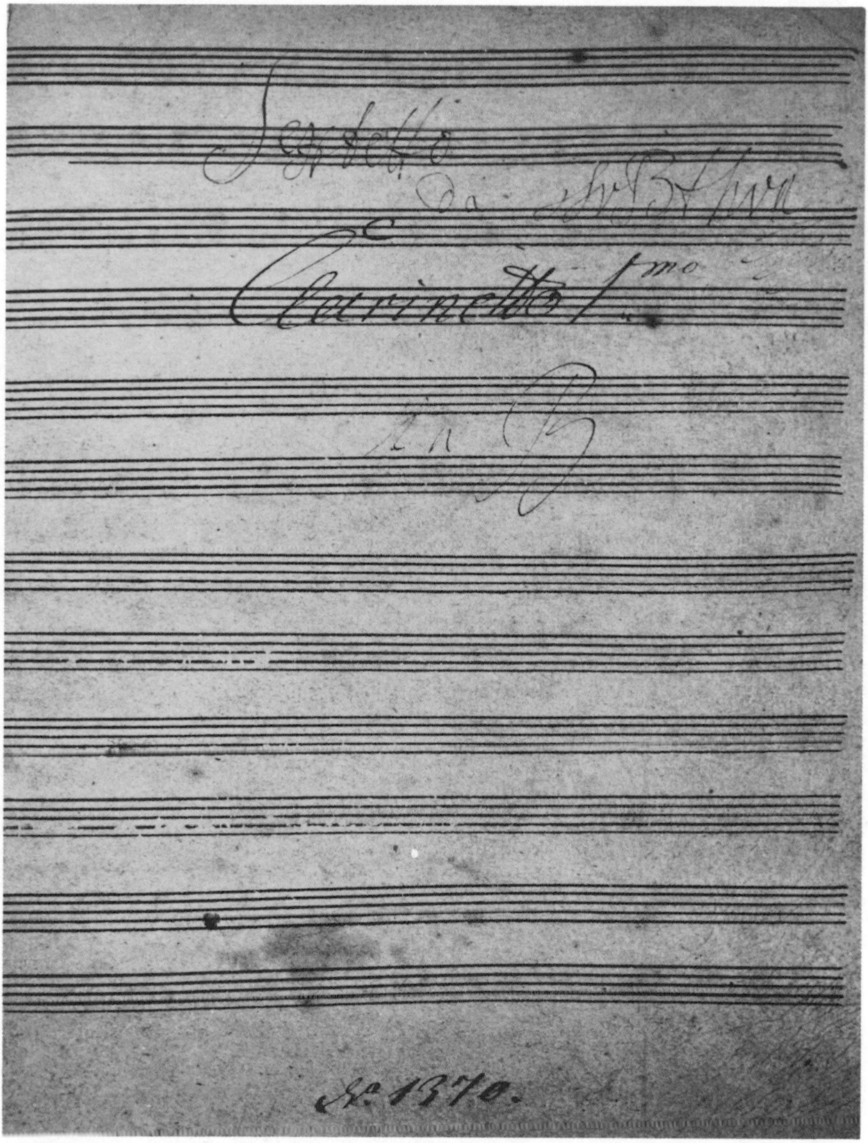

Facsimile 1. *Title page (and title page of first clarinet) of Beethoven's Op. 71 in the authentic manuscript parts from the Hummel Archives in Florence. Beethoven added the words "Sextetto / da LvBthvn" and "in B" (pitch of the clarinet).*

Facsimile 2. *A page of the first horn part of the first movement, showing a cancelled passage and Beethoven's holograph correction at the bottom of the page.*

Facsimile 3. *The last page of the second horn part, showing another cancelled passage with Beethoven's correction ("Vi-de" and "#"). The dynamic marks on this page are all in Beethoven's hand.*

Eisenstadt Archives. But there is, again, no music by Haydn in the wind-band collection. It is clear that dance music and wind-band *Parthien* (as they were called in those days) were treated as music of secondary importance: it is no accident that Haydn's own Catalog of 1805 (the so-called *Haydn-Verzeichnis*) contains no dance music whatever.

Beethoven was a guest of the Prince at Eisenstadt in the summer of 1793, when he was studying with Haydn. Beethoven also preserved a friendly relationship with the Esterházy family for some years thereafter: in 1795 Prince Nicolaus was a subscriber to Beethoven's Opus 1 Trios[3]—he bought three copies—, and the Esterházy Archives own manuscript copies (which have, rather fantastically, never been examined textually by any Beethoven scholar) of Beethoven's Symphonies Nos. 1, 2 and 3. It is well known that Beethoven was also invited to compose the Mass in C for Eisenstadt in 1807, but the visit was a fiasco.

It is presumed that the *Sextetto* was composed in 1796, the first two movements perhaps earlier.[4] Sketches to the third and fourth movements are found in the "Kafka Sketchbook," together with "Ah! perfido" (1796) and the Piano Sonata Op. 49, No. 2. In a letter to Breitkopf & Härtel of 8 August 1809, Beethoven refers to the *Sextetto*:

> . . . The Sextet is one of my earlier works and written in one night at that—one can't say anything else about it but that it is by an author who has at least written some better works—yet for some people these works are the best—. . . .[5]

[3] Facsimile in H.C. Robbins Landon, *Beethoven: A Documentary Study*, trans. Richard Wadleigh and Eugene Hartzell (London: Thames and Hudson, 1970), p. 64f. The Beethoven symphonies are listed in the Hummel catalog of 1806 (printed in *Haydn Yearbook* 9 [1975]:95-116). We examined the Esterházy copies of Beethoven's Symphonies Nos. 1-3 in Budapest in 1958 and 1959. Concerning Beethoven's unhappy visit to Eisenstadt in 1807, see Landon, *Beethoven*, p. 217ff.

[4] *Das Werk Beethovens: Thematisch-Bibliographisches Verzeichnis seiner sämtlichen vollendeten Komposition von Georg Kinsky*. Nach dem Tode des Verfassers abgeschlossen und herausgegeben von Hans Halm (Munich-Duisburg: G. Henle Verlag, 1955), p. 169f. See also J.S. Shedlock, "Beethoven's Sketch Books," *Musical Times* 33 (1892):651. The Minuet in clean copy (score) is in the so-called Kafka Sketchbook in the British Museum (facsimile ed., *Ludwig van Beethoven, Autograph Miscellany from* circa *1786 to 1799, British Museum Additional Manuscript 29801, ff. 39-162 [The 'Kafka Sketchbook']*, ed. Joseph Kerman, vol. 1, *Facsimile* [London: Oxford University Press, 1970]), fols. 104v and 105r.

[5] *Beethovens sämtliche Briefe*, ed. Alfred C. Kalischer, vol. 1 (Berlin and Leipzig: Schuster & Loeffler, 1909), p. 287f. See also *Selected Letters of Beethoven*, trans. Emily Anderson, ed. Alan Tyson (London: Macmillan & Co., 1967), p. 90f. We have translated directly from the German.

The first edition appeared with Breitkopf & Härtel in April 1810 and was entitled: "Sestetto / Pour 2 Clarinettes, 2 Cors / et 2 Bassons / par / L. v. BEETHOVEN. / Pr. 1 Rthlr. / à Leipsic / chez Breitkopf & Härtel."

Can the *Sextetto*, as Beethoven entitled the work in his curious mixture of German ("Sextett") and Italian ("Sestetto"), have been composed in 1796 for the Princely Esterházy *Feldharmonie* (wind band)? From the evidence of Haydn's dated Masses of 1796 (*Missa Sancti Bernardi de Offida* and *Missa in tempore belli*),[6] we know that in 1796 and 1797 Haydn's *Feldharmonie* included two clarinets, two bassoons and two horns. We assume that if this had been the case, Hummel later "appropriated" the source, which after all had Beethoven's signature and was heavily corrected by him, when Hummel left Eisenstadt in 1811. By then, this *Sextetto* was an "old-fashioned" work and no longer in the repertoire; probably no one would have missed it. If this is not the true explanation of the work's origin, perhaps Hummel asked for a keepsake from Beethoven in 1827 and received this work, though in the circumstances, this seems very doubtful: Beethoven would surely have given Hummel some kind of autograph ms., as he usually did when faced with requests of this kind, particularly from a fellow musician (e.g., in the cases of John Cramer and Sir George Smart).

The ms. itself consists of the separate parts. The most immediately striking fact is that the "Menuetto quasi allegretto" was obviously added after the parts had been completed. The separate parts for the Minuet are "laid in," and the first clarinet part is by another copyist (the other Minuet parts are by the principal copyist). It is significant that the above-mentioned "Kafka Sketchbook" includes a clean copy of this Minuet and Trio in score (see note 4). The Hummel source (except for the first clarinet part for the Minuet) is written on 4° opaque Viennese paper (watermarks illegible except for chain lines) of twelve staves (Minuet, clarinet I on fourteen-stave paper). The copyist seems to have been working from a score, probably Beethoven's (now lost) autograph, for in bar 51 of the first movement, horn II has *both* horn parts, i.e.,

horns I and II: 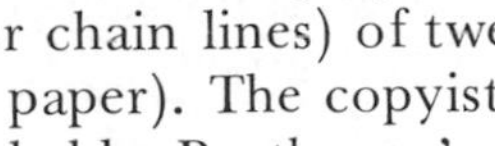 . This reading is probably from Beethoven's autograph score, where presumably both horns were written on one stave.

Textually, the ms. shows in its final, revised state a very clear

[6] *Joseph Haydn Werke*, ser. 23, vol. 2, *Messen Nr. 5-8*, ed. H.C. Robbins Landon (Munich-Duisburg: G. Henle Verlag, 1958); see also miniature score reprints, Bärenreiter Taschenpartituren nos. 93 and 94 (Kassel, 1961).

relationship to the first edition of Breitkopf & Härtel. In the manuscript parts the copyist made numerous larger and smaller errors: larger errors in jumping a section while copying from the score (see Facsimile No. 2 for one such case), smaller errors in wrong notes, etc. Beethoven labouriously corrected most of these errors. The other and principal source of Beethoven's additions was added dynamic marks and phrasing: it would seem that the autograph contained rather sparse indications of dynamic marks and slurs, staccati, and the like. If we examine the authentic sources of the Piano Sonatas Opus 49, Nos. 1 and 2, we will note an almost total absence of dynamic marks (the *Urtext* state may be examined conveniently in the Henle edition); so there is a precedent for this state of affairs in other works of ca. 1796.

There follows a short list of the principal textual differences between the known, established *Urtext* (as represented by the first edition) and our source. For convenience, references are to the easily available Edition Eulenburg No. 1239 (taken from the Breitkopf & Härtel *Gesamtausgabe*).

First pages of the manuscript parts: Clarinetto 1mo (see Facsimile No. 1), B (= additions in Beethoven's hand, so abbreviated hereinafter): title and "in B." Clarinetto 2do, B: "in B." Corno Primo in Dis: B changed "Dis" to "Es" (a proper linguistic emendation, which he later suggested should be made in the title of the "Eroica," i.e., from "in D-sharp" to "in E-flat"; "Dis" was a bad scribal habit in Austria of those days). Corno Secondo, B: "in Es."

First Movement

1: Clar. II first two bars = Clar. I. B: "in 8va." Fag. I, B: title at head of part "Sextetto/Adagio."
4: Fag. II 4th note corrected (in future these many corrected scribal errors are not noted unless of some textual significance. Similarly, the occasional missing dynamic mark [e.g., Cor. II missing *p* at bar 5 is not listed]).
6: Clar. I, II, Cor. I, II no stacc.
9: Clar. I, II *ff* by B (Fag. I no *ff*).
10: Clar. I, II *fp* by B (none in other parts!).
Upbeat to 11: B added "Allo" to Fag. I, "Allegro" to Fag. II.
11: Clar. I first note also stacc.
15/18: Fag. I no slurs; at 176/9 B added slur 
18: Cor. II *ff* (no *f* Clar. I, II & Fag. I).
23/25: *cresc.* fork (only Clar. I, II reaches into middle of 24, *decresc.* fork continues to end of 25).
26: Clar. I slur begins on 2nd note.
29: Cor. II *p* on 2nd note.
32/33: Fag. I, Cor. I no slur.
33: Fag. II first note also stacc.
34/35: Fag. II slurs bar-wise.

41: *ff* only Clar. I, II; Fag. I *f* on 2nd note; otherwise no dynamic marks.

43: Clar. I *sf* instead of *fp* and Fag. I no *p*; also Cor. I no *p* at 45, and no *p* in Fag. at 47.

49: Clar. I, II *sf* for *ff*; at 50 Clar. I *ff* on first note (B), Clar. I *f*.

58: Clar. I appoggiatura is clearly an eighth note, at 66 a sixteenth, Fag. I at 71 an eighth, Clar. I at 75 a sixteenth.

72ff: Clar. I no accents (but accents present Fag. I, 69ff.).

73: Cor. II originally had  (cancelled by B).

80: *cresc.* begins here in Clar. II (B), Fag. I, II (B). In Clar. I it begins at 81 (B), in Cor. I, II at 82 (B).

84: Clar. II, Fag. I *sf* for *ff* (B).

99: instead of *sf, rinf:* (or *mf* or *rf:*).

127/8: Clar. I slur 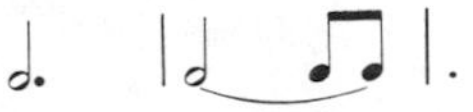.

136: Cor. II *p* again.

151: Fag. I eighth notes stacc.

155: Fag. I eighth notes slurred.

159: Fag. I *pp* (B), again at 162, 2nd note.

171: Clar. I *fp* for *ff*, Clar. II *ffp*, Fag. I nothing, Cor. I *ff*^{mo} (B), Cor. II *fp* (B).

178 (with upbeat): Clar. II slur only within 178; 178/9: Clar. I slur across bar-line.

179ff: Cor. I wrongly copied bars 194-211, the cancelled version of which helps us to reconstruct the original reading of bar 204; see facsimile (No. 2) of this section. B added the correct horn part at the bottom of the page but at 181, first note written e'' instead of (correct: first edition) e'.

183/5: Clar. II originally had reading of Clar. I, bars 184/6; cancelled by B.

192: Clar. I *cresc.* by B.

195: Cor. I no *sf* and at 199 *f* (instead of *sf*) but wiped out; in these same bars, no slurs in Fag. I.

204: it would seem that the original reading of this passage was as follows:

—in other words, a bar shorter. The horn parts at 213ff. were also quarter notes and not eighths: curiously, Cor. I was originally  but changed by B to read , whereas Cor. I originally read as in the latter example and was changed by B to read as in the former (an oversight, obviously).

210: Clar. I appoggiatura sixteenth note, at 218 an eighth, Clar. II at 227 an eighth.

220ff. (Clar. I), 225ff. (Clar. II) no accents, but present in other parallel passages; Clar. II at 225, 226 first note stacc., also Clar. I at 229, 230.

234/6: Clar. I slurred 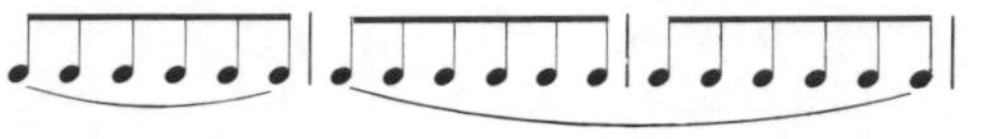 ; at 237 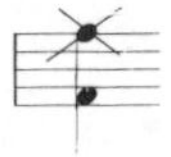 ,

241, 253: some of *ff* are *sf*.

243, 255: Cor. II wrongly  (not corrected!).

256: Fag. II *p* (B), should be added to other accomp. instr. at 257.

275: some of the *ff* are on the 2nd note (B).

Second Movement

9: Fag. I stacc. (B).

19: Clar. II first 3 notes stacc., also first and eighth notes of 20.

28: Fag. I slur over whole bar.

31: Fag. I slurs 4+4+4.

33: Fag. I slur only over last 4 notes (but cf. Clar. I), Fag. II slurs 12+2.

34: *pp* only Fag. I (B) and II (B on 2nd note).

36: Cor. I, II quarter notes.

37: Cor. II *p*.

44: Fag. II first 4 notes stacc. (B).

45/46: Cor. no tie.

59: Fag. I first note also b-flat (not octave lower); *pp* only Clar. II, but at 62 Fag. I *pp* (B).

66/7: between these bars Clar. I had 

(cancelled).

Third Movement ("Menuetto" added later)

1: Cor. I stacc. (B).

2: Cor. I appoggiatura eighth.

30: Cor. II (B) (to be added to Cor. I as well).

Trio: many of the *sf* added by B (34, 35, 38, etc.).
59: Fag. II no slur.
60: Clar. II f' (written).

Finale

Fag. II has 'Rondo / All[egr] o/maestoso' ("maestoso" not in other parts but likely).

6: Fag. I last 2 notes not dotted (but dotted at bar 64).
8: Clar. I stacc.
11: Clar. II 2nd quarter of bar two equal eighth notes (*sic*).
12: Clar. I slur ends at fourth note, last 4 notes slurred.
14: no *sf*.
15: Fag. I 2nd half of bar reads  , also at bars 77 & 115.
17: Clar. I, II no *p* (only Fag. here but not at 21).
28: Fag. I after this bar are three bars, cancelled.
37: Cor. I last note *sf*.
39: Clar. II *rf* for *sf*.
43: Clar. I, II *sf*, other instr. *ff* (B).
47: Cor. I, II *ff*^{mo} (B).
55: Fag. II after 55 a bar cancelled.
57: Clar. II some stacc., Fag. II last 6 notes stacc. Many of the dynamic marks here were added by B.
79ff: Cor. II slurred 79/80, 81/2.
82: Fag. II no *p*, *p* at 83; 83ff. Fag. II slurred 83/4, 85/6; Cor. II 91ff. slurred 91/2, 93/4.
102: Clar. I  (uncorrected! mixture of bars 101/2).
111: Clar. II 2nd beat 2 equal eighth notes (undotted).
119: Clar. I *f* (B) and no *cresc.*; Clar. II, Fag. *cresc.* (B) nearer beginning of bar.
120: Fag. I, II *ff* (B).
123: *cresc.* (B) at beginning of bar (except Cor. II), *f* at 124 by B.
126/9: Cor. II four bars heavily cancelled (B) and corrected by B at bottom of page by "Vi-de" and # sign (see Facsimile No.3). In these bars, all the *sf* in the other instr. added by B.
131: Clar. I ~ instead of *tr* (but with the "tail").
134: Fag. II and Cor. I corrected (earlier reading cannot be determined).
135ff: all the dynamic marks added by B.

Michael D. Williams

Rodolphe Kreutzer vs. Beethoven and Berlioz

Throughout the history of music, conservative administrators, critics, performers, composers, and teachers in positions of power in the musical world have attempted to place obstacles in the paths of younger, more innovative composers. The methods employed by the conservatives include issuing derogatory and inflammatory statements, refusing to program new works, and emphasizing older musical styles at educational institutions. In general these attempts have met with only temporary success, as is illustrated by the relationships of Ludwig van Beethoven and Hector Berlioz, two avant-garde composers in their day, with Rodolphe Kreutzer—violinist, conductor, composer, pedagogue, and administrator.

Rodolphe Kreutzer (1766-1831) was a leading member of the French violin school in the late eighteenth and early nineteenth centuries.[1] Although this was a time of great upheaval in French life, Kreutzer was able to adapt to the changing governments and retained his high position in the musical life of Paris until declining health forced his retirement in 1826.

Kreutzer had a variety of careers during his lifetime. As a concert violinist, he carried on the traditions of the French style of playing. His career as a soloist lasted from his debut at the Concert spirituel in 1782 until a badly broken arm forced his retirement from the concert stage in 1810.[2] As a teacher, Kreutzer was one of the first violinists on the faculty of the Paris Conservatoire, and his influence can be traced to the twentieth century through a series of

[1] For a fuller survey of Kreutzer's life and works, see the author's "The Violin Concertos of Rodolphe Kreutzer" (Ph.D. diss., Indiana University, 1972).

[2] *Allgemeine Musikalische Zeitung* 12 (1810): 968; 13 (1811): 735.

direct teacher-student relationships.[3] He wrote over one hundred musical works, including nineteen solo violin concertos for his own use on the concert stage, over forty operas and other stage works, and the famous *42 Etudes ou caprices,*[4] used as the basic set of violin exercises by most advanced violinists even today. As conductor and later administrator of the Paris Opéra, Kreutzer had great influence over the selection of works to be performed by the various musical institutions in that city.

Kreutzer's only personal contact with Beethoven occurred in 1798 in Vienna. Although he did not travel extensively as a violin soloist, Kreutzer did undertake one lengthy trip, beginning in 1796. It was a common practice of the Revolutionary governments to send scholars, artists, and musicians to countries conquered by the French army to secure art objects and musical scores, or to make copies of them, for use in French museums and libraries. Kreutzer either accompanied the army or was sent to join it in Italy, where he remained for nearly two years, having copies made of numerous manuscripts which were sent to the library of the Paris Conservatoire.[5] After the Peace of Campo Formio, Kreutzer left Italy and toured Germany and Holland.

On January 11, 1798, General Jean Baptiste Bernadotte was named French ambassador to Vienna. He presented his credentials to the Emperor on March 2. Bernadotte was a successful soldier who had taken part in the Italian campaign under Napoleon. Later in his life Bernadotte became King of Sweden.[6]

Accompanying the ambassador to Vienna was Rodolphe Kreutzer. While there is no direct evidence concerning Kreutzer's exact position there, it is likely that he performed the same duties in Vienna as he had in Italy—collecting and copying manuscripts for French libraries. Beethoven was a frequent visitor to the French embassy, and a friendship between the composer and the ambassador grew quite strong. In fact, Bernadotte may have suggested to Beethoven the idea of a symphony in honor of Napoleon.[7]

Beethoven met and heard Kreutzer play during these visits to

[3]Walter Kolneder, "Die Gründung des Pariser Konservatoriums," *Die Musikforschung* 20 (1967): 56-57.

[4](Paris: Imbault, 1796); modern edition: *42 Etudes, pour Violon*, rev. and annotated Lucien Capet (Paris: Editions Salabert, 1915).

[5]J.G. Prod'homme, "Napoleon, Music and Musicians," trans. Frederick H. Martens, *Musical Quarterly* 7 (1921): 583.

[6]Alexander Wheelock Thayer, *Life of Beethoven*, rev. and ed. Elliot Forbes, 2 vols. (Princeton: At the University Press, 1964), 1:203.

[7]J.G. Prod'homme, *Les Symphonies de Beethoven (1800-1827)*, 2nd ed. (Paris: Delagrave, 1906), p. 76.

the embassy. That the two remained on friendly terms was not evident until the following letter from Beethoven to his publisher Nikolaus Simrock concerning the dedication of the Sonata in A major for Violin and Piano, Op. 47 came to light:

Vienna, October 4, 1804

> . . . I will send you at once a little note for *Kreutzer*; and you will be so kind as to enclose it when you send him a copy (since in any case you send your copies to Paris or they may even be engraved there)—This *Kreutzer* is a dear kind fellow who during his stay in Vienna gave me a great deal of pleasure. I prefer his modesty and natural behavior to *all the exterior* without *any interior*, which is characteristic of most virtuosi —As the sonata was written for a competent violinist, the dedication to Kreutzer is all the more appropriate—Although we correspond (that is to say, he gets one letter a year from me), yet—I trust that he has not yet heard anything about my dedication. . . .[8]

Although Beethoven states that he wrote yearly letters to Kreutzer, he implies that they were not answered.

While Beethoven eventually dedicated the published version of Op. 47 to Kreutzer, the work was originally written for the mulatto violinist George Polgreen Bridgetower (1779-1860), the son of Prince Nikolaus (I) Esterházy's page, August. After spending several years as a popular violinist in London and Paris, Bridgetower visited Vienna on a European tour in April and May of 1803. Evidently Beethoven and Bridgetower rapidly developed a close friendship. Bridgetower was scheduled to give a recital at the Augarten on May 24, 1803, and the Op. 47 sonata was written for this occasion. As was so typical of Beethoven, the work was not finished on time. The third movement had originally been the finale of the Sonata in A major for Violin and Piano, Op. 30, No. 1. Bridgetower had to play the variation movement from the manuscript, and the piano part, played by the composer, was only sketched out.[9]

The dedication on the manuscript of Op. 47 is as follows: "Mulattick Sonata. Composed for the mulatto Brischdauer, great lunatick and mulattick composer."[10] But when the work was published by Simrock in 1805, there was no reference to Bridgetower, and the work was dedicated to Rodolphe Kreutzer:

[8] *The Letters of Beethoven*, collected, trans., and ed. Emily Anderson, 3 vols. (New York: St. Martin's Press, 1961), 1:120.

[9] Otto Jahn, "George Bridgetower and the 'Kreutzer' Sonata," *Musical Times* 49 (1908): 305.

[10] H.C. Robbins Landon, *Beethoven: A Documentary Study*, trans. Richard Wadleigh and Eugene Hartzell (London: Thames and Hudson, 1970), p. 148.

Sonata / per il pianoforte ed un violino obligato / Scritta in un stile molto concertante / quasi come d'un concerto / composta e dedicata a / suo amico / R. Kreutzer / membro del Concervatorio di musica di Parigi, primo Violino dell' academia delle arti e della camera imperiale / da L. van Beethoven Op. 47 / Bonn, presso N. Simrock, Prezzo 6 Frs (proprieta del editore).[11]

Why did Beethoven change his mind about the dedication? Several explanations have been offered. Schindler reports that the sonata was originally written for Bridgetower, "but with the appearance of Rodolphe Kreutzer, the co-founder of the rightly named 'great French violin school,' Beethoven changed his mind and dedicated the work to the French master (Beethoven frequently changed his dedications)."[12] But Kreutzer's appearance in Vienna had been in 1798, and there is no record of another visit to that city before the publication of the sonata.

Emery states that the dedication was changed because of a quarrel between Beethoven and Bridgetower concerning some changes Bridgetower wanted to make in the work.[13] There is no evidence to support this opinion.

Fortunately, Bridgetower himself informed the publisher of *The Musical World*, J.W. Thirwall, of the reasons for the change:

Bridgetower, when advanced in years, talking with Mr. Thirwall about Beethoven, told him that at the time the Sonata, Op. 47, was composed, he and the composer were constant companions, and that the first copy bore a dedication to him; but before he departed from Vienna they had a quarrel about a girl, and Beethoven then dedicated the work to Rudolph Kreutzer.[14]

Another question about the "Kreutzer" Sonata (as Op. 47 is now commonly known) is whether Rodolphe Kreutzer ever played the work. There is no record of Kreutzer's acknowledging the dedication or performing the work in public. Hector Berlioz gives the following account:

C'est à ce même homme [Kreutzer] (dont nous ne contestons point du reste le talent), que Beethoven venait de dédier l'une de ses plus sublimes sonates pour piano et violon; il faut convenir que l'hommage était bien adressé. Aussi le célèbre violon ne put-il jamais se décider à jouer cette composition *outrageusement inintelligible*.[15]

[11]Theodor Frimmel, *Beethoven-Handbuch*, 2 vols. (1926: reprint ed., Wiesbaden: Breitkopf & Härtel, 1968), 1:303.

[12]Anton Felix Schindler, *Beethoven As I Knew Him*, ed. Donald MacArdle, trans. Constance S. Jolly (London: Faber & Faber, 1966), p. 119.

[13]Frederic B. Emery, *The Violin Concerto* (Chicago: Violin Literature Publishing Co., 1928), p. 106.

[14]Reported in Thayer/Forbes, *Beethoven*, I:333.

[15]Hector Berlioz, *Voyage musical en Allemagne et en Italie*, 2 vols. (Paris: Jules Labitte, 1844), I:264.

Various other reasons, besides his conservative musical tastes, can be offered for Kreutzer's refusal to play the work in public. (Surely he must have read through the violin part in private.) First of all, Kreutzer must have known that the sonata was originally written for another violinist, and he may have resented the fact that he was a second choice. Also, much of Beethoven's "Kreutzer" Sonata requires short staccato (separated) and spiccato (bouncing) bowings. This style of writing is quite uncommon in Kreutzer's own works. As is the case with most performers writing music for their own use on the concert stage, Kreutzer emphasized playing techniques that came easiest to him and de-emphasized those at which he was less adept. Contemporary accounts, such as the following, praise Kreutzer's long bow strokes, clean execution, and full tone:

> Die Manier des Viottis ist auch ganz die seinige. Eben der starke Ton und eben der lange Bogenstrich characterisieren auch sein Allegro; wobey er die schwierigsten Passagen deutlich und ausserordentlich rein vorträgt. Im Adagio zeigt er sich wo möglich noch mehr als Meister seines Instruments. Dies spielt er so schön und mit so richtig gefühlten und durchdachten Manieren, dass es schwer zu begreifen ist, wie es ihm möglich ist, seine Manier im Vortrage des Rondo so ganz verleugnen zu können.[16]

Another facet of Beethoven's respect for Kreutzer can be seen in the similarity of themes in Beethoven's violin works and those of Kreutzer and, to a lesser extent, those of the other members of the French violin school (Rode, Baillot, and Viotti). In every case, Beethoven's work was composed after the French model. Boris Schwarz has located several examples of similar themes and figural passages;[17] the most striking example may be seen by comparing the main themes of the opening movements of Kreutzer's Concerto No. 2 in A major (1784-85) and Beethoven's Sonata in F major for Violin and Piano, Op. 24 ("Spring," 1800-1):

Example 1a. Kreutzer, Concerto No. 2 in A major, Mvt. I, mm. 1-4, Violin I

[16]Ernst Ludwig Gerber, *Neue historisches-biographisches Lexicon der Tonkünstler*, 4 vols. (1812-14; reprint ed., 4 vols. in 2, Graz, Austria: Akademische Druck- und Verlagsanstalt, 1966), 1: 118. For further information on Kreutzer's style of playing and its influence on his violin concertos, see Williams, "The Violin Concertos," chaps. 4-6.

[17]"Beethoven and the French Violin School," *Musical Quarterly* 44 (1958): 431-47.

Example 1b. Beethoven, Sonata in F major for Violin and Piano, Op. 24 ("Spring"), Mvt. I, mm. 1-4, Violin

While the overall rhythmic and melodic shape of the two themes is similar, Beethoven's has a much greater sense of direction than Kreutzer's rather static presentation.

Further study of Kreutzer's concertos reveals additional examples of possible sources for the main theme of the "Spring" Sonata from three Kreutzer concertos written in the late 1790s—the time of Kreutzer's and Beethoven's meetings in Vienna: Concertos No. 9 in E minor, No. 10 in D minor, and No. 11 in C major (Examples 2a-c).

Example 2a. Kreutzer, Concerto No. 9 in E minor, Mvt. I, mm. 72-75, Solo Violin

Example 2b. Kreutzer, Concerto No. 10 in D minor, Mvt. I, mm. 73-76, Solo Violin

Example 2c. Kreutzer, Concerto No. 11 in C major, Mvt. I, mm. 51-54, Solo Violin

Again, the style of these themes is quite similar to that of the opening theme of the "Spring" Sonata, quoted above (see Example 1b).

This lyric style of opening theme used by Kreutzer in Concertos Nos. 9-11 may also have served as the model for the opening theme of Beethoven's Romance in F for Violin and Orchestra, Op. 50 (1798-99):

Example 3. Beethoven, Romance in F for Violin and Orchestra, Op. 50, mm. 9-12, Violin I

Finally, Kreutzer's Concerto No. 15 in A major (1804) and Beethoven's Violin Concerto in D major, Op. 60 (1806) both have themes consisting of ascending and descending scales in uniform note values:

Example 4a. Kreutzer, Concerto No. 15 in A major, Mvt. I, mm. 1-8, Violin I

Example 4b. Beethoven, Violin Concerto in D major, Op. 60, Mvt. I, mm. 43-50, Oboe I

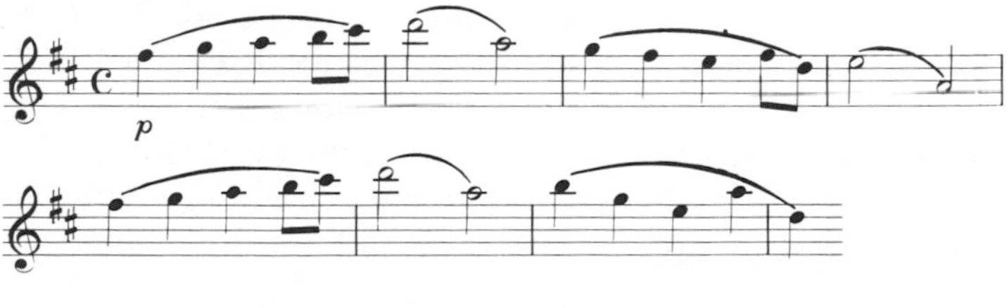

While it may be argued that these similarities are purely coincidental, the fact remains that none of Beethoven's violin works written before the "Spring" Sonata uses the lyric type of opening theme so common in Kreutzer's works. Although no documentary evidence exists showing that Beethoven studied Kreutzer's violin works before writing his own, he did have the opportunity to hear and examine Kreutzer's works in 1798 in Vienna. Furthermore, Kreutzer's concertos written after 1798 were published one or two years before Beethoven composed his similar works, and these publications were advertised, and concert reviews of the works appeared, in the *Allgemeine Musikalische Zeitung* shortly after publication.

Any attempt to locate examples of Beethoven's influence on Kreutzer's violin works is in vain. Although Beethoven's works written before 1810 do not seem far removed from contemporary musical style, they do show advances in harmonic language, formal procedures, and writing for the violin in comparison to Kreutzer's conservative style, which is firmly rooted in the eighteenth century. It is unlikely that Kreutzer would imitate works that he considered "outrageously unintelligible."

If Beethoven were aware of Kreutzer's reaction to his works, he must have overcome any feelings of anger or disappointment, for several years later he wrote the following adulatory and friendly letter to Kreutzer:

> [Vienna, Sept. 1825]
>
> Monsieur!
>
> C'est dans l'espérance que vous vous souveniez encore de votre ancien ami, que j'ose vous recommander le porteur de cette lettre, Monsieur ---un des artistes les plus distingués, en vous priant de ne point lui refuser vos conseils ni votre----Je profite de cette occasion pour vous témoigner ma considération et mon amitié perpetuelle.
>
> Je suis Monsieur votre très humble serviteur.
>
> L.v.B.[18]

After 1810, when Kreutzer's career as a solo violinist ended, he turned his attention more fully to the world of opera. He had served as concertmaster of the Paris Opéra since 1801. In 1816 he was asked to take over the baton of an indisposed conductor and supposedly conducted with such ability that he was appointed assistant conductor. He succeeded Habeneck, the principal conductor, the following year and was named musical director in 1824.[19]

During this period the Opéra was underwritten by great sums of money from the government. Therefore, political control of the

[18] *The Letters of Beethoven*, 3: 1416.

[19] Franz Farga, *Violins and Violinists*, trans. Egon Larsen (London: Rockliff, 1950), p. 154.

Opéra management was extensive, and personnel changes were frequent. Also, as is common whenever government becomes involved in the arts, there was a very conservative outlook towards new music. In Rodolphe Kreutzer, the Opéra had just the person to convert this attitude into actual practice. He had vast influence over the selection of music to be performed, not only at the Opéra, but also at the Concert spirituel, the series of concerts which replaced dramatic productions during Lent. During the period in which Kreutzer was principal conductor and musical director of the Opéra (1817-26), the majority of the works performed were by the old guard of French composers.

The young Hector Berlioz was at that time an unknown composer attempting to induce the musical establishment to perform his rather radical works. The following letter from Berlioz to Kreutzer extols with effusive language the latter's opera *The Death of Abel.* It is difficult to believe that the young composer is serious.

[Paris, ? Spring 1823]

O genius!

I succumb! I die! Tears choke me! *The death of Abel*! Heavens! What an infamous public! It feels nothing! How can one move it?

O genius! and what shall I do myself if one day my music should depict passion? How shall I be understood if the public does not crown, carry in triumph or prostrate itself before the author of everything that is beautiful?

Sublime, heart-rending, pathetic!

Ah! I cannot stand any more: I must write! Whom shall I write to? To the Genius! No, I dare not.

I write to the man, to Kreutzer . . . he will laugh at me . . . I don't care—I would die if I kept silence.

Ah! if I could only see him, talk to him, he would listen to me, he would see what is happening in my ravaged soul; perhaps he would restore to me the courage which I have lost, seeing the insensitivity of these lepers, who are hardly worthy of listening to the buffooneries of that jack-in-a-box Rossini.

If the pen did not fall from my hands I should never finish.

AH! GENIUS!!!

Hector Berlioz
Pupil of M. Lesueur[20]

Berlioz's efforts proved fruitless, however. The young composer became quite bitter towards the musical establishment and, especially, Kreutzer. When Kreutzer was asked by his colleague

20*Hector Berlioz: A Selection from His Letters*, selected, ed., and trans. Humphrey Searle (New York: Harcourt, Brace & World, 1966), p. 13.

and Berlioz's teacher Lesueur to perform Berlioz's "Heroic Scene: The Greek Revolution," he is said to have replied gruffly, "What would happen to us if we helped newcomers?"[21]

Berlioz also reports on Kreutzer's "contemptuous disdain for everything German," especially the works of Beethoven. It was common practice at the Concert spirituel to alter and cut Beethoven's symphonies. Kreutzer supposedly shut his ears with his hands while attending a rehearsal of Beethoven's orchestral works and fled the hall on his first hearing of Beethoven's Symphony No. 2.[22]

Kreutzer's dislike for the works of Beethoven and Berlioz had a greater effect on Berlioz than on Beethoven at the time. By the early 1800s, Beethoven, only four years younger than Kreutzer, was a composer with an established reputation, and, though refusing to perform his works, Kreutzer had little influence in preventing their general acceptance. Even in Paris, Beethoven had strong champions for his music, including the prominent conductor François-Etienne Habeneck.

Berlioz, on the other hand, was a young radical attempting to gain a foothold in the musical sphere where Kreutzer's influence was strongest and at the time when that influence was at its peak. Thus, Kreutzer was able to block performances of Berlioz's works and to have some effect on public acceptance of them.

Because of these differences, it is easy to understand why Beethoven remained friendly towards Kreutzer (he may also have been unaware of Kreutzer's opinions of his music, since the two were separated geographically), and why Berlioz was quite bitter about the treatment he received (the 1823 letter quoted above notwithstanding).

In the long run, however, Kreutzer's opinions had little effect on the final acceptance of the works of either Beethoven or Berlioz. While their music has "stood the test of time," Kreutzer's works have for the most part been forgotten. Perhaps this fact can be of some reassurance to composers facing the same reactions and obstacles today.

[21]Jacques Barzun, *Berlioz and the Romantic Century*, 3rd ed., 2 vols. (New York: Columbia University Press, 1969), 1:68.

[22]*Memoirs of Hector Berlioz from 1803 to 1869*, trans. Rachel and Eleanor Holmes, annotated and ed. Ernest Newman (1932; reprint ed., New York: Dover Publications, 1966), pp. 63, 64, 77; Barzun, *Berlioz*, 1: 88, 422.

Austin Caswell

Anton Reicha on Vocal Embellishment

During the past few years I have followed a trail of evidence which hopefully will lead toward greater illumination of nineteenth-century performance practices. In general, I have been interested in discovering evidence concerning embellishment practice as applied to the operatic aria, specifically, the degree to which virtuosic ornamentation was approved of (or even encouraged) by the operatic composer. If embellishment can be shown to bear the approval of the composer in whose opera it was applied, the traditional view of the composer standing in adamant opposition to the prima donna on this issue begins to be thrown into doubt.

In a recent article I demonstrated that the soprano for whom Rossini wrote the leading roles in all four of his Paris operas applied a rich and wide variety of embellishments to his arias—and evidently did so with his approval.[1] Another article examined Parisian reactions to the abundant use of this Italian technique and viewed the cultural schizophrenia which it engendered: French cultural chauvinism in conflict with Italian melodic glory.[2] A third article looked at a number of vocal treatises from the first half of the nineteenth century and found that there was a widespread acknowledgement of embellishment as essential to the singer's technique.[3] Such an

[1]"Mme Cinti Damoreau and the Embellishment of Italian Opera in Paris: 1820-1845," *Journal of the American Musicological Society* 28 (1975): 459-92.

[2]"Vocal Embellishment in Rossini's Paris Operas: French Style or Italian?" *Bollettino del Centro Rossiniano di Studi . . .* 1975, nos. 1-2 (Pesaro: For the Foundation, 1976): 5-21.

[3]"Embellishment in Rossini: a Survey of Sources and a Re-examination of Assumptions," *19th Century Music*, forthcoming.

influential pedagogue as Manuel Garcia (1805-1906) devoted large sections of his treatises to the teaching of cadenzas for specific arias as well as to the providing of embellishment patterns for study.

One of my most exciting discoveries during the course of the latter research was the composition treatises of Anton Reicha, a teacher, composer and theorist who was a friend and contemporary of Beethoven and who spent his mature years in Paris. Since Reicha's writings on embellishment are extensive and detailed, it is to the further examination of his thinking in this area that this article will be devoted. It is hoped that the observations of this theorist-pedagogue will offer enlightening contrasts to the performer-oriented statements which dominate the literature on embellishment.

First, a look at Anton Reicha's life and professional career, both of which are well-documented.[4] A number of articles in our own century reveals that musicologists have given him some notice as a theorist,[5] a teacher of a number of famous composers,[6] a com-

[4]Maurice Emmanuel's 1937 biography *Antonin Reicha* (Paris: Librairie Renouard), while subtitled a "biographie critique," is an introduction to the life and works of Reicha rather than an extensive examination of it. Ernst Bücken's 1912 doctoral dissertation (University of Munich) *Anton Reicha* was unavailable to me. Additional contributions are found in J.-G. Prod'homme, "From the Unpublished Autobiography of Antoine Reicha," *Musical Quarterly* 22 (1936): 339-53; and Norman Demuth "Antonín Reicha," *Music and Letters* 29 (1948): 165-72.

[5]While only one article can be found which deals solely with Reicha the theorist (Ernst Bücken's "Anton Reicha als Theoretiker," *Zeitschrift für Musikwissenschaft* 2 [1919/20]: 156-69), Reicha's conceptions of tonal forms have been featured rather prominently in the continuing discussion of this issue over the past generation. A chronological list of those contributions which make mention of Reicha's thinking would include:

William S. Newman, "The Recognition of Sonata Form by Theorists of the 18th and 19th Centuries," *Papers of the American Musicological Society*, Annual Meeting, 1941 (1946): 21-29.

Leonard Ratner, "Harmonic Aspects of Classic Form," *Journal of the American Musicological Society* 2 (1949): 159-68.

William S. Newman, "Communications," *Journal of the American Musicological Society* 20 (1967): 513-15.

Piero Weiss, "Communications," *Journal of the American Musicological Society* 21 (1968): 233-34.

William S. Newman, *The Sonata Since Beethoven* (Chapel Hill: University of North Carolina Press, 1969).

Malcolm S. Cole, "Sonata-Rondo, the Formulation of a Theoretical Concept in the 18th and 19th Centuries," *Musical Quarterly* 55 (1969): 180-92.

Peter Bloom, "Communications," *Journal of the American Musicological Society* 27 (1974): 161-62.

Jane R. Stevens, "Theme, Harmony and Texture in Classic-Romantic Descriptions of Concerto First-Movement Form," *Journal of the American Musicological Society* 27 (1974): 25 60.

[6]Daniel Lazarus, "Anton Reicha et Berlioz," *La Revue Musicale*, 1 June 1922,

poser of wind quintets and monumental fugues,[7] or an acquaintance of Beethoven.[8] At his death in 1836 Berlioz (among others) wrote testimonial articles in various Parisian journals,[9] but little of his music survived him in the concert repertoire.[10] Fétis (his colleague on the faculty of the Paris Conservatoire) treated him with patronizing disdain in the *Biographie universelle des musiciens,*[11] and of his hundreds of compositions only a few chamber works and piano pieces are available today. If his music made little or no impact upon his times or his environs, a rather different picture presents itself by tracing the success of his theoretical and pedagogical treatises. Reicha was an indefatigable explainer, exemplifier and cataloguer, the popularity of whose treatises is demonstrated by their adaptation, translation and republication throughout all the major countries of western Europe.[12]

Antonín Josef Reicha was born 26 February 1770 in Prague. His father Simon was a municipal wind-player, who died when Anton was less than a year old. By age eleven the boy had received

---

p. 255; and C. Gardavsky, "Liszt und seine tschechischen Lehrer," *Studia Musicologica* 5 (1963): 69-76.

[7]Udo Sirker, "Die Entwicklung des Bläserquintetts in der ersten Hälfte des 19. Jahrhunderts" (Ph.D diss., University of Cologne, 1968); Stefan Kunze, "Anton Reichas 'Entwurf einer phrasirten Fuge.' Zum Kompositionsbegriff im frühen 19. Jahrhundert," *Archiv für Musikwissenschaft* 25 (1968): 289-307; and Gerard Werker, "Een Fantastisch Fugaschrijver: De 36 Fugás van Antonin Reicha," *Mens en Melodie* 30 (1975): 118-21.

[8]Ernst Bücken, "Beethoven und Reicha," *Die Musik* 12 (1913): 344 ff.; and Václav Sýkora, "Beethovens Jugendfreund Anton Reicha und der künstlerische Wert seiner Fugen," cf. *Bericht über den Internationalen Musikwissenschaftlichen Kongress Bonn 1970*, ed. Carl Dahlhaus et al. (Kassel: Bärenreiter-Verlag, 1971), p. 592.

[9]For a list of such articles see Emmanuel, *Antonin Reicha*, p. 123.

[10]Reicha's oeuvre includes eleven operas or partial operas (only two of which ever saw the public stage), approximately fifteen orchestral works (symphonies and overtures), seven concerti and a vast amount of chamber music of all possible combinations, among them at least twenty-five string quartets and a prodigious quantity of works for various combinations of winds—especially wind quintet. His keyboard output is also extensive and is dominated by works whose titles indicate a pedagogical intent, e.g., "XXXVI Fugues," "L'Art de Varier," and large numbers of etudes. A minority of these works were published, many of those by the composer himself.

[11]2nd ed., s.v. "Reicha, Antoine." The only successful effort of Reicha's admitted by Fétis is that of his wind quintets: "He was the first in France to write serious works for wind instruments, in which their particular resources are employed with skill. His quintets for flute, oboe, clarinet, horn and bassoon had some popular success around 1815 . . . . One is astonished that, among so many works written by a skillful man, nothing remains and that the majority of his compositions had fallen into deep oblivion, even before his death."

[12]Reicha's treatises are listed and summarized below.

almost no formal education and evidently realized its lack, since at that tender age he left home to seek broader experience in the world. He found a second home in Wallerstein, Swabia with an uncle Josef Reicha (1746-95), who was a cellist in the orchestra of Count Öttingen-Wallerstein. Here he plunged into the eager acquisition of the basic cultural and professional necessities of the court musician, learning German and French and studying violin, flute and piano. In 1785 his uncle was appointed director of the court orchestra of Prince Maximilian of Austria, Elector of Cologne, and Anton was brought into the orchestra as second flutist, where he became closely acquainted with his contemporary, a violist named Ludwig Beethoven. The two of them attended lectures in philosophy and mathematics at the University of Bonn beginning in 1789 and taught themselves counterpoint, harmony and composition by the study of Kirnberger and Marpurg. As members of the orchestra, they had ample opportunity to come into contact with the best of the current repertoire: Handel, Haydn and Mozart are specifically mentioned by Reicha in later years. With only grudging support from his uncle, he became an active and proficient composer, producing cadenzas for his orchestral colleagues, a "Scenes Italiennes" for tenor, and a symphony by age seventeen.

Late in 1794 the forces of the French Revolution took control of the Cologne electorate, and Prince Maximilian's court was disbanded. Reicha, urged by his uncle (who was in poor health and lived scarcely two more months, dying in February of 1795), moved to Hamburg, where he spent the next five years studying (algebra, physics, astronomy and philosophy) and composing. During his last year in Hamburg he completed his first two operas, *L'Ermite dans l'île Formose* and *Obaldi ou les Français en Egypte.*[13] Finding no opportunity for publication or performance for either of these works, he left Hamburg on 25 September 1799 for Paris, where he hoped their language, plots, and musical style might find a better reception. During his two years in Paris (late 1799 to early 1802) he had no success in getting his operas staged but gained some favorable attention through the performance of several of his instrumental works. He also gained a foothold as a teacher, became acquainted with many Parisian musicians and wrote another opera *(L'Ouragan* [1800]).

Evidently his professional beginnings in Paris were not promising enough to induce him to stay: in the summer of 1802 he left for Vienna in hopes of studying with Haydn. While he never achieved this goal (he studied with Albrechtsberger and Salieri instead), he

[13]The title of the latter work reveals an attempt at political relevance, for in 1799 Napoleon was in the midst of his Egyptian campaign.

claimed to have become closely acquainted with Haydn as a friend and disciple. His worship of Haydn's style shows itself throughout his treatises, where the examples taken from Haydn's works outnumber those of all other composers combined.[14]

In Vienna as in Paris he tried–but with limited success–to gain recognition as a composer. Prince Lobkowitz did arrange a private performance of parts of his opera *L'Ouragan*, and Empress Maria-Theresa commissioned an opera on the story of *Argine* in 1805. He had gained enough renown within a year of his arrival to receive (and to reject) an offer of a court position from Prince Ferdinand of Prussia. During the six years Reicha stayed in Vienna he seems to have composed large works at a considerable rate. The most often cited is a set of thirty-six fugues for piano (dedicated to Haydn) in which he demonstrated his lifelong penchant for complexity of design. More than one writer notes that Reicha's works display more of the mathematician-philosopher than of the inspired creator.

In the fall of 1808 Reicha left Vienna to return to Paris, where he spent the rest of his life. This time he met with greater success and within a few years became a well-known teacher of composition and counterpoint. Among his pupils were Berlioz, Gounod, Franck, Adam, Thomas, Onslow and Liszt. Although only two of the eight operas he wrote after settling in Paris ever saw the stage, he gained some recognition as a composer of instrumental music, with his wind quintets receiving favorable notice quite frequently. By all accounts he wrote twenty-six of them. In 1818 he married a Frenchwoman and was appointed by Cherubini to the post of Professor of Theory and Composition at the Conservatoire. The accounts of Reicha the professor left to us by students and colleagues consistently show him as a loner: a man who (either by personal inclination or as insulation from the repeated rebuffs of the operatic world) worked at what he pleased when he pleased and made little effort to secure its public acceptance. As he said in his unpublished autobiography, "I have never been interested in writing for the popular demand. To instruct the public has been my aim; not to amuse it."[15]

In an article commemorating the life of his teacher, Hector Berlioz drew this portrait:

14Why did Reicha almost completely ignore the works of his close friend Beethoven? Berlioz, in his testimonial article "Antoine Reicha," which appeared in *Le Journal des Debats* on 3 July 1836, guesses that Reicha found Beethoven's compositional style too free, too irregular.

15Prod'homme, "Unpublished Autobiography," p. 339.

> He tranquilly wrote what it pleased him to write—arranging performances of some when he could, engraving others when his resources permitted, entrusting the health of the rest to his star, and always tranquil in his progress, deaf to the voice of the critic, almost insensible to praise; he paid no evident attention to the prizes or successes of the young artists whose education had been entrusted to him at the Conservatoire and to whom he gave his lessons with such care and with all the attention imaginable.[16]

This independence also manifested itself in a lack of diplomacy on Reicha's part vis-à-vis his colleagues and their opinions. In direct opposition to the policy advocated by the Conservatoire's director Cherubini, Reicha opposed the required mastery of the "school fugue" and proposed its replacement by the "free fugue." Open expression of such opinions (along with others directed at his colleague Fétis) had the effect of factionalizing the students into three "nationalities": the "Bohemians" (followers of Reicha), the "Netherlanders" (followers of the Belgian Fétis) and the "Italians" (adherents of Director Cherubini).

Naturalized a French citizen in 1829, he was presented for election to the Academy of Beaux Arts the same year but lost to Auber. Presented again in 1831, he lost to Paer. On a third presentation in 1835 he was elected but had little time to enjoy his new prestige, dying in Paris on 28 May 1836, almost exactly one year after his election.

He was remembered by his students as the lone champion of the Germanic rigors of counterpoint and fugue (as compositional technique as well as intellectual discipline) in an age when all about him had discarded these approaches in favor of those of grand opera and *opéra comique*. The violinists Baillot and Rode both studied counterpoint with him as well as did Habeneck, the famed conductor whose disciplined interpretations of the Beethoven symphonies made such an impression on the young Wagner. His influence upon Berlioz would seem to have been in the area of orchestration. Although Berlioz did not admit such influence, the extension of orchestral forces and the experimentation with their placement is a recurrent subject in Reicha's treatises, and a comparison of the ideas of teacher and pupil would seem to prove of interest.

Reicha's treatises are without doubt his most significant legacy. In them one finds a puzzling combination of the conservative traditionalist and the startling innovator. The influence of the treatises per se can be seen by the number of different editions and translations they underwent, a popularity corroborated by

[16] Berlioz, "Antoine Reicha."

Reicha in his unpublished autobiography in which he virtually chortles with glee over their healthy sales and gloats that they are sold as far away as Calcutta. The major treatises are these:

I. *Traité de mélodie: abstraction faite de ses rapports avec l'harmonie; suivi d'un supplément sur l'art d'accompagner la mélodie par l'harmonie, lorsque la première doit être prédominante* (Paris: By the author, 1814); also in Italian translation as:

Trattato della melodia considerata fuori de' suoi rapporti coll' armonia . . . , 2 vols. (Milan: Ricordi, n.d.)

A comparatively short treatise, it deals with the analysis and structure of melody as a musical parameter per se, i.e., not as one which is dependent upon harmony (viz., Rameau). As Reicha says in the opening statement of the introduction, "The great structure of music rests on two columns of the same height and of equal importance, melody and harmony." He then explains that in recent generations there have been many treatises which have dealt with harmony but none dealing with melody and that he intends to rectify that imbalance.

Reicha's approach is surprisingly similar to that used by mid-twentieth-century textbooks. He reduces a melody to its hierarchy of components: period, phrase, subphrase and motive, shows good and bad structure through numerous examples,[17] and takes the student step by step in "work-book" fashion toward the goal of successful melodic writing. He displays an illuminating awareness of tonal shape and is able to transmit its complexities in an admirably lucid way. The entire treatise was reissued as part of a later publication (see IIIc below).

II. *Cours de composition musicale ou traité complet et raisonné d'harmonie pratique* (Paris: Gambaro, 1816); two translated editions exist:

a. *Corso di composizione musicale . . . tradotto dal francese . . . Luigi Rossi* (Milan: Lucca, n.d.)
b. *Course of Musical Composition (with Remarks by C. Czerny)*, trans. A. Merrick (London: J. Bishop, 1854)

A much larger treatise of some 350 pages, it proceeds in a

[17]In addition to composing his own examples, he uses melodies by Handel, Gluck, Haydn, Mozart, Piccini, Sacchini, Sarti, Paisiello, Cimarosa, Giordanello, Grétry, Dalayrac, Della Maria and Zingarelli.

methodical way from the classification of intervals and inversions to cadential formulae, part-writing and a taxonomy of chords. Toward the end of the volume, having covered all aspects of harmony and part-writing (with the exception of canon and fugue), Reicha goes on to orchestration, incorporating earlier examples into his observations on instrumental tone-quality in solo and in combination. The entire treatise was reissued as part of a later publication (see IIIc below).

III. *Traité de haute composition musicale*, 2 vols. (Paris: Costallat, 1824-26); three translated editions make use of this treatise:

a. *Trattato d'armonia . . . compendiato e recato . . . da Pietro Tonassi* (Milan: Ricordi, n.d.)

b. *Practical Harmony and Composition*, trans. C. Rudolphus (London: n.p., n.d.)

c. *Cours de composition musicale ou traité complet d'harmonie pratique, de mélodie, de l'emploi des voix et des instrumens, de haute composition et du contrepoint double, de la fugue et du canon . . ./ Vollständiges Lehrbuch der musikalischen Composition oder ausführliche und erschöpfende Abhandlung über die Harmonie (den Generalbass), die Melodie, die Form und Ausarbeitung der verschiedenen Arten von Tonstücken, den Gebrauch der Gesangstimmen, die gesamte Instrumentierung, den höheren Tonsatz im doppelten Contrapunct, die Fuge und den Canon, und über den strengen Satz im Kirchenstyl* . . . (Vienna: A. Diabelli, [1834])

(This is an immense opus of more than 1200 pages. The format is that of parallel columns of French and German, the German translation having been done by Carl Czerny. It incorporates Reicha's two previous treatises, the entire *Cours de composition musicale* of 1816 and the *Traité de mélodie* of 1814. Thus, the new material of the *Traité de haute composition musicale* is found only in the later portion of the work.)

This treatise consists of an intellectual extension of the Germanic discipline of strict counterpoint into undreamed-of regions. After having laid the foundations of counterpoint for every possible texture, rhythm and direction, Reicha goes on to canons of every conceivable sort, concluding with a chapter "Des canons énigmatiques, polymorphus, circulaires, en augmentation, en diminution, et des canons à deux parties qui peuvent se changer en trio et en quatuor." The next two parts of the treatise deal with fugue, which was obviously Reicha's favorite intellectual and musical diversion. The first portion deals with fugal processes in a normal enough manner, but the second concerns itself with the idea of fugue carried to the point of speculative science or metaphysical inquiry. He deals with triple and quadruple fugues, fugues in as many as eight parts, fugues in which each statement enters in a different key, fugues in irregular meters, fugues in the church modes and fugues involving incredible combinations of augmentation and diminution. In the area of fugal composition, Reicha gave free rein to his penchant for intellectual and systematic investigation. A conservative musician who was disturbed by Beethoven's disruption of traditional forms and procedures, he found in the fugue cohesion enough to allow him to experiment freely without danger of structural collapse. It was this fugal experimentation which earned him the enmity of his colleagues at the Conservatoire.

The final section of the treatise deals with closed tonal forms. Reicha's discussion of the sonata structure ("la grande coupe binaire") has afforded many researchers with interesting evidence of his perceptions of this form.[18]

IV. *Art du compositeur dramatique, ou cours complet de composition vocale* (Paris: Costallat, 1833); Czerny also did a German translation of this treatise entitled:

Die Kunst der dramatischen Composition oder vollständiges Lehrbuch der Vocal-Tonsetzkunst . . . (Vienna: A. Diabelli, n.d.)

This is a manual for the composition and production of opera. Ironically, the composer whose operas never achieved success turns opera-pedagogue, dealing with every last problem and detail of musical theatre. He concerns himself with all styles of vocal, choral and ensemble composition appropriate to French grand opera and chooses the best examples from the operas of Auber, Cherubini, Lesueur, Méhul, Meyerbeer, Rossini and Spontini. It is in this treatise that he takes most specific aim at what he considers the self-indulgent formlessness of Romanticism, in particular at the version espoused by his erstwhile friend Beethoven. But, although opposed to rhapsodical or improvisatory composition, Reicha demonstrates himself very much in favor of rhapsodical improvisation per se. More than approving of it, he actually gloried in it as long as it was kept distinct from the art of composition:

> Improvisation is something entirely different than composition: the necessity constantly to move onward with no opportunity to stop, reflect and search for the right solution places the spirit in an entirely different position, and one must use whatever one's imagination affords. By contrast, in composition one has the time to reflect on what one

[18]See the list of articles and books in n. 5 supra.

should do, to seek out, develop and arrange one's ideas and materials. In improvisation there is no selecting of ideas to perplex or impede the performer; if one has the ideas one's success is assured. On the other hand, in composition it is primarily the choice of ideas which constantly holds the composer back. A great deal of time is necessary to write them down, to combine them, to utilize them, to unify them, etc.: the composer must repeatedly go back over his material in the creation of his work. The best improvisation remains constantly outside of all these principles as long as it is not inferior, not merely mediocre composition.[19]

This statement of reverence for the gifts of the natural improviser was written in the early 1830s, but even more detailed evidence of the significance he attached to this art appears in his first treatise, *Traité de mélodie* of 1814. Naturally, considering the subject of this treatise, Reicha deals with melodic improvisation, in particular with the type associated with the Italian operatic tradition of the embellishment of the *da capo* aria. In addition to giving us a most detailed and meticulous description of the improvising virtuoso's art, Reicha includes three valuable examples of what he considers the epitome of this art. Here is the text in full:[20]

Concerning Styles of Melodic Performance and the Art of Melodic Embellishment

It is not enough to invent charming (vocal) melodies; they must also be performed in a perfect style. If it is difficult to compose them, it is no less difficult to perform them well. One must never equate the art of singing with that of simple declamation: out of a hundred people who declaim well enough, one can scarcely find two who can sing passably. To be an excellent singer one must have:

1. a voice which is rich and at the same time sweet, flexible and pleasant, with a range which is wide enough and consistent in tone throughout
2. deep sensitivity
3. fine taste
4. perfect training
5. a well-trained, sharp and subtle sense of hearing.[21]

It is agreed that it is a rare phenomenon to find all these qualities united

[19]Translated from Klaus Blum, "Bemerkungen Anton Reichas zur Aufführungspraxis der Oper." *Die Musikforschung* 7 (1954): 429.

[20]Translated from *Cours de composition musicale/Vollständiges Lehrbuch*, pp. 489-500.

[21]The consistency of the descriptions of the vocal equipment required for skillful embellishment gives us some sense of direction, even though specificity is impossible. Lightness and flexibility are the characteristics stressed by every writer on vocal embellishment from Caccini to Garcia.

in one individual. How many composers are victims of performances without subtlety, without taste, without emotion, or even without a voice capable of charming or interesting the listener! The result is like attempting to declaim the verse of Racine in the Gascon dialect.

It is also quite remarkable that no climate has produced such excellent voices, such perfect singers, and both in such great quantity as has Italy. It is also true that no nation has had such excellent vocal schools as has Italy. Among singers of both sexes in that happy climate, there are those who, with their heavenly voices and their incomparable style of melodic performance (such as Farinelli), have renewed the marvels and the extraordinary powers of the music of the Greeks.[22]

There is a living example of a style of performance which, if it were known among all singers, would exclude all other styles: the celebrated Mme Todi would be the singer of all the ages; other styles of singing could not come close to hers; they would merely pass in and out of style.[23] It would be essential for all to follow and learn from this living proof, but, alas, this is just as impossible as it would be to extend throughout the entire world the luminous rays of great truth which shine from the humble dwellings of true philosophers. This is the reason that there is one style of singing in Italy, another in France and a third in Germany. In Italy they still sing, but not like they used to, and the great schools there have begun to decline. In France they still shout more than they sing. In Germany they do both, i.e., in general they don't shout too much, but they don't sing too well either.[24] From the days of Allegri, Palestrina, Corelli, Handel, Leo, Durante, Marcello and Jomelli down to the time of Hasse, they sang in the simplest, most affecting and most noble style. The singer didn't allow himself anything but the addition here and there of some appoggiaturas (grace notes), trills and other small melodic ornaments, with a cadenza only on the penultimate or antepenultimate note (i.e., at the end of an aria). The composers of those times had at least as much to do with the success of an aria as did the singer. After that epoch the situation reversed itself completely; rather than singing in this simple style, singers began to embroider everything. Composers became slaves to singers and in the end, so to speak, ceased to exist. They would create nothing but melodic skeletons to which the singers would add color and life by the style in which they embroidered them. Novelty has always had a great attraction for us. We were unable to see at the time how much damage we were doing to music by applauding these types of arias in such an enthusiastic

22 The inference that the vocal type necessary for skillful embellishment (as well as the improvisatory skill itself) is of Italian provenance needs no commentary. Even the most chauvinistic Frenchmen (Bacilly, Rousseau et al.) admit that the *fons et origo* of skillful vocalism is Italy.

23 Luiza Todi (1753-1833; née d'Aguiar) was a Portuguese mezzo-soprano whose career (1778-96) was divided among the stages of London, Paris, Berlin, St. Petersburg and Italy.

24 This somewhat simplistic categorization of national schools of singing follows the formula adhered to by almost every writer of the 18th century.

and general way, for it is from this epoch that one must date the decadence of composition in Italy.[25]

[Here follows a three-line note by Czerny (in the German text only) to the effect that the reader must keep in mind that Reicha's comments were written before 1813 and thus before the healthy influence of Rossini and others upon Italian singing.]

Since well-sung ornamented arias have always had a great many partisans, and since at the same time they have had a damaging effect upon composition, it will be of some use to make the following remarks:

When an artistic phenomenon wins almost universal approval, it must be that it has some sort of merit. It is of some interest to the art to find out what this merit consists of. To reject such a phenomenon without examination is just as foolish as it would be to reject everything but it.

One must never confuse a phenomenon with its abuse, for there is a great difference between the two. One must also distinguish between the talented singer who, with a flexible and pleasant voice, embellishes an aria with rare subtlety and exquisite taste and those miserable hacks and pitiful caricatures who do the worst possible job of it. Furthermore, if the former has the intelligence to place his embellishments appropriately, he must be distinguished from the latter who throw them around helter-skelter.

It is natural for mankind to admire the person who overcomes difficult challenges; and if his efforts are at the same time accompanied by charm, the admiration is increased and very often transformed into enthusiasm. I have often been a witness to this universal enthusiasm, and I will say frankly that I have participated in it.

To attract us in this way, a singer must

1. possess a voice which is pleasing, flexible and well-suited to this style of singing
2. have fine taste and delicate subtlety
3. have overcome all the difficulties of this technique through long training so that he has acquired the art of embellishment correctly.[26]

It is agreed that finding all these qualities combined in one individual is very rare. The simple tones of a beautiful voice are already of great charm for us. But when these tones are divided into many different rhythmic values with meter maintained, with cadences symmetrically distributed, with regular and well-connected scales, with rhythms and phrases well-proportioned, and when finally all this is accompanied by simple, sweet harmony, the charm must necessarily become irresistible.

I will include here the following three pieces (which I heard embellished by a skillful Italian singer) with the original above for the purpose of comparing the two versions. This virtuoso had the grace to

[25]While the literary cliché which bemoans current artistic decline and nostalgically hails a golden age of the past is endemic, there is ample evidence from the late 18th century that the performer's freedoms were seen as excessive. See Marcello, Tosi, Rousseau and Gluck, among others.

[26]Reicha is essentially restating the advice with which he begins his essay. That his literary style is rambling and often ill-organized will become evident to anyone who attempts to wade through his treatises.

sing them for me in private so that I could notate them more exactly. They may serve composers as examples of arias to be embellished* and singers as examples of performance in this style [see Facsimiles 1-4].[27]

*the more so since these embellishments are no more than variations of the melody, which composers themselves often employ with success, as Haydn has done in a majority of his andantes; finally one must make sure that a well-varied melody always remains the melody by maintaining its rhythm, its cadences, its phrases and the same melodic concepts.

Observations on These Three Arias for Composers and Singers

1. One does not vary or embellish in this style except in very slow movements (and in $\frac{4}{4}$ meter, which is the slowest); it is for this reason that I have not included the allegros which follow these arias.[28]

2. The form of these adagios must be the small ternary form which the Italians call the *rondeau*.[29]

3. Since in the *rondeau* the motive is repeated (because one returns *da capo* for the third section) skillful singers vary its repeat with different nuances than were performed the first time.[30]

[27]The three arias are identified by composer and title but not as to source. Of particular value is the fact that Reicha regards these three embellished arias as pedagogically "good" examples: i.e., they are not transcriptions of the inventions of a particular prima donna on a particular occasion but, rather, are the recommendations of a conservative pedagogue who is admittedly skeptical of the art of embellishment by reason of its potential for abuse.

[28]This specificity of tempo and meter is interesting: the requirement of a "very slow" tempo is one of the very few written confirmations of a generally accepted criterion; however, the limitation to $\frac{4}{4}$ meter does not correspond to 18th-century ornamentation practice.

[29]The use of the term *rondeau* for the *da capo* form makes sense when we recall that 1) ABA form was often called "simple" or "first-class" rondo and 2) Reicha was writing in French, which produced the spelling we associate with the *forme fixe* of the 14th and 15th centuries. (Czerny's German translation used "rondo.")

[30]All three of the examples presented by Reicha show two embellishments of the *da capo* section—the first to be used initially and the second to be applied to the repetition of the same section. The points of interest are these: 1) it again confirms the accepted opinion that the *da capo* repeat was never sung the same as it had been at the opening of the aria, and 2) even the conservative and skeptical Reicha presumed that the initial performance of the opening section should be embellished (albeit in a constrained fashion). This evidence is corroborated by a number of currently available examples, e.g.,

a. "Sempre piango" by Giovanni B. Bononcini, a duet for two altos with embellishments written by Carlo Antonio Benati; printed in Ernest T. Ferand, *Improvisation in Nine Centuries of Western Music*, Anthology of Music no. 12 (Cologne: Arno Volk Verlag, 1961), pp. 118-22.

b. "Sulla ruota di Fortuna" from the opera *Rinaldo* by G.F. Handel (1711); printed in Hellmuth C. Wolff, *Original Vocal Improvisations from the 16th-18th Centuries*, Anthology of Music no. 41 (Cologne: Arno Volk Verlag, 1972), pp. 101-8.

Such examples may serve to correct the current opinion that the opening section of the *da capo* must be performed strictly as is.

A 2

Nº 1. { AIR DE CIMAROSA : ARIE VON CIMAROSA .

("Ah! serena il mesto ciglio.")

Mélodie simple .
Einfache Melodie .

Même mélodie brodée ou variée par le chanteur .
Dieselbe Melodie vom Sänger verziert oder varirt .

Variée pour la 2de fois en prenant le motif Da-capo après la 2de Période .
Zum zweitenmal varirt, indem das Motif nach der 2ten Periode wieder Da capo vorkommt .

Facsimile 1. *Reicha,* Cours de composition musicale/Vollständiges Lehrbuch, *from p. 493.*

Nº 2. { AIR DE GIORDANELLO.
ARIE VON GIORDANELLO.

("Partirò dal caro bene.")

Largo.

Mélodie simple.
Einfache Melodie.

1re manière de la broder ou de la varier.
1te Art der Verzierung oder Variation.

2de manière de la varier.
2te Art der Variation.

Facsimile 2. *Reicha*, Cours de composition musicale/Vollständiges Lehrbuch, *p. 494.*

1/2 cad.
1/2 Cad.
1/2 cad.
5
1/2 Cad.
3
1/2 Cad: forte sur la dominante.
starke 1/2 Cad: auf der Dominante.
Da Capo.
3
conduit qui ramène au motif.
Führer zum Thema.
1/2 cad.
Fin de la 3me Période ou du Dacapo.
Ende der 3ten Periode oder des Da Capo.
6
1/2 Cad.
tr
cad: parf:
vollk: Cad:
tr
cad: parf:
vollk: Cad:

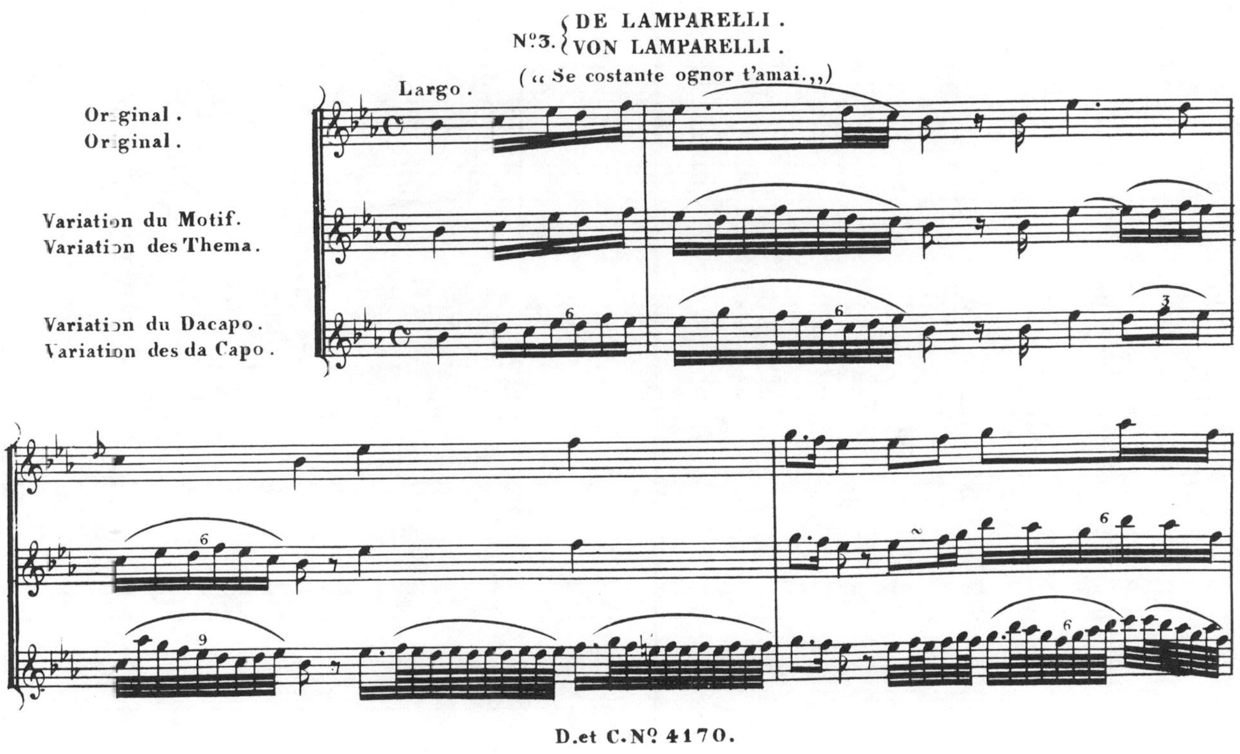

Facsimile 3. *Reicha*, Cours de composition musicale/Vollständiges Lehrbuch, *p. 495.*

1/2 Cad:
1/2 Cad:
1/2 Cad:
cad: parf:
vollk: Cad:
cad: parf:
vollk: Cad:
cad: parf:
vollk: Cad:
2de PÉRIODE.
2te PERIODE.
1/2 Cad:
1/2 Cad:

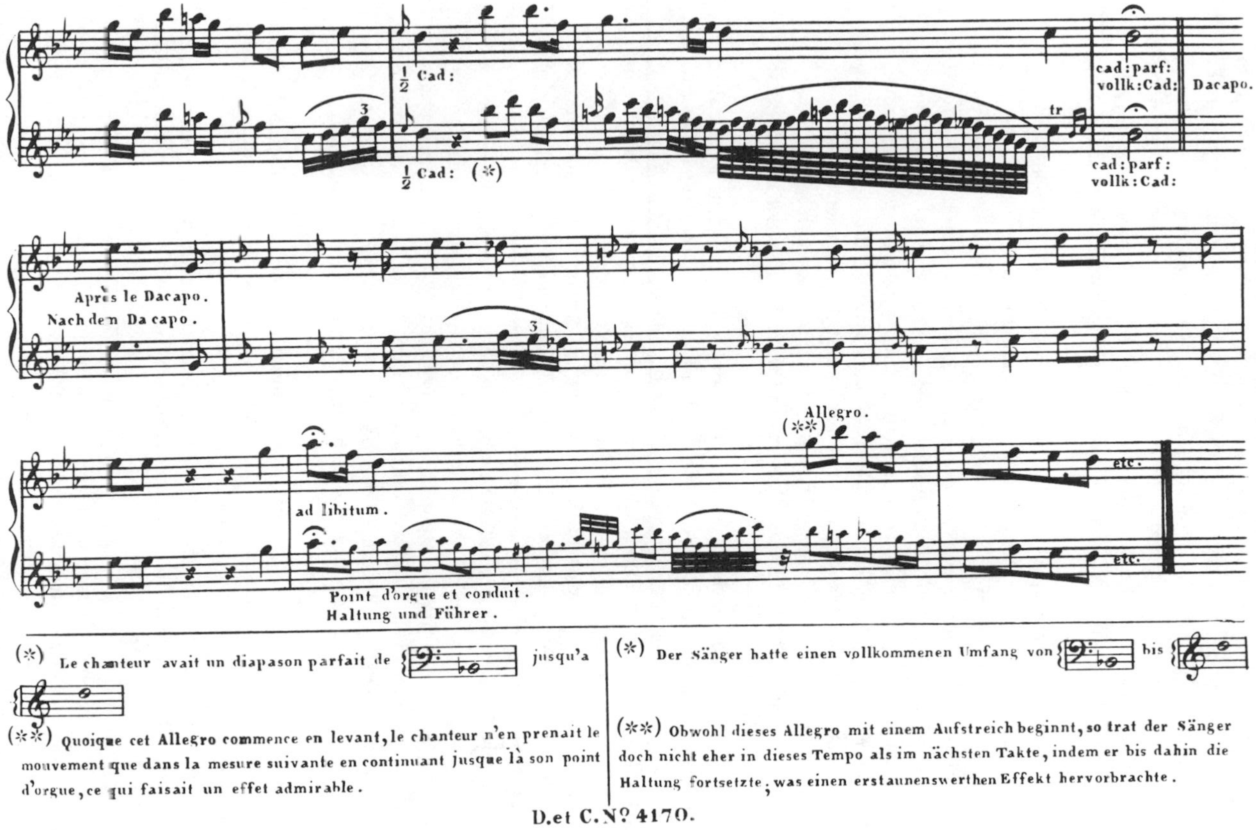

Facsimile 4. *Reicha*, Cours de composition musicale/Vollständiges Lehrbuch, *p. 496.*

4. The melody must be as slow and simple as possible. In laying out the melody the composer must observe the rhythm [*sic*] rigorously and articulate the cadences strongly.

5. The singer must observe the cadences strictly and never alter them nor change them through embellishment, i.e., he must never make a perfect cadence out of a half-cadence, nor vice versa, nor sing through one, which is an unpardonable fault. Finally, one must be able to recognize the outlines of the composer's melody in the embellishments, particularly its rhythm. All skillful singers must observe these important principles.[31]

6. The opening section (the motive), which should not be too long, must stay within the tonic key and must be accompanied by the simplest harmonies, i.e., by major and minor triads and dominant sevenths, which must not succeed each other too rapidly. All these chords must be within the diatonic scale, for can one imagine singers, who usually have no abilities other than their voices, correctly embellishing an aria which has intellectual and studied harmonies which modulate endlessly? It would be a very skillful composer indeed who would attempt such a thing. It is also for this reason that one should always compose arias in the major mode since it is harder to embellish in the minor mode.[32]

7. The second section, which exists only to lead back to the first one again, must modulate a little, at least to the dominant. Also this second section is embellished much less because of the modulations it contains. But since it is felt that a largo of this length cannot stay constantly in the same key, one must adapt oneself to this.

8. Singers love to stop in these arias at the end of the second section on the tonic triad or the dominant seventh and take the opportunity to sing a cadenza followed by a conduit.[33]

If these kinds of embellished arias on the one hand have created a great deal of pleasure, on the other they are strongly detrimental to the art, especially among the Italians, who nowadays do nothing but repeat them endlessly. The reason is that composers, being forced to sacrifice art to whim, carelessness and frivolity, compose nothing but arias made to be embroidered by singers who have only two modulations and two

[31]Here is evidence of Reicha's fear of the dictatorship of the embellishing virtuoso. Examples of what Reicha warns against can be found in ample supply in the two anthologies referred to in n. 30 supra.

[32]Reicha the theorist-composer offers us observations on harmonic structure which are all but unique in the literature on embellishment. Since most other writers on the subject were performers rather than composers or theorists (with such exceptions as Tartini and Quantz), they expressed themselves in melodic terms only. It is odd, however, that Reicha, having expressed this concern for harmonic structure, chooses to omit the accompaniment from these examples.

[33]The cadenza at the end of the B section is (grudgingly?) allowed by Reicha. The term "conduit" is a French one which refers to the simple (or lightly ornamented) ascent from the dominant pitch to the tonic, one which occurs at such a place as a means of "leading" back to the *da capo* (see Example 1, m. 13; Example 2, m. 23; and Example 3, m. 24).

chords in their ears and cannot embellish anything else. Composers, by working in this way, have forgotten the immense resources of their art and have allowed the Italian school to degenerate so that they now move in a very small circle in which they do nothing but repeat themselves endlessly. There everyone composes, ignorant of what composition is (this is currently being noticed in other countries, too). The Leos, Durantes, Jomellis and Maios disappeared long ago.

Singers, in this epoch of decadence, want nothing but arias to be embellished, and one can say that for the past nearly forty years we have been living in the epoch of musical embroidery, of which the three arias just cited can serve as examples for the purpose of passing on the history of this art: it can be assumed that, because of the abuse of this style of singing, it will go out of fashion or at least be restrained within reasonable limits by employing these arias very rarely and then only when they can be sung by an excellent and appropriate type of voice, and only by singers with excellent taste.[34] If this were to happen, one could envisage such arias being recognized as a separate genre of vocal composition, distinct from others and called "embellishment arias."*

But couldn't the composer of such an aria embellish it himself and thus vary the harmony and employ richer modulations? Yes, if he composes only for instruments, but I must warn him to beware of attempting to specify everything for the singer. First of all, a composer is not a singer; what he would compose for his own voice or by means of his own voice would fit neither the talent nor the tone-quality of the skilled singer. Thus, written embellishments almost invariably sound bad. A skilled singer creates his ornamentation most often by inspiration, which is always worth more in this case than the studied care of the composer. The singer shapes his embellishment according to the nature of his voice and its range and changes it frequently; all this is lost if the composer prescribes everything.[36]

*For the history of music and the interest of their performance it would be important to fix in notation the different epochs in the style of singing and of the art of embellishment as employed by celebrated virtuosos for the purpose of comparing their methods and choosing those which relate to the best schools and to the most perfect taste. How interesting it would be to performers and amateurs to compare the methods of a Farinelli, a Durastanti, a Faustina, a Gabrielli, a Todi, a Cafarelli, etc.[35]

[34] Following a diatribe against then-current abuses of virtuosity, Reicha recommends the very solutions that are attributed to Rossini during his Parisian activity of the 1820s. Rossini's implementation of the solutions are traced in my articles cited in nn. 1-3 supra.

[35] N.B.: This plea for historical style-consciousness was written in 1813!

[36] This is perhaps the most significant paragraph of Reicha's entire statement on embellishment. Even the conservative structuralist recognizes that improvisation yields a different musical fruit than does composition. The performer's involvement in the creative process through his own voice is so far superior to the efforts of the composer to duplicate such spontaneity that Reicha categorically rejects the latter.

> But in bravura arias (another type of aria), which are composed of a simple melody with runs and roulades and which must stick close to the melody by observation of the rhythms and thus the cadences, the composer must prescribe everything; it is too bad if he hasn't the talent for it.
>
> Concerning varied melody in instrumental music in which the composer must create everything, where he can employ all at once all the resources of his art, I can only refer one to the works of Haydn and counsel one to analyze them and study them endlessly. By means of all these resources a melody can be varied to infinity. This subject could furnish the material for an immense volume.[37]

It is of interest to note the style of embellishment displayed in Reicha's three examples, especially in the *da capo* sections, where we find two different embellished versions, one for the opening section and the other for its repeat. Throughout the three arias, Reicha adheres scrupulously to the then-centuries-old rules that governed the addition of passaggi or diminutions to a melodic line. These rules were founded in the belief that the shape, direction and phrase-contour of the original melody should not be obscured by the embellishment and that the surest way to preserve the integrity of the original melody was to begin and end each ornamental passage with the first and last notes of the corresponding original melodic segment. Reicha's adherence to this formula can be seen by looking at any measure of any of the three examples. In the A sections it is interesting to note that the more elaborate embellishment for the *da capo* repeat is as carefully crafted as is the simpler one and, thus, that both versions almost invariably touch the first and last notes of every melodic motive of the original. In the few cases in which Reicha disregards this practice (see, e.g., Example 1, m.8), which is also one of the few places in which he allows himself to alter the rhythmic structure, he does so only for the purpose of dealing with a larger melodic unit–i.e., of creating a passage which encompasses two, three, or four beats rather than the more customary single beat.

It is also interesting to note the type and placement of cadenzas. We can thus see how often and under what circumstances Reicha considers it permissible to bring the regular flow of rhythm, melody and harmony to a standstill in order to focus on the singer's virtuosity. In Example 1 there are two small cadenzas specified within the body of the B section (mm. 12 and 13), although, oddly enough, there is no cadenza at the end of it nor at the close of the *da capo* repeat. In Example 2, on the other hand, the only cadenza

[37]At this point Reicha begins to wander off into a discussion of different approaches to recitative.

in the entire aria is one specified as a second ending for the A section. This particular cadenza leaves one somewhat puzzled, however, since it is not an unmeasured embellishment placed at the hiatus created by a fermata but rather is measured and even supplied with a simple "original" version of itself. In Example 3 we find yet a different arrangement, one which combines the patterns of the first two examples: there is a cadenza (albeit a measured one) at the close of the B section as well as another to be used as a second ending for the *da capo* repeat.

Reicha's style of embellishment can be labeled completely Italian. There is little evidence of the use of the rhythmic and language-oriented formulas associated with the French style of ornamentation of the 17th and 18th centuries. It is perhaps this Italian orientation which allowed him to omit the texts of the three arias, a practice which would be anathema in the case of a French air or a French style of ornamentation.

Reicha's very careful and meticulous pedagogy on the subject of vocal embellishment shows us that, contrary to prevalent opinion, embellishment was not a clandestine art surreptitiously propagated by singers in spite of the righteous wrath of composers. Although Reicha shows a healthy apprehension about its misuse, he acknowledges that in certain places and in the hands of skilled singers, improvised embellishment is not only necessary but also unique since the composer cannot duplicate its effects. Is not this a fairly accurate prediction of the position taken on this subject by Italian opera throughout the course of the 19th century?

Wilbur R. Maust

The American Indian in the Orchestral Music of Anthony Philip Heinrich *

Anthony Philip Heinrich enjoyed a dominant position as an American composer of orchestral music between 1830 and 1860. Since Heinrich's life spanned almost the entire period between the Revolution and the Civil War—a period of intense national consciousness—it is worth noting the themes that he felt were important. One theme that is most frequently found in his orchestral works is that of the American Indian. A contemporary of Heinrich called attention to his treatment of the American Indian:

> Father Heinrich passed several years of his life among the Indians that once inhabited Kentucky, and many of his compositions refer to these aboriginal companions. He is a species of musical Catlin, painting his dusky friends on the music staff instead of the canvas, and composing laments, symphonies, dirges, and war-songs, on the most intensely Indian subjects. He would be the very one to set Hiawatha to music.[1]

In spite of Heinrich's popularity during his lifetime, his music was all but forgotten following his death in New York in 1861. In 1917, when Heinrich's music was deposited in the Library of Congress, Oscar G. Sonneck, who catalogued it, noted that Heinrich was probably the first symphonic composer to utilize Indian themes,[2] and later William Treat Upton, in his biography, called Heinrich "... a true pioneer ..." in his role as interpreter of the Indian in orchestral works of large dimensions.[3] Many historians

*The assistance of a Canada Council Research Grant for the study of Heinrich's orchestral music is gratefully acknowledged.

[1]*Criterion*, 24 May 1856, p. 58.

[2]Editor's note to César Saerchinger's "Musical Landmarks in New York," *Musical Quarterly* 6 (1920):249, n. 2.

[3]*Anthony Philip Heinrich: A Nineteenth-Century Composer in America* (New York: Columbia University Press, 1939; reprint ed., New York: AMS Press, 1967), p. 251.

following Sonneck and Upton have called attention to the importance of Heinrich's compositions on Indian themes. It may therefore be useful and informative to look more closely at the historical context of these early nineteenth-century works which are virtually unique in American orchestral music.

Heinrich first arrived in America as a Bohemian immigrant in the years just preceding the War of 1812. By 1817, only a few years after the war had ended, he arrived on the Kentucky frontier. Thus he experienced first-hand the exuberance of a growing nation in an era of strong national consciousness. He was a part of the western expansion of the nation, which involved the defeat of the British army and the Indian tribes who resisted the efforts of the U.S. Government to take their lands by means of treaties of cession. The westward movement brought increasing conflicts between the interest of the Indians and the whites with the result that the "Indian Removal" gained momentum in the decades following the War of 1812.

It is possible that Heinrich may have come into contact with Indians during his years in Kentucky. Newspapers there frequently carried accounts of relationships between the Indians and the whites. Several books on Indians and Indian customs were familiar to him, particularly John McIntosh's *The Origin of the North American Indians*,[4] which is the source of some of his titles on orchestral themes and occasionally of the programs printed in his scores.

His interest in Indian and other American themes is shared by many other artists in this era, particularly writers and painters. As the cultural life of the growing nation began to take shape, they began to search for native, indigenous topics and themes that would express their own aspirations.

The goals of American literature in this era are outlined, for example, by Nye, who says:

> What Americans wanted most was a culture of their own after the Revolution. Critics, editors, and authors clamored for the immediate creation of a native, indigenous, original American art. Having proved their political genius, the U.S. must now demonstrate its eminence in art and literature.[5]

Topics that seemed suitable were the Indian, the frontier, U.S. history, the Revolution, characters of American society, and nature in America—the vast, various, fascinating land itself.[6]

[4]New York: Nafis and Cornish, 1843.

[5]Russel Blaine Nye, *The Cultural Life of the New Nation 1776-1830* (New York: Harper and Row, 1960), p. 239.

[6]Ibid.

In nineteenth-century painting, also, many of the themes associated with the American character first appeared, especially those of Indian life and the landscape. The subject matter demanded a new kind of treatment. According to Wilmerding, paintings increased in size; canvases became larger "in an effort to equate size with grandness."[7] The American "love of fact" and the depiction of specific events resulted in such works as "The Exhuming of the Mastodon." A new emphasis on improvisation and casualness is found in the painting of this era. Wilmerding notes:

> The life of the American Indian was given as its symbol that of the Noble Savage, an incarnation of brutal force and ideal beauty that was also seen in the environment. Some painters like George Catlin sought to record the physiognomy and dress of the Indian with the accuracy a journalist might use.[8]

When one compares Heinrich's lengthy descriptive titles, his interest in recording fact, his employment of a large orchestra as well as his "improvisational" compositional techniques and his disregard for classical formal principles with the themes and techniques of literature and painting, the analogies are striking indeed. The comparison of Heinrich to George Catlin was made in an earlier quotation. The similarities of the careers of John J. Audubon and Heinrich are even more remarkable. Both were immigrants to America in the early 1800s. Audubon arrived from France in 1803, Heinrich from Bohemia in 1805. Both had little formal training. Heinrich was a successful businessman before he arrived in the U. S. but lost his fortune in the Napoleonic Wars. Audubon made several unsuccessful business ventures in Kentucky. After 1819 Audubon devoted himself entirely to drawing birds, and in 1820 he conceived the idea of making and publishing drawings of all the birds of America. Heinrich's earliest works were composed between 1817 and 1820, and he published his *Dawning of Music in Kentucky* in 1820. The two artists met at Farmington at the Speed home just outside Louisville, Kentucky in the years between 1818 and 1820, and probably they were aware of each other's plans for these first publications.

In 1826 both Audubon and Heinrich left for England to further their careers. Audubon achieved success when the King purchased a portfolio of his plates. Heinrich was successful in having some of his vocal and piano works published. His first orchestral works were completed in England, but he was not successful in having them performed there. Audubon returned to the U. S. a famous

[7]John Wilmerding, *Audubon, Homer, Whistler and Nineteenth-Century America* (New York: McCall Publishing Co., 1970), p. 1.

[8]Ibid.

man in 1831. Heinrich returned by February 1832 but with less claim to fame. After 1837 Heinrich made his home in New York when he was not travelling in Europe. Audubon bought land on the Hudson River and lived in New York between 1841 and his death in 1851. Heinrich died ten years after Audubon in 1861 and was buried in the Audubon vault.[9]

American writers such as Cooper and Emerson, and American painters such as J.J. Audubon and George Catlin are widely recognized for their attempts to create an American tradition, but the musical achievements of their contemporary A.P. Heinrich are familiar to only a few today. Although known and acclaimed in his lifetime, Heinrich failed to have his orchestral music published. Many works were also not performed.

Heinrich's choice of the American Indian as the theme for nine of his orchestral works was probably made for the same reasons that writers and painters chose the theme. To Heinrich, the Indian was clearly one of the most "American" topics he could find. In a "Proposal" to publish a work for the piano entitled "The Musical Week," dated November 11, 1838, five of the seven works were to be based on Indian themes. His intentions are clear from his announcement: "This Publication is intended expressly for the piano-forte; and all the subjects and associations connected with it, will be exclusively American."[10] Three of these pieces, *Pocahontas, The Treaty of William Penn*, and *The Landing of the Pilgrims*, were based on previously composed orchestral works.

Heinrich continued to be interested in the theme of the American Indian throughout his lifetime. His first orchestral work, *Pushmataha*, completed in 1831 in London, is based on an Indian theme. Between 1835 and 1837 four more orchestral works on Indian themes—*William Penn, Logan, Pocahontas*, and *The Indian War Council*—were completed. By 1845 he composed three more, all called "symphonies:" *Manitou Mysteries, Mastodon*, and the *Indian Carnival*. Finally, in 1859 one of his last orchestral works, *Felsen von Plymouth*, was completed in Prague.

9 Factual details regarding Audubon's career are taken from Wilmerding, *Audubon*. For biographical details of Heinrich's life, see Upton, *Heinrich*. Heinrich's burial in the Audubon vault is registered in the interment records of Trinity Church, New York City.

10 The "Proposal" was published in New York. A copy is found in a Scrapbook belonging to Heinrich which contains letters, newspaper clippings, music, etc., now located in the Music Division of the Library of Congress, Washington, D.C. (shelf no.: ML96.H42), p. 1067. The five works on Indian themes in Heinrich's "Proposal" are *Osceola, Pocahontas, The Cherokee's Lament on Quitting Their Native Homes for Arkansas, The Landing of the Pilgrims*, and *The Treaty of William Penn*. The orchestral scores used as the basis of this study are also located in that library.

In his compositions on Indian themes Heinrich showed an interest in three areas of their life: 1) historical events based on early meetings of Indians and whites, 2) portraitures of Indian leaders, and 3) the customs and religion of the Indians.

Three orchestral works which celebrate historical events all commemorate early meetings of the Indians and the white settlers. All three reflect a spirit of reconciliation and good relationships. The first composition centered on Pocahontas, the celebrated daughter of Powhatan, head of the Powhatan confederacy in Virginia. Her extreme heroism in sparing the life of Captain John Smith by placing her head over his when he was about to be executed by her father would appear to be the reason for Heinrich's lengthy title, *Pocahontas—The Royal Maid and Heroine of Virginia, the Pride of the Wilderness. Fantasia Romanza.* In 1614 Pocahontas married the English gentleman, John Rolfe, in Jamestown. The union was regarded as a bond of friendship between the English and the Indians. The marriage helped to bring peace and was an aid in establishing the colony on a firm basis.[11] No additional programmatic details other than the title are given in the score, which was completed in 1837. A waltz on the same subject published in New York two years later is "dedicated to descendants of Pocahontas."

This "Fantasia Romanza" takes on a festive character, with Heinrich's usual large orchestra[12] augmented by contrabassoon and, particularly, by the "Cornetto concertante," to which Heinrich calls attention on the title page of the work. The work includes several cornetto cadenzas but also uses solo woodwind instruments as well: flute, oboe, and clarinet. The work, which begins in C major and ends in F major, is a set of free variations.

The second composition celebrating a historical event characterized William Penn's treaty with the Indians. William Penn was noted for his fair dealings with the Indians. He made every effort to satisfy them in his negotiations for their lands, and they were loyal to him and respected him. Several treaties were signed between Penn and the Indians. Tradition, according to Kelsey, has "fused these treaties into one great treaty 'Under the elm tree at Shackamaxon,' made famous by the brush of Benjamin West."[13]

[11]*Dictionary of American Biography*, s.v. "Pocahontas," by Thomas Jefferson Wertenbaker.

[12]Heinrich's usual orchestra includes triangle, cymbals, tambourine, side and bass drums, timpani, piccolo, 2 flutes, 2 oboes, 2 clarinets, 2 bassoons, 3 trombones, ophicleide, serpent, 4 horns, 4 trumpets, and strings (instruments listed in the order in which they appear in his scores).

[13]*Dictionary of American Biography*, s.v. "Penn, William," by Rayner W. Kelsey.

Heinrich's orchestral work was completed in 1834 in London and was revised in New York in 1847.[14] As the title indicates, the work is in six sections. Heinrich supplied not only a lengthy descriptive title but also provided titles for each of the six sections which make the program very explicit: *The Treaty of William Penn with the Indians.* Concerto Grosso. An American National Dramatic Divertissement, for a Full Orchestra, Comprising Successively 6 Different Characteristic Movements United in One:

(1) The Meeting of William Penn and his associates with the Delaware Indians;
(2) The Treaty;
(3) Smoking of the Calumet;
(4) The Presentation of Gifts to the Indians;
(5) The Grand Dance of the Calumet;
(6) Coda Volante. The Manitou Air Dance.

In this work, a relatively short one for Heinrich (totalling only forty-nine pages), each of the six sections is related musically to the program in a highly subjective way, that is, the tempo, thematic material, and instrumentation seem to "fit" the program. Each uses one motive primarily, and the different sections of the work are related. The descriptive titles probably help to make the work more coherent.

The landing of the Pilgrims and their meeting with the Indians is the subject of the third of the historical themes. This was one of Heinrich's last orchestral works. It was composed in Prague during the winter season of 1858 and 1859. Heinrich's note in the score indicates that it was written ". . . in a desolate comfortless chamber, without any fire whatsoever, during great sufferings of cold, as also without the aid and solace of a pianoforte."[15] With its lengthy main title plus descriptive titles for each of the sections of the work, this score resembles *William Penn.* In fact, a comparison of the last four sections with sections one, four, five, and six of *William Penn* reveals many similarities. The full title and the subsections are in German, as follows: *Der Felsen von Plymouth, oder Die Landung der Pilger Väter in Neu-England A.D. 1620.*

1) Animato. Die Einschiffung der Puritaner in Europa auf dem Barke: "Mayflower" (Maiblume);
2) Der Abschied (Cadenza);

[14] In addition to the full score, the Library of Congress possesses a "trombone part," which is in reality the parts for trumpets 3 and 4 in F (located in vol. 8 of Heinrich's 37-volume collection of mss. and printed music deposited there).

[15] Annotation on the final page of the score.

3) Concertante grazioso: Eine Mondlichtscene auf dem Ocean;
4) Adagio sublime: Gebet;
5) Tremolante molto agitato: Die Landung and feierliches Entgegenkommen der Indianer;
6) Baletto indico nazionale: Freudentänze der Squaws nach erhaltenen Geschenken;
7) Andante e Fuga: Das Calumet oder die Friedenspfeife der Indianer dem grossen Geiste (Great spirit Manitou) geweiht.

In this work Heinrich is at his best in finding a suitable musical expression for each of the seven sections, which provide considerable programmatic variety. The fourth section opens with an effective prayer-like theme played by the trombones in F minor. The fifth is presented as a solemn occasion. Heinrich captures well the air of suspense and excitement by means of an unexpected modulation from F minor to E major at the opening of the section, the "tremolante" atmosphere by the use of pizzicato strings, the chromatic coloring, and sudden pauses. The sixth section, a dance, is as close as he comes to the employment of native Indian music. He uses the harmonic minor scale but concentrates the melodic movement around the first, third, fourth, and fifth degrees or, sometimes, around the first, second, fifth, and sixth degrees of the scale. The ostinato nature of the rhythm and the static and repetitive nature of the orchestration add to this "primitive" atmosphere. The fact that the section has a static, non-modulatory character also adds to the effectiveness of this dance. Thematic material for this section was used in two earlier orchestral works,[16] but it has been fittingly recast here as a dance. Sections one, two, and three as well as the finale are also appropriate mood pieces, but the musical relationship to the program is a much more generalized and subjective, although suitable, one.

Portraitures form a second topic of Heinrich's Indian themes. These compositions depict Indian leaders celebrated for their eloquence and their courage. All were active in the period from the Revolutionary War until the years following the War of 1812. This was an era of increasingly strained relations between the whites and the Indians because of the westward movement and the consequent "Indian removal." All five of the chiefs which Heinrich characterizes in his orchestral works were involved in one way or another in support of, or in opposition to, the U.S. Government. The fact that Heinrich does not choose his "heroes" from only

[16]*The Columbiad, Grand American National Chivalrous Symphony*, composed in 1837, and *The Jubilee. A Grand National Song of Triumph*, composed in 1841. The program of the *Jubilee* has many similarities with that of the *Felsen von Plymouth*.

one side may reveal that their heroic qualities were more important to him than their political affiliations. In this respect his treatment of the Indian is not unlike that of the "Noble Savage" in American literature of this era, that is, he romanticizes the intrinsic beauty and wildness, or unspoiled quality, of the native.

Pushmataha, a Venerable Chief of a Western Tribe of Indians. Fantasia Instrumental, Heinrich's first orchestral work, was completed in April 1831 in England. The score was revised in New York, the revision bearing the date "Feb. 3, 1855." As has been noted earlier by Sonneck, this was probably the first treatment of the American Indian in a large orchestral work. In addition to the lengthy title, a note in the score provides the "program" which forms the basis for Heinrich's composition:

> In a work entitled "Origin of the North American Indians," p. 255, by John McIntosh, occurs the following: Not less felicitous was the close of a speech made by *Pushmataha*, a venerable chief of a Western Tribe, at a Council held, we believe, in Washington, many years ago. In attending to his extreme age, and to the probability that he might not even survive the journey back to his tribe, he said: "My children will walk through the forests, and the *Great Spirit* will whistle in the treetops, and the flowers will spring up in the trails, but *Pushmataha* will hear not–he will see the flowers no more. He will be gone. His people will know, that he is dead. The news will come to their ears, *as the sound of the fall of a mighty oak in the stillness of the woods*."

Pushmataha's words were prophetic. He never returned to his tribe. He was elected chief of the Choctaw tribe in 1805. In 1811 he opposed Tecumseh, who tried to form an Indian Confederacy. He led a band of warriors in Andrew Jackson's forces and fought with William Weatherford against the Creek Indians. After the peace, he signed treaties of cession in 1816 and 1820. It was during his visit to Washington, D.C. in 1824, where he met Lafayette, that he made the speech recorded in McIntosh. While in Washington he became ill and died. Because of his patriotism he was buried in the Congressional Cemetary according to the rites of the white civilization.[17]

This one-movement "fantasia" uses Heinrich's full orchestra plus Bassett Horn. It is written in one of two tonalities throughout: either C (minor or major) or E-flat (major). At least ten different motives are introduced before the Coda, which contains Heinrich's own version of "God Save the King"–the only quotation of a national tune in the nine works on Indian themes. The reason for his introduction of this tune may be due to the facts that Push-

[17]*Dictionary of American Biography*, s.v. "Pushmataha," by Katherine E. Crane.

mataha was an ardent supporter of the U.S. and that he was honored at his funeral "with a great procession and booming guns."[18]

The composer prefixed the following note to the score: "The author composed this fantasia under peculiar circumstances which have given it great wildness . . . ." The work is in typical "Heinrich style," which may indicate that all his works were composed under "peculiar circumstances."

The Indian War Council. Gran Concerto Bellico. A Grand Divertissement for 41 Instrumental Parts is a portraiture of the Shawnee Chief, Tecumseh, who was one of the most outspoken Indians in support of Indian rights. As noted earlier, he opposed Pushmataha in his efforts to form an Indian Confederation, an alliance which would have rejected the white man's culture and returned to the Indians land lost through treaties of cession. He has been called

> one of the most dynamic individuals in the annals of American history, . . . certainly the outstanding leader of the American Indians of his time, and the equal of any white luminary of the period.[19]

With the outbreak of the War of 1812 Tecumseh fought with the British army and participated in skirmishes which preceded General William Hull's surrender at Detroit. He was killed in the Battle of the Thames on October 5, 1813 near Chatham, Ontario.

Although there is no reference to Tecumseh in the Library of Congress score, the work was performed in Boston on June 13, 1846 with the following program:[20]

> Tecumseh – or the Battle of the Thames—a Martial Overture—for full Orchestra.
>
> Introduction – The Indian War Council
> Allegro Eroico – The Indian War Dance –
> Advance of the Americans – Skirmishing –
> Battle and Fall of Tecumseh

Following a six-page "Adagio" introduction which features an unusual instrument, the harmonicon or glassichord, the march-like "Allegro piu tosto moderato" dominates the greater part of the movement. In the final section the tempo returns to "adagio," and

[18] Ibid.

[19] Frank W. McGill, ed., *Great Events from History: American Series*, vol. 1 (Englewood Cliffs, N.J.: Salem Press, Inc., 1975), p. 500.

[20] The complete program, preserved in Heinrich's Scrapbook, is reprinted in Upton, *Heinrich*, following p. 196. In the 1857 "Nomenclature" of Heinrich's works, no. 24 is *Tecumseh—Chief of the Shawnee Tribe, etc. Heroic Overture*, and no. 27 is *The Indian War Council. Gran Concerto Bellico*. The two works were combined into one by Heinrich.

the harmonicon is again heard (although a note indicates that the piano may be used as a substitute) before the final brief "Allegro." While the score has no program, Heinrich's inclusion of one for the audience when the work was performed indicates that he wanted the theme to be known in an explicit way.

In a note preceding the score of *Logan, the Mingo Chief. Grand Fantasia*, which he completed in 1834 in London and revised in New York in 1851, Heinrich specifies his source of inspiration for the work: "In perusing Milton's *Samson Agonistes* the composer conceived the idea of this work–hence its title." Logan's family was massacred at Yellow Creek, Ohio in April 1774. This act set Logan on a path of vengeance against the colonists. It is undoubtedly the vengeance motif in *Samson* that fired Heinrich's imagination. Logan refused to be reconciled after his defeat in November 1774 but sent his speech to be read at the conference where the treaty was signed. His speech was copied in many colonial newspapers and later was made famous through Jefferson's *Notes on the State of Virginia*:

> I appeal to any white man to say, if ever he entered Logan's cabin hungry, and he gave him not meat; if ever he came cold and naked, and he clothed him not. During the course of the last long and bloody war Logan remained idle in his cabin, an advocate for peace. Such was my love for the white, that my countrymen pointed as they passed and said, "Logan is the friend of white men." I had even thought to have lived with you, but for the injuries of one man. Colonel Cresap, the last spring, in cold blood, and unprovoked murdered my women and children. There runs not a drop of my blood in the viens of any living creature. This called on me for revenge. I have sought it: I have killed many: I have fully glutted my vengeance: for my country I rejoice at the beams of peace. But do not harbour a thought that mine is the joy of fear. Logan never will fear. He will not turn on his heel to save his life. Who is there to mourn for Logan?–not one.[21]

The tragic heroism added to the motif of vengeance must have been in Heinrich's mind as he composed this lengthy, 155-page movement which is permeated with driving rhythmic motives and chromatic movement that give an intensity and unrelenting forward momentum appropriate to the subject. Following a nine-page "Adagio quasi largo" opening, the "Allegro piu tosto Moderato" begins and continues uninterrupted and with increasing motion to page 101 of the score, where Heinrich inserts two bars rest before a section marked "Andante Sostenuto," which modulates frequently by means of a series of augmented-sixth chords. The rhythmic drive begins again on page 116, marked "Allegro Primo," and con-

[21]Thomas Jefferson, *Notes on the State of Virginia*, ed. William Reden (Chapel Hill: University of North Carolina Press, 1955), pp. 253-54.

tinues until the final two pages of the movement, which return to "Andante." The long stretches of the "Allegro" sections are normally in C major or minor, with only brief and infrequent modulations to other keys. This static harmonic idiom seems to add greater insistence to the movement and drives home the theme even more forcefully.

The *Mastodon* is a symphony in three movements, called "musical portraitures" by Heinrich. The title of the work may have been suggested to him by Charles Wilson Peale's painting, "Exhuming the Mastodon," of 1806. Peale played an important part in the exhuming, which took place in New York shortly after Heinrich's first trip to America in 1805. It is also possible that Heinrich was aware of the fact that bones of a mastodon had been found in Kentucky. These were taken to Thomas Jefferson's home, Monticello, outside Charlottesville, Virginia, and they were also sent to Paris as proof that America possessed such ancient treasure.[22]

The first and final movements of the *Mastodon* are portraits of Indian chiefs. The first movement is entitled "Black Thunder, the Patriarch of the Fox Tribe." It was probably Black Thunder's courage and eloquence that attracted Heinrich's attention. Black Thunder's speech was given at a council held at Portage, Wisconsin during July 1815. In it he replied to charges made by the American commissioners regarding a breach of treaties and of hostile intentions. His speech shows strong resistance to the loss of his lands—his country:

> My father, restrain your feelings, and hear calmly what I shall say. I shall say it plainly. I shall not speak with fear and trembling. I have never injured you, and innocence can feel no fear. . . . You are acquainted with my removal from Prairie du Chien. I went and formed a settlement, and called my warriors around. We took counsel, and from that counsel we never departed. We smoked, and resolved to make common cause with the United States . . . . I have nothing now to say here in your councils, except to repeat what I said before to my Great Father, the President of your nation. You heard it, and no doubt remember it. It was simply this. My lands can never be surrendered; I was cheated, and basely cheated in the contract; I will not surrender my country, but with my life.[23]

Heinrich uses no program as such with this movement, but in it he quotes his own "Tyler's Grand Veto Quick Step," a work for piano which was published in 1844, the year before he completed

[22]This information appears on a note identifying the bones of a dinosaur on display at Monticello.

[23]McIntosh, *Origin*, pp. 283-84.

his *Mastodon*. This movement has a single theme which is used throughout. The key of B-flat persists for the greater part of the movement, with only brief modulations to the subdominant, E-flat, and to the distant key of F-sharp major. The latter tonality occurs in the middle of the movement, which is marked "Andantino con grazia" and contrasts with the "Allegro" which forms the greater part of the movement.

The third movement of this symphony is a portrait of "Shenandoah, an Oneida Chief." Shenandoah fought with the Americans in the Revolutionary War, and he was known as "the white man's friend." Shenandoah's speech is written on the first page of the final movement. Heinrich cites McIntosh as the source of his program:

> He lived to a great age, and in his last oration in council, he opened with the following sublime and beautiful sentence:
>
> "Brothers, I am an aged hemlock. The winds of a hundred winters have whistled through my branches, and I am dead at the top!"
>
> Every reader who has seen a tall hemlock with a dry and leafless top surmounting its dark green foliage, will feel the force of the simile, "I am dead at the top." His memory, and all the vigorous fervor of youth, had departed for ever.[24]

This movement opens and closes with a "concertante" texture and "Adagio" and "Larghetto" tempi. Otherwise, it is a march-like movement in B-flat (either major or minor) with only brief modulations to D and E-flat major.

Heinrich's interest in the American Indian led him to compose works which portray aspects of their religious and social customs. The second movement of the *Mastodon*, "The Elkhorn Pyramid or the Indian's Offering to the Spirit of the Prairies," was based on Prince Maximilian de Wied's *Travels in the Interior of North America*, which Heinrich cites in the score on the title page of the movement.[25] The portrait describes a ceremony of the Blackfoot Indians which was performed in order to give them success in the hunt. This through-composed movement introduces seven melodic themes. The second one is a variation of the first movement theme, i.e., of "Tyler's Grand Veto Quick Step." But the other themes which are introduced are successively stated and then abandoned. This "piling up of themes" may be analogous to the Blackfoot ceremony of piling up elks' horns to form a pyramid. The move-

[24]Ibid., p. 222.

[25]Maximilian, Prince of Wied, *Travels in the Interior of North America, 1832-1834* (London, 1843; reprinted in Reuben G. Thwaites, *Early Western Travels, 1748-1846*, vol. 23 [Cleveland: Arthur H. Clark Co., 1906]), pp. 34-35.

ment, which opens in E-flat major, ends in B-flat major. There is much melodic chromaticism in the movement.

The one-movement symphony *The Indian Carnival: or, the Indian's Festival of Dreams* depicts some of the more exotic elements of the Indian's religious ceremonies. The orchestral work uses only a descriptive title, but Heinrich also composed and published in 1849 a composition for piano based on this symphony, which he dedicated to Heinrich Marshner. In the work for piano McIntosh is cited as the source for his "program," and a note on the title page gives a more explicit description of the festival of dreams: "A Bacchanal among the North American Indians, which commonly lasts 15 days, and is celebrated about the end of Winter." This festival of dreams is, according to McIntosh, the occasion for all kinds of fooleries, ridiculous disguises, tricks and confusion.[26] The work is highly chromatic, and the rondo-like form is one of Heinrich's most balanced and symmetrical ones. The introduction and the final section, or "Coda," are based on the same themes–both in C minor. Thematically the form can be outlined as ABACDA, and the key scheme also presents a similar pattern of repetition.

The idea for his symphony *Manitou Mysteries or the Voice of the Great Spirit. Gran Sinfonia Misteriosa Indiana* may also have been taken from McIntosh, who writes:

> The religion of the Indians is very simple, for it consists of few doctrines and fewer ceremonies. The Supreme Deity, they call the Great Spirit, whose power they believe to be infinite . . . . But, beside the Supreme Being, they believe in an infinite number of subaltern spirits, who are the objects of worship. These they divide into good and bad. The good spirits are called . . . by the Algonquins, *Manitous*. They suppose them to be the guardians of men, and that each has his tutelary Deity. In fact, every thing in nature has its spirit, though all have not the same rank nor the same influence. The animals they hunt have their spirits. If they do not understand anything, they immediately say *it is a spirit* . . . .[27]

Heinrich provided no program for this work, and it is the only one of his orchestral pieces on Indian themes that has no subtitles for the individual movements. It is, in fact, his only orchestral work that resembles the traditional, four-movement symphony. The movements are called "Sinfonia," "Minuetto," "The Adagio," and "Finale." The music itself is not "traditional." The work begins in F major, the Minuetto is in A-flat major, and the final two movements are in C major. The Finale is based on a theme from the third movement, and C major is maintained throughout the entire

[26]McIntosh, *Origin*, p. 170.
[27]Ibid., p. 104.

movement. The Minuetto opens like a dance, but a new theme replaces the return to the opening section.

It may be seen from the foregoing discussion that lengthy titles, and usually subtitles, are found in all orchestral works on Indian themes. In addition, occasional programs and—in two works—detailed tableaux are added to provide further explanation of his themes. These observations are valid for all his orchestral music. In the case of *The Indian War Council*, the only one of the nine works under discussion which was performed during his lifetime, he gave additional details which helped to clarify the program in the minds of the audience. In each work the title primarily provides an indication of the general mood or character of the music.

In his use of descriptive titles Heinrich is in step with his European contemporaries—Mendelssohn, Berlioz, Liszt, and others. By comparison, Heinrich's titles are often longer, more factually oriented, and are often more directed toward topics which are identified with American themes. It may well be that Heinrich would have agreed with Liszt, who felt that the musician could "give in a few lines the spiritual sketch of his work, and, without falling into petty explanations, convey the idea which served as the basis for the composition . . . ."[28]

In contemporary accounts his programs were frequently lauded for their appropriateness to the music. They found ready acceptance by both European and American audiences. However, the Boston journalist and critic John S. Dwight was critical of Heinrich's descriptive programs in his review of Heinrich's 1846 Boston concert, which included as the first work *The Indian War Council*:

> Mr. Heinrich belongs to the romantic class, who wish to attach a story to every thing they do. Mere outward scenes and histories seem to have disturbed the pure spontaneous inspiration of his melodies. We are sorry to see such circumstances dragged into music as the "Indian War Council," the "Advance of the Americans," the "Skirmish," and "Fall of Tecumseh." . . . A series of historical events may have unity enough in themselves to make a very good story; but it does not follow that just that series of subjects, translated into so many musical themes or passages, will still have unity as music.[29]

Heinrich's reply is humorous and clever,[30] but he does not give a clear defense for his program. His claim that he never took

[28]Paul Henry Lang, *Music in Western Civilization* (New York: W.W. Norton and Co., 1941), p. 868, quoting *Gesammelte Schriften von Franz Liszt*, vol. 2, ed. and trans. L. Ramann (Leipzig: Breitkopf & Härtel, 1881), p. 130.

[29]*Harbinger*, 4 July 1846, p. 58.

[30]Letter to J. Libby, dated July 11, 1846, in Heinrich's Scrapbook, p. 517.

Beethoven or anybody else as a pattern may, however, help to explain why Dwight failed to find unity in Heinrich's music. Heinrich, as a romantic individualist, was the product of an environment unlike Beethoven's. The cultural conditions to which Heinrich was sensitive demanded a new mode of expression. Dwight was an ardent advocate of the German tradition of absolute music, and Heinrich's idiom may not have provided the kind of musical "unity" that he expected. If by "unity" Dwight meant thematic development and a traditional formal scheme, then he would have been disappointed because Heinrich created his own modes of expression.

Heinrich's titles and programs, as is the case with all program music, do not provide musical unity in themselves. Thus, the final success of the works must rest on the effectiveness of the music itself. Heinrich's individualistic tendencies led him to compose music in unorthodox ways, and the strange or unusual qualities of his music were noted by his contemporaries. His most concentrated efforts were put into his orchestral scores. The distinctive musical qualities of these works can only be summarized here.

First of all, his sensitive ear for appropriate orchestral color led him to choose a large orchestra which provided him with a wide range of instrumental combinations. Sometimes his imagination demanded unusual instruments, such as the harmonicon or glassichord in *The Indian War Council.* In some of Heinrich's scores one also finds passages where there is a predominance of shimmering orchestral color for its own sake. When these passages are found in highly chromatic sections where the sense of tonality is temporarily abandoned, as in the third movement ("Adagio") of the *Manitou Mysteries*, the effect is not unlike that found in the works of Impressionistic composers more than fifty years later. Heinrich's expansion of the orchestra is analogous to the increase in the size of the canvas that American painters required in the nineteenth century in order to depict grand scenes adequately.

Heinrich's orchestral works on Indian themes demonstrate a variety of forms. Most of the works are through-composed, that is, they introduce themes or motives which are stated, varied, and then gradually dissolved. Other movements, such as the first movement of the *Mastodon*, are based principally on a single theme which is varied and "developed" in a free manner. In *Pocahontas* Heinrich uses one principal theme as the basis for a set of free variations.

The freedom with which he approached his forms recalls a statement made by Charles Ives about the prose style of Emerson: "As thoughts surge to his mind, he fills the heavens with them, crowds them in, if necessary, but seldom arranges them along the ground first."[31] In this almost "stream-of-consciousness" mode of expression Heinrich was undoubtedly ahead of his time, as his contemporaries noted.

Heinrich's harmonic materials were quite conventional, but his key schemes and modulations frequently were not. He often achieved surprising results through the deceptive resolution of the dominant seventh and through the use of augmented-sixth chords built on virtually any degree of the scale. Heinrich seldom uses the dominant key as a key of contrast. In many sections there is an equal emphasis on parallel major and minor keys. In some multimovement works as well as in certain ones in a single movement he ends in a different key than the one in which he began. In some movements Heinrich was so radical as to maintain the same key throughout with no, or only very brief, digressions to other tonal centers. At other times, such as in the third movement of *Manitou Mysteries*, he created tonal ambiguity by means of rapid modulations through a series of keys with little reference to the tonic chord of each new key.

During the nineteenth century Heinrich's orchestral music was seldom heard, or when it was, it was performed without adequate rehearsals. *The Indian War Council* was the only one of the nine orchestral works on Indian themes programmed during his lifetime. There were probably several reasons for such infrequent performances: 1) his music was too difficult; 2) orchestras in the U.S. lacked an established tradition; 3) the music required unusually large orchestras; 4) the attitude in Europe and America toward American musicians and music was generally negative; and 5) as many of Heinrich's contemporaries noted, "He was ahead of his time."

Four of Heinrich's orchestral works have, however, been heard in the twentieth century, among them two on American Indian themes. In 1951 Robert Whitney conducted the Louisville Orchestra in three concerts which included Heinrich's overture, *The Wildwood Troubadour*. On December 6, 1958 the *Manitou Mysteries* was performed by the Columbia University Orchestra under Howard Shanet's direction. Shanet also conducted the same orchestra in a performance of *Pushmataha* on December 9, 1961. More recently, on January 18, 1976, Michael Tilson Thomas conducted the Buffalo Philharmonic in the first of two concerts

[31]Charles Ives, *Essays Before a Sonata and Other Writings*, ed. Howard Boatwright (New York: W.W. Norton and Co., 1962), p. 108.

featuring *The War of the Elements and the Thundering of Niagara.*[32]

Scholars, editors, conductors, and performers who have studied or performed Heinrich's orchestral music have found his music to be original and effective. New performances of his orchestral works would provide the opportunity for a more complete critical assessment of this unusual repertoire. Heinrich was a keen observer of American life and manners. He felt deeply about her ideals, history, the physical environment, and about the Indians who were at one with the land and who defended their rights so courageously and eloquently. In his orchestral works on Indian themes he created a musical idiom which is original and suitable to the themes that captured his imagination. His titles and programs and their musical expression effectively reflect the unique character of the American Indians. These works form a musical complement to the novels of Cooper and the paintings of Audubon and Catlin. Possibly the more abstract language of these orchestral scores may be the most effective artistic medium in helping us to understand the "spiritual essence" of America's first inhabitants.

[32]Two critics reviewed the January 18 performance. John Dwyer said ". . . the work and performance must be counted a huge success" (*Buffalo Evening News*, 19 January 1976). Thomas Putnam, however, found the work to be "mostly polite commentary, neither fearsome nor sublime in its evocations. A postcard view" (*Buffalo Courier-Express*, 19 January 1976).

William Hopkins

The Solo Piano Works of Robert Volkmann (1815-1883)

The Saxon composer Friedrich Robert Volkmann (April 6, 1815-October 29, 1883) is numbered among the followers of Robert Schumann. Son of the cantor and schoolmaster in Lommatzsch, young Robert received early musical instruction from his father and other local musicians before traveling to Leipzig in 1836.[1] At the conservatory there he studied with Robert Schumann and C. F. Becker and was also influenced by Mendelssohn.

The years 1839-42 were spent in Prague as music master to the family of Countess Stainlein-Saalenstein[2] at Szemeréd (near Jpolyság), following which he settled in Buda. There Volkmann led a simple bachelor existence among friends, who included the lawyer Balthasar Elischer, the composer Karl Thern, and Gustav

[1]Sources consulted in preparing the biographical summary include Louis Ehlert, *From the Tone World: A Series of Essays on Brahms, Chopin, Gervinus, Gounod, Mendelssohn, Offenbach, Schumann, Tausig, Volkmann, and Wagner*, trans. from the German by Helen D. Tretbar (New York: C. F. Tretbar, 1885); Viktor von Herzfeld, "Robert Volkmann," *Musical Quarterly* 1 (1915): 336-49; Cornelius Preiss, *Robert Volkmann: Kritische Beiträge zu seiner Schaffen* (Graz: n.p., 1912); Gerhard Puchelt, *Verlorene Klänge: Studien zur deutschen Klaviermusik, 1830-1880* (Berlin-Lichterfelde: Robert Lienau, 1969); Reinhold Sietz, "Volkmann, Friedrich Robert," *Die Musik in Geschichte und Gegenwart*; Hans Volkmann, *Robert Volkmann: Sein Leben und seine Werke* (Leipzig and Dresden: H. Seemann nachf., 1903); *Briefe von Robert Volkmann*, comp. and ed. Hans Volkmann (Leipzig: Breitkopf & Härtel, 1917); and *Thematisches Verzeichnis der Werke von Robert Volkmann (1815-1883)*, comp. Hans Volkmann (Dresden: W. Ramisch, 1937).

[2]There is some confusion in the spelling of the name. Most sources use this spelling; however, Herzfeld has "Stainlein *G*aalenstein," while Sietz names only a *Count* Wilczek in Szemeréd.

Heckenast,[3] his patron and publisher. As a member of the "Roastbeef Club," the composer contributed quaint and occasionally satiric entries to its social journal[4] while enjoying a life of *Gemütlichkeit*. During this period he was organist and choir director of the Israelite congregation and wrote occasional compositions and criticism.

In 1854, through the generosity of his friend Heckenast, he moved to Vienna, where he resided for four years and wrote much of his piano music.[5] He returned to Buda in 1858, remaining there—in spite of calls to positions at the *Thomaskirche* in Leipzig and in Vienna—until his death in 1883.

In 1875 Volkmann was appointed Professor of Harmony and Counterpoint at the National Academy of Music. His duties included conducting a ninety-minute, bi-weekly master class, which he taught in a relaxed but conscientious manner. A significant measure of his reputation is that his statue—one of three, the others being those of Franz Liszt and Franz Erkel—later graced the Academy.[6] Unfortunately, his music, which enjoyed great popularity and renown during his lifetime, sharply declined in esteem after his death. The purpose of this essay is to evaluate Volkmann's solo piano works in the context of the success he enjoyed during his lifetime as opposed to the neglect he suffered almost immediately following his death.

Volkmann's compositions were issued by prominent publishers of his day, including Breitkopf & Härtel, August Cranz, and Friedrich Kistner of Leipzig; Gustav Heckenast and Rózsavölgi & Co. of Pest; Henry Litolff of Braunschweig; and B. Schott's Söhne of Mainz. All of the works with opus numbers were published shortly after their composition (usually within twelve months), a measure of the esteem in which the composer was held by his contemporaries. His 108 works span a creative life of nearly fifty years (1834-83) and encompass the standard nineteenth-century genres with the exceptions of opera and oratorio. They include seventy-six works with opus numbers and thirty-two divided evenly between those

[3]Numerous letters from Volkmann to these friends are found in his *Briefe*: fourteen to Elischer (1854-65) and nine to Heckenast (1855-71). Correspondence (friendship?) with Karl Thern seems to have begun after Volkmann's return to Buda in 1858. The thirteen letters to his colleague, dating from 1864-67, indicate a briefer duration.

[4]Two examples, from February and March 1869, are found in the *Briefe* (nos. 126-27).

[5]Puchelt, without documentation, dates the Viennese stay 1853-57; however, this is contradicted by all other sources.

[6]Franz Erkel (1810-93), the "creator of Hungarian national opera," was the founder and director of the Philharmonic Concerts and first Professor of Piano at the National Academy of Music.

without opus and unpublished works. More than half (sixty-two) of these works are instrumental, twenty-seven of which are for piano (twenty-one for piano solo and six for piano four-hands).

In contrast to the large output of lyrical piano pieces by keyboard composers of this period, Volkmann wrote only nine groups of short solo pieces, the remaining works comprising pairs or single compositions. Two of the nine collections carry titles reminiscent of Mendelssohn (e.g., *Lieder der Grossmutter*, Op. 27), while four are similar to ones used in the character cycles of Robert Schumann.[7] One of these is Volkmann's first published work, the *Sechs Fantasiebilder*, Op. 1, composed in 1837 and published by G. Schubert in 1840 (see the Appendix for further information regarding this work). This collection, Volkmann's third completed work,[8] was written during his study with Schumann in Leipzig. Although it was composed during the same year as his teacher's *Phantasiestücke*, Op. 12, it has little in common with Schumann's work except for the title. In fact, the titles of the individual pieces ("Nachtstück," "Idylle," "Walpurgis-Nachts-Scene," "Hexentanz," "Humoreske," and "Elegie,") resemble those of Mendelssohn. The second and third of these also reveal stylistic affinities with the music of that composer, as the opening measures of No. 3, reflecting the "elfin" character of Mendelssohn's *Midsummer Night's Dream* overture, show:

Example 1. Volkmann, "Walpurgis-Nachts-Scene," *Fantasiebilder*, Op. 1, No. 3, mm. 1-6

[7]Opp. 18 and 22 are dances; Op. 20 consists of folksong arrangements.

[8]It was preceded by "Im Wiesengrün," Verz. No. 81, for mixed chorus (composed in 1834 but not published until 1912), and an unpublished *Variationen für drei Violoncelli*, Verz. No. 98, of March 1836.

Stylistic indebtedness to Mendelssohn is less obvious in "Hexentanz." An original feature of this work is its use of five-measure phrases, a favorite Volkmann technique. This device is often combined with unusual meters such as $\frac{5}{4}$, which may be an influence of Hungarian folk music. In contrast to the somewhat colorless "Idylle," "Humoreske" shows Schumannesque modelling except for the B section, which is more characteristic of Volkmann. "Nachtstück" is original in melody and technique. Its melancholy anticipates Volkmann's masterful Piano Trio, Op. 5 (1850). Easily the most original work in the collection, "Nachtstück's" quality justifies the composer's decision to place it at the head of his first published work (Example 2).

Example 2. Volkmann, "Nachtstück," *Fantasiebilder*, Op. 1, No. 1, mm. 1-7

The works from the 1850s—years of his greatest productivity in the short keyboard piece—continue characteristics noted in Opus 1.

Two single solo pieces, Opp. 6 and 8, the *Musikalisches Bilderbuch*, Op. 11, for piano duet, and his only piano sonata, Op. 12,[9] were written prior to the years in Vienna. Collections composed during the Viennese stay (Opp. 17-27, see Appendix) open with the *Buch der Lieder*, whose title is reminiscent of Mendelssohn's, and culminate with *Visegrád*, Op. 21, and the Handel Variations, Op. 26.

The nine pieces of Op. 17 contain only one with a title: "Die Savoyardin" (No. 9). Lyrical right-hand melodies with supporting broken-chord accompaniments—traits of Mendelssohn's *Songs without Words*—are found in several pieces, No. 2 being especially characteristic. On the other hand, the opening piece clearly resembles Schumann's *Album for the Young* in melody and texture. Its lyrical phrases with their antecedent-consequent phrase structure strengthen this resemblance while reflecting Volkmann's gift for lyrical melody (Example 3).

Example 3. Volkmann, *Buch der Lieder*, Op. 17, No. 1, mm. 1-10

[9] Its last movement has a decidedly Mendelssohnian quality.

The $\frac{5}{4}$ metrical pattern of the earlier "Hexentanz" is found here in No. 3, but the latter's melodic and harmonic traits are much more typical of Volkmann's Hungarian style (Example 4).

Example 4. Volkmann, *Buch der Lieder*, Op. 17, No. 3, mm. 1-8

No. 8, in E-flat minor, contains textural and melodic features later seen in the *Lyric Pieces* by Grieg.

A change in character may be observed in the five *Deutsche Tanzweisen*, Op. 18, pieces revealing the charm of the Viennese waltz. Especially noteworthy are the melodic lines, enhanced by many striking harmonic effects, such as the chromatically moving bass in No. 5 (mm. 17-24). As a collection, they are graceful and ingratiating works, similar in style to Brahms' *Waltzes*, Op. 39 (published in 1867). However, they are lengthier than Brahms' works because of the larger number of individual sections and greater duration of those sections; structurally they are cast in ternary forms in which most subsections are repeated. Of the five waltzes, the first is superior.

The following year the character cycle *Visegrád, musikalisches Dichtungen*, Op. 21, was composed and published. Its twelve pieces are prefaced with a few remarks by the composer given "to provide for a better understanding of these small tone pictures."[10] The title page includes a portrait of the royal castle at Visegrád in its heyday—during the reign of King Matthias I Corvinus.[11]

These twelve pieces, Volkmann's finest collection, have been compared favorably with Schumann's *Kreisleriana* and *Phantasiestücke.*[12] The composer dedicated them to Gustav Heckenast in a letter to his friend and publisher, in which he notes several errors in the copy, comments on the circumstances of composition, and states that this collection is his first to contain metronome markings.[13] The works are short (averaging seventy-one measures), mostly in ternary forms, and feature contrasting tempos and characterizations (see Table 1).

Dramatically the story of life at the castle is divided into four parts: chivalry (Nos. 1-3), love (Nos. 4-6), character pieces (Nos. 7-9, in which the newly married couple hear the prediction of tragedy), and fulfillment of destiny (Nos. 10-12). The tonalities of the first three numbers (f/d-D/A-a) outline, collectively, the components of a D-minor triad; those of the last three (B-flat/g-G/e-flat-E-flat), an E-flat-major triad. The idyllic No. 4—in the most distantly related key—reflects the tonal distance of "love" to life at the castle. Internal key relationships feature modulations to parallel keys.

Characteristics already noted are frequent in these pieces, but, in contrast to the earlier works, quality is higher and more consistently found. While there are no weak pieces, the concluding numbers are appropriately culminating. Juxtaposition of "Der Page" (No. 10) with the march-like "Solimon" ("Suleyman," No. 11) leads to the battle "Am Salomons Thurm" (No. 12)[14] and elegie for the slain warriors. Throughout, the musical level is equivalent to Schumann's best; technically, however, the work is less demanding.

[10]The extensive remarks take an entire page.

[11]Matthias Corvinus (Matyas Hunyndi, 1443-90) was the only national king to reign over all Hungary after the Arpads. He is noted for successfully resisting the Turkish invaders and reforming the Hungarian state. Visegrád, north of Budapest, is situated at the top of a narrow, canyon-like gorge overlooking the Danube river. It was conquered by the Turks under Suleyman (Soliman II) the Magnificent in 1529. During the following century it was the scene of much warfare with the Turks, finally being reduced to ruins.

[12]Preiss, *Beiträge*, p. 10.

[13]*Briefe*, no. 53 (dated December 9, 1855).

[14]As Volkmann states in the preface, the tower on the left of the castle was built during the reign of Ladislaus the Holy and was named in 1081 for his cousin King Salomon.

Table 1

Schematic Analysis of Volkmann's *Visegrád*, Op. 21

	Chivalry			Love			Character Pieces			Destiny Fulfilled		
	1. Der Schwur	2. Waffentanz	3. Beim Bankett	4. Minne	5. Blumenstück	6. Brautlied	7. Die Wahrsagerin	8. Pastorale	9. Das Lied vom Helden	10. Der Page	11. Solimon (Suleyman)	12. Am Salomons Thurm
Measures	58	71	61	53	77	89	60	99	49	100	65	73
Tempo/ Character	Mit Würde ♩ =80	Gemessen 𝅗𝅥 =96	Frisch ♩ =120	Langsam ♩ =60	Etwas Lebhaft — —	Munter ♩ =112	Mässig Langsam ♩ = 72	In mässi-ger Be-wegung ♩ =112	Mässig bewegt ♩ =100	Einfach nicht schlep-pend ♩ =96	Ungestüm 𝅗𝅥 =112	Langsam doch nicht zu sehr ♩ =80
Form	a-b-a	A-B-A	a-b-a	a-b-a	a-a^1	a-a^1	a-b-a	A-B-A	a-a^1	a-b-a	a-b-a	a-b-a
Meter	C	$\frac{3}{2}$	$\frac{2}{4}$	$\frac{2}{4}$	$\frac{6}{8}$	$\frac{2}{4}$	C	$\frac{3}{4}$	C	C	$\frac{3}{2}$	C
Key	f-f	d-D-d	A-a-A	f♯-F♯	B	G	e	C	F	B	g-G	e♭-E♭-e♭

Several keyboard collections from these years incorporate Hungarian stylistic elements. In addition to *Visegrád*, they include the *Ungarische Lieder*, Op. 20, keyboard arrangements of Hungarian folksongs; the *Ungarische Skizzen*, Op. 24, for piano duet, which use individualized Magyar rhythmic and melodic traits; and the *Trauerphantasie*, Op. 41, which quotes the Szózat. These works, along with metrical and rhythmic traits of earlier pieces, reflect the growing influence of his years in Hungary.

The *Variationen über ein Thema von Händel*, Op. 26, parallels *Visegrád* in importance. An introduction of improvisatory character, a theme and seven variations of varying length, and an extensive fantasy-like coda are found in this work. Although posing fewer technical difficulties than Brahms' "Handel" variations on a different theme (Op. 24, 1862), it incorporates extensive chromaticism and pedalpoint, anticipating the variation technique of turn-of-the-century composers such as Reger. These traits, which pervade even the borrowed theme, are shown in Example 5.

Volkmann's piano collections and single pieces reflect traits found in similar works by German composers of the second half of the nineteenth century. Hungarian and independent stylistic

Example 5. Volkmann, *Variationen über ein Thema von Händel*, Op. 26, mm. 41-54

features are blended with the traditions of Mendelssohn and Schumann. His hybrid style matured rather quickly and did not develop significantly. The Viennese years showed a more intensified effort, with several collections achieving the consistently high quality of *Visegrád*. These works influenced diverse composers such as Grieg, Reger, and the composer's pupils.[15] However, his style is rather self-contained, with a historicizing tendency similar to that in other minor masters such as Kirchner, Kiel, and Bargiel. It is this tendency, combined with uneven quality, that accounts for Volkmann's fading significance.

[15]The "Volkmann School" includes Gyula J. Major and Mór Vavrinecz, composers of stage and symphonic works.

Appendix

The Solo Piano Works of Robert Volkmann

Opus	Date of comp.	Title	Original publisher	Publ. date	Dedication/ remarks
1	1837	Sechs Fantasiebilder	G. Schubert[a]	1840	
4	1851	Dithyrambe (und Toccata)	Rózsavölgyi	1852	
6	1852	Souvenir (de Maróth)[b]	Spina	1852	
8	1852-53	Nocturne	F. Kistner	1853	
12	1853	Sonate (1840 for Mvt. I)	F. Kistner	1854	
17	1854-56[c]	Buch der Lieder	Spina	1855-57	
18	1854	Deutsche Tanzweisen	Rózsavölgyi	1854	
19	1854	Cavatine und Barcarole	Müllers Wwe.	1854	
20	1855	Ungarische Lieder[d]	Rózsavölgyi	1855	arr. of Hungarian folksongs
21	1855	Visegrád	Rózsavölgyi	1855	Gustav Heckenast[e]
22	1855[f]	Märsche	F. Kistner	1855	
23	1855[g]	Wanderskizzen	F. Kistner	1856	Frau Emilie Feldinger[h]
25a	1857	Phantasie	E. Hallberger[i]	1858	
25b	1857	Intermezzo	E. Hallberger[j]	1859	
26	1856	Variationen über ein Thema von Händel	Schott[k]	1857	
27	1855-56	Lieder der Grossmutter	Schott	1857	
36	1858	Improvisationen—Rögtonzések[l]	Schott	1859	Fräulein Helene von Bajza
41	1860	Trauerphantasie[m]	Schott	1860	
51	1860 1866	Ballade und Scherzetto[n]	Schott	1866	
Vz.79	1852	Die Variationen über J. Andres Rheinweinlied[o]	Rózsavölgyi	1852	
Vz.80	1855	Capriccietto	*Neue Zeitschrift für Musik*, No. 24[p]	1855	

Notes to Appendix

[a]A "new, revised edition" was published in Vienna by P. Mechetti in 1854, the first year of Volkmann's four-year sojourn in that city. Publication of this edition was later assumed by A. Cranz of Leipzig (no date; plate no. 12061). The Library of Congress has a print of the Cranz edition. The first edition contrasts to the second in the following points: No. 1, "Nachtstück," is called "Nach dem Verlust" in the first edition; No. 2, "Idylle," in A major, is entitled "Seelenfrieden" and written in E major in the first edition; No. 6, "Elegie," is "Vereitelte Hoffnung und Trost" in the first edition. In the "new, revised edition" the middle section of No. 6, "Elegie," has been expunged by the publisher.

[b]The year 1852 marked the beginning of the friendship and patronage of the publisher Gustav Heckenast, at whose palace, Maróth, Volkmann spent that summer.

[c]No. 5 was composed in 1840; the remainder in 1854-56.

[d]For the sources of the lieder, see Hans Volkmann's biography, p. 63. According to the composer, the first lied is reminiscent of the Szózat, the "Rule Britannia" of Hungary, as he termed it (*Briefe*, p. 297).

[e]According to the composer's letter to Heckenast (*Briefe*, p. 130); however, there is no dedication given in the first edition.

[f]No. 4 was composed in 1837.

[g]No. 4 was composed in 1838; the remainder in 1855 in Vienna.

[h]According to the composer's correspondence (*Briefe*, nos. 50 and 57); however, it was published the following year without dedication.

[i]Appeared in the sixth book of the second *Jahrgang* of *Das Pianoforte*, edited under the direction of Franz Liszt.

[j]At the request of the publisher Hallberger for a "pretty and popular" piece, Volkmann composed this work in November, 1857 as a companion to the more difficult *Phantasie*.

[k]According to the *Verzeichnis*, p. 4, all works published by Schott were initially issued by Heckenast.

[l]These pieces are set to verses by J. von Bajza, which are quoted in Hungarian and German on the title page.

[m]Count Stephan Széchenyi died on April 8, 1860. The *Phantasie* was composed on May 12, 1860 and published a few months later.

[n]The Ballade was composed in May, 1860 and published separately (October 23, 1860) in "Album van de Maatschappy tot Bevordering der Toonkunst," Amsterdam, without opus number. The Scherzetto was composed on March 7, 1866. The pieces were published together as Op. 51 by Schott and by Jurgenson of Moscow in the fall of that year.

[o]Volkmann gave the work to the publisher Rózsavölgyi in 1852 under the pseudonym "Otto Döring," In the second edition, also published by Rózsavölgyi (no date), it was attributed to Volkmann. This (second) edition has the following foreword: "These variations, which appeared earlier under the pseudonym 'Otto Döring,' owe their origin to the concerts that Fräulein Therese Milanollo gave in Pest, to which they form a reminiscence, especially the fourth variation, which is an imitation of one of that artist's performances."

[p]Originally published as a supplement to the *Neue Zeitschrift für Musik* (June 8,1855), it was later published by C. F. Kahnt as No. 6 of the *Album für Musik* (no date).

Hans Busch

Apropos of a Revision in Verdi's *Falstaff*

In *The Music Review* of 1941 the great musician Hans Gál, whose friendship I treasure, discussed a change Verdi made in the second finale (act II, scene 2) of *Falstaff*. Professor Gál's article, "A Deleted Episode in Verdi's Falstaff," deserves to be rcmembered, and I am citing it with the author's consent:

> Let us remember the situation in the second finale of Verdi's masterpiece. Falstaff's *rendezvous* with Alice has been suddenly interrupted by Ford and his friends who break in to catch the philanderer; the gallant knight has been stowed away in a laundry basket; Ford and his gang, making a tremendous row, are searching the whole house; the young lovers, Nanetta and Fenton, amongst all that turmoil, have found a peaceful refuge behind a fire-screen; they make love and are happy. A hearty kiss, resounding during a pause, draws the general attention to the screen. No doubt, it is he, the fat rogue! So with all measures of precaution necessary to be taken against such a formidable adversary, a surprise attack is prepared against the criminal behind the screen. It is a situation of high dramatic tension, asking for quick development and solution. But Verdi would not have been Verdi had he not used such a situation for inserting one of his glorious pieces of concerted music, and there is no doubt he was acting in the best tradition of Italian opera when he did so. [*Andante, pianissimo.*] It starts as a slow scherzando, with tittering triplets and nervous, sudden accents. Subsequently a broad, beautiful melody takes the lead, sung by Nanetta and Fenton, the young lovers behind the screen, who in a close embrace have forgotten everything around them. Ford and his men encouraging each other for the dangerous enterprise, the merry women choking with repressed laughter—everything *sotto voce*—give a kind of lining to it, in the well-known manner of Italian *ensemble*, as it had been already developed by Rossini. It is a delicious little oasis of rest and euphony in

the frolicsome turbulence of the finale, dying away in the softest pianissimo and cut off finally when Ford's gang rush up and overthrow the screen. Do you remember it? No, you don't. I am afraid I am the only lover of that opera who knows this admirable little gem, a most characteristic specimen of Verdi's latest style of melody and harmony. Many years have passed, but I still remember my wrath and grief, when as a young student I first heard a performance of *Falstaff* and this episode, one of my favourites in that beloved masterpiece, was cut short. I had studied with infinite delight my vocal score, rather a torn copy I had hunted up in an antiquarian's shop. I had been looking forward to that glorious moment of beauty and loveliness, and it did not come!

Example 1.

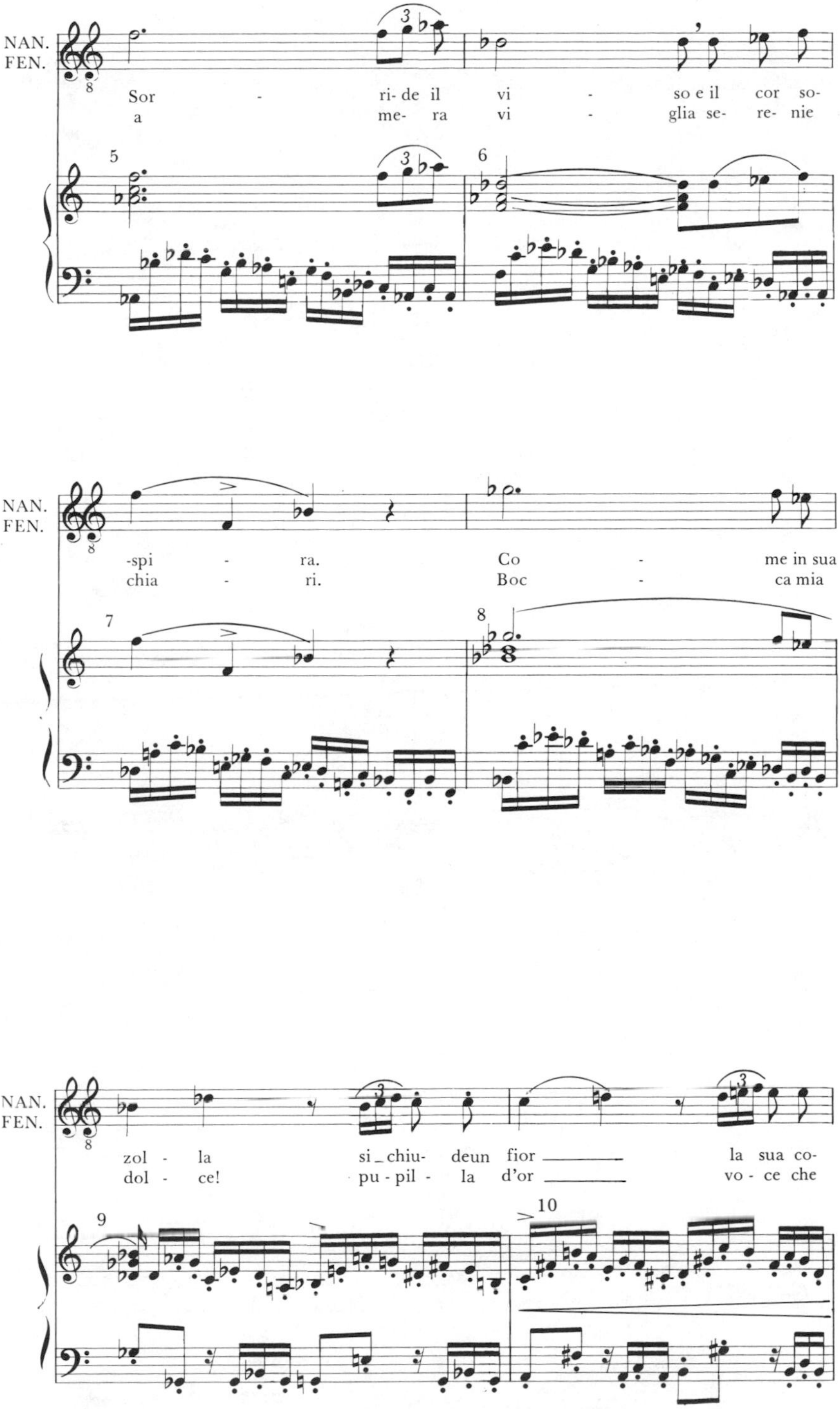
NAN.
FEN.
Sor - ri- de il vi - so e il cor so-
a me- ra vi - glia se- re- nie
5
6
NAN.
FEN.
-spi - ra. Co - me in sua
chia - ri. Boc - ca mia
7
8
NAN.
FEN.
zol - la si _ chiu- deun fior _____ la sua co-
dol - ce! pu - pil - la d'or _____ vo - ce che
9
10

dolce
NAN.
FEN.
-rol - - la svol - veil mio
mol - - ce co - m'ar - pa il
11
12
p
cor, la sua co - rol - la
cor, vo - ce che mol - ce
dolciss
13
14
(Pistola, Coro)
ff
p (Ford)
svol - ve il mio
dolciss
co - m'ar - pa il
15
16
dim.

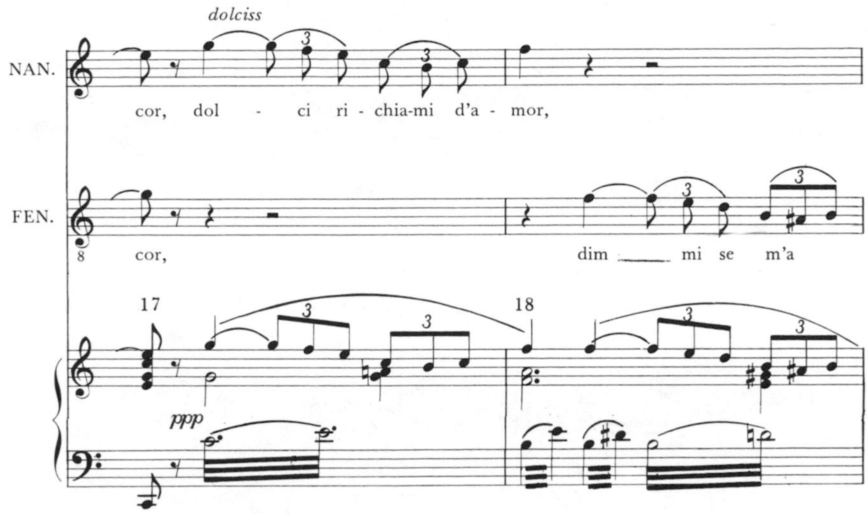

I think I might have killed the conductor, had I known how to get at him. But it would have been a deplorable act of youthful rashness. For some time later, when I got hold of a full score, I realised that Verdi's enemy and mine would have died guiltless. His performance was in strict accordance with the score.

Example 2.

63
NANETTA
FENTON
(unis.)
p espr.
(Nan) Tut - to de - li - ra,
(Fen) Fra quel - le ci glia
p
NAN.
FEN.
so - spi - ro e ri - so.
ve - do due fa - ri
(etc. see Ex. 1
bars 17-21)
NAN.
FEN.
Sor - ri - de il vi - so e il cor so - spi - ra.
a me - ra - vi - glia se - re - ni e chia - ri.

The cut, no doubt, was made by Verdi himself, and he must have had his reason. My vocal score, apparently, was a remainder of a first edition, printed before the first performance in Milan in 1893, and revised subsequently by the composer, as later editions show the correspondence with the full score. There is nothing uncommon in that fact, and there is another substantial alteration at the end of the first part of the last act which results in a considerable musical improvement. The first edition of an opera, printed before the crucial test of the stage, is generally restricted to a limited number of copies, as the publisher knows by experience the probability of at least some slight alterations. So this first edition is likely soon to be superseded by a new, final one.

Since then I have heard many performances of *Falstaff*, good and bad, culminating in the unforgettable perfection achieved by Toscanini at Salzburg. But I cannot help feeling the same sensation of discomfort every time at that moment, a shock of something awkward and out of proportion in the musical texture. To-day, as an experienced musician, I find no difficulty in analysing the reasons for that feeling. As a result, for the first time in my life, I have to plead against the final decision of a great composer and for the restoration of his original version.

If Verdi had simply eliminated the whole episode, one might deplore it, but one could put up with it as with a sacrifice for higher reasons of unity and dramatic flow. But he seems to have felt the necessity for an oasis of music in that scene, as he left part of it. He replaced sixteen bars (1-16 of Example No. 1) by a new invention of six bars, which have always given me an impression of something abrupt and inconsistent in the context. [See Ex. 2.]

These six bars, though masterly and refined, have a definite defect: they do not match the following melodious appendix (bars 17-21 of Example 1). The new invention starts very promisingly; a broad melody seems to unfold its wings (bars 1-4). But it does not rise; the following two bars turn round to the tonic again, as if it were not worth taking the trouble. The result is a shortwinded, incomplete period. Its deficiency is betrayed by that delightful little appendix, which also has the same harmonic object of revolving round the tonic as a melodious cadence, a typical codetta. Such a codetta has an organic, necessary function after the spacious range of harmony covered by the original tune, but it is hopelessly out of place after the shortwinded period which has replaced it. Imperfections of a similar kind are not rare in operatic music, since opera in the nineteenth century got more or less emancipated from the formal and aesthetic postulates of absolute music. But when music takes the lead in an opera—and it does so definitely wherever a lyrical invention is developing—the claims of musical architecture are pitilessly exigent, exposing the patchwork. Any musician with a sharp ear and a sense of proportion, I fancy, would feel something to be wrong here.

The question remains: why did Verdi do it? Well, I think I can give a plausible explanation. I have mentioned above the dramatic problem with which the composer was confronted. That lyric *ensemble* undoubtedly involves a kind of deadlock in the progress of the action,

> although standstills of that sort are inevitable within the conventions of Italian opera. Remember the great second finale in *Aida*, or the third finale in *Otello*, or the glorious quartet in *Rigoletto*. It is a problem which concerns the producer who, if he is resourceful and experienced in opera, will find a way of coping with it. In any case it can easily be imagined that the old maestro when attending a rehearsal was made nervous by the impression that something was dragging in one of the most decisive scenes of his opera. Only an amateur is sufficiently in love with his work to be easily satisfied. A master will be ten times more sensitive to any shortcoming than the most critical listener can be; and no true opera composer was ever afraid of a sacrifice of music for scenic reasons. Verdi may have found that scene somewhat lengthy. As we know from other examples, he was as callous as an experienced surgeon in cutting out whatever he found unsatisfactory. In this case, I am afraid he has gone too far in mutilating the product of his invention to quicken the dramatic flow. The cut, no doubt, has shortened the scene. But it has definitely spoiled a precious musical climax.
>
> Here is a suggestion. It is not unlikely that the missing pages can be found in Verdi's manuscript at Ricordi's. And if not, it would be no difficult job for an able musician to orchestrate the eliminated sixteen bars with all the necessary piety and observance of style. Here is an opportunity for a conductor to acquire merit by risking a restoration! At least there could be no harm in trying it as an experiment. Sixteen bars of one of the most precious scores ever written should be worth the trouble.[1]

In 1970 I tried unsuccessfully to recover those missing pages of Verdi's original orchestration (not contained in the facsimile score). Verdi himself might have destroyed them, as he did many others. Thereupon Hans Gál made me the gift of his own orchestration, done "with all the necessary piety and observance of style" but still waiting to be played. Since then the House of Ricordi generously made available to me photocopies of Verdi's letters to his publisher Giulio Ricordi (1840-1912) pertaining to this correction and other changes the old maestro had made in his *Falstaff* after the première at La Scala on 9 February 1893. Except for some quotes in Franco Abbiati's *Giuseppe Verdi*,[2] these letters have, to the best of my knowledge, not been published and translated before. With the permission of the House of Ricordi I have translated—as literally as possible—the parts concerning the above-mentioned changes so that we may appreciate Verdi's own thoughts and the great pains he took in these matters.[3]

[1] Hans Gál, "A Deleted Episode in Verdi's Falstaff," *Music Review* 2 (1941): 266-72. Reprinted by permission of W. Heffer and Sons, Ltd.

[2] 4 vols. (Milan: G. Ricordi, 1959), 4:499-501, 503, 509.

[3] I have tried to maintain Verdi's distinctive, very simple and informal style because I think that any attempt to "improve" his writing would distort it.

Genoa, 7 March 1893

. . . Once more to *Falstaff*.

I don't know if you know that when at an orchestra rehearsal I went to hear the opera from the auditorium, I was so displeased with the final *concertato* [act II, scene 2] that I said to all the artists gathered together: "This piece does not work like that; either you perform it more *piano*, totally *sotto voce*, with each group detached from the other, or it must be cut and changed!" Nobody breathed, but these words did not make a good impression, as they can tell you. The next night they performed it better and nothing was said anymore! But at the performances I saw that on the stage that section is long and too much of a *concertato* piece. I wanted to change it in Milan, but I never had an hour of complete tranquillity. I say, change it, because I am an enemy of cuts. A section that is cut is like an arm, the belly, the legs, etc., etc. cut from a body . . . . In pieces conceived too broadly the cut becomes necessary, but it is always a monstrosity; it's a body without head or without belly, or without legs.

In the *concertato* of *Falstaff* it was easy to cut and jump right away to *Dolci richiami d'amor*; but the musical piece was gone, the belly was missing. I have rewritten 6 bars and the piece is shortened by 10 bars. I'll send it to you tomorrow . . . . I would like it to be done before the performances at La Scala are over . . . . And do you get it in time for the second edition [of the vocal score] ?

It is learned very easily. A little half-hour call for the singers (instead of their going for a walk) and 5 minutes with the orchestra, when it is assembled for another rehearsal, will suffice.

One can do [the rehearsal] without Maurel[4] . . ., that is: if he comes also, one can go over those *parlandos* that he does no longer in *tempo*. . . .

[Genoa, 8 March 1893]

Here is the section of the finale I wrote you about yesterday. It's not a cut but a section that ties in well with:

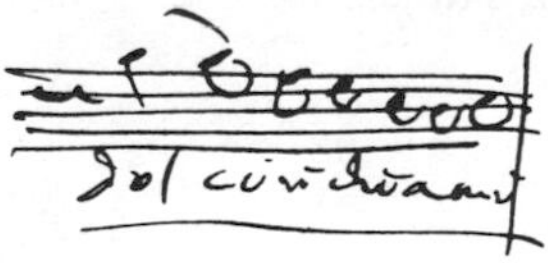

Ten long bars are out. And that's a lot!

For the action this is better; for the music I don't know . . . , unless the recall of the wives' phrase

is good, and then neither the stomach nor the legs are missing in the piece.

Do with it as you please. Look it over with Mascheroni and Boito;[5] actually Boito must perhaps adjust some verses.

[4]The French baritone Victor Maurel (1848-1923), Verdi's first Jago and Falstaff.

[5]Edoardo Mascheroni (1859-1941) conducted the première of *Falstaff* at La Scala; Arrigo Boito (1842-1918) was the opera's librettist.

The singers know that I was not happy with that section, and so they won't mind coming for half an hour to the foyer. I'll be there too, since (if advised half an hour before) I'll arrive as quick as a flash.[6]

When you decide to perform it, send me the original section to be adjusted.

Amen.

Greetings to you all. *Addio*

G. Verdi

Saturday [Genoa, 11 March 1893]

Dear Giulio,

My presence indispensable!!

What the devil! For such a little thing??

It would be outright ridiculous on my part to come to Milan to hold a rehearsal of *six* bars!!!! Oh Giulio, Giulio, . . . how could you ever say such a thing!!

If there is (how shall I say this?) even the slightest controversy, obstacle, etc., etc., leave things as they are! . . .

Genoa, 14 March 1893

Dear Giulio,

As I telegraphed, if you believe there is [too much] responsibility for you (which I do not believe), let's not talk about it anymore.

However, since you have written out the parts of the singers, hold a rehearsal with the singers only, maybe without Maurel, and you will see the result. Mind you, though, that this little rehearsal must be held on the stage with the *screen* and with the *basket* so that you will be able to judge. Hold the stage rehearsal after they have learned the notes.

With a little bit of good humor and good will you will do it fast and well . . . .

In any event there always is the supreme remedy: *the old* [version].

Addio, addio Yours,

G. Verdi

Genoa, 18 March 1893

Dear Giulio,

Looking again and again over the section of the finale [act II, scene 2], I have seen other bars that should be revised. Furthermore, I have never liked that sort of mazurka which concludes the first part of the third act, . . . and there I had a [musical] motive at hand (*avrò con me dei putti*)[7] that, well played and well modulated, would have made a better effect; and it was also more fitting and more musical. It was the continuation of the plan for the masquerade . . . *che fingeran folletti . . . Spiritelli . . . Farfarelli*,[8] etc., etc. It was such an easy thing to do!

[6]There is no equivalent for Verdi's expression "arriverò d'urgenza a cavallo del telegrafo" meaning "I shall arrive as fast as possible astride the wire."

[7]Verdi quotes from Alice's lines in act III, scene 1.

[8]Verdi again quotes from Alice's lines in act III, scene 1.

. . . Ah, what poor heads we have!!! It would be better to throw them against a wall . . . and good night . . . .

P.S. *Torno all'assalto.*[9] . . . For the time being let's not make any changes in *Falstaff* . . . . Later, who knows? . . . Perhaps for a revival . . . .

[Genoa,] 1 April 1893

Dear Giulio,

For a long time, ever since the first orchestra rehearsals in Milan, I had planned to make two changes. Many nuisances distracted me. This morning, angered by the latest events, I threw myself down to write.

I send you the section [act II, scene 2] (I don't know what it's like). Have the little vocal parts copied right away; then I'll rehearse it here with the artists: not to have it performed in a theatre, neither here nor elsewhere, at least not for now, but for my own artistic satisfaction . . . . *Addio*

G. Verdi

Wednesday [Genoa, 5 April 1893]

Dear Giulio,

I received your letter which I cannot answer at the moment.

Afterwards I received the parts of the changed sequence . . . .

If you come tomorrow night, bring along the bundle of the original score in which I made the change of the finale [act II, scene 2] so that I can orchestrate it.

Genoa, Friday [*probably* 28 April 1893]

Dear Giulio,

Since I expected other observations, I was surprised that I should add a bar to the section I sent you.

We do not speak of [*undecipherable*] nor of 8 bars . . ., but here I really feel that by adding a bar the phrase would be limping. The musical movement goes in two-bar phrases:

Thus the phrase two-by-two is right. By lengthening it one would have to add not one but two bars, and it would become cold.

But perhaps there is a reason for you and Boito to be right. The little *cantilena* for soprano and tenor above the movement of the basses requires a larger development in the last two bars; making that phrase shorter, it can go well like this:

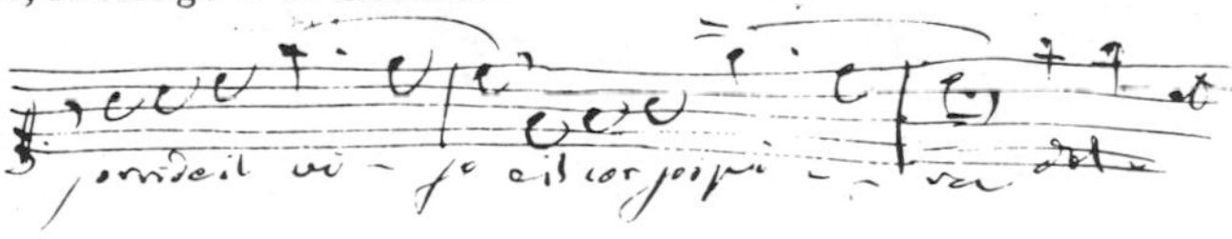

[9]Verdi quotes Fenton in act I, scene 2.

Anyway, try it with the singers, and if you still have the impression that a bar is missing after you have tried it, well, let's not talk about it anymore and leave it as it has been until now.

Genoa, 30 April 1893

. . . It's all right to redo the parts in the original orchestral score; but I'll do this little job at St. Agata. . . .

St. Agata, 23 May 1893

Dear Giulio,

This morning I sent you the last notes of *Falstaff*.[10] Peace to his soul! . . .

***

Who was right? Verdi the dramatist, or Verdi the musician?

Postscript

Since these pages went to press, I received photocopies of hundreds of letters to Verdi from his publisher, Giulio Ricordi. On 9 March 1893 Ricordi wrote to Verdi that Arrigo Boito, the librettist of *Falstaff*, respectfully objected to the change the Maestro proposed in the second finale. Boito's reasons were the same as Hans Gál's.

Verdi's letter from "Genoa, Friday," which I previously presumed to have been written on 28 April 1893, was the answer to Ricordi's letter of 9 March and was definitely written on the 10th.

[10]The last corrections of the orchestral score.

David Fenske

Contrapuntal Textures in the String Quartets, Op. 51, No. 2 and Op. 67 of Johannes Brahms

Allusions are commonly made in the literature about Brahms to a specifically Brahmsian texture. While these statements seemingly refer to a characteristic feature of Brahms's style, there is no agreement defining the nature or descriptors of this stylistic trait. Occasionally, the remarks about texture in Brahms's chamber works are given in a derogatory tone, the authors observing, for example, the symphonic nature of the textures. Rey M. Longyear states in a textbook on nineteenth-century music that "a few of his chamber works have an almost 'orchestral' sound . . . ."[1] Longyear goes on to describe Brahms's instrumentation as characterized "by a rather dark brown, somber coloring thanks to the importance of the violas, the blended tone-colors, and the doubling of notes, particularly the thirds of chords, in the low register . . . ."[2] Paul Henry Lang states, while discussing the Op. 51, No. 1 String Quartet, that "his C minor quartet is already plainly symphonic in texture and sonority . . . ."[3] It is apparent from these few quotations that there is little unanimity in definition or descriptors.

The musical concepts of density, chord spacing, contrapuntal usage, instrumentation and sonority are easily associated with the idea of texture. The profusion of the above listed terms in the literature about music is related to the common usage of the term texture. One of the few definitions of texture is contained in the *Harvard Dictionary of Music*:

[1] *Nineteenth-Century Romanticism in Music* (Englewood Cliffs, N.J.: Prentice-Hall, 1969), p. 137.

[2] Ibid., p. 138.

[3] *Music in Western Civilization* (New York: Norton, 1941), p. 902.

> Much like woven fabric, music consists of horizontal ("woof") and vertical ("warp") elements. The former are the successive sounds forming melodies, the latter the simultaneous sounds forming harmonies. It is these elements that make up the texture. The texture stands out particularly clearly in part music, i.e., music written in a given number of parts. Each part represents a horizontal line of individual design, connected with the other lines by the (vertical) relationship of consonance or harmony. Such music is said to have a *contrapuntal* or *polyphonic* texture . . . .[4]

Textural analysis, characterized by an inclusiveness of ideas, is more of a concept than a term.

As defined in this study, textural analysis is concerned with the relative importance of different parts (i.e., contrapuntal density) and with the rate of change in the number of contrapuntal parts (i.e., textural rhythm). Contrapuntal density will be presented as follows:

1. The relative importance of each of the instruments
2. The relative importance of various combinations of part writing

For example, in a given measure, the first violin and the viola may have parts of melodic or contrapuntal interest while the other instruments accompany them. This measure would be counted as one for the first violin and the viola in category one above, and it would have the value of two in the second category above because there are two such parts in this measure. For the purposes of this study, it is assumed that the greater the number of simultaneous contrapuntal parts, the more dense is the texture.

Textural rhythm is defined in this study as the rate of change in the number of simultaneous contrapuntal parts (derived from category two above) as represented in beats for each change. For instance, the textural rhythm may change twenty-five times in a movement having 250 beats. The composite mean beat value would be 10.00. Similarly, mean beat values are determined for each of the major formal sections of a movement to establish how fluctuations in the rate of change may be linked to formal sections or may be used as a device for contrast between large formal sections.

The three string quartets, which constitute all of the extant quartets of Brahms, were published in 1873 (both of the Op. 51 Quartets) and in 1876 (the Op. 67 Quartet). Most of the intrinsic chronological and historical problems revolve around two factors: 1) the time lag between composition and publication; 2) the actual number of string quartets.

On one occasion, Brahms told Alwin Cranz that he had written

[4]2nd ed., s.v. "texture."

and destroyed twenty string quartets.[5] Little is known about when these quartets were actually written but Brahms did withdraw an early string quartet from a list that Schumann proposed for publication twenty years before the publication of the Op. 51 Quartets.[6] Brahms did not clearly state his reasons for discarding the quartets. Speculation centers around two ideas: 1) the traditionalism of the medium itself; 2) the review to which all Brahms's works were subject. Most of Brahms's earlier chamber works involved the keyboard in some way and reflected Brahms's familiarity with piano performance. The major exceptions to the preceding observation are the two String Sextets, Op. 18 and Op. 36. The conclusion perhaps follows that Brahms had difficulty in reducing his sound and texture to a level appropriate to four strings. A partial explanation for the destruction of so many string quartets can also be found in Brahms's self-criticism. While the well-known examples of the Op. 8 Trio and the several arrangements of the First Piano Concerto and the Piano Quintet tend to support this explanation, Brahms is not known to have destroyed a similar quantity of works of any other genre. A combination of the above factors probably led to Brahms's decision to destroy the other string quartets.

The time lag between the composition of the Op. 51 Quartets and their publication adds credence to the view that Brahms attached special importance to the publication of his first quartets. Clara Schumann heard the Quartet in C minor, Op. 51, No. 1, in the summer of 1866.[7] Hermann Deiters played both of the Op. 51 Quartets with Brahms in 1868 in Bonn.[8] However, both of the Quartets received their first public performance in the year of their publication, 1873.[9] A seven-year time lag such as the one described above is not typical during this period of Brahms's life—when he had no difficulty in obtaining a publisher for his works.

While all of Brahms's chamber works have been subjected to the same textural analysis described above (including all three string quartets), only the Op. 51, No. 2 and the Op. 67 Quartets have been included in this study. These two last-named works have some unusual features from the point of view of contrapuntal texture.

[5]Henry S. Drinker, *The Chamber Music of Johannes Brahms* (Philadelphia: Elkan-Vogel, 1939), p. 68.

[6]Florence May, *The Life of Johannes Brahms*, 2nd ed., 2 vols. (London: William Reeves, n.d.), 2:463.

[7]Ibid., 2:474.

[8]Ibid.

[9]Ibid.

Quartet for 2 Violins, Viola, and Violoncello in A minor, Op. 51, No. 2

The Op. 51, No. 2 Quartet was dedicated to Theodor Billroth and received its first public performance by the Joachim Quartet in Berlin on October 18, 1873.[10] The data for the first movement, marked "Allegro non troppo" and in 2/2 meter, are as follows:

Number of measures containing important melodic or contrapuntal material for each instrument

Vln. I	279 of 335	83.28 percent
Vln. II	236 of 335	70.45 percent
Vla.	209 of 335	62.39 percent
Vc.	164 of 335	48.96 percent

Number of measures with textures involving varying numbers of important melodic or contrapuntal parts

4	108 of 335	32.24 percent
3	55 of 335	16.42 percent
2	113 of 335	33.73 percent
1	59 of 335	17.60 percent

Textural Rhythm

Composite mean beat value		9.23
mm. 1-128	Exposition	11.73
mm. 129-182	Development	6.35
mm. 183-277	Recapitulation	10.67
mm. 278-375	Coda	6.82

In many respects the first movement is, from a textural viewpoint, the most conservative of the eight movements examined in this study: 1) the sonata form is fairly straightforward; 2) the profile of the relative contrapuntal importance of the four instruments shows a first violin domination and relatively little importance for the viola and violoncello parts; and 3) the textural distribution pattern suggests the equal importance of two- and four-part writing and does not suggest a particularly dense contrapuntal texture. Texture is used to delineate various sections through the contrasting of instrumental combinations, which in no way affect the dominant role of the first violin. Three major combinations emerge from this movement: 1) first violin or first and second violins with the other parts providing accompanimental material (e.g., exposition of theme A, m. 1ff.); 2) second violin and viola, often with the viola above the second violin (e.g., m. 62ff.); and 3) first violin and violoncello, often at the extremities of their respective tessituras

[10]Ibid.

and often in contrary motion (e.g., m. 35ff.). Other less frequent combinations include: 1) the three upper parts having one important melodic idea versus the violoncello having another melodic part (i.e., the usual arrangement when the violoncello has an important, unique part); and 2) the two violin parts versus the viola and the violoncello. The second violin, while present in several of the above combinations, is usually subservient to another part. In contrast, the first violin is rarely without important material and often in a register considerably above the other three parts, making its predominance even more apparent. When four-part texture is found in this movement, it is often initiated by imitative contrapuntal devices, including canon and inversion. Although rhythmically not the most notable example, a good instance of four-part imitative entrances can be found in m. 321ff.

The textural rhythm in this movement serves to delineate and contrast the various sections. The exposition and recapitulation have virtually the same rate of textural change. While the development and the coda also have the same rate of change, it is twice as fast as that found in the other two sections.

The data for the second movement, which is marked "Andante moderato" and in 4/4 meter, are as follows:

Number of measures containing important melodic or contrapuntal material for each instrument

Vln. I	109 of 124	87.90 percent
Vln. II	72 of 124	58.06 percent
Vla.	75 of 124	60.48 percent
Vc.	80 of 124	64.52 percent

Number of measures with textures involving varying numbers of important melodic or contrapuntal parts

4	49 of 124	39.52 percent
3	26 of 124	20.97 percent
2	13 of 124	10.48 percent
1	36 of 124	29.03 percent

Textural rhythm

Composite mean beat value		15.03
mm. 1-42	A	15.27
mm. 43-76	B	15.11
mm. 77-110	A	15.11
mm. 111-124	Coda	14.00

Although the melodic characteristics of the A and B sections are quite dissimilar, they share the same textural principle of construction: a less dense texture at the beginning and in the middle of the section is followed in each case by a more dense texture. When the denser structure is present, it tends to fluctuate between three and four parts (found in over sixty percent of the movement). The similarity of construction explains the lack of variation in the textural rhythm, which is quite unusual. The A section is initiated by one-part texture, while the B section starts in two-part texture. Most listeners, however, would perceive the B section to be considerably more dense than the A section despite a similarity in the frequency with which three- and four-part textures occur. That perception is due not only to the two-part texture at the opening of the B section but also to the nature of the two-part counterpoint and the tessituras of the two parts. The first violin and the violoncello play the B theme in canon at the upper and lower extremities of their respective tessituras, thus creating the illusion of a denser texture than actually exists.

The second movement, in addition to being texturally denser than the first, is also noteworthy for a greater equality and balance of important material between the four parts. Although the first violin continues to have important melodic material throughout most of the movement (87.90 percent), the viola and violoncello both have significant percentages (60.48 and 64.52 respectively). It should be noted that, while the second violin has a lower percentage of importance than any other part, it is, in most instances, an independent part when it has melodic material. The four-part textures in this movement are truly contrapuntal. Voice crossing between all parts is common throughout the movement, which further supports the contrapuntal and linear structure.

The data for the third movement, which is marked "Quasi Menuetto, moderato" and in 3/4 meter, are as follows:

Number of measures containing important melodic or contrapuntal material for each instrument

Vln. I	156 of 178	87.64 percent
Vln. II	140 of 178	78.65 percent
Vla.	158 of 178	88.76 percent
Vc.	105 of 178	58.98 percent

Number of measures with textures involving varying numbers of important melodic or contrapuntal parts

4	81 of 178	45.50 percent
3	63 of 178	35.39 percent
2	4 of 178	2.24 percent
1	30 of 178	16.85 percent

Textural rhythm

Composite mean beat value		11.43
mm. 1-39	A	19.50
mm. 40-133	B	7.32
mm. 134-169	A	27.00
mm. 170-178	Coda	13.50

The third movement is a fascinating study in contrasting textures and contrapuntal techniques. The A section, which is marked "Quasi Minuetto moderato," is in 3/4 meter. The second A section is nearly a written out *da capo* of the first A section. The B section is marked "Allegretto vivace" and is in 2/4 meter with two short, but important, insertions of 3/4 meter in mm. 73-78 and 122-133. The change of meter between the A and B sections is only one way in which the sections are contrasted with one another and otherwise delineated. The basic texture of the A section is three-plus-one, the first and second violins and the viola all having important parts set against the violoncello, which normally has a static part employing double-stopping and pedal point. The A section is dominated by the three-measure phrase that is found in mm. 1-3. The B section, excluding for the moment the two insertions mentioned above, is built around the principle of equal contrapuntal parts. The most common grouping is two lower parts doubling the same line against another contrapuntal line in an upper part (e.g., m. 4ff., m. 48ff., and m. 57ff.).

While the two "Tempo di Menuetto" insertions in mm. 73-78 and 123-133 are not exactly the same, they do share the same material at the outset. Both insertions contrast markedly with the portions of the B section which precede them and resemble the A section in terms of meter and of rhythm. The insertions are built on two contrapuntal lines, each of which is imitated at the interval of three beats, creating, therefore, four equal contrapuntal parts. Line one is an ornamented version of theme A in that the relative sequence of pitches occurring on beat one is the same as in the A theme. The situation is even more subtle than that statement would imply because the same can also be said of its relationship to theme B. A thematic relationship between themes A and B which would otherwise not be apparent is made clear by the insertions. Line two consists of the first five pitches of the A theme, repeated once. The ending of the second insertion, mm. 128-133, is particularly noteworthy because it involves double-stopping in a low tessitura for all parts, creating one of the densest vertical and horizontal textures found in the chamber works of Brahms.

The data for the number of measures containing important melodic and contrapuntal material demonstrate that the viola has a higher percentage (88.76) than the first violin (87.64), a very unusual occurrence. The relatively high and approximately equal percentages for the first violin, second violin, and viola as compared to the relatively low percentage for the violoncello (58.98 percent) are reflective of the three-plus-one contrapuntal groupings noted above. The highest percentage for the distribution of important melodic and contrapuntal parts is that for four-part writing (45.50 percent), an unusually high percentage. When the percentage for four-part writing is combined with that for three-part writing (35.39 percent), the resulting 80.89 percent is indicative of the dense contrapuntal writing found in this movement.

The composite mean beat value of the textural rhythm for this movement (11.43 beats) is slightly slower than one might expect, but there are strong contrasts between sections. The relatively static quality of the A sections is reflected in their slow textural rhythm (19.50 beats for the first A section, 27.00 beats for the second). This slow textural rhythm contrasts markedly with the fast rate of textural change found in the more contrapuntal B section (7.32 beats).

The data for the fourth movement, which is marked "Allegro non assai" and in 3/4 meter, are as follows:

Number of measures containing important melodic or contrapuntal material for each instrument

Vln. I	297 of 359	82.73 percent
Vln. II	209 of 359	58.22 percent
Vla.	259 of 359	72.14 percent
Vc.	223 of 359	62.12 percent

Number of measures with textures involving varying numbers of important melodic or contrapuntal parts

4	172 of 359	47.91 percent
3	42 of 359	11.70 percent
2	48 of 359	13.37 percent
1	93 of 359	25.91 percent
0	4 of 359	1.11 percent

Textural rhythm

Composite mean beat value		17.37
mm. 1-44	A	22.00
mm. 45-115	B	21.30
mm. 116-143	A'	7.00
mm. 144-197	B'	11.57
mm. 198-237	A"	20.00
mm. 238-293	B	28.00
mm. 294-333	A'''	30.00
mm. 334-359	Coda	19.50

The fourth movement is in the form of a complex rondo. Contrasts in this movement are achieved primarily through differentiation in thematic materials, but textural characterizations also play an important role. Both A and B sections start with one-part texture, which is also true of most of the complete thematic statements in the movement. Most other occurrences of one-part texture are reserved for short-term contrast, usually within transitions. Four-part textures are used frequently in the last half of A sections and for the majority of B sections after the initial statements of the B theme. The B theme, which is very lyrical (in marked contrast to the jagged contour of the A theme), does not dominate B sections. In most cases, after the statement of the B theme the remainder of the section is devoted to the development of both the A and B material in predominantly four-part texture. When one-part texture is prevalent, it does not always mean that the first violin has the important material. The viola and violoncello both have instances of exposed, important passages in this movement (e.g., m. 13ff. and m. 238ff. respectively).

The contrast between one-part textures at the beginning of sections and the prevalence of four-part texture throughout most of the rest of the sections is reflected in the data. Four-part texture occurs most often (nearly forty-eight percent of the time) with one-part texture having the second highest rate of incidence (nearly twenty-eight percent). The combined percentage for one- and four-part textures is nearly seventy-five percent, indicating that two- and three-part textures are reserved for only occasional use. Of course, the unusually high percentage for four-part texture is indicative of a contrapuntally dense texture throughout most of the movement.

The data for the relative importance of each part indicate the dominant role played by the first violin part but also the importance of the viola and violoncello (72.14 and 62.12 percent respectively). The relatively close percentages for the second violin (58.22 percent) and for four-part texture (47.91 percent) indicate that the second violin rarely has important material in textures other than those for four voices.

The data for textural rhythm reveal that textures do not change radically between sections and that the rate of change is not a prime factor of contrast between sections. Instead, sections seem to be paired, and the rate of change is a matter of some contrast between pairs of sections (e.g., between the A' and B' sections).

Quartet for 2 Violins, Viola, and Violoncello in B-flat major, Op. 67

The String Quartet in B-flat major, Brahms's third and last published string quartet, was completed in February 1876.[11] The first performance of the Quartet was given on October 30, 1876 by the Joachim Quartet in Berlin.[12] The Quartet was published during 1876 and dedicated to Theodor W. Englemann. All we know of Brahms's string quartet style is restricted to the decade (between the start of the Op. 51 quartets and the completion of the Op. 67 quartet) in the middle of Brahms's creative years.

The data for the first movement, which is marked "Vivace" and in 6/8 meter, are as follows:

Number of measures containing important melodic or contrapuntal material for each instrument

Vln. I	278 of 340	81.76 percent
Vln. II	261 of 340	76.76 percent
Vla.	278 of 340	81.76 percent
Vc.	208 of 340	61.18 percent

Number of measures with textures involving varying numbers of important melodic or contrapuntal parts

4	165 of 340	48.53 percent
3	55 of 340	16.18 percent
2	83 of 340	24.41 percent
1	36 of 340	10.59 percent
0	0 of 340	.29 percent

[11] Ibid., p. 504.

[12] Ibid., p. 505.

Textural rhythm

Composite mean beat value		11.85
mm. 1-103	Exposition	10.04
mm. 104-204	Development	12.57
mm. 205-307	Recapitulation	10.18
mm. 308-340	Coda	31.60

In terms of symmetry, the first movement is one of the most balanced sonata forms in Brahms's chamber works. The exposition, development, and recapitulation are each approximately one-hundred measures long, followed by a coda of some thirty measures. Even within the exposition, the A and B themes are of approximately the same length, and the development is divided into four nearly equal segments. The above is not to imply that the movement is without inventiveness, since the movement's thematic ideas are presented through frequent changes between 6/8 and 2/4 time. Occasionally, both signatures are present simultaneously. In addition, 3/4 meter is frequently implied when both 6/8 meter and A material are present. In part as a result of the metric experimentation, two-against-three, three-against-four, and syncopated rhythms are common throughout the movement.

Within this framework of metric and rhythmic inventiveness, texture plays an important part in delineating thematic ideas and in lending cohesion to the movement as a whole. The A theme in both the exposition and in the recapitulation is characterized by terraced, two-measure alternations between two- and four-part textures, often initiated in the two inner parts. The B theme is first stated in the inner parts, accompanied by a first-violin obbligato. It is apparent that the movement features all instruments and highlights the inner parts to a significant degree. As these statements imply, changes of texture are frequent.

The percentages of melodic and contrapuntal importance for the first violin, second violin, and viola are quite similar and high. Although the violoncello has a much lower percentage, it is still relatively high. The most unusual percentage is that for the viola, which equals that for the first violin. The above percentages speak to the equal treatment of all parts in this movement, and it can be truly stated that no one part dominates the movement as a whole. In previous quartet movements, the percentages for the second violin part often revealed a correlation to another part, usually the first violin part, or a correlation to a type of texture. In this movement, the second violin part is on equal footing with the other parts of the quartets.

With such high percentages for the upper three parts, and even for the violoncello, it is not surprising to find that four-part texture is the prevalent one. The second highest percentage is that for two-part writing, caused in part by the importance of two-part texture in A material. The combined percentages for four- and three-part writing indicate that these textures dominate nearly two-thirds of the movement. In contrast to the above, one-part texture plays a relatively minor role (10.59 percent), and it is frequently found in transitional passages. Given the predominance of four-part texture, the high combined percentage of four- and three-part textures, and the high percentage of two-part over one-part texture, it is fair to conclude that this movement is contrapuntally dense.

The data for textural rhythm are very interesting and, given the relatively fast tempo of the movement, imply a rapid rate of change. The data require some further explanation. The collection of data on textural rhythm in this study was based on a strict interpretation of the meter (i.e., 6/8 meter equals six beats per measure regardless of performance beat, which in this case would equal two beats per measure). While the composite mean beat value (11.85) is quite fast, it is based on six beats per measure when 6/8 meter is present. The perceived rate of change is obviously much faster than 11.85. From the above, it is possible to conclude that the rate of change is quite rapid and uniform for the exposition, development, and recapitulation (10.04, 12.57, and 10.18 beats respectively), in marked contrast to the slow rate of change in the coda (31.60 beats).

The data for the second movement, which is marked "Andante" and in 4/4 meter, are as follows:

Number of measures containing important melodic or contrapuntal material for each instrument

Vln. I	90 of 95	94.74 percent
Vln. II	68 of 95	71.58 percent
Vla.	65 of 95	68.42 percent
Vc.	54 of 95	56.84 percent

Number of measures with textures involving varying numbers of important melodic or contrapuntal parts

4	43 of 95	45.26 percent
3	21 of 95	22.11 percent
2	5 of 95	5.26 percent
1	26 of 95	27.37 percent

Textural rhythm

Composite mean beat value		12.32
mm. 1-28	A	9.33
mm. 29-56	B	14.25
mm. 57-84	A'	11.20
mm. 85-95	Coda	44.00

The designation of this movement as an ABA-plus-coda form does not begin to represent the nearly experimental complexity found in the movement. Indeed, one is tempted to label this movement as through-composed but with two contrasting thematic ideas. The introduction (mm. 1-2) anticipates the motivic material of the A theme, but the introductory material occurs two more times in the movement (at mm. 27-28 and 81-82). It is usually associated with the A material: its appearance in mm. 27-28 is here regarded as the conclusion of the A section, but it could also be considered an introduction to the B section. Similarly, the start of the A' section is best described as a continuation, without thematic restatement, of material primarily from the A section, containing also, however, some material from the B section. The A theme itself does not reappear until m. 73ff. The initial statements of the A and B themes, however, are clearly delineated. The A theme is stated in the first violin part with the other parts accompanying. The melodic contour of the A theme is best visualized as a high arch. The B theme is initially stated in four-part texture and is characterized by a jagged contour and smaller subdivisions of the beat.

The second movement is unusual in that the first violin part dominates the writing to an extent rarely found in Brahms's chamber works (94.74 percent). Normally, such an occurrence would indicate that the movement is not very contrapuntally dense and that the other parts are not particularly important. The anticipated correlation is not the case in this movement, however. The second violin and viola (71.58 and 68.42 percent respectively) both have relatively high percentages of contrapuntal importance. Only the violoncello has a moderately low percentage (56.84), but even that percentage is not unusually low.

The relatively high percentages for the second violin and the viola and the very high percentage for the first violin are in part reflected in the unusually high percentage for four-part texture (45.26 percent). When this percentage is combined with that for three-part writing (22.11 percent), the combined percentage is actually slightly above that found for the first movement. On the other hand, the percentage for two-part writing is relatively low (5.26 percent), and the high percentage for one-part writing does correlate with the high first violin percentage and the nature of this movement as a slow, lyrical movement. It is fair to conclude that the contrapuntal texture for this movement is moderately dense.

The rate of textural change is quite slow (12.32 beats), and the contrasts between the ABA' sections are at best moderate. The coda, however, has an even slower rate of change (44.00 beats).

The data for the third movement, which is marked "Agitato (Allegro non troppo)" and in 3/4 meter, are as follows:

Number of measures containing important melodic or contrapuntal material for each instrument

Vln. I	151 of 203	74.38 percent
Vln. II	132 of 203	65.02 percent
Vla.	180 of 203	88.67 percent
Vc.	85 of 203	41.87 percent

Number of measures with textures involving varying numbers of important melodic or contrapuntal parts

4	66 of 203	32.51 percent
3	62 of 203	30.54 percent
2	26 of 203	12.81 percent
1	49 of 203	24.14 percent

Textural rhythm

Composite mean beat value		18.45
mm. 1-129	A	14.92
mm. 130-185	B (Trio)	24.00
	A (*da capo*)	14.92
mm. 186-203	Coda	9.00

The form of the third movement is a straightforward scherzo-trio-scherzo (*da capo*) with coda. The gentle and subdued mood of the movement is created by the predominance of melodic material in the viola (usually in the lowest part of its tessitura) and the use of mutes on all instruments except the viola. The texture of the A section (i.e., of the scherzo) is often one part, usually with the viola stating the thematic ideas. In contrast, the trio is predominantly in three- and four-part texture, but even in this setting the viola often has the melody with the other three parts playing countermelodies.

The pattern of percentages indicating melodic and contrapuntal importance are extremely unusual and reflect the importance of the viola part. The viola has important melodic material nearly eighty-nine percent of the time, which is an unusually high percentage for any part. This percentage is also significantly higher than those for the first and second violins. The percentage for the violoncello is low (41.87 percent), reflecting the secondary role of the violoncello in this movement. Most of the important melodic material for the violoncello is found in the trio.

Given the predominant importance of the viola in this movement, it is somewhat surprising to find that the percentages for four- and three-part writing are fairly high (32.50 and 30.54 percent respectively). These percentages combined, however, are not as high as in the preceding movements of this quartet, and they are in part a result of the texture in the trio. Also, the percentage for four-part writing is over fifteen points less than in the first and second movements. There is a significant percentage for one-part texture (24.14 percent), which nearly always features the viola as bearer of the thematic materials.

The composite mean beat value for this movement (18.45 beats) is somewhat slow for a movement that is usually performed at a moderate tempo. There are strong contrasts between the A and B sections (14.92 and 24.00 beats respectively). The coda differs markedly with the rest of the movement and has the fastest rate of change (9.00 beats).

The data for the fourth movement, which is marked "Poco Allegretto con Variazioni" and in 2/4 meter, are as follows:

Number of measures containing important melodic or contrapuntal material for each instrument

Vln. I	190 of 224	84.82 percent
Vln. II	168 of 224	75.00 percent
Vla.	174 of 224	77.68 percent
Vc.	144 of 224	64.29 percent

Number of measures with textures involving varying numbers of important melodic or contrapuntal parts

4	123 of 224	54.91 percent
3	30 of 224	13.39 percent
2	22 of 224	9.82 percent
1	49 of 224	21.88 percent

Textural rhythm

Composite mean beat value		10.44
mm. 1-10	Theme	5.00
mm. 11-23	Var. I	8.67
mm. 24-38	Var. II	10.00
mm. 39-52	Var. III	7.00
mm. 53-66	Var. IV	5.60
mm. 67-80	Var. V	5.60
mm. 81-94	Var. VI	9.33
mm. 95-121	Var. VII	11.57
mm. 122-149	Var. VIII	24.00
mm. 150 221	Coda	9.38

The fourth movement of this quartet is a theme with eight variations plus a coda. The theme consists of a four-measure plus a six-measure phrase, each of which is repeated for a total of twenty measures. The first six variations are each twenty measures long, consisting of varying combinations of repeated and non-repeated sections. Starting with variation seven, the tempo marking is "Doppio Movimento." Variations seven and eight are each approximately forty measures long—or twice as long as the theme—, but, if the "Doppio Movimento" is taken literally, the length in terms of time elapsed is approximately the same as that of the theme and the early variations. In addition, variations seven, eight, and the coda introduce the opening phrase of theme A of the first movement.

Texture and instrumentation are employed to delineate the theme and each of the variations. The theme is presented by the two violin parts in duet. Variation I features the viola in predominantly one-part texture. The viola is also very prominent in the second variation. The first violin is featured in the third variation. The fourth variation is primarily a first violin and violoncello duet. The dominant textures in each of the variations can be summarized as follows:

1. Three- and four-part textures: variations two, five and six plus the coda.
2. Two- and four-part textures: variations four, seven and eight
3. Two-part texture: the theme
4. One-part texture: variations one and three

The data reflect the importance of all of the instruments. The percentages for the first violin, second violin, and viola parts are all quite high and fairly uniform. While the percentage for the violoncello (64.29 percent) is lower than those for the other instruments, it is still quite high.

The data for the distribution of different types of texture confirm many of the observations made above. Given the large number of variations using three- and four-part textures, it is not surprising to find a significant percentage for four-part texture (nearly fifty-five percent). It is the highest percentage for four-part texture in any quartet movement. Although the percentage for three-part texture is not particularly high (13.39 percent), the combined percentage for three- and four-part textures indicate that these textures are found in nearly seventy percent of the movement. The combined percentage and the dominance of four-part texture makes this movement one of the contrapuntally densest movements in Brahms's quartets. It would probably be the densest except for the high percentage for one-part texture. The percentages for two- and one-part textures (9.82 and 21.88 percent respectively) reflect the use of these textures in the theme (two-part texture) and the first and third variations (one-part texture).

Each section of this movement contrasts markedly with its neighbors in terms of textural rhythm with the exception of variations four and five, which have the same rate of change. The variations that have the slowest rate of change are the seventh and eighth, which are marked "Doppio Movimento." The addition of thematic material from the first movement also tends to slow down the rate of change.

In addition to being one of the densest movements contrapuntally of Brahms's quartets, the movement is also noteworthy for its use of texture to delineate sections and for the relative equality of all parts.

***

The preceding portion of this study has detailed Brahms's use of contrapuntal density and texture in specific movements. At this point a profile of Brahms's textural usage in these two string quartets should be developed in order to facilitate the understanding of Brahms's compositional process. A previous study established that the string quartets of Brahms are contrapuntally the most dense examples of all of his chamber works.[13] The Op. 51, No. 1 String Quartet was omitted from this study because it is significantly less dense contrapuntally than either the Op. 51, No. 2 or the Op. 67 String Quartets.[14] To facilitate the presentation, the summaries will be organized as follows: 1) contrapuntal density as related to the individual instruments; and 2) contrapuntal density as related to the distribution of part writing.

In terms of the melodic and contrapuntal importance of each part, the normal pattern is for the highest percentage to occur in the first violin. In two instances, the viola has the highest percentage, and it is tied for the highest in another movement. The viola part has the highest or second highest percentage in five of the eight movements, which compares to only two movements where the second violin has the second highest percentage. The normal pattern is for the violoncello part to have the lowest percentage. Only two movements deviate from this pattern. Furthermore, in three of the movements the violoncello part is approximately twenty percentage points lower than the highest percentage. The above indicates that the violoncello part does not play a role that is equal to that of the other parts in most of the movements.

Based on the percentages indicated for each instrument of the movements included in this study, a model based on mean percentages may be established:

[13]David Fenske, "Texture in the Chamber Music of Johannes Brahms" (Ph.D. diss., University of Wisconsin, 1973), p. 527.

[14]Ibid.

	Mean	Normal Range
Vln. I	84.66	80-90
Vln. II	69.22	65-75
Vla.	75.04	70-80
Vc.	57.34	50-60

The mean percentages indicate that the first violin and viola are the most important and that the upper three parts are significantly more important than the violoncello.

Earlier in this study, percentages were given for each instrument indicating that part's activity. In order to judge the relative equality of the instruments in a given movement, a measure needs to be presented that is not affected by the size of the percentages, only by the comparative closeness of the terms. The standard deviation for each movement is given below. The lower the standard deviation, the greater the equality of treatment.

Op. 51, No. 2		Op. 67	
1st movement	12.42	1st movement	8.44
2nd movement	11.87	2nd movement	13.75
3rd movement	11.94	3rd movement	17.02
4th movement	9.51	4th movement	7.39

The preceding table demonstrates that the fourth movements of each quartet have the least variability among the percentages for each instrument and therefore the greatest equality of treatment. The first movement of the Op. 67 Quartet also has a similar degree of equal treatment. On the other hand, the rest of the movements, particularly the interior movements, have the greatest degree of variability.

The author's study cited earlier established that the mean combined percentage for combinations of more than half of the available parts for all of Brahms's chamber works is forty percent.[15] The following table gives the mean percentage for both of the quartets considered in the present study for each type of part writing and for combinations of more and less than half of the number of available parts.

4	43.30 percent
3	20.83 percent
combined 3 & 4	64.13 percent
2	14.11 percent
1	21.67 percent
combined 1 & 2	35.78 percent

[15] Ibid., p. 523.

It is apparent from the above percentage for three- and four-part writing (64.13 percent) that these two quartets greatly exceed the average for contrapuntal density of all Brahms's chamber works. Indeed, the percentage for four-part writing alone exceeds the norm.

The following table gives the combined percentages for each of the movements:

Op. 51, No. 2	3 & 4 parts	1 & 2 parts
1st movement	48.66 percent	51.34 percent
2nd movement	60.49 percent	39.51 percent
3rd movement	80.89 percent	19.11 percent
4th movement	59.61 percent	40.39 percent
Op. 67		
1st movement	64.71 percent	35.29 percent
2nd movement	67.37 percent	32.63 percent
3rd movement	63.05 percent	36.95 percent
4th movement	68.30 percent	31.70 percent

The preceding table establishes: 1) that no movement of these quartets has less contrapuntal density than the norm found in all Brahms's chamber music; and 2) that, while the third movement of the Op. 51, No. 2 Quartet has the highest degree of contrapuntal density, the four movements of the Op. 67 Quartet have the most consistent degree of contrapuntal density. Interestingly, there is not a correlation between the degree of contrapuntal density and the equality of treatment of the instruments.

In a recent study, Bernard Jacobson stated: "Linear freedom in Brahms is a resource that informs and aerates the entire warp of the musical texture, rather than being pressed into service on an occasional basis as a special effect."[16] The conclusions of the present study certainly established the degree of contrapuntal density and usage in these two quartets and support Jacobson's statement. The fact that these works exceed the norm for Brahms, who is perhaps one of the finest nineteenth-century polyphonists, supports the significance that Brahms attached to his few published string quartets.

[16]*The Music of Johannes Brahms* (Rutherford, N.J.: Fairleigh Dickinson University Press, 1977), p. 70.

Malcolm H. Brown

Skriabin and Young Prokofiev, 1905-15: Promethean vis-à-vis Pragmatist

This essay proposes to examine the impact of Skriabin's highly idiosyncratic mature style and singular aesthetic vision on the youthful Prokofiev, who began to gain modest recognition just as his elder contemporary approached the zenith of public acclaim. Confronted by the force and assurance of Skriabin's late works, Prokofiev countered with his own stylistic idiosyncracies. Rejecting Skriabin's musical style, Prokofiev rejected as well his Promethean vision of an art that would transfigure mankind, positing in its stead a pragmatic art of immediate, even crude effect.

The measure of Skriabin's power in Russian cultural life during the early twentieth century can be gauged by the furor attendant on his sudden death on 14/27 April 1915. Not yet 44, the audacious reach of his creative imagination commanded the attention of Russia's cultural vanguard; his vision of an apocalyptic synthesis of the arts with *music* the nucleus resonated with the grand aesthetic theories formulated by his contemporary poets, writers, and philosophers. Then a pimple appeared on his upper lip, and a week later he was dead of massive strepto- and staphylococcus infection. The poet Osip Mandelshtam voiced the shock and grief of his countrymen when he declared:

> Pushkin and Skriabin—two incarnations of one sun, two incarnations of one heart. Twice the death of an artist rallied the Russian people and ignited a sun above them. . . . In dying, personal identity waxed into a symbol of an entire people, and the sun-heart of him who died stopped forever at the zenith of suffering and glory. . . . To vanquish

oblivion, though it cost death–that was Skriabin's motto, that the heroic aspiration of his art.[1]

Skriabin had indeed aspired to vanquish oblivion. As early as 1893, just 21, he started speaking about his art in metaphor:

> . . . but my star is so beautiful, and I so love it, that should I not gaze on it, should it not light me in life and I not strive toward it, thought would perish and with it everything. Better I vanish in a fit of madness, but thought remain and be triumphant.[2]

By the turn of the century, the character of Skriabin's thought reflected more and more the artistic-philosophical currents of its milieu. His close friendship with Prince Sergei Trubetskoy may have supplied the essential catalyst.

Professor on the Faculty of Philosophy at Moscow University and an editor of the journal *Voprosy filosofii i psikhologii* [Questions of philosophy and psychology], sometime music critic and an ardent advocate of Skriabin's genius, Trubetskoy was as well a disciple of Vladimir Solovyov and a persuasive spokesman for Solovyov's doctrine of art as theurgy or divine force.[3] Trubetskoy

[1]Osip Mandel'shtam, "Pushkin i Skriabin (Fragmenty)," *Sobranie sochinenii* [Collected works], ed. G.P. Struve and B.A. Filippov, 2 vols.; vol. 2. *Stikhotvoreniia, proza* [Poems, prose] (New York: Inter-Language Literary Associates, 1966), pp. 355, 359-60. The editors of the collected works relate this article to the period immediately or soon after Skriabin's death but say that it was finished somewhat later, in 1919 or 1920 (p. 607). Nadezhda Mandelstam asserts that the article was read at the Petersburg Religious-Philosophical Society and explains, "I still have the manuscript, though someone (alas, I know not who) has walked off with the first page. There were two first pages, completely identical except for the title. On one the title was: 'Pushkin and Skriabin,' and on the other: 'Skriabin and Christianity.' It is the first which has disappeared" (Nadezhda Mandelstam, *Hope Abandoned*, trans. Max Hayward [New York: Atheneum, 1974], pp. 104-5). In this and subsequent notes, authors' names and titles *of sources in Russian* are transliterated according to the Library of Congress system, simplified. All other references to Russian proper names reflect this writer's personal preference in transliteration.

[2]Skriabin to Natalia Valerianovna Sekerina, 30 May/11 June 1893, in A. Skriabin, *Pis'ma* [Correspondence], comp. and ed. A.V. Kashperov (Moscow: Muzyka, 1965), p. 56.

[3]Although the complexity of Trubetskoy's personal philosophy suffers in the simplification, it may be characterized as an attempt to reconcile Hegel's objective idealism and Solovyov's mystical idealism. Vladimir Sergeevich Solovyov [Solov'ev] (1853-1900) viewed art as an avenue to the universal unity that embraced Human Individuality, Nature, and the Divine Principle in a single transcendent reality; thus for Solovyov true art possessed religious significance. Sergei Nikolaevich Trubetskoy [Trubetskoi] (1862-1905) elaborated Solovyov's view of art as divine force in his own writings, which he introduced to Skriabin. Trubetskoy's writings were published posthumously: *Uchenie o Logose, v ego istorii* [A study of logos in history] (Moscow: Lissner

sponsored Skriabin's membership in the Moscow Philosophical Society around 1902; there and in Trubetskoy's private circle Skriabin encountered ideas that challenged him to examine his thought more carefully, to question the nature of his "star."[4] Something of the depth of his interest in philosophy about this time can be inferred from remarks to a friend in a letter of 1904:

> I was very pleased to learn that you're studying philosophy a great deal. You should learn Kant as quickly as possible, then acquaint yourself a little with Fichte, Schelling and Hegel, if only as a part of the history of philosophy. Fouillée's textbook is no good at all. German philosophy is very poorly presented there. Get hold of a copy of Überweg-Heinze's History of New Philosophy.[5] The work is rather dull, but very complete and, the main thing, concise, which for you is most important right now. Kuno Fischer[6] can acquaint you with Kant. When you have assimilated all of this, it will be easy for me to work with you and you will quickly grasp my teaching [*uchenie*].[7]

The direct reference to his emergent doctrine ("my teaching")

---

i Sobko, 1906); *Sobranie sochinenii* [Collected works], 2 vols. (Moscow: Lissner i Sobko, 1907-8).

[4]Boris Schloezer, Skriabin's brother-in-law, maintains that despite Skriabin's fondness for Trubetskoy and awe of his great erudition, Skriabin held aloof from the ideas and attitudes prevalent in Trubetskoy's "tea" circle. Schloezer admits, however, that had Skriabin's acquaintance with Trubetskoy taken place a few years later (i.e., ca. 1907-8, after Trubetskoy's death), the two would have established "significantly more intimate spiritual bonds" (Boris Fëdorovich Shletser, *A. Skriabin*, vol. 1, *Lichnost'; misteriia* [Personality; mystery] [Berlin: "Grani," 1923; vol. 2 was never published], pp. 17-18). Schloezer's opinion notwithstanding, the claim that Trubetskoy may have supplied the catalyst for Skriabin's emergent mysticism seems logically defensible.

[5]Friedrich Überweg's *Geschichte der neuern Philosophie*, revised and edited by Max Heinze, appeared in a Russian edition published in St. Petersburg in 1889. Skriabin's personal copy contains copious notes that substantiate his careful study of the volume (V. Iu. Del'son, *Skriabin: Ocherki zhizni i tvorchestva* [Skriabin: essays on his life and work], ed. S. Aksiuk [Moscow: Muzyka, 1971], p. 340, n. 3).

[6]Kuno Fischer, *Geschichte der neuern Philosophie*, vols. 4-5, *Immanuel Kant und seine Lehre* (Heidelberg: C. Winter, 1898-99). A Russian translation of this *jubilee* edition—the original ten volumes appeared in Heidelberg between 1897 and 1903—was published in St. Petersburg by Zhukovsky between 1901 and 1909. I have been unable to ascertain the date when the Russian edition of the volumes on Kant appeared, but since their German publication occurred in 1898 and 1899, they may well have been available in Russian by early 1904. Skriabin would surely have preferred reading the Russian edition, since unlike his French his German was anything but fluent.

[7]Skriabin to Margarita Kirillovna Morozova, 3/16 April 1904, in A. Skriabin, *Pis'ma*, pp. 307-8.

deserves note; by this time (1904) it had already affected aspects of his musical output.

Before the period when his inchoate eschatological ideas started to strain toward definition, the piano had sufficed the scope of Skriabin's creative utterance.[8] Then, about 1900, he delved tentatively into opera, sketching a plot based on the myth of Eros and Psyche: in a transcendent artistic act, the Hero ("a young unknown philosopher-musician-poet") opens up to mankind a new, beautiful and better world[9]—an obvious prefiguring of the later Promethean vision that makes himself the artist-hero whose "Mystery" transfigures mankind. But he abandoned the operatic project. Instead, still determined to intensify his musical expression, he undertook to wield the massive forces of the post-Wagnerian orchestra. He composed his First Symphony, Op. 26, in 1900, his Second, Op. 29, in 1901, and the leap in complexity between the two prompted Anatoly Liadov to exclaim about the Second:

> What a symphony! The devil only knows!! Skriabin could offer Richard Strauss a hand without a qualm. Lord, where is music headed? Decadents crawling out of every nook and cranny. Saints preserve us!! Help!!! . . . After Skriabin, Wagner seems nothing but a suckling babe babbling sweetly.[10]

Liadov was confronting the musical consequences of Skriabin's emergent doctrine. In compositional terms this meant a style whose antecedents were found in Wagner and Liszt. The stylistic innovations of both Wagner and Liszt had been grounded in philosophical attitudes (cf. Wagner's idea of the "re-education" of mankind by means of the *Gesamtkunstwerk* or Liszt's notion that music might embody the "entire history of the world")—attitudes congenial to Skriabin's own incipient doctrine; where better to find compositional models for intensifying his musical expression.

The elements of Skriabin's mature personal style and methodology of composition started to coalesce coincidentally with the coming into focus of his eschatological vision. The image of Wagner and Liszt dimmed and receded in the progression from the *Divine*

[8]All of Skriabin's completed works before 1900, through the Nine Mazurkas for Piano, Op. 25 (1899), were for solo piano, with the exception of the Piano Concerto in F-sharp minor, Op. 20 (1897), and *Rêverie* for Orchestra, Op. 24 (1898).

[9]*Russkie propilei* [Russian propylaea], vol. 6, *Zapisi A. N. Skriabina* [A. N. Skriabin's notebooks], comp. and ed. M. Gershenzon (Moscow: M. and S. Sabashnikov, 1919), p. 125.

[10]M.K. Mikhailov, *A. K. Liadov* (Leningrad: Muzgiz, 1961), p. 141, as quoted in A. Skriabin, *Pis'ma*, p. 251, n. 1.

Poem [*Bozhestvennaia poema*] , Op. 43 (1903-4), to the Fifth Piano Sonata, Op. 53 (1907), and the *Poem of Ecstasy* [*Poema Ekstaza*] , Op. 54 (1905-7). In the same period, Skriabin's vision of himself as hero-theurgist clarified, permitting him to declare confidently in a letter of 18 April/1 May 1906:

> The *political* revolution in Russia in its present phase [he refers here to the lingering unrest following "Bloody Sunday" in 1905] and the overthrow I want are different things, although, certainly this revolution, as any unrest, hastens the approach of the desired moment. Using the word *overthrow [perevorot]*, I err. *It's not the actualization of anything whatever* I want, but the eternal exaltation of creative activity which will be evoked by my art. That means first of all my main work must be finished. . . . *My* moment has not yet come. But it's getting closer. There will be a celebration! Soon![11]

By "main work," Skriabin had in mind his "Mystery." As the details of its projected realization formed over the next few years, he shared with friends his vision of an artistic work in which

> there will be not a single spectator. All will be participants. . . . The performing group will include an orchestra, of course, a large mixed chorus, an instrument for lighting effects, dances, cavalcades, processions, incense, rhythmic recitation of texts. . . . There will be no décor of any kind, only the necessary musical instruments, some sort of special attire for the participants, draperies, lighting effects. . . . Smoke from incense will be introduced as an essential effect for the "Mystery." . . . The form of the temple in which the "Mystery" will always be taking place will not be monotonously fixed forever, but will be forever changing, together with the mood and movement of the "Mystery"—all that, of course, with the aid of the smoking incense and the illumination, which will alter architectural lines and contours. . . .
>
> . . . Just as people now travel to Bayreuth, . . . so they will travel to this temple.[12]

Such was Skriabin's vision of an eschatological artistic synthesis that would transcend Wagner's *Gesamtkunstwerk*. How was the young, ambitious Prokofiev to contend with this *éminence* who loomed over the Russian musical scene like one of Mikhail Vrubel's

[11]Skriabin to M.K. Morozova, 18 April/1 May 1906, in A. Skriabin, *Pis'ma*, pp. 422-23.

[12]Anna Alekseevna Gol'denveizer, Diary, State Central Museum of Musical Culture (Moscow), Gol'denveizer Filial, quoted in A. Skriabin, *Pis'ma*, pp. 611-12, n. 3.

brooding titans[13] and spoke about a "Mystery" that would transfigure mankind?

Still a teenager when he first encountered Skriabin's music, Prokofiev succumbed:

> ... the first performance [in St. Petersburg on 23 February/8 March 1906] of Skriabin's Third Symphony (the *Divine Poem*) ... remains vividly imprinted in my memory. I went to all the rehearsals and was terribly interested in Skriabin's new symphony.... Much in the symphony seemed remarkable to me, but much I simply did not understand.[14]

Not quite fifteen years old, even a prodigy of Prokofiev's calibre could scarcely be expected to grasp fully the novelties of Skriabin's score, much less the philosophical program that accompanied it.

Skriabin's piano works appealed more directly to young Prokofiev. He studied and played the mazurkas and the preludes; fellow student composer Nikolai Miaskovsky insisted that he detected traces of Skriabin's *Satanic Poem* [*Satanicheskaia poema*], Op. 36 (1903), for piano, in the harmonic pungencies of Prokofiev's Fourth "School" Sonata for Piano from about 1907.[15]

But when Prokofiev confronted a later revelation of Skriabin's evolving musical-philosophical vision on 19 January/1 February 1909, a note of skepticism tempered his earlier enthusiasm:

> Sitting together [at the Russian première], Miaskovsky and I devoured the *Poem of Ecstasy* with tremendous enthusiasm, though we were

[13]Mikhail Aleksandrovich Vrubel' (1856-1910), distinguished Russian artist, painted a series of powerful canvases between 1890 and 1902 devoted to images of titans inspired by Lermontov's story *Demon*. Vrubel shed some light on his obsession by declaring that his Demon "personifies the eternal dilemma of the bewildered human spirit ... that finds no answer either in heaven or earth to its doubts" (quoted in E.P. Gomberg-Verzhbinskaia, "Iskaniia v russkoi zhivopisi, 1890-1900 godov" [The quest in Russian painting, 1890-1900], in *Russkaia khudozhestvennaia kul'tura, kontsa XIX–nachala XX veka [1895-1907]* [Russian artistic culture, the end of the XIX–the beginning of the XX century (1895-1907)], ed. A.D. Alekseev et al., Book Two: *Izobrazitel'noe iskusstvo, arkhitektura, dekorativno-prikladnoe iskusstvo* [Graphic arts, architecture, decorative-applied arts] [Moscow: Nauka, 1969], p. 110). By 1901, the character of the titan image had become, in the words of Vrubel's wife, "no longer Lermontov-like, but a kind of modern Nietzschean" (quoted ibid., p. 117).

[14]Sergei Prokof'ev, *Avtobiografiia*, ed. M.G. Kozlova (Moscow: Sovetskii kompozitor, 1973), pp. 335-37.

[15]Vasilii Mitrofanovich Morolev, "Vospominaniia o Serëzhe Prokof'eve" [Recollections of Seryozha Prokofiev], in *S. S. Prokof'ev: Materialy, dokumenty, vospominaniia* [Materials, documents, recollections], 2nd ed., enl., comp. and ed. S.I. Shlifshtein (Moscow: Muzgiz, 1961), p. 344; Prokof'ev, *Avtobiografiia*, pp. 287, 441.

> puzzled in spots by the novelty of the music. We had expected an "improved" *Divine Poem*, so to speak, which we knew and loved so well; instead, the harmonic and thematic material and the manner of voice leading were entirely new. Skriabin had mainly attempted to find new harmonic resources. The principles discovered were very interesting, but to a degree their complexity hung like a millstone around Skriabin's neck, hampering his inventiveness in the areas of melody and, more important, counterpoint.[16]

For a number of years now, the elements of Skriabin's musical language had been responding to the pressure of powerful emotions associated with the composer's philosophical formulations. He sought systematically to invent unusual sonorities whose tonal content could be combined and recombined in chords with subtly graduated "harmonic timbres."[17] A particularly favored tonal matrix seems to have been derived from the tritonal linkage of two major-minor seventh chords, each with a flat fifth (the French-sixth sound).[18] Enharmonically the tones in both chords were the same, but, as altered dominants, their theoretical tonics lay a tritone apart. Successions of such chords, usually enriched by added tones, diffused the sensation of decisive gravitation toward a key note. Skriabin described such harmonic inventions as possessing "an astral cast," and playing some of them once, he declared, "an aura appears."[19] Permutations of these chordal complexes produced a musical discourse of ambiguous sonorities whose ebb and flow was articulated by seemingly capricious, at times almost spasmodic rhythms. Melodic ideas derived from the matrix often appeared as fragmentary lines whose character ranged from the languorous to the impetuous in the context of complex rhythms and exaggerated tempo rubatos (for example, the Fifth Piano Sonata, Op. 53 [1907], Two Pieces for Piano, Op. 59 [1910], *Prometheus, the Poem of Fire* [*Prometei, poema ognia*], Op. 60 [1909-10], Two Poems for Piano, Op. 63 [1911-12]). As a conse-

16 Prokof'ev, *Avtobiografiia*, p. 557.

17 "Harmonic timbre" is a term coined by the writer to describe the change in timbre that results, regardless of any change in instrumentation, when the disposition of tones within a sound complex is rearranged. The change in timbre is accounted for by the acoustical consequences of different partials cancelling each other out. The effect is far more striking when the sound complex contains dissonant elements because the partials of the constituent tones are less congruent within the audible hearing range.

18 The most persuasive explication of Skriabin's systematic approach to harmonic invention appears in Varvara Pavlovna Dernova's *Garmoniia Skriabina* (Leningrad: Muzyka, 1968).

19 Leonid Leonidovich Sabaneev, *Vospominaniia o Skriabine* [Recollections of Skriabin] (Moscow: Muzykal'nyi sektor gosudarstvennogo izdatel'stva, 1925), p. 102.

quence of striking juxtapositions of fluctuating tempos and contrasted rhythms, subtle harmonic graduations with ambiguous tonal references, and a diversity of texture typified by extreme ranges and uncommon spacing, Skriabin's music seemed to become more and more imbued by hyperexpressiveness and encumbered by philosophical significance.

Prokofiev was eighteen when he first encountered Skriabin's Fifth Piano Sonata in 1909:

> I love Skriabin's Fifth Sonata (= a perfected Fourth). I even want to memorize it. Only I finally get worn out and fed up with its continuous morbidity throughout nineteen pages; it seems to me the sonata is too drawn out and loses form.[20]

Clearly, young Prokofiev had already started to feel impatient with Skriabin's characteristic manner, finding the emotional indulgence ("continuous morbidity") incompatible.

Even as a youngster Prokofiev had shied away from overt emotionalism, expressing his feelings with reserve and at times a touch of cynicism.[21] Such an innate character trait inevitably impinged on his musical taste. At fourteen he remarked condescendingly, "Chopin is like a mulberry"[22] (meaning that he found him sickly sweet), and he faulted him as well for "sentimentality."[23] This anti-romantic bias gained encouragement in 1908 when Prokofiev auditioned for the founders of the St. Petersburg Evenings of Modern Music. Never before had his music elicited such enthusiasm. One of the group exclaimed, "the antithesis of Skriabin, and thank God that antithesis has appeared!"[24] The flattery of such an extravagant statement was seductive to the youth (Prokofiev was seventeen at the time). He liked the idea that he might actually be in competition with Skriabin, the dominating presence in contemporary Russian music.

The most distinctive elements in young Prokofiev's style seemed to validate his role as "the antithesis of Skriabin"—a role he laid

[20] Prokofiev to Nikolai Iakovlevich Miaskovskii, 6/19 June 1909, quoted in Prokof'ev, *Avtobiografiia*, p. 594.

[21] Iulii Anatol'evich Kremlev, *Esteticheskie vzgliady S. S. Prokof'eva* [S. S. Prokofiev's aesthetic views] (Moscow and Leningrad: Muzyka, 1966), p. 14.

[22] Mariia Ksenofontovna Moroleva, "Vospominaniia o S. S. Prokof'eva i ego roditeliakh" [Recollections of S. S. Prokofiev and his parents], in *S. S. Prokof'ev: Materialy, dokumenty, vospominaniia*, p. 346.

[23] Vera Al'pers, "Iz proshlogo" [From the past], in *Sergei Prokof'ev: Stat'i i materialy* [Sergei Prokofiev: Articles and materials], 2nd ed., rev. and enl., comp. and ed. I.V. Nest'ev and G. Ia. Edel'man (Moscow: Muzyka, 1965), p. 244.

[24] Prokof'ev, *Avtobiografiia*, p. 482.

claim to in three of the works performed on 18/31 December 1908 at his first public appearance for the Evenings of Modern Music: *Flurry* [*Poryv*], *Despair* [*Otchaianie*], and *Obsession* [*Navazhdenie*].[25] These short pieces announced the arrival on the Russian musical scene of a vigorous, new voice whose characteristic accent would be heard again and again in a series of original statements between 1910 and 1915 (for example, the two sets of Four Pieces for Piano, Op. 3 [1911] and Op. 4 [1910-12], The First Piano Concerto, Op. 10 [1910-12], the Toccata for Piano, Op. 11 [1912], the *Sarcasms* for piano, Op. 17 [1912-14]). Skriabin had preferred refined and subtly graduated sonorities in which dissonance was attenuated into a component of harmonic timbre. Prokofiev opted for chords of a more classic cast in which ample dissonance clashed sharply with the predominantly consonant, often triadic, harmonic structure. Skriabin's ambiguous sonorities had moved within a veiled, non-directive tonal ambience. Prokofiev's harmonies often implied directed motion, but he bridled the motion with cadential articulations that wrested the movement away from implicit goals toward unexpected but decisively defined local tonics. Prokofiev's deliberately simplistic, sharply punctuated, predictable rhythms and precisely regulated pulse dispelled all traces of Skriabin's dissolute rhythm.

Prokofiev's personality may well have predestined his eventual disenchantment with Skriabin as a model, but his fortuitous role as "the antithesis of Skriabin" surely hastened the process. Later he was to maintain: "Scriabin [*sic*] cannot have disciples. Scriabin must stand alone—he is a solitary genius."[26] Respect could still prompt Prokofiev in 1910 to dedicate his Symphonic Poem, *Dreams* [*Sny*], Op. 6, "to the composer who began with *Rêverie*" (*Rêverie* was Skriabin's first purely orchestral work).

Skriabin, on his part, could not reciprocate with the slightest approbation for Prokofiev's work. Its musical substance and implicit philosophy struck him as alien and incomprehensible. Shown a Prokofiev score (possibly that of the First Piano Concerto, which was published in 1913), Skriabin examined it pensively, picked out at random one of the more dissonant harmonic episodes and declared:

> What filth! . . . I seem to be getting like Anatoly Konstantinovich

[25]These three pieces were eventually revised and included in the Four Pieces for Piano, Op. 4. *Obsession* is better known by its French title, *Suggestion diabolique*, which was chosen deliberately to associate the piece with Liszt's *Mephisto-Walzer* and Skriabin's *Poème satanique* (Prokof'ev, *Avtobiografiia*, p. 513).

[26]Israel V. Nestyev, *Prokofiev*, trans. Florence Jonas, with a foreword by Nicholas Slonimsky (Stanford: At the University Press, 1960), p. 455.

> [Liadov] in my aversion to filth . . . and a little like Sergei Ivanovich [Taneev] . . . . Besides that, *what a minimum of inspiration*! . . .
>
> The saddest part is that this music actually expresses something very successfully, but that "something" is horrible.[27]

The dead seriousness with which Skriabin judged Prokofiev's music supplies a key to understanding these two creative artists within the context of their eras. Skriabin approached his art solemnly and hieratically. The seriousness of his theurgic purpose demanded that, and virtually precluded humor as a component of his creative attitude or his music. This tendency to slight the comedic characterizes as well those sources from which Skriabin drew in formulating his creative vision. There is nothing light-hearted about the Orphic objectives of Wagner's *Gesamtkunstwerk*, the eschatological concerns of the Russian Mystic Symbolists, or the tone of nineteenth-century German philosophy.

Young Prokofiev approached his art not as a priest but as a pragmatist. He was an artist who could revel in growing mastery and still thumb his nose at the conventions of his craft for the sake of a good joke. He never conceived of himself as a philosopher attempting to explicate transcendent visions in musical microcosms. His respect for the finite musical moment, his classically regulated meters and predictable rhythms, his preciseness and directness in expressing more objective, unencumbered emotional states, all suggest parallels with the Acmeist and Futurist movements in Russian poetry during the early twentieth century. But Prokofiev showed little interest in or understanding of the artistic, creative trends around him. An ultimate synthesis of the arts, an "omniart" [*vseiskusstvo*] as conceived by Skriabin, the Mystic Symbolists, or even to some extent the adherents of the "World of Art" [*Mir iskusstva*], never seems to have engaged Prokofiev's thinking, despite his eventual association with Diaghilev's *Ballets Russes*. Here, indeed, stood the pragmatist, concerned primarily with the immediate and practical consequences of his musical conceptions, indifferent to Skriabin's Promethean dream of transfiguring mankind through the fervor of artistic vision.

[27]Sabaneev, *Vospominaniia*, p. 248.

Bibliography of Walter Kaufmann's Works

I. COMPOSITIONS

Unless otherwise indicated, the composition exists only in manuscript. Manuscripts of those titles preceded by an asterisk have been deposited in the Music Library of Indiana University, Bloomington.

A. For Orchestra

*Symphony No. 1 for Strings (1931).
Prag, Suite (1932).
Concerto No. 1 for Piano and Orchestra (1934).
Symphony No. 2 (1935).
Symphony No. 3 (1936).
Symphony No. 4 (1938).
Two Bohemian Dances (1942). London: Arcadia, 1948.
Concerto No. 1 for Violin and Orchestra (1943).
**Six Indian Miniatures* (1943). London: Arcadia, 1948.
Concerto No. 2 for Violin and Orchestra (1944).
Picturebook for Katherine (1945).
Navaratnam, Suite for Piano and Chamber Orchestra (1945).
Phantasmagoria (1946).
*Variations for Strings (1947).
Concertino for Piano and Strings (1947).
**Dirge* (1947).
**Madras Express* (1947).
Fleet Street Overture (1948). London: Arcadia, 1948.

*_Strange Town at Night_ (1948).
*_Faces in the Dark_ (1948).
Andhera for Piano and Orchestra (1942-49).
*Sinfonietta No. 1 (Symphony No. 5) (1949).
*Divertimento for Strings (1949).
Concerto No. 2 for Piano and Orchestra (1949).
Concerto for Violincello and Orchestra (1950).
*_Chivaree Overture_ (1950).
Main Street for Strings (1950).
Kalif Storch, Fairy-tale for Speaker and Orchestra (1951).
Arabesques for Two Pianos and Orchestra (1952).
*_Vaudeville Overture_ (1952).
Sewanee River Variations (1952).
Short Suite for Small Orchestra (1953).
*_Nocturne_ (1953).
Pembina Highway (1953).
Four Skies (1953).
*_Three Dances to an Indian Play_ (1956).
Symphony No. 6 (1956).
Four Essays for Small Orchestra (1956).
*Sinfonietta No. 2 (1959).
Concerto for Timpani and Orchestra (1963).
Festival Overture (1968).
Concertino for Violin and Orchestra (1977).

B. For Piano

Concertino (1932).
Sonatina No. 1 (1948).
Sonata (1948-51).
*_Arabesques_ for Two Pianos (1952).
Sonatina No. 2 (1956).
Suite (1957).

C. For Organ

Prelude (1960).

D. Chamber Works

Ten String Quartets (1935-46).
Three Piano Trios (1942-46).
Six Pieces for Piano Trio (1957).
String Quartet (1961).
Partita for Woodwind Quintet (1963). Delaware Water Gap, Penn.: Shawnee Press, 1966.
*_Arabesques_ for Flute, Oboe, Harpsichord and Bass (1963).

Eight Pieces for Twelve Instruments (1967).
Passacaglia and Capriccio for Brass Sextet (1967). Delaware Water Gap, Penn.: Shawnee Press, 1967.
Sonatina for Piccolo/Flute Solo (1968).

E. Ballets

Visages, in 1 act (1950).
The Rose and the Ring, in 2 parts (1950).
Wang, in 1 act (1956).

F. Operas

(The names appearing in brackets are those of the librettists.)

Der grosse Dorin [P. Eisner], in 3 acts (1932).
Der Hammel bringt es an den Tag [W. Kaufmann], chamber opera in 2 acts (1932).
Esther [H. Politzer], in 2 parts (1931-32).
Die weisse Göttin [F. Kahler and K. Juhn], operetta in 3 acts (1933).
The Cloak [W. Kaufmann], in 11 scenes (1933-50).
A Parfait for Irene [W. Kaufmann], in 2 acts (1951).
The Research [W. Kaufmann], in 1 act (1951).
The Golden Touch [J. M. Sinclair], short opera for children in 2 acts (1953).
Christmas Slippers [B. Marsh], television opera in 1 act (1955).
**Sganarelle* [W. Kaufmann], in 2 acts (1955).
George from Paradise [W. Kaufmann], in 1 act (1958).
**Paracelsus* [W. Kaufmann], in 1 act (1958).
**The Scarlet Letter* [W. Kaufmann], in 3 acts (1960).
**A Hoosier Tale* [W. Kaufmann], in 3 acts (1965).
Rip van Winkle [W. Kaufmann], short opera for children in 1 act (1966).

G. Cantatas

Galizische Bäume for Chorus and Orchestra (1932).
Coronation Cantata for Soloists, Chorus and Orchestra (1953).
Rubayyat for Soloist and Orchestra (1954).

H. Songs

Six Orchestral Songs (1933).
Four Songs [H. Hesse] (1933).
Six Songs [H. Politzer] (1935).
Aus meines Vaters Garten [H. Politzer] (1936).

I. Film Scores

Numerous scores for "Information Films of India" (1935-40).
Scores for commercial films, Bombay (1935-40).
Scores for documentary films of Arthur Rank Co., Denham, England (1947).

J. Radio Dramas

Numerous scores for the Canadian Broadcasting Corporation (1948-54).

II. SCHOLARLY WRITINGS

A. Books

Musical Notations of the Orient. Bloomington: Indiana University Press, 1967.
The Ragas of North India. Bloomington: Indiana University Press, 1968.
Tibetan Buddhist Chant (with translations by Thubten Norbu). Bloomington: Indiana University Press, 1975.
Involvement with Music: The Music of India. New York: Harper's College Press, 1976.
Musical References in the Chinese Classics. Detroit: Information Coordinators, 1976.
The Rāgas of South India. Bloomington: Indiana University Press, 1976.

B. Articles

"Folk-Songs of the Gond and Baiga." *Musical Quarterly* 27 (1941):280-88.
"Prehistoric Music in India." In *Dalhousie Review*, pp. 226-32. Halifax, Nova Scotia: Dalhousie University, 1948.
"The Classification of Indian *Ragas.*" In *Asia and the Humanities*, edited by Horst Frenz, pp. 131-45. Bloomington: Comparative Literature Committee, Indiana University, 1959.
"The Forms of the *Dhrupad* and *Khyal* in Indian Art Music." *Canadian Music Journal* 3, no. 2 (1959):25-35.
"The Songs of the Hill Maria, Jhoria Muria and Bastar Muria Gond Tribes." *Ethnomusicology* 4 (1960):115-28.
"The Musical Instruments of the Hill Maria, Jhoria Muria and Bastar Muria Gond Tribes." *Ethnomusicology* 5 (1961):1-9.

"The Folksongs of Nepal." *Ethnomusicology* 6 (1962):93-114.

"Rasa, Rāga-Mālā and Performance Times in North Indian Rāgas." *Ethnomusicology* 9 (1965):272-91.

"The *Mudrās* in Sāmavedic Chant and Their Probable Relationship to the *Go-on Hakase* of the Shōmyō of Japan." *Ethnomusicology* 11 (1967):161-69.

"The Problem Concerning a Chinese Ming Bronze." *Ethnomusicology* 12 (1968):251-54.

"Some Reflections on the Notations of Vedic Chant." In *Essays in Musicology: A Birthday Offering for Willi Apel*, edited by Hans Tischler, pp. 1-18. Bloomington: Indiana University School of Music, 1968.

"The Application of the Kaṭapayādi Sankhya in South Indian Music." In *American Oriental Society, Middle West Branch, Semi-Centennial Volume: A Collection of Original Essays*, edited by Denis Sinor, pp. 127-33. Bloomington: Indiana University Press, 1969.

"India." In *Harvard Dictionary of Music*, 2nd ed. (1969).

"The Mathematical Determination of the Twelve Lü as Performed by Prince Liu An in His Huai-nan Tzu (Second Century B.C.)." In *Essays in Ethnomusicology: A Birthday Offering for Lee, Hye-ku*, pp. 371-82. Seoul: Korean Musicological Society, 1969.

"Parallel Trends of Musical Liturgies and Notations in Eastern and Western Asia." *Orbis musicae* 2 (1973-74):97-119.

"Die Melodie der Gesaenge des Bulgan-Schamanen"(in collaboration with Friedrich A. Bischoff). *Zentralasiatische Studien* 10 (1976):311-25.

C. Reviews

Karan Singh, comp. *Shadow and Sunlight: An Anthology of Dogra-Pahari Songs. Ethnomusicology* 8 (1964):74-75.

Inde du nord; râgas du matin et du soir and *Chants et danses populaires du Bengale* [sound recordings]. *Ethnomusicology* 9 (1965):341-42.

Ustad Ali Akbar Khân: Master Musician of India: Râga Chandranandan; Râga Gauri Manjari and *Yoga Music of India* [sound recordings]. *Ethnomusicology* 10 (1966):242-44.

Musique Indienne du Rajasthan: Painted Ballads [sound recording]. *Ethnomusicology* 10 (1966):355-61.

Classical Music of India [sound recording]. *Ethnomusicology* 12 (1968):473-75.

Folk Music of India [sound recording]. *Ethnomusicology* 13 (1969):189-93.

Martin Gimm. *Das Yüeh-fu tsa-lu des Tuan An-chieh. Studien zur Geschichte von Musik, Schauspiel und Tanz in der T'ang-Dynastie. Journal of Asian History* 3 (1969):65-66.

The Anthology of Indian Music [sound recording]. *Ethnomusicology* 13 (1969):577-81.

The Music of India [sound recording]. *Ethnomusicology* 14 (1970):184-88.

D. Manuscripts

The Art-Music of Hindusthan (1944). Copy deposited in the New York Public Library.

Index

Compiled by Paul W. Borg